YOTSUBA&!

15

KIYOHIKO AZUMA

CONTENTS

YOTSUBA&!
KIYOHIKO AZUMA

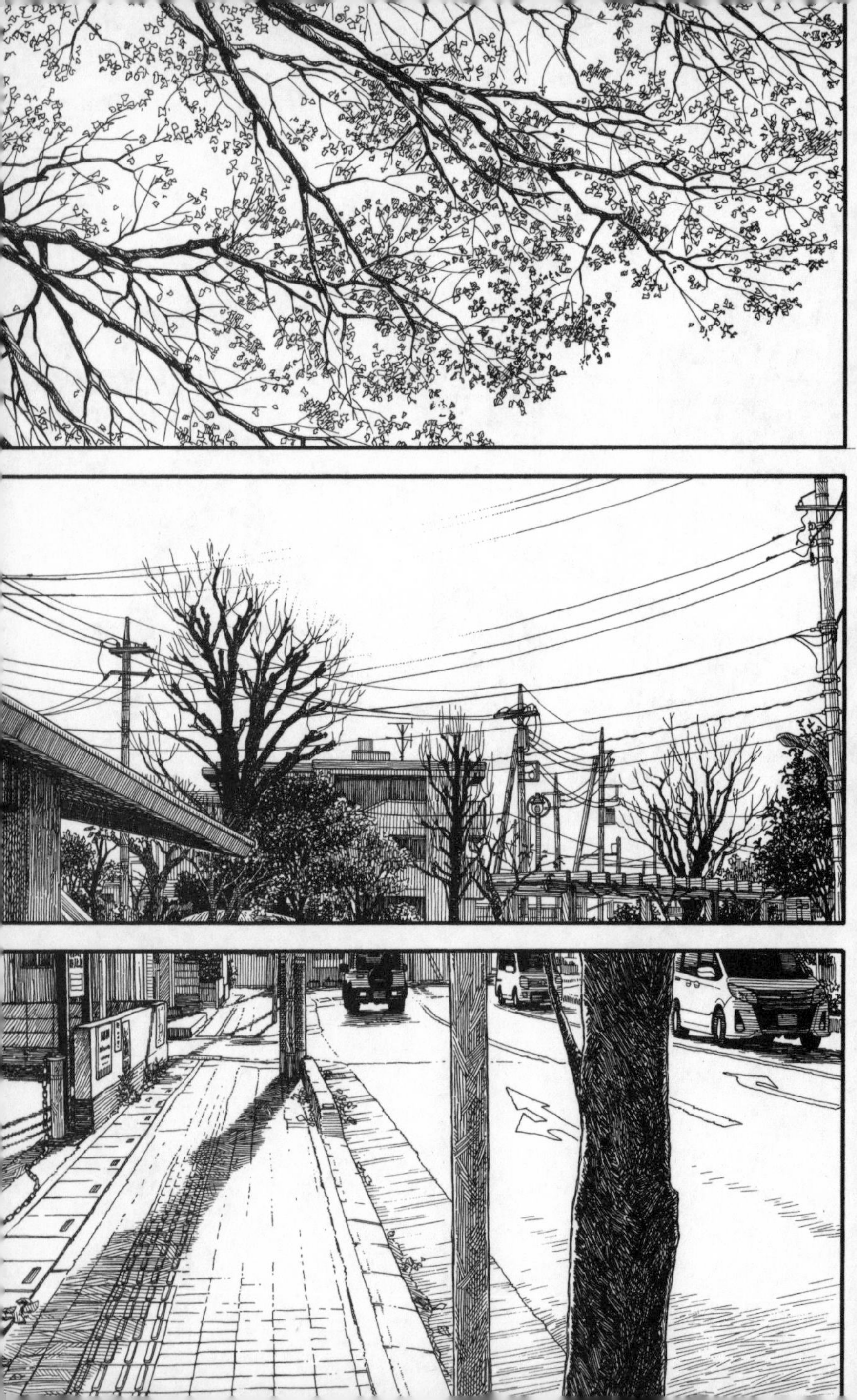

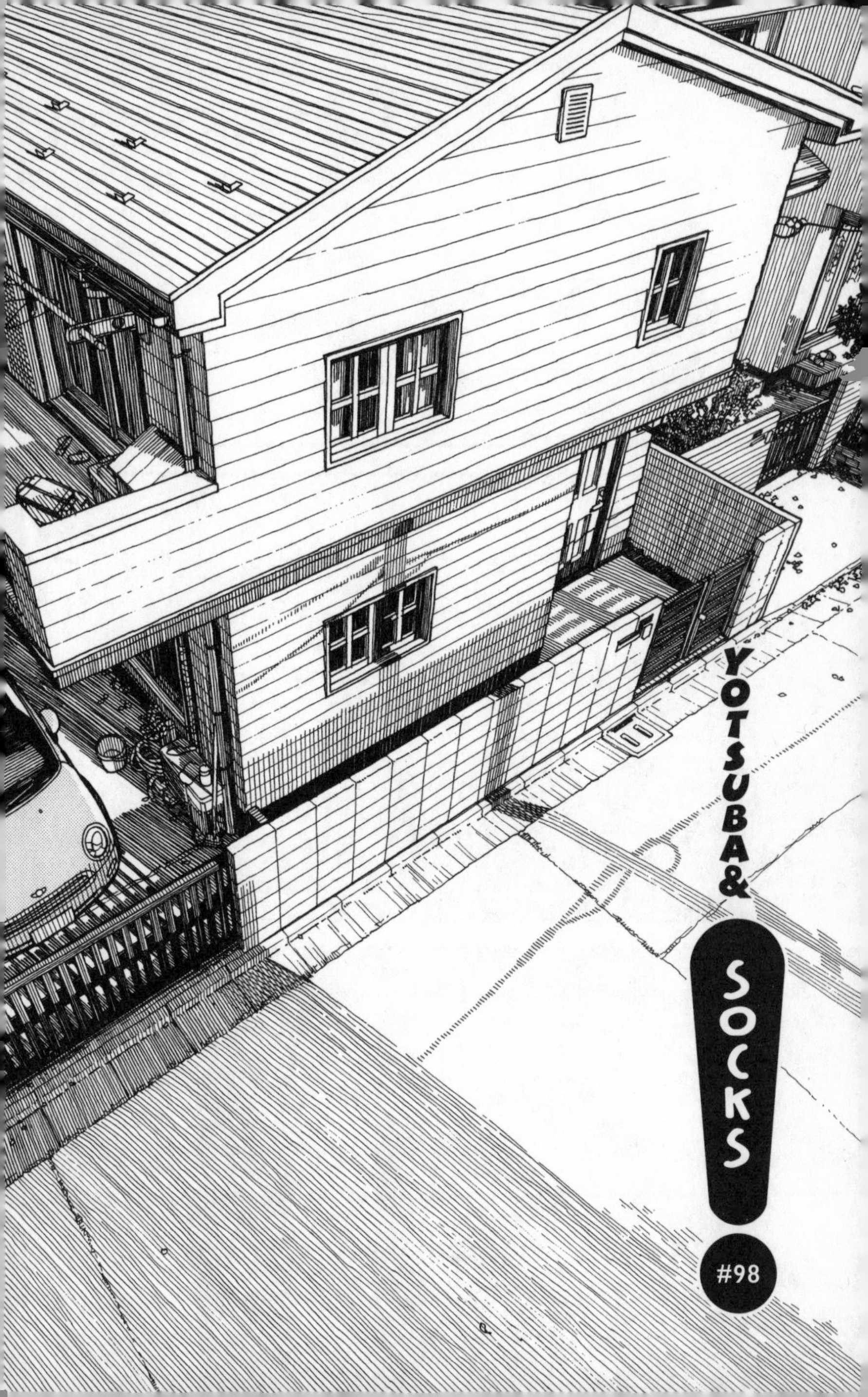
YOTSUBA&
SOCKS
#98

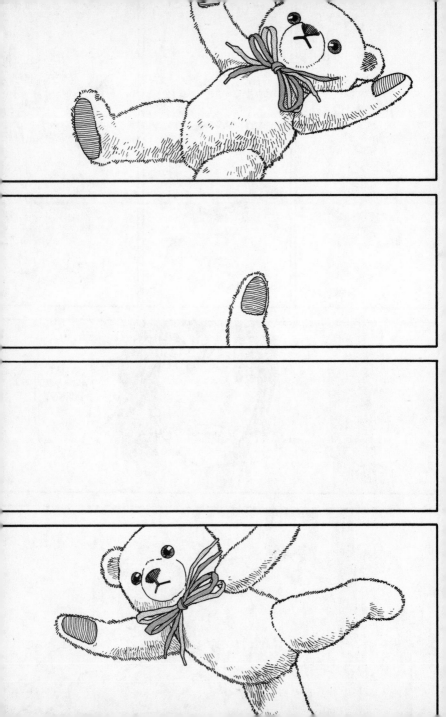

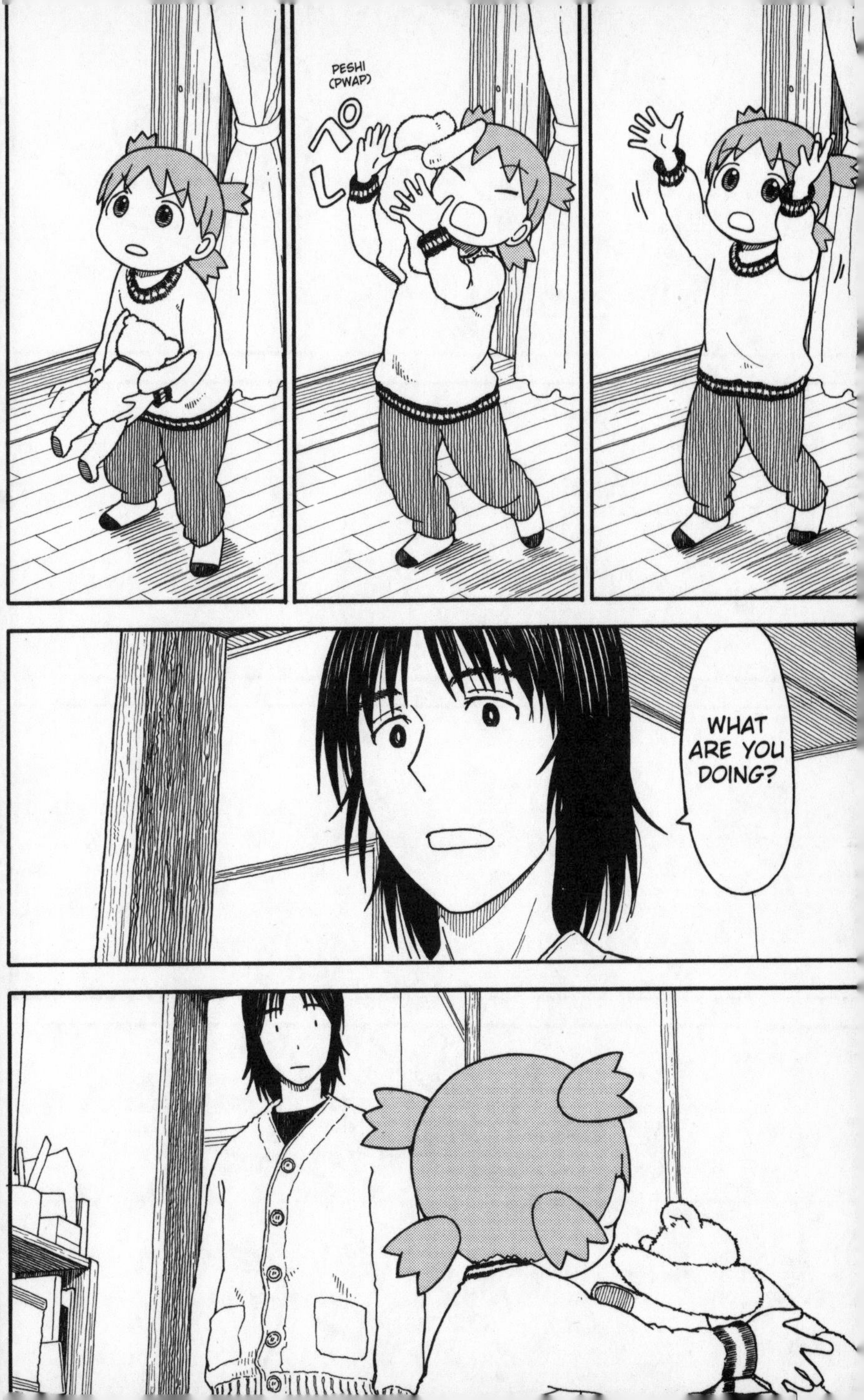
PESHI (PWAP)
WHAT ARE YOU DOING?

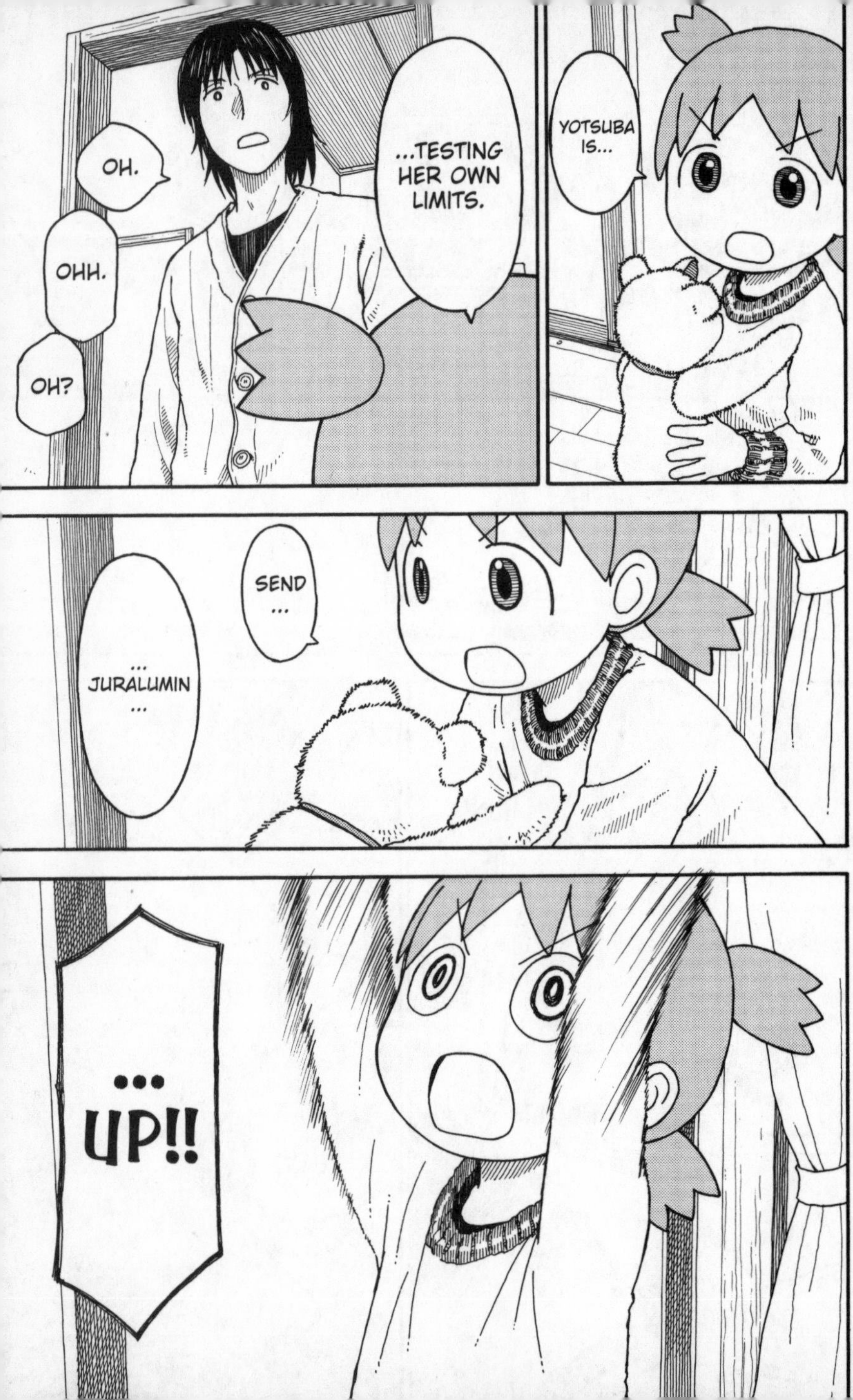
YOTSUBA IS...
...TESTING HER OWN LIMITS.
OH.
OHH.
OH?
SEND ...
... JURALUMIN ...
... UP!!

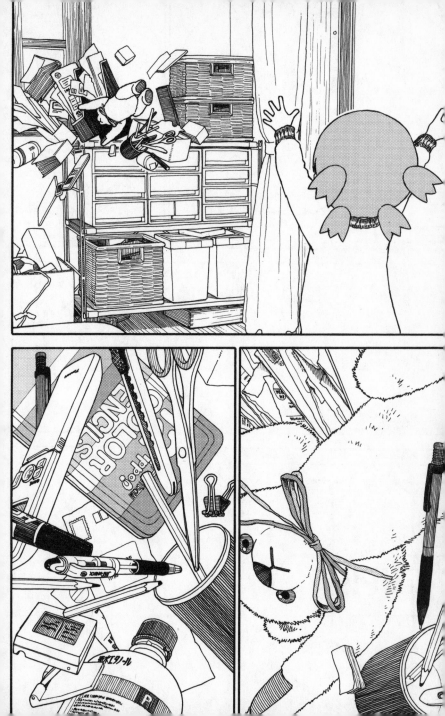

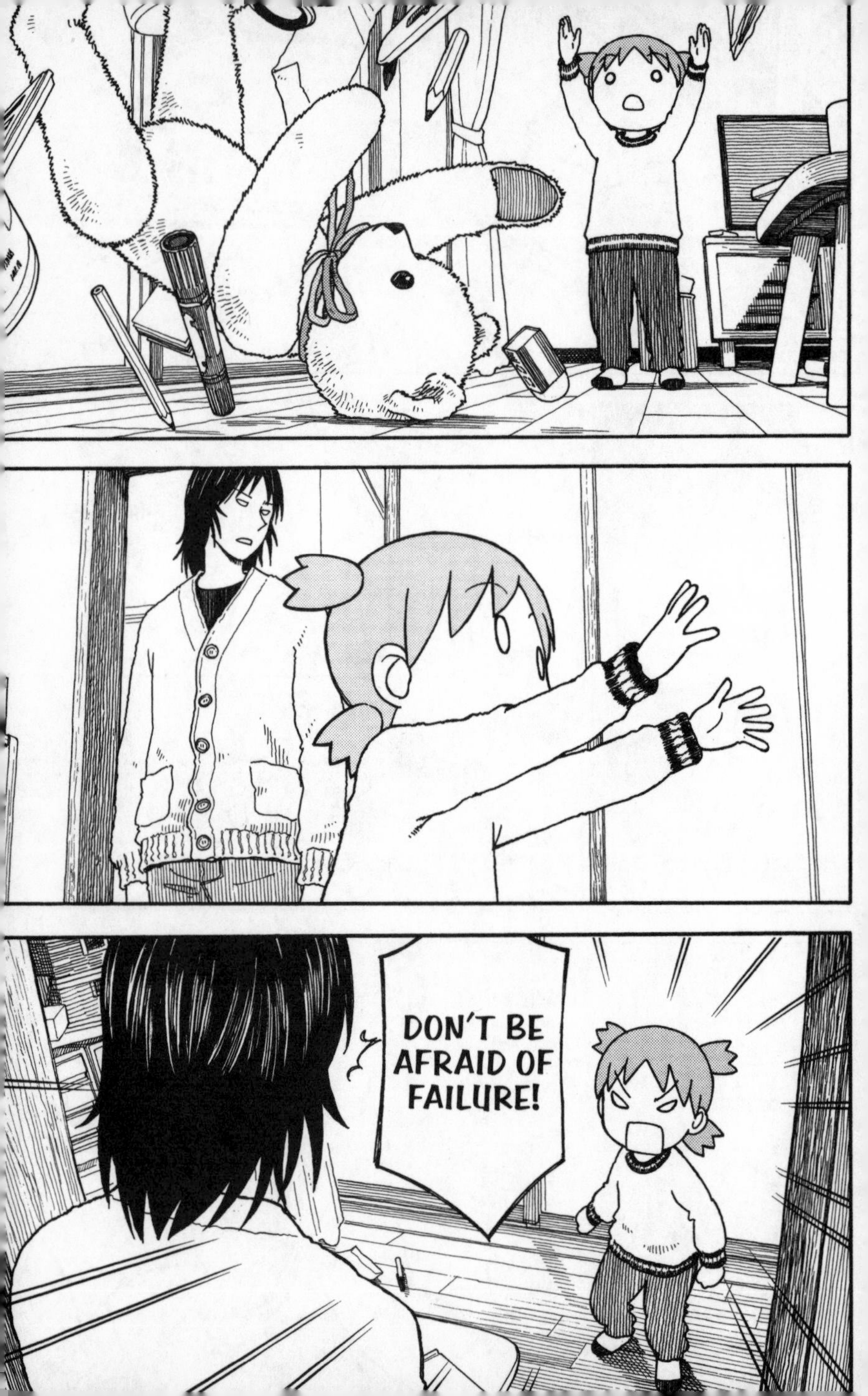
DON'T BE AFRAID OF FAILURE!

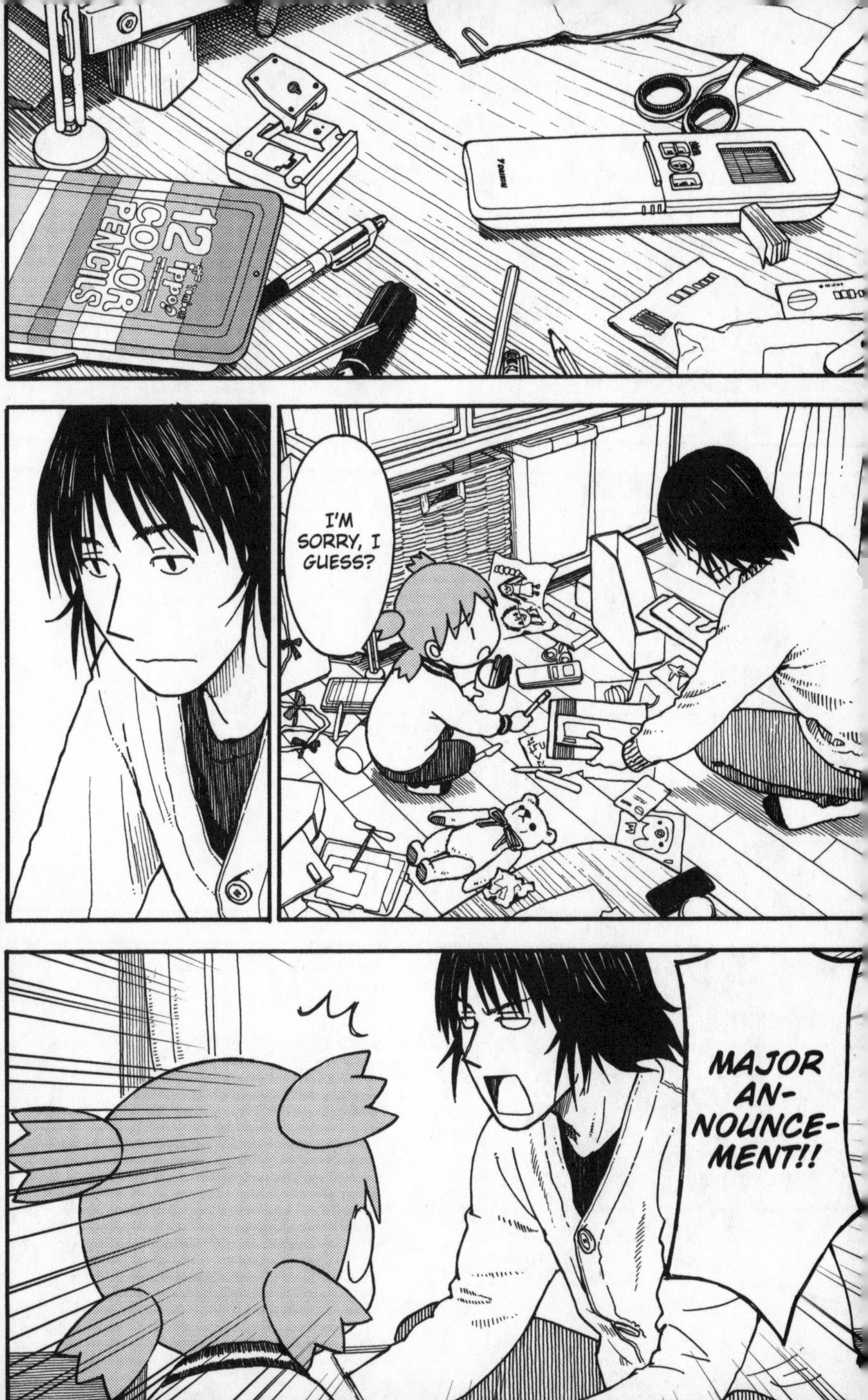
12 COLOR PENCILS
I'M SORRY, I GUESS?
MAJOR AN-NOUNCE-MENT!!

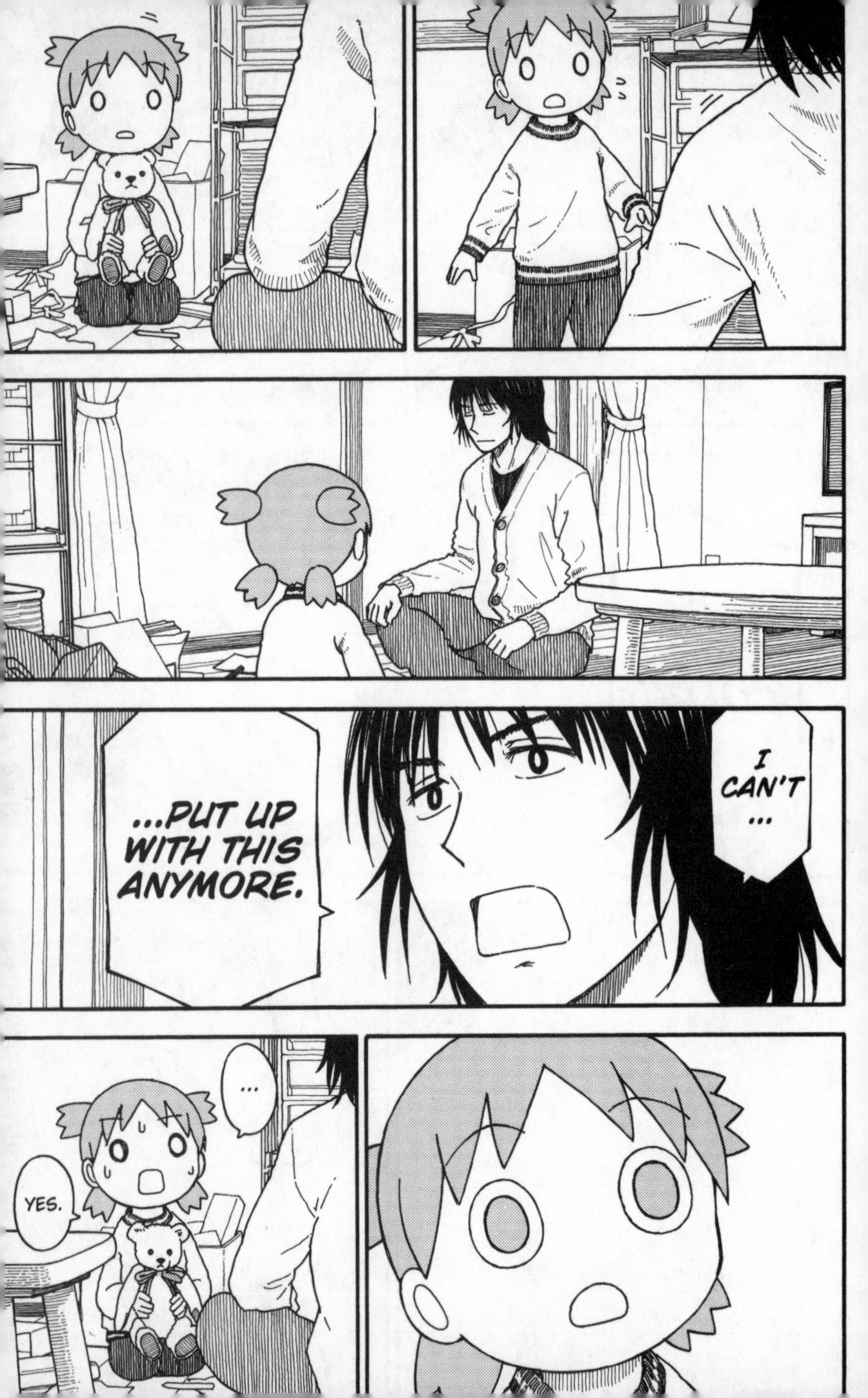
I CAN'T ...
...PUT UP WITH THIS ANYMORE.
...
YES.

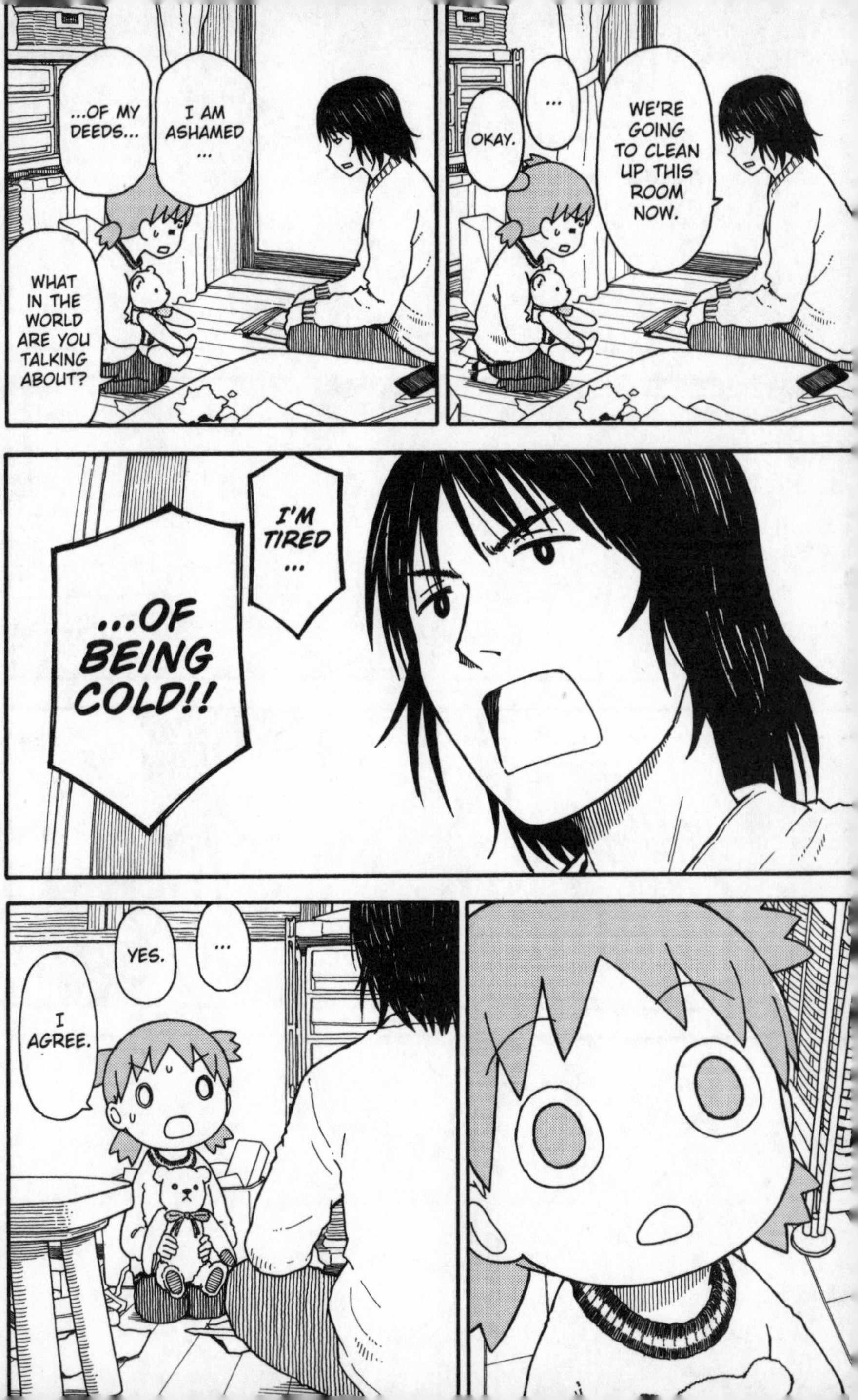
WE'RE GOING TO CLEAN UP THIS ROOM NOW.
...
OKAY.
I AM ASHAMED ...
...OF MY DEEDS...
WHAT IN THE WORLD ARE YOU TALKING ABOUT?
I'M TIRED ...
...OF BEING COLD!!
...
YES.
I AGREE.

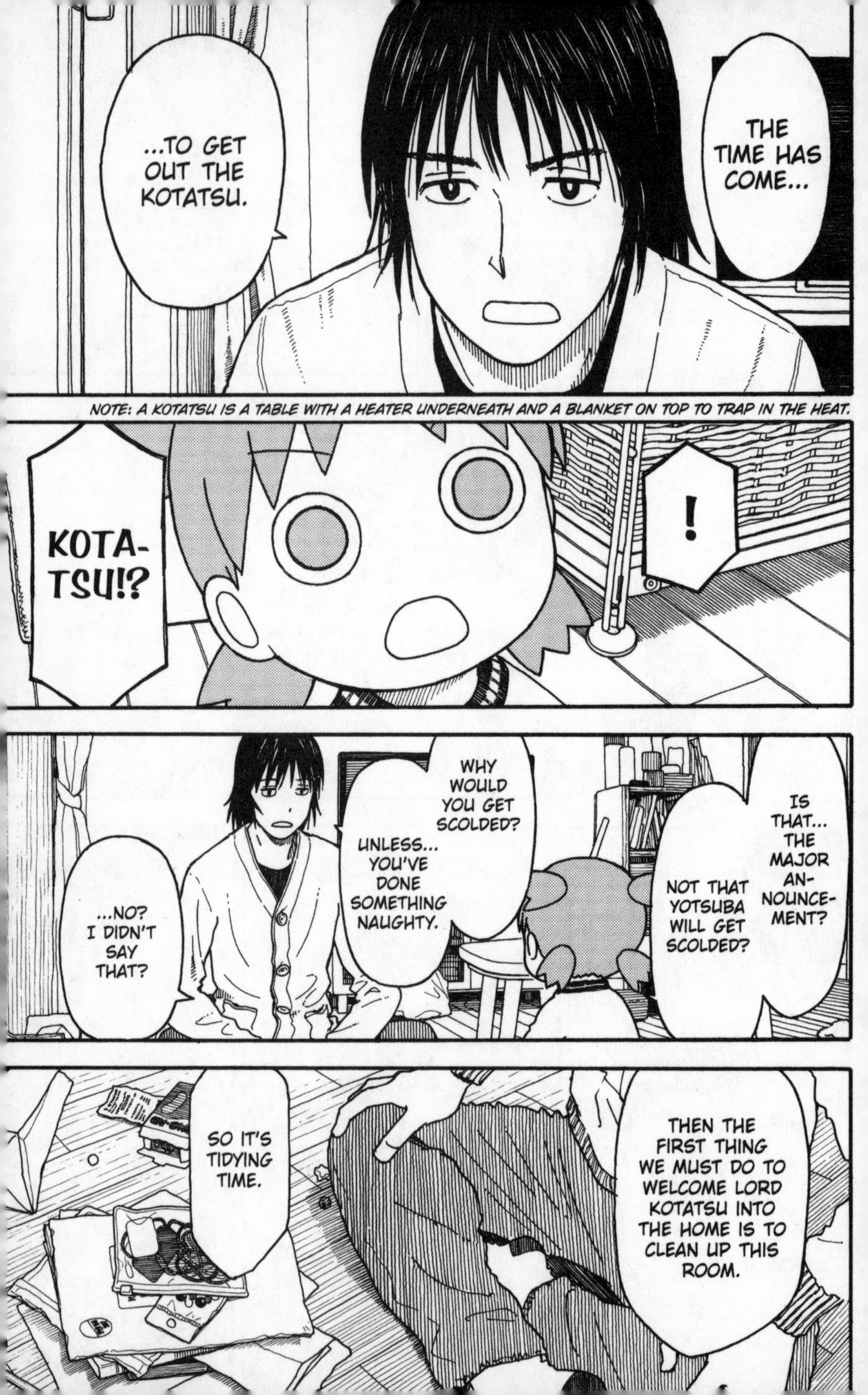
THE TIME HAS COME...
...TO GET OUT THE KOTATSU.
NOTE: A KOTATSU IS A TABLE WITH A HEATER UNDERNEATH AND A BLANKET ON TOP TO TRAP IN THE HEAT.
!
KOTA-TSU!?
IS THAT... THE MAJOR AN-NOUNCE-MENT?
NOT THAT YOTSUBA WILL GET SCOLDED?
WHY WOULD YOU GET SCOLDED?
UNLESS... YOU'VE DONE SOMETHING NAUGHTY.
...NO? I DIDN'T SAY THAT?
THEN THE FIRST THING WE MUST DO TO WELCOME LORD KOTATSU INTO THE HOME IS TO CLEAN UP THIS ROOM.
SO IT'S TIDYING TIME.

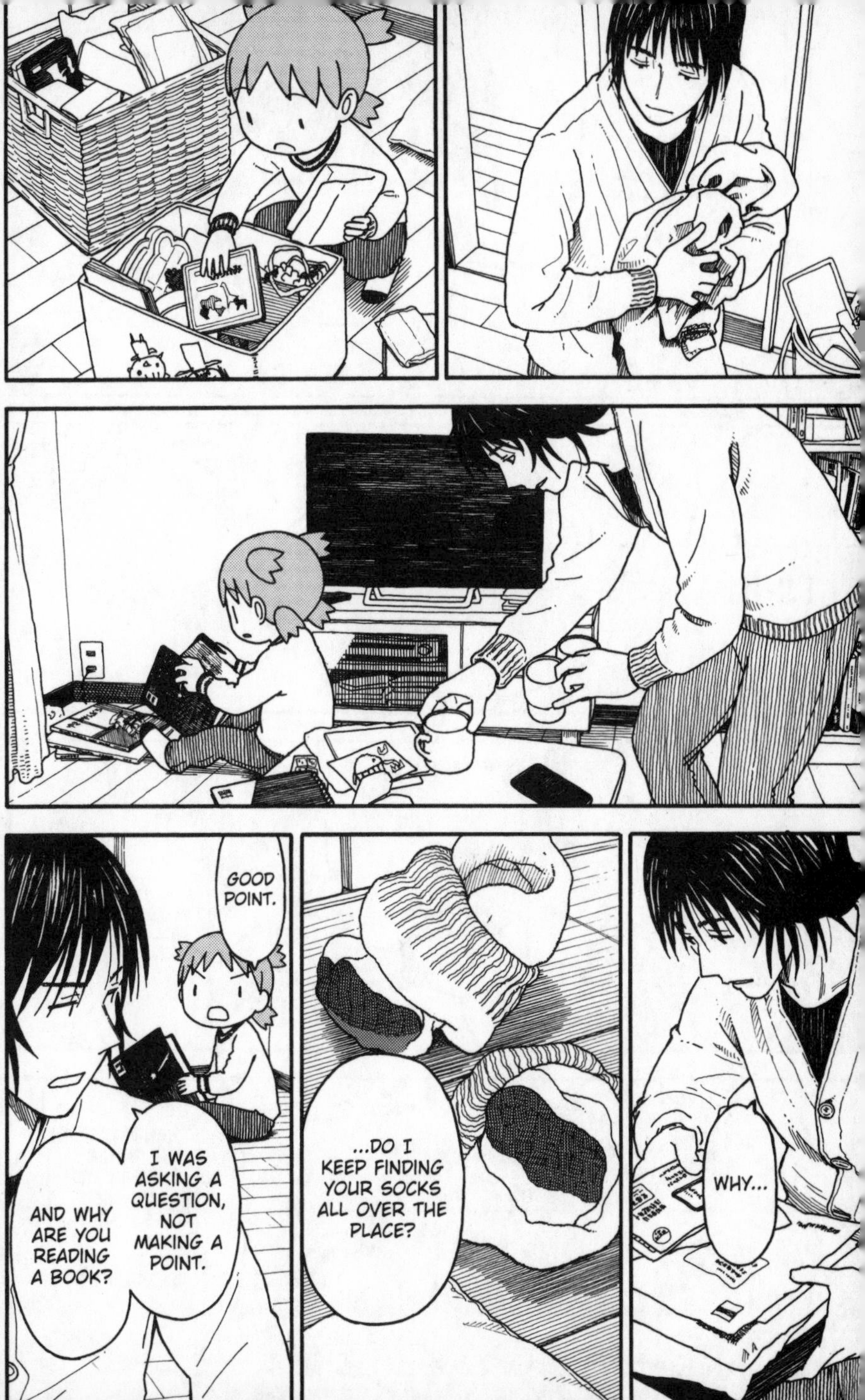
WHY...
...DO I KEEP FINDING YOUR SOCKS ALL OVER THE PLACE?
GOOD POINT.
I WAS ASKING A QUESTION, NOT MAKING A POINT.
AND WHY ARE YOU READING A BOOK?

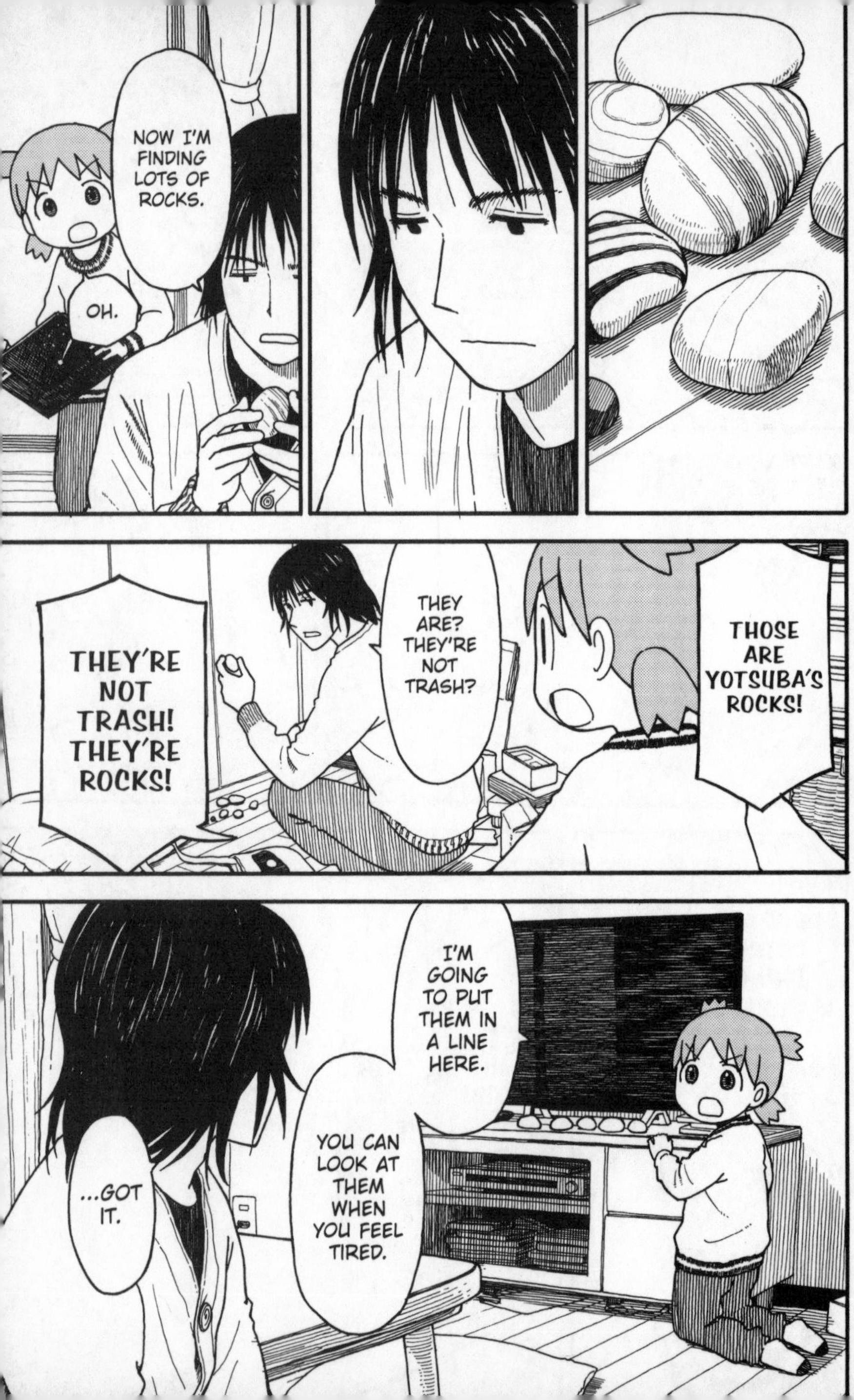
NOW I'M FINDING LOTS OF ROCKS.
OH.
THOSE ARE YOTSUBA'S ROCKS!
THEY ARE? THEY'RE NOT TRASH?
THEY'RE NOT TRASH! THEY'RE ROCKS!
I'M GOING TO PUT THEM IN A LINE HERE.
YOU CAN LOOK AT THEM WHEN YOU FEEL TIRED.
...GOT IT.

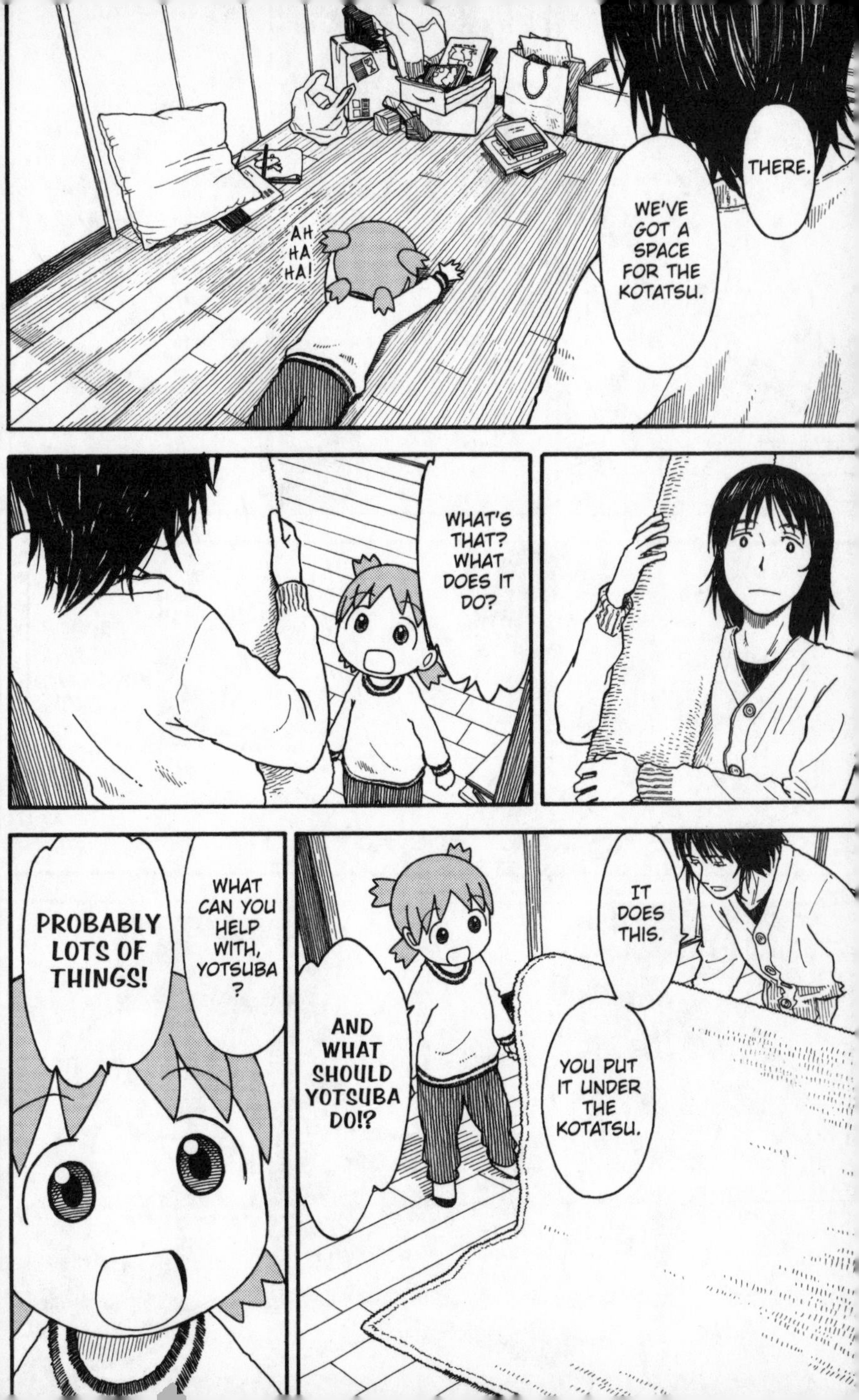
THERE.
WE'VE GOT A SPACE FOR THE KOTATSU.
AH HA HA!
WHAT'S THAT? WHAT DOES IT DO?
IT DOES THIS.
YOU PUT IT UNDER THE KOTATSU.
AND WHAT SHOULD YOTSUBA DO!?
WHAT CAN YOU HELP WITH, YOTSUBA?
PROBABLY LOTS OF THINGS!

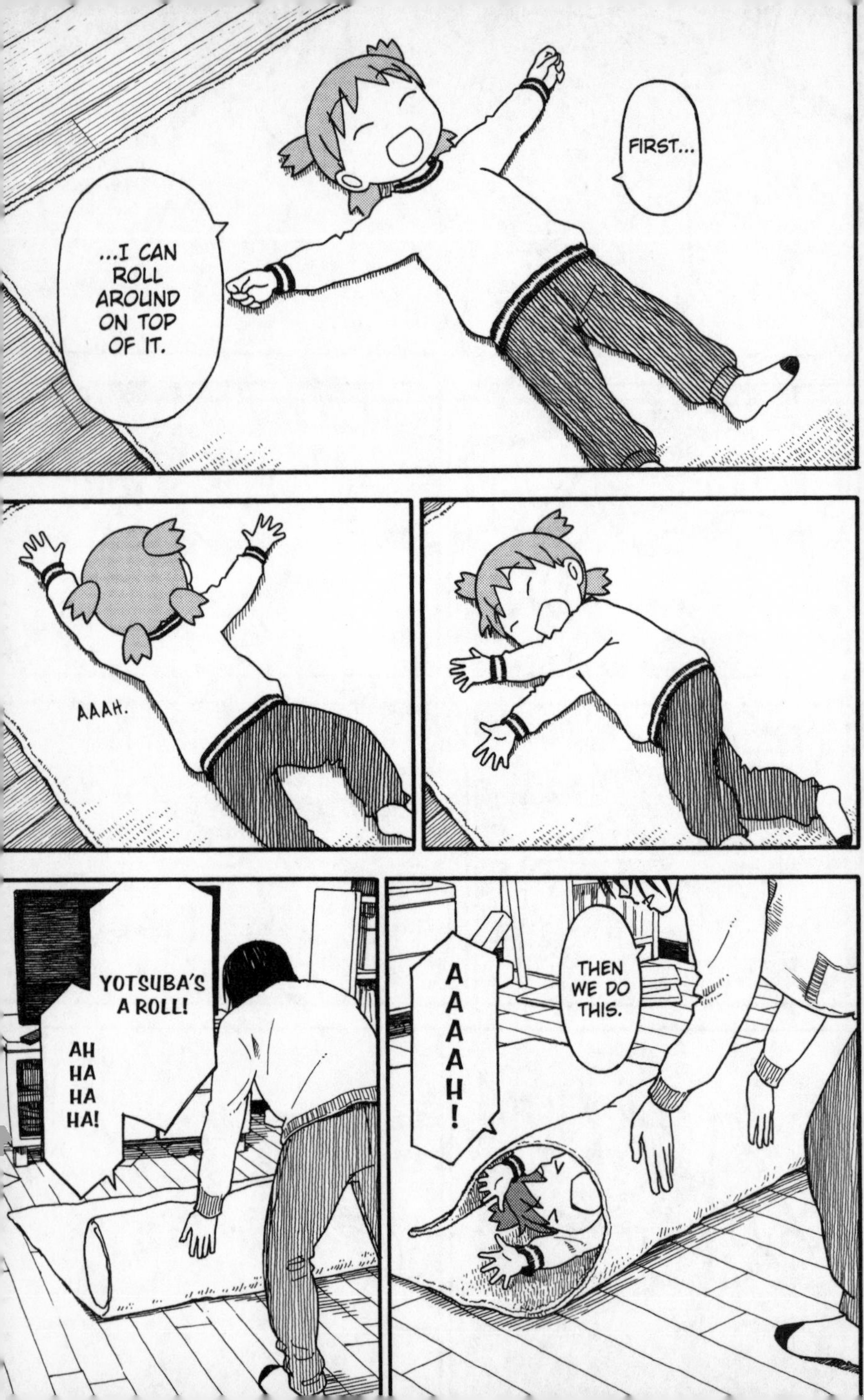
FIRST...
...I CAN ROLL AROUND ON TOP OF IT.
AAAH.
THEN WE DO THIS.
AAAAH!
YOTSUBA'S A ROLL!
AH HA HA HA!

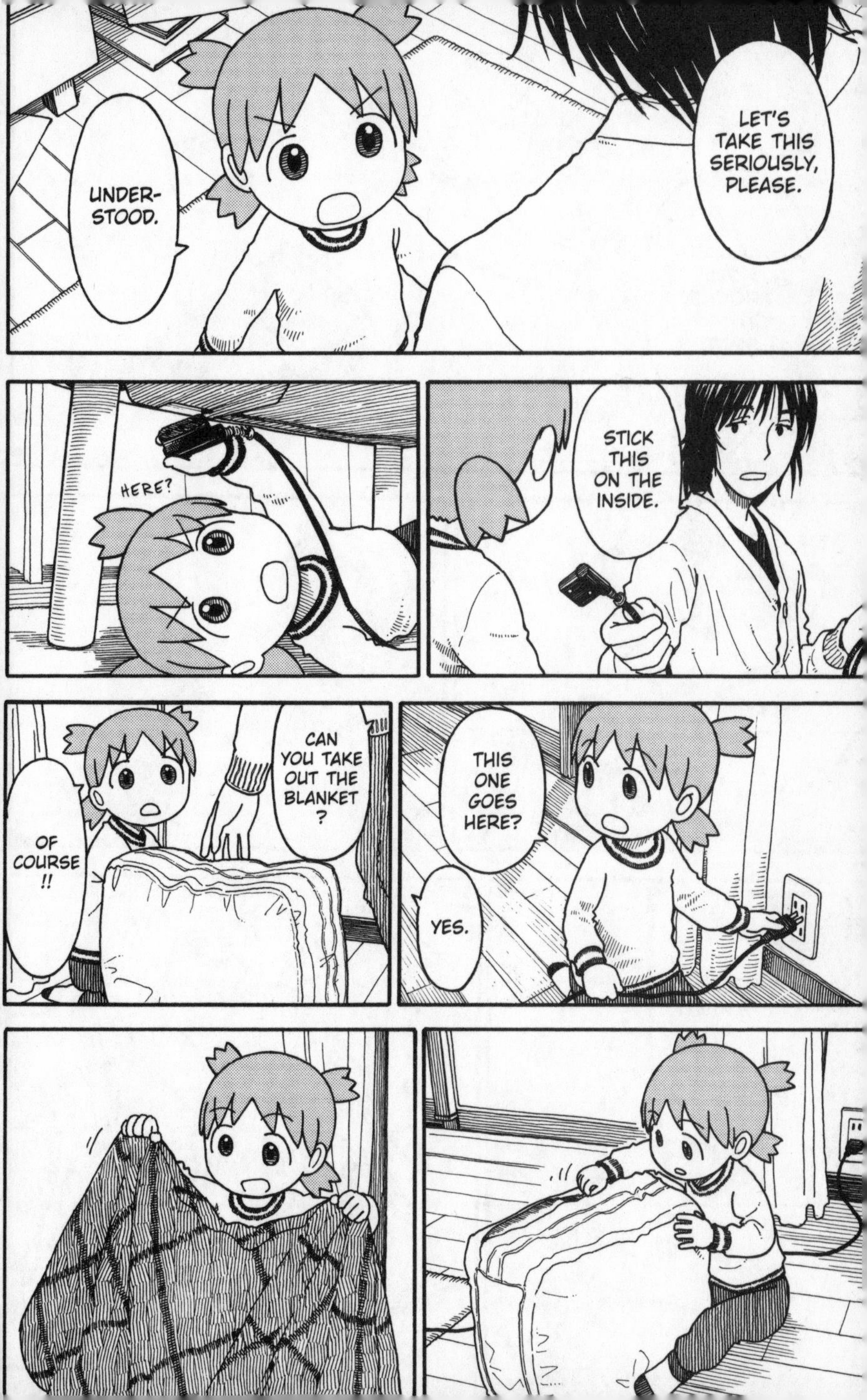
LET'S TAKE THIS SERIOUSLY, PLEASE.
UNDER-STOOD.
STICK THIS ON THE INSIDE.
HERE?
THIS ONE GOES HERE?
YES.
CAN YOU TAKE OUT THE BLANKET?
OF COURSE!!

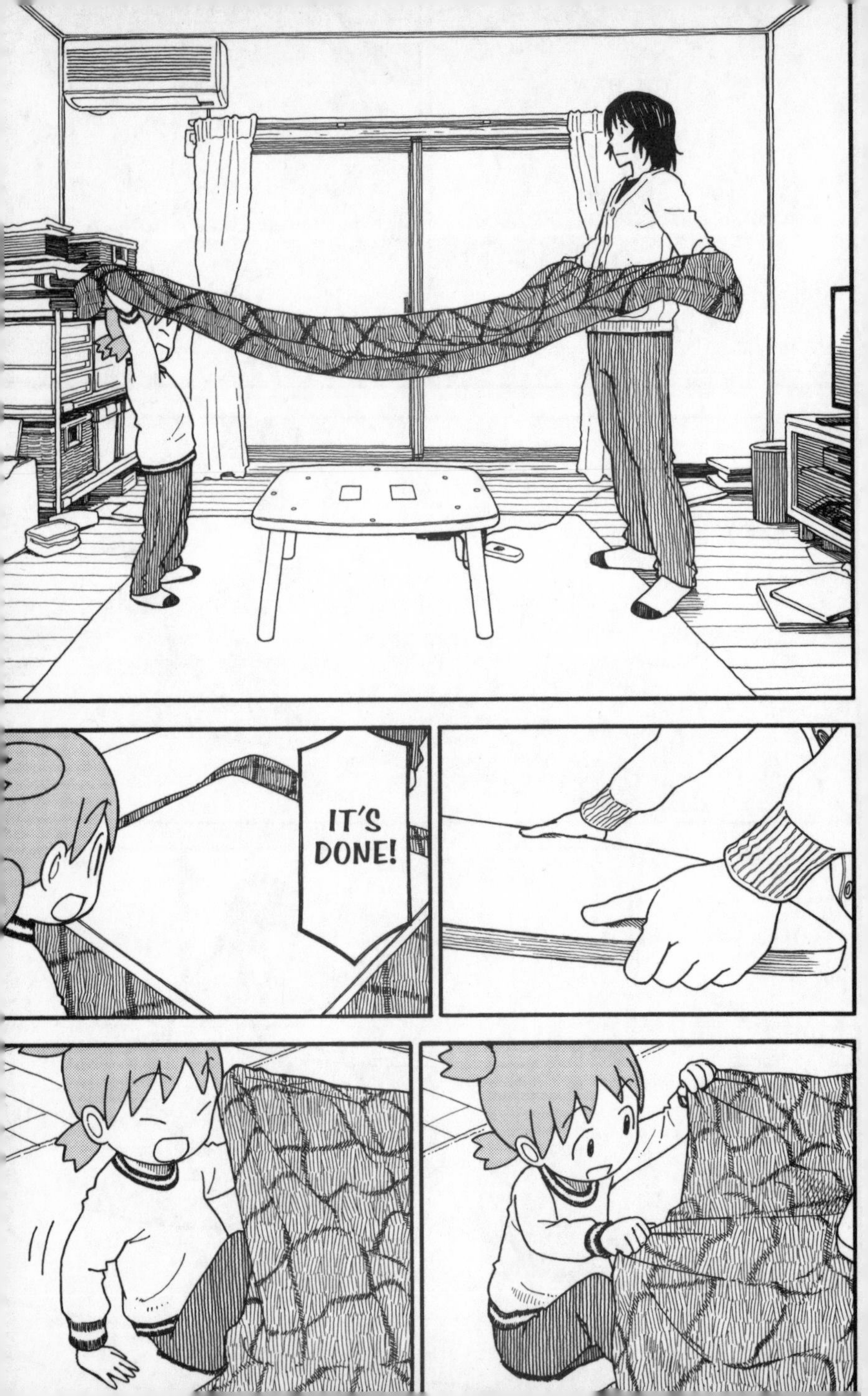
IT'S DONE!

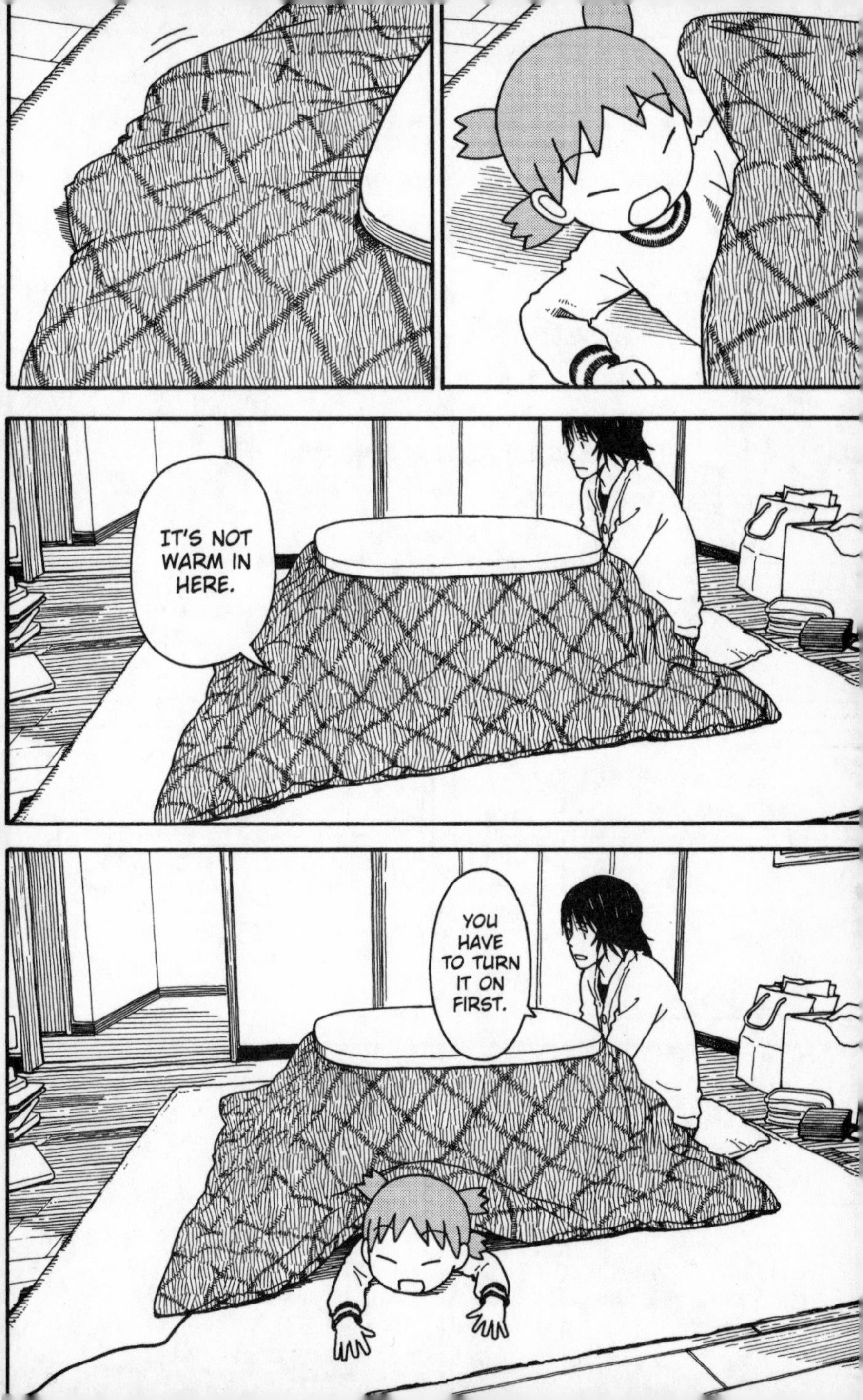
IT'S NOT WARM IN HERE.
YOU HAVE TO TURN IT ON FIRST.

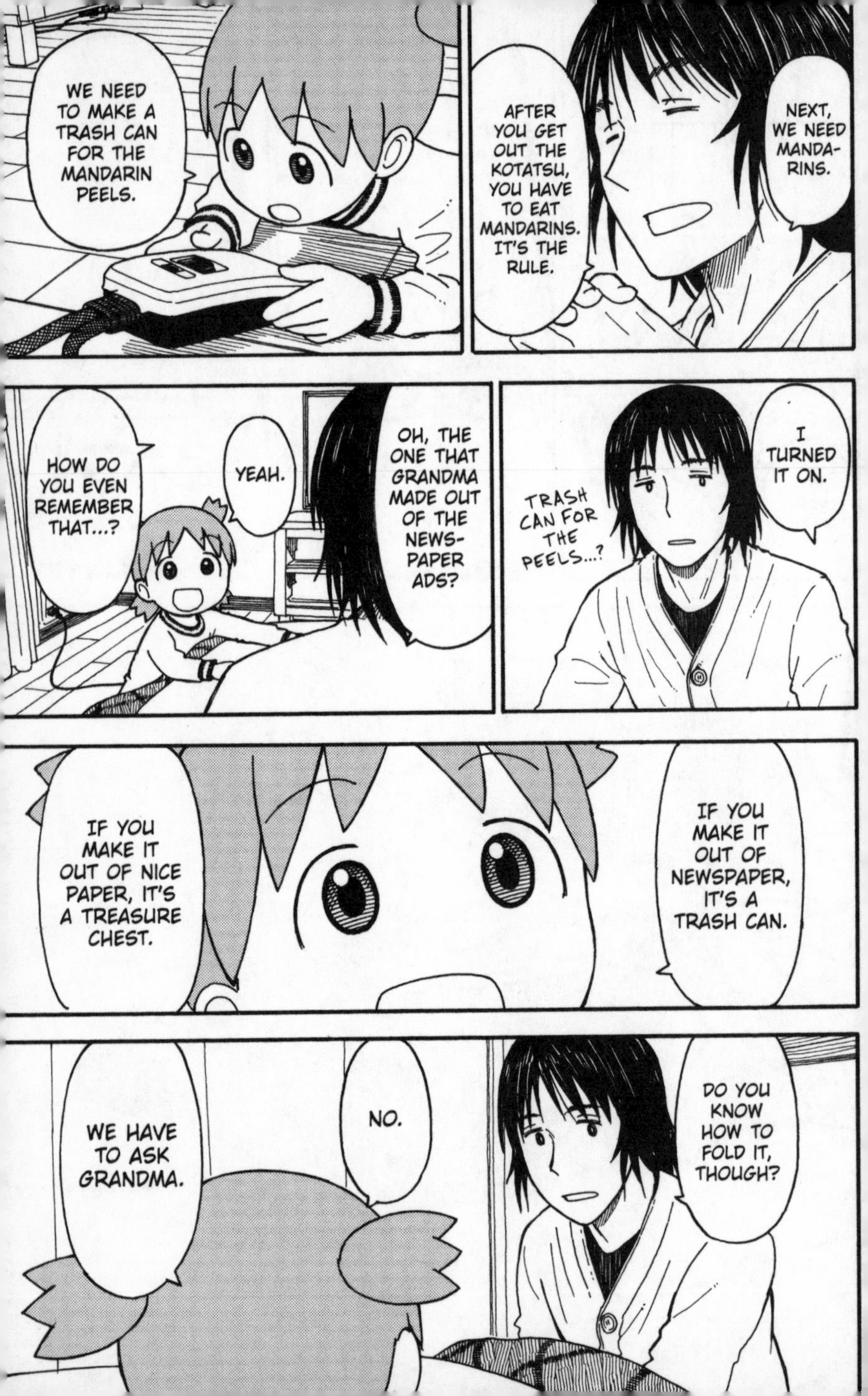
NEXT, WE NEED MANDA-RINS.
AFTER YOU GET OUT THE KOTATSU, YOU HAVE TO EAT MANDARINS. IT'S THE RULE.
WE NEED TO MAKE A TRASH CAN FOR THE MANDARIN PEELS.
I TURNED IT ON.
TRASH CAN FOR THE PEELS...?
OH, THE ONE THAT GRANDMA MADE OUT OF THE NEWS-PAPER ADS?
YEAH.
HOW DO YOU EVEN REMEMBER THAT...?
IF YOU MAKE IT OUT OF NEWSPAPER, IT'S A TRASH CAN.
IF YOU MAKE IT OUT OF NICE PAPER, IT'S A TREASURE CHEST.
DO YOU KNOW HOW TO FOLD IT, THOUGH?
NO.
WE HAVE TO ASK GRANDMA.

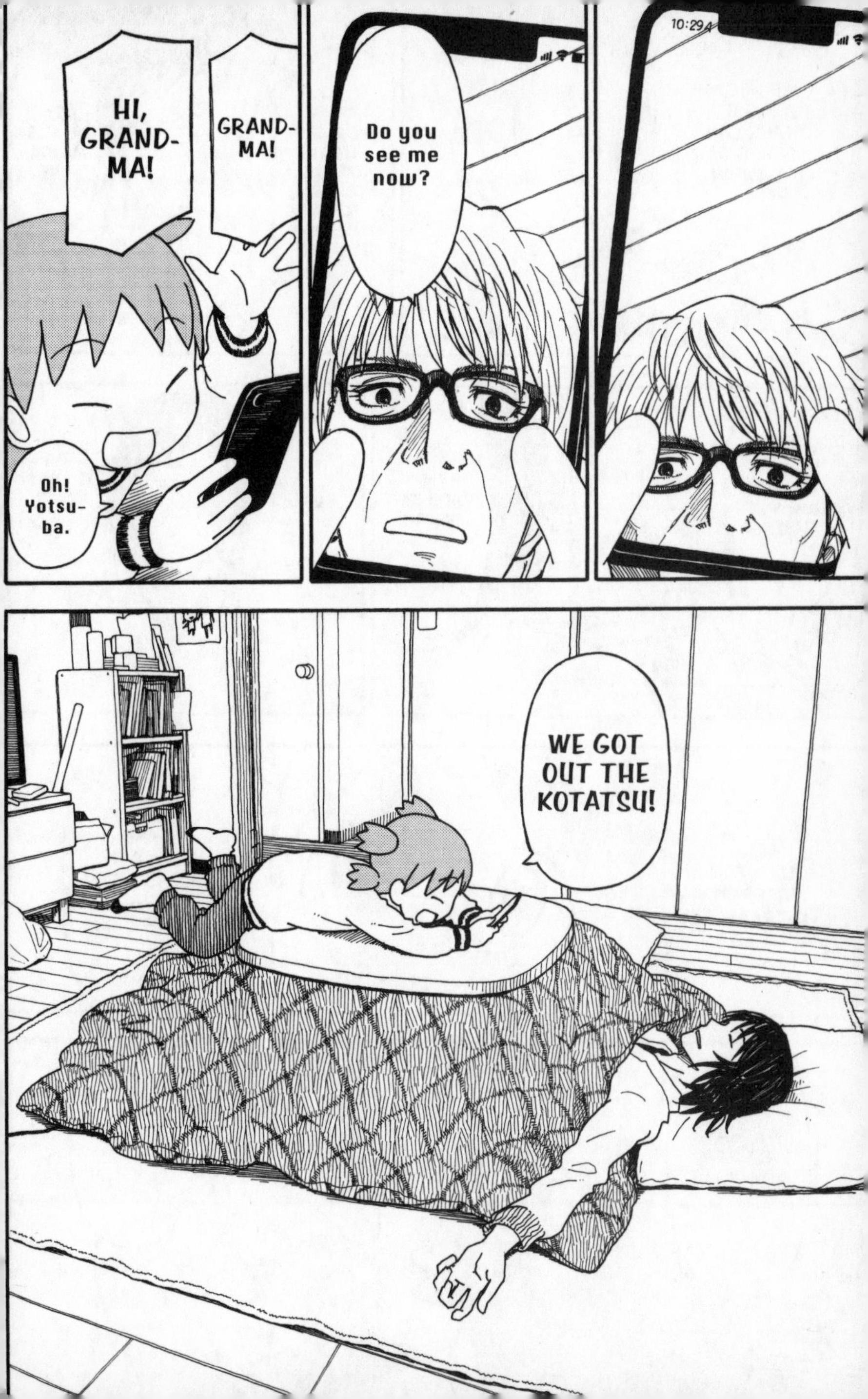
10:29
Do you see me now?
GRAND-MA!
HI, GRAND-MA!
Oh! Yotsu-ba.
WE GOT OUT THE KOTATSU!

YOTSUBA&!

TRY TO
THROW IT
RIGHT UP
TO THE
CEILING.

IF IT
TOUCHES,
YOU
LOSE.

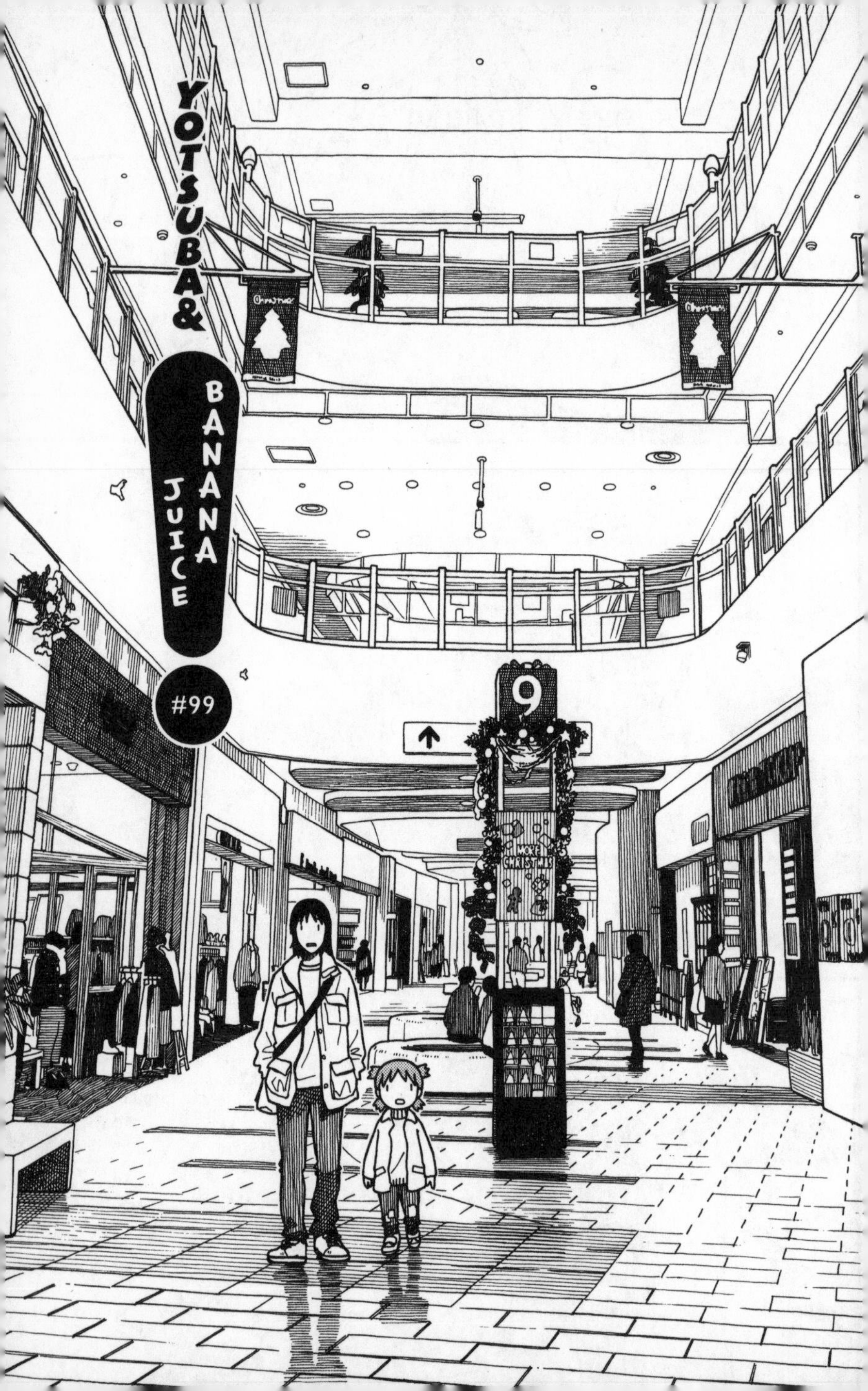
YOTSUBA&
BANANA JUICE
#99
9
MORE CHRISTMAS

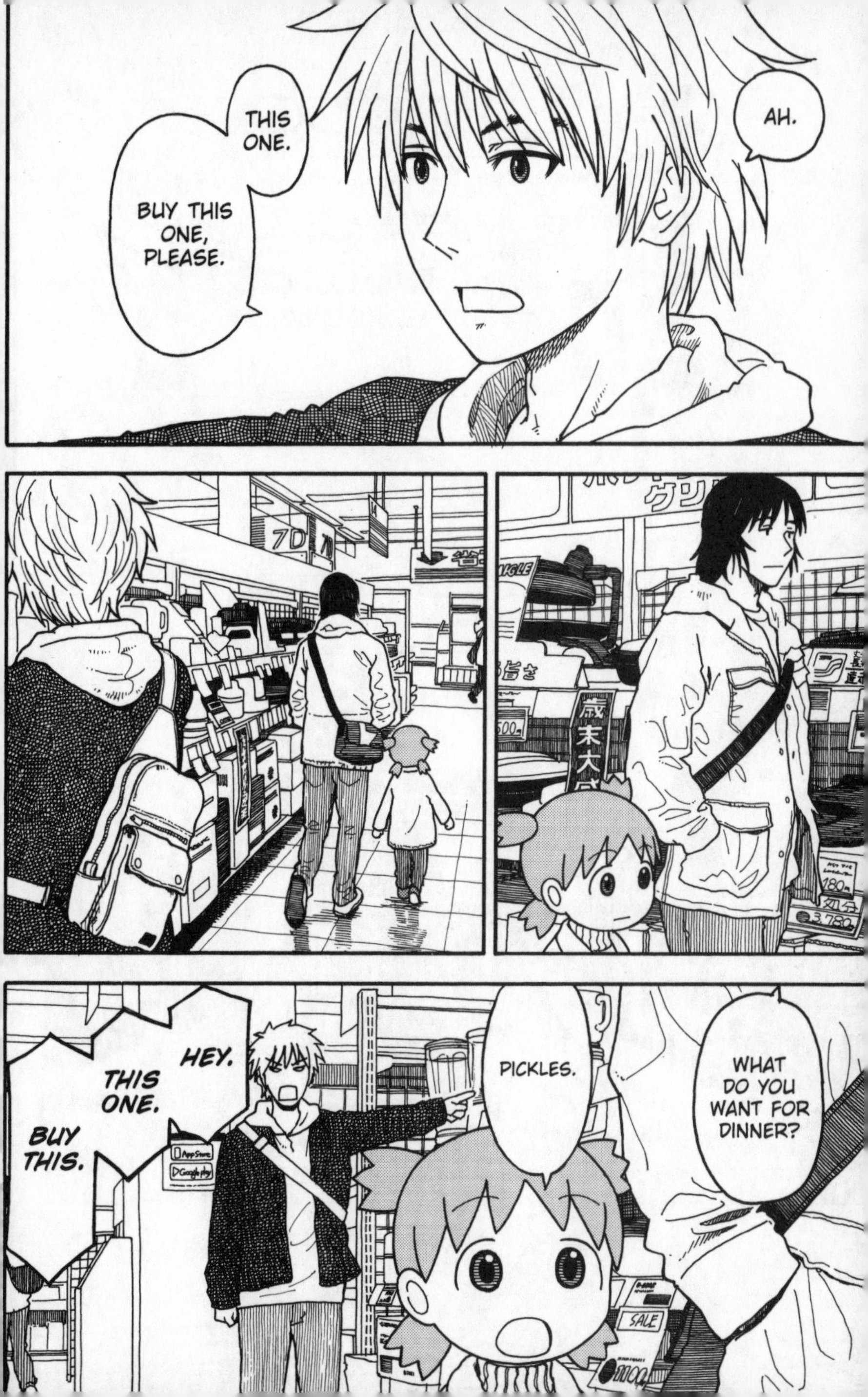
AH.
THIS ONE.
BUY THIS ONE, PLEASE.
WHAT DO YOU WANT FOR DINNER?
PICKLES.
HEY.
THIS ONE.
BUY THIS.

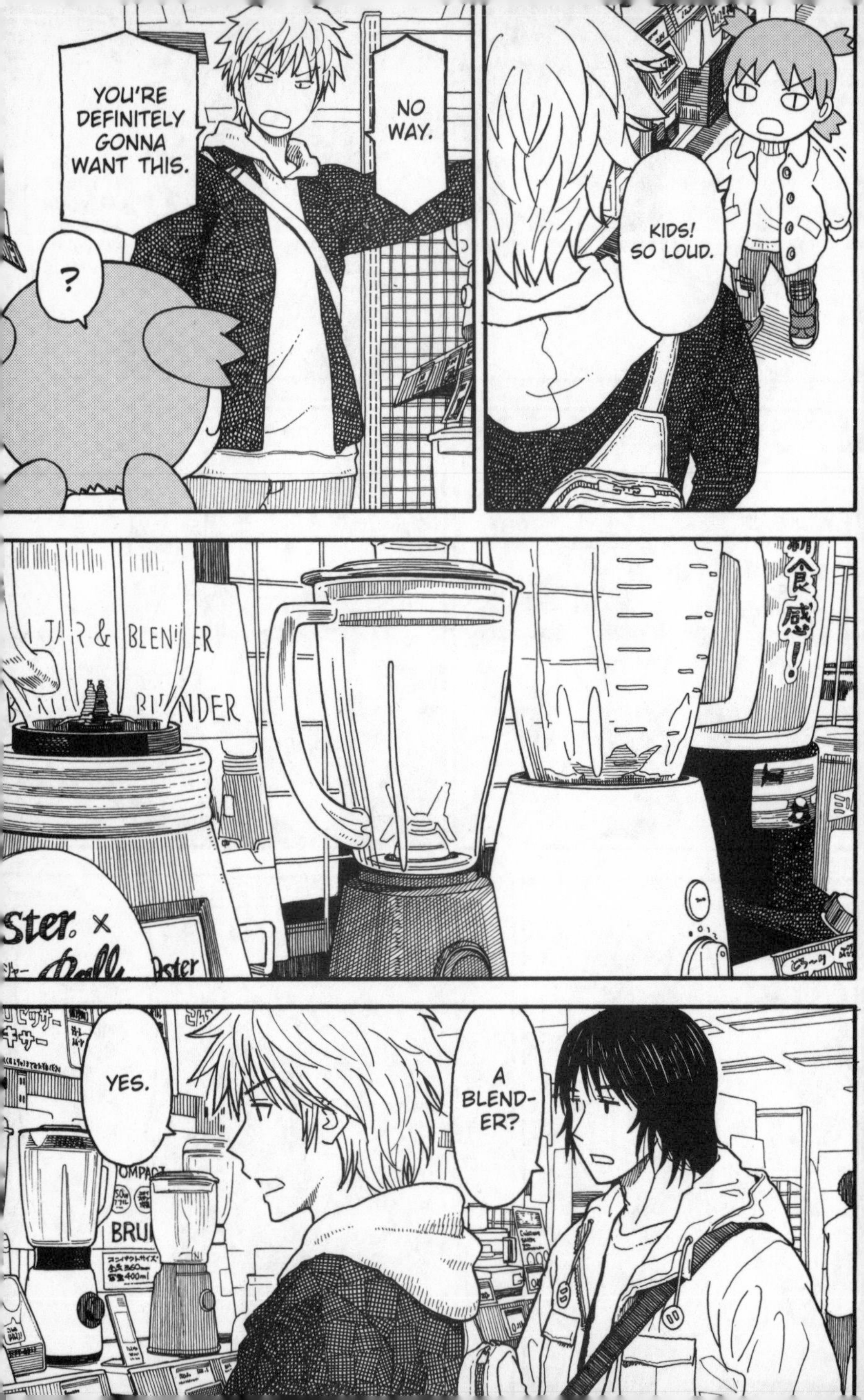
KIDS! SO LOUD.
NO WAY.
YOU'RE DEFINITELY GONNA WANT THIS.
?
新食感!
A BLENDER?
YES.

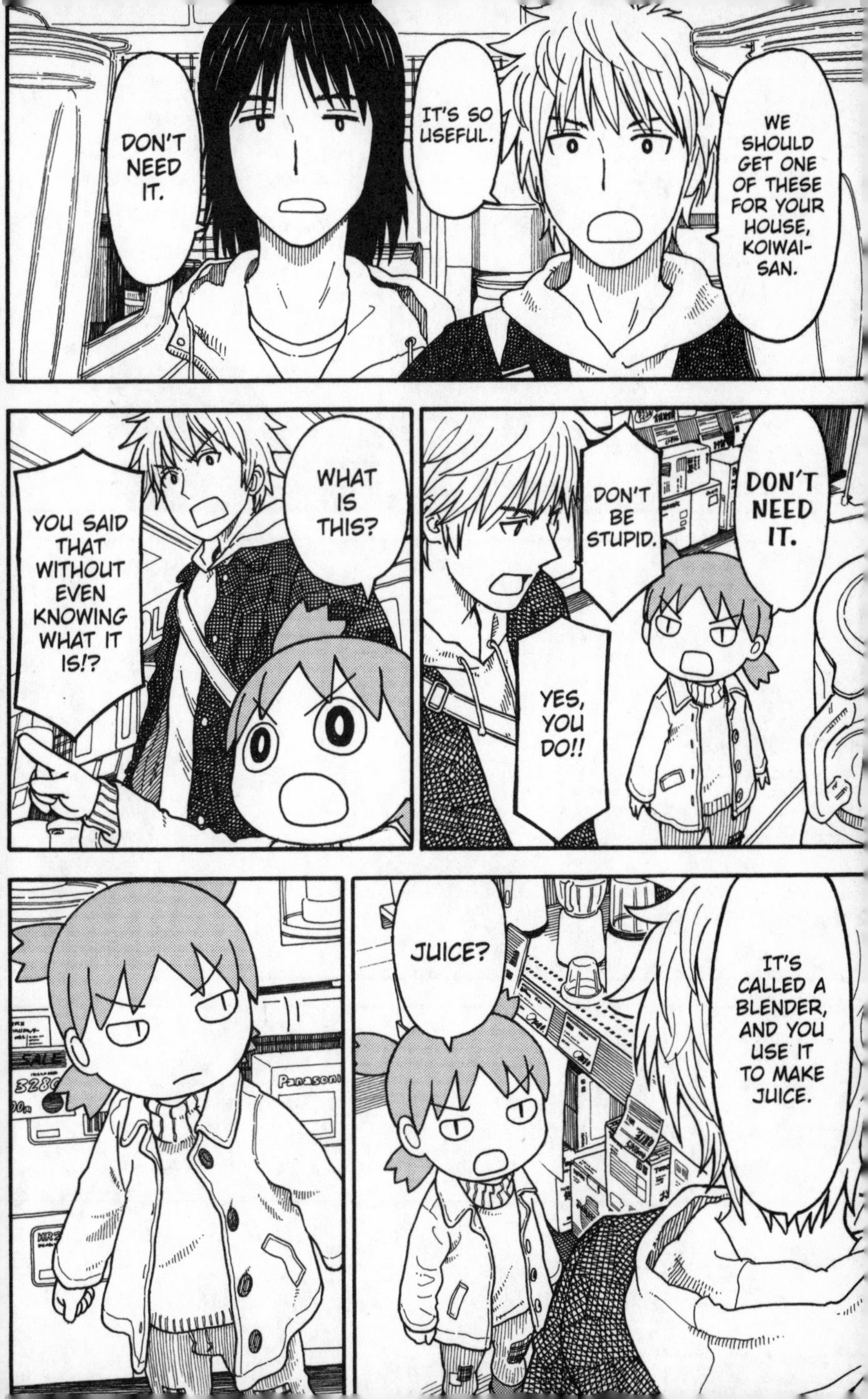
WE SHOULD GET ONE OF THESE FOR YOUR HOUSE, KOIWAI-SAN.
IT'S SO USEFUL.
DON'T NEED IT.
DON'T NEED IT.
DON'T BE STUPID.
YES, YOU DO!!
WHAT IS THIS?
YOU SAID THAT WITHOUT EVEN KNOWING WHAT IT IS!?
IT'S CALLED A BLENDER, AND YOU USE IT TO MAKE JUICE.
JUICE?
SALE

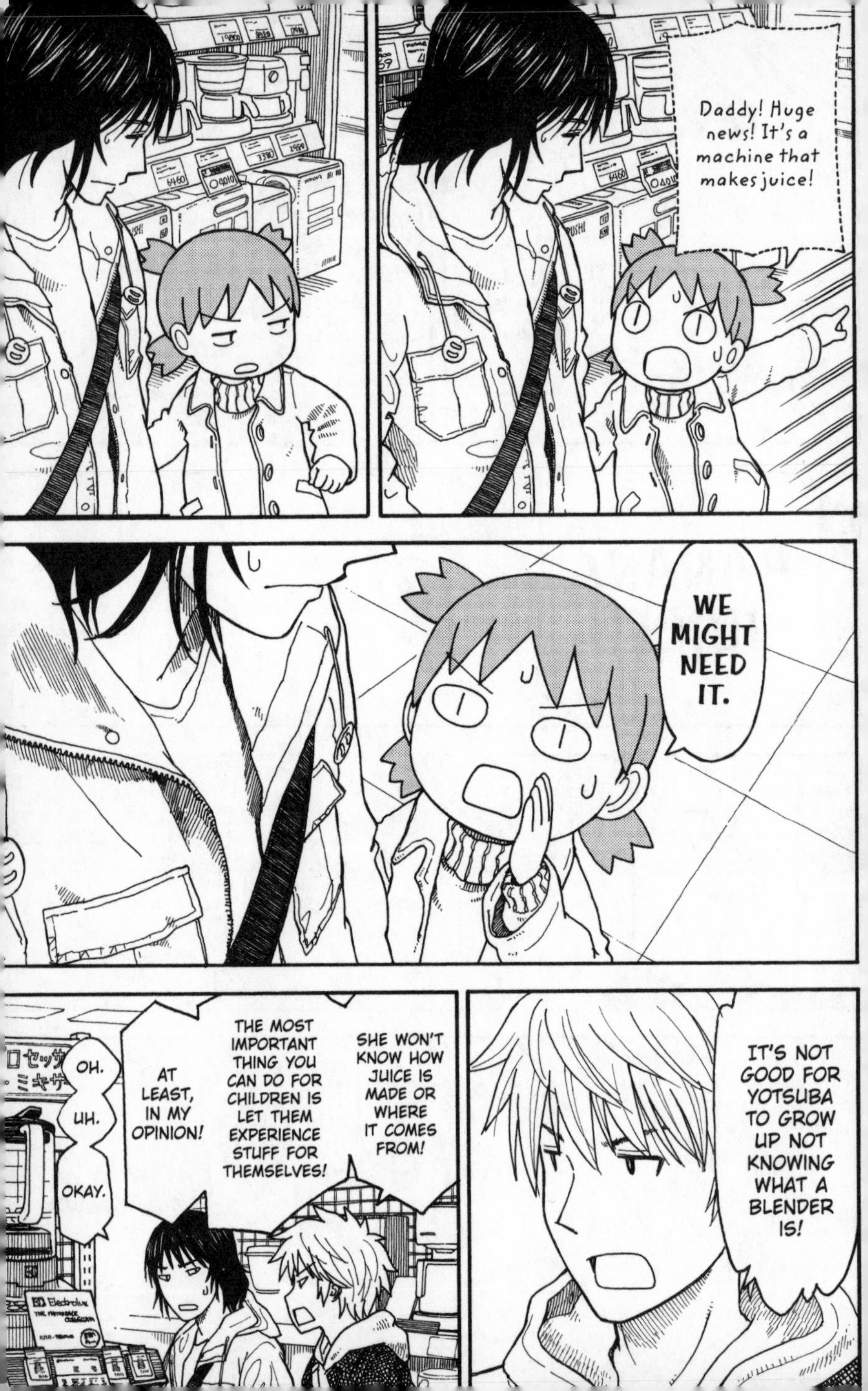
Daddy! Huge news! It's a machine that makes juice!
WE MIGHT NEED IT.
IT'S NOT GOOD FOR YOTSUBA TO GROW UP NOT KNOWING WHAT A BLENDER IS!
SHE WON'T KNOW HOW JUICE IS MADE OR WHERE IT COMES FROM!
THE MOST IMPORTANT THING YOU CAN DO FOR CHILDREN IS LET THEM EXPERIENCE STUFF FOR THEMSELVES!
AT LEAST, IN MY OPINION!
OH.
UH.
OKAY.

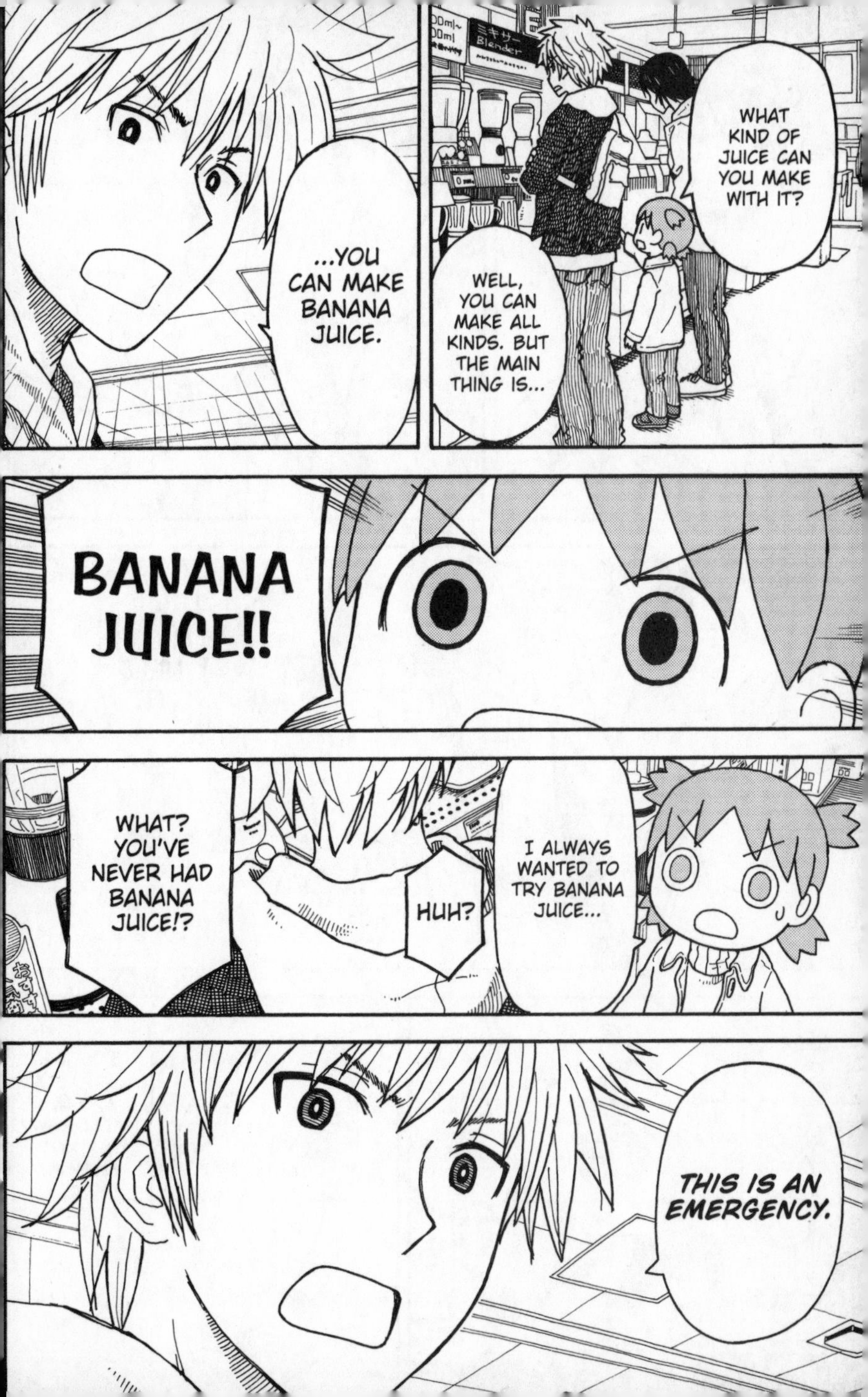
ミキサー
Blender
WHAT KIND OF JUICE CAN YOU MAKE WITH IT?
WELL, YOU CAN MAKE ALL KINDS. BUT THE MAIN THING IS...
...YOU CAN MAKE BANANA JUICE.
BANANA JUICE!!
I ALWAYS WANTED TO TRY BANANA JUICE...
HUH?
WHAT? YOU'VE NEVER HAD BANANA JUICE!?
THIS IS AN EMERGENCY.

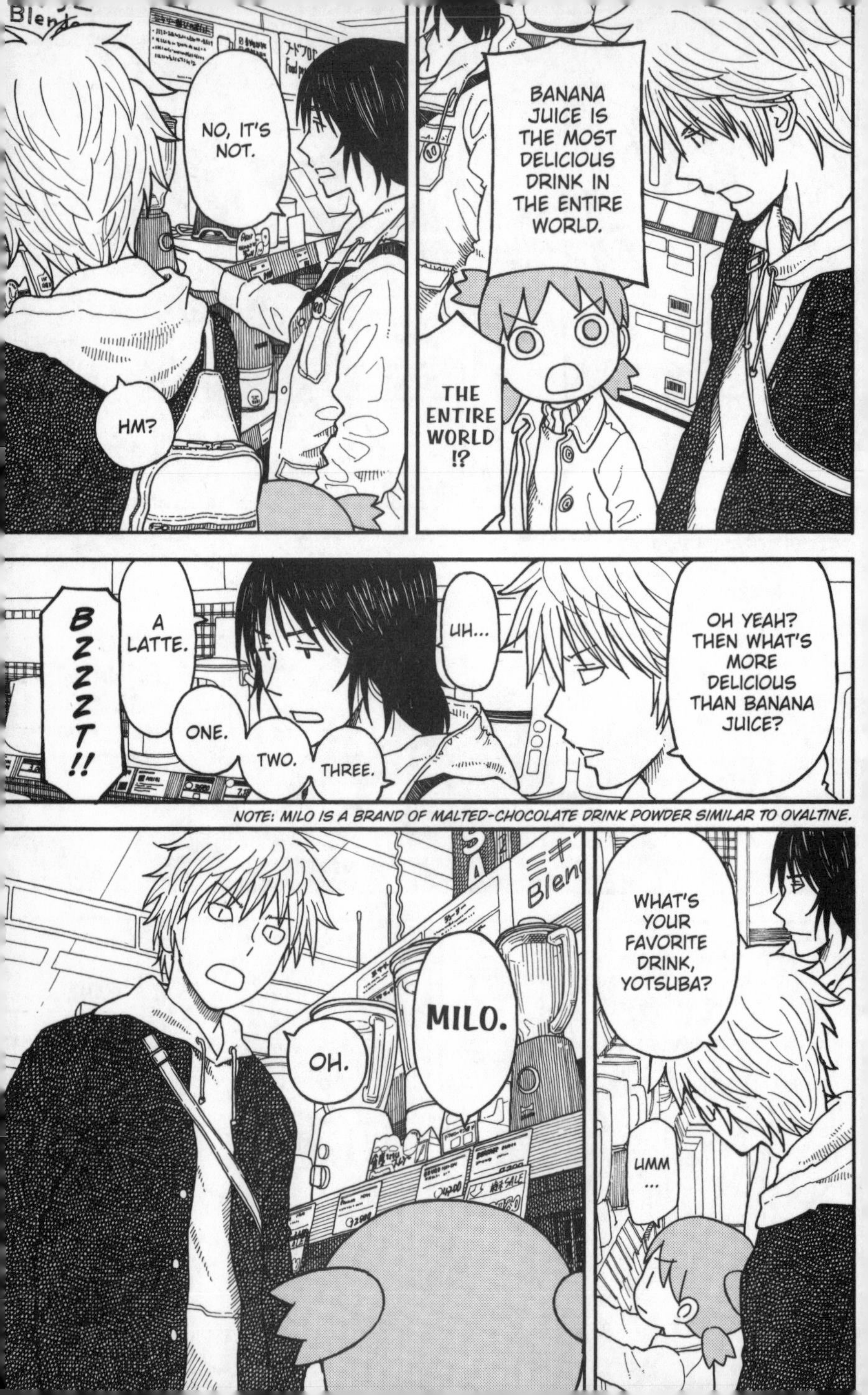
BANANA JUICE IS THE MOST DELICIOUS DRINK IN THE ENTIRE WORLD.
THE ENTIRE WORLD!?
NO, IT'S NOT.
HM?
OH YEAH? THEN WHAT'S MORE DELICIOUS THAN BANANA JUICE?
UH...
A LATTE.
ONE.
TWO.
THREE.
BZZZZT!!
WHAT'S YOUR FAVORITE DRINK, YOTSUBA?
UMM ...
MILO.
OH.

NOTE: MILO IS A BRAND OF MALTED-CHOCOLATE DRINK POWDER SIMILAR TO OVALTINE.

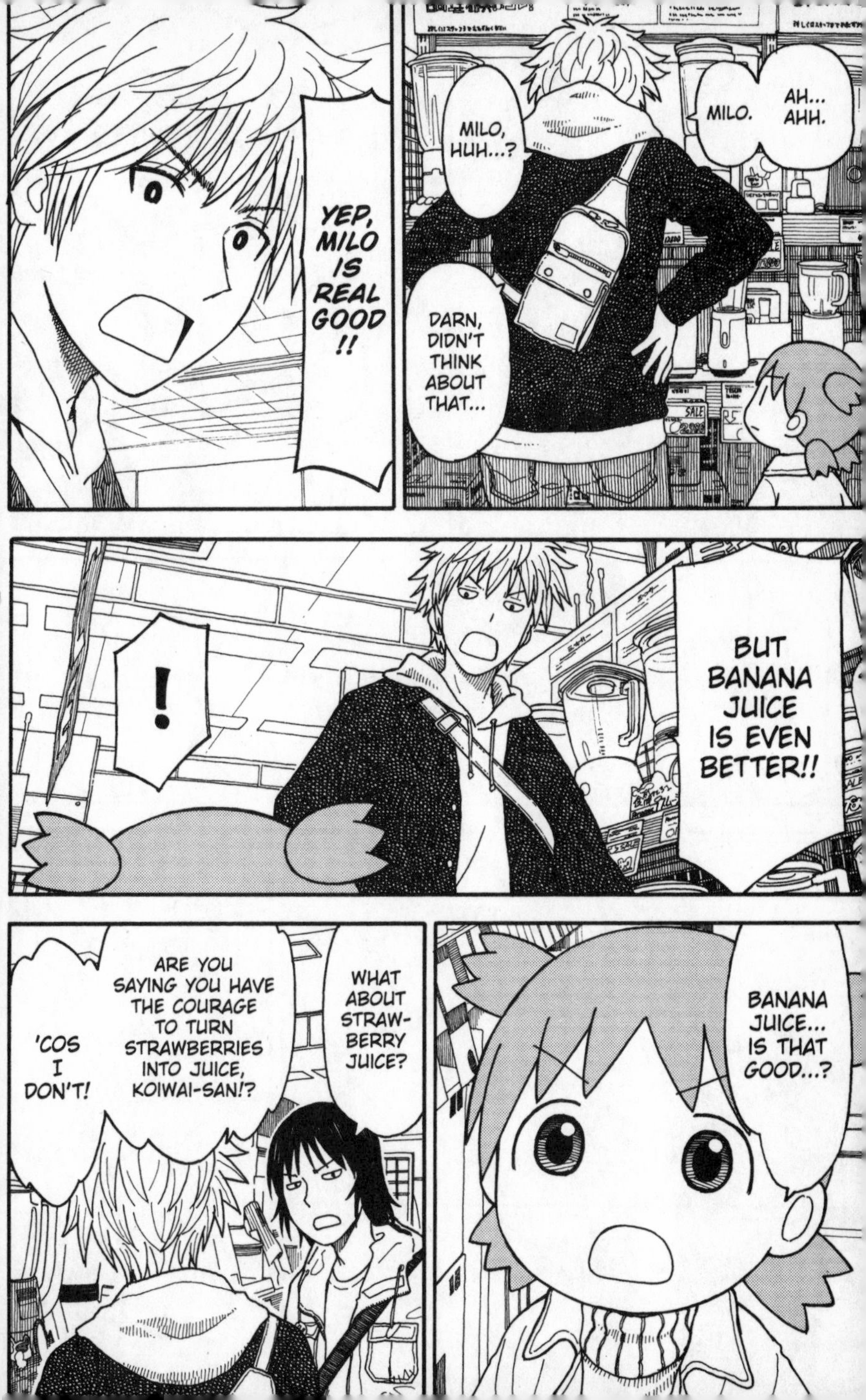
AH... AHH.
MILO.
MILO, HUH...?
DARN, DIDN'T THINK ABOUT THAT...
YEP, MILO IS REAL GOOD!!
BUT BANANA JUICE IS EVEN BETTER!!
!
BANANA JUICE... IS THAT GOOD...?
WHAT ABOUT STRAW-BERRY JUICE?
ARE YOU SAYING YOU HAVE THE COURAGE TO TURN STRAWBERRIES INTO JUICE, KOIWAI-SAN!?
'COS I DON'T!

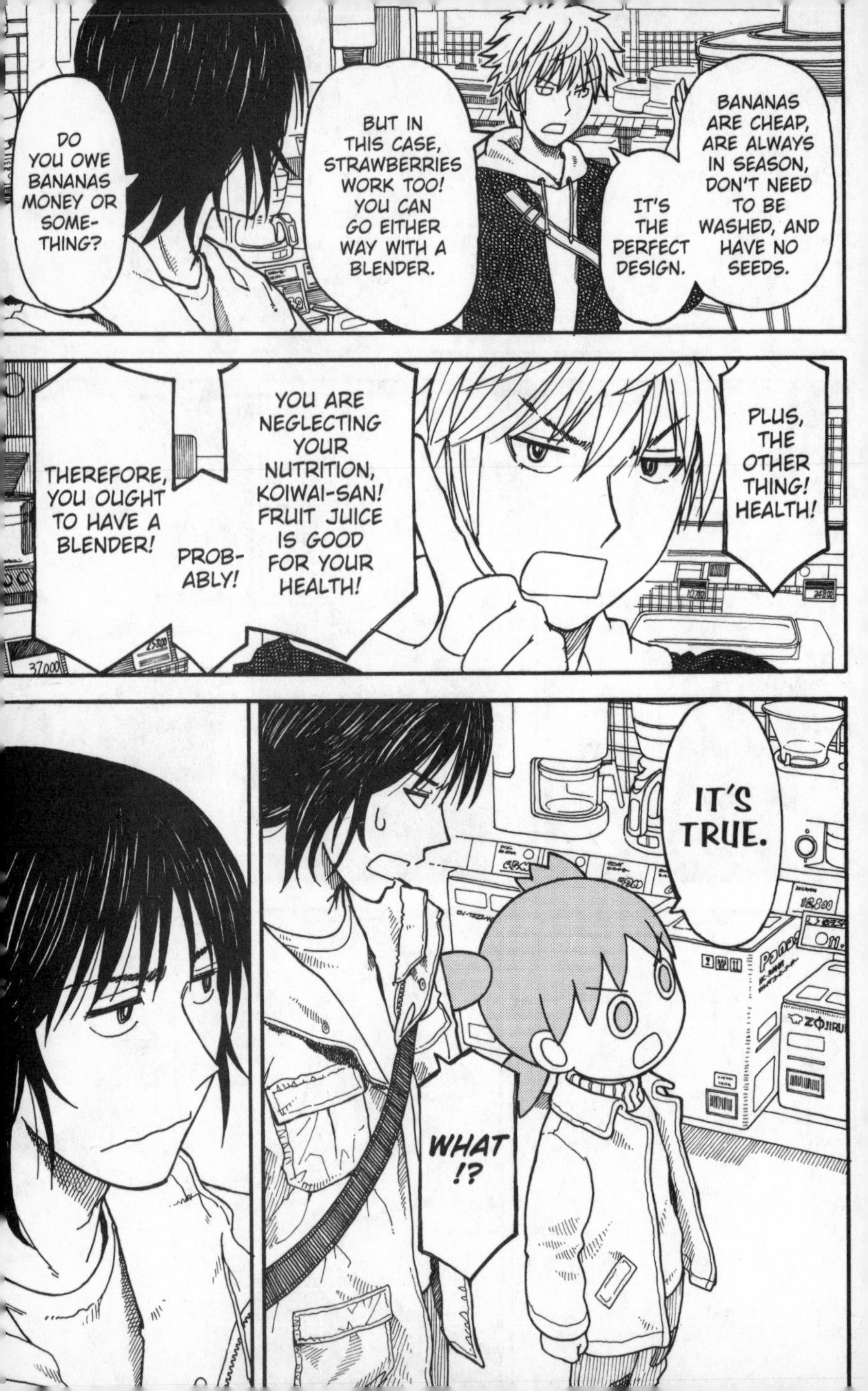
BANANAS ARE CHEAP, ARE ALWAYS IN SEASON, DON'T NEED TO BE WASHED, AND HAVE NO SEEDS.
IT'S THE PERFECT DESIGN.
BUT IN THIS CASE, STRAWBERRIES WORK TOO! YOU CAN GO EITHER WAY WITH A BLENDER.
DO YOU OWE BANANAS MONEY OR SOMETHING?
PLUS, THE OTHER THING! HEALTH!
YOU ARE NEGLECTING YOUR NUTRITION, KOIWAI-SAN! FRUIT JUICE IS GOOD FOR YOUR HEALTH!
PROBABLY!
THEREFORE, YOU OUGHT TO HAVE A BLENDER!
IT'S TRUE.
WHAT!?

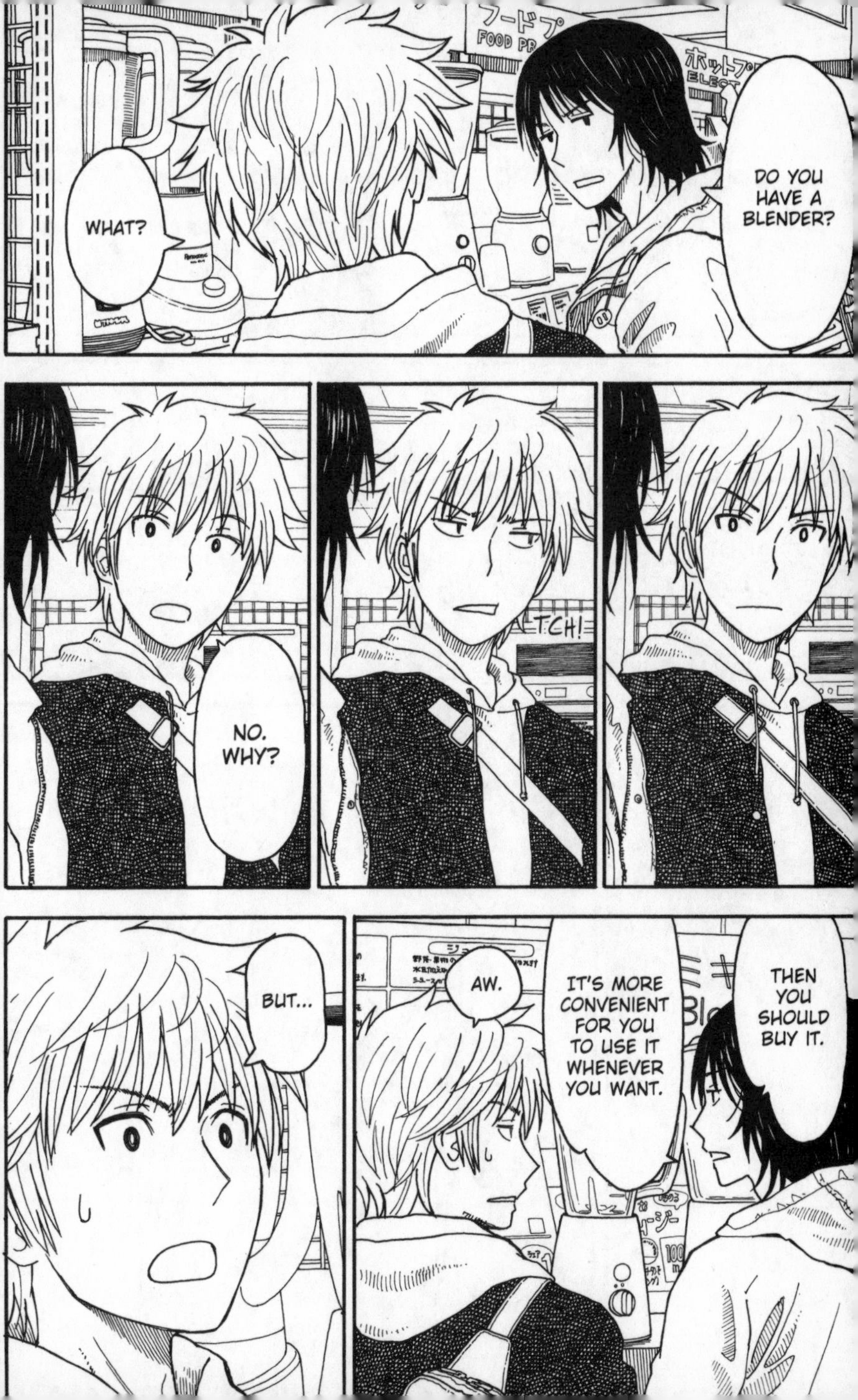
DO YOU HAVE A BLENDER?
WHAT?
TCH!
NO. WHY?
THEN YOU SHOULD BUY IT.
IT'S MORE CONVENIENT FOR YOU TO USE IT WHENEVER YOU WANT.
AW.
BUT...

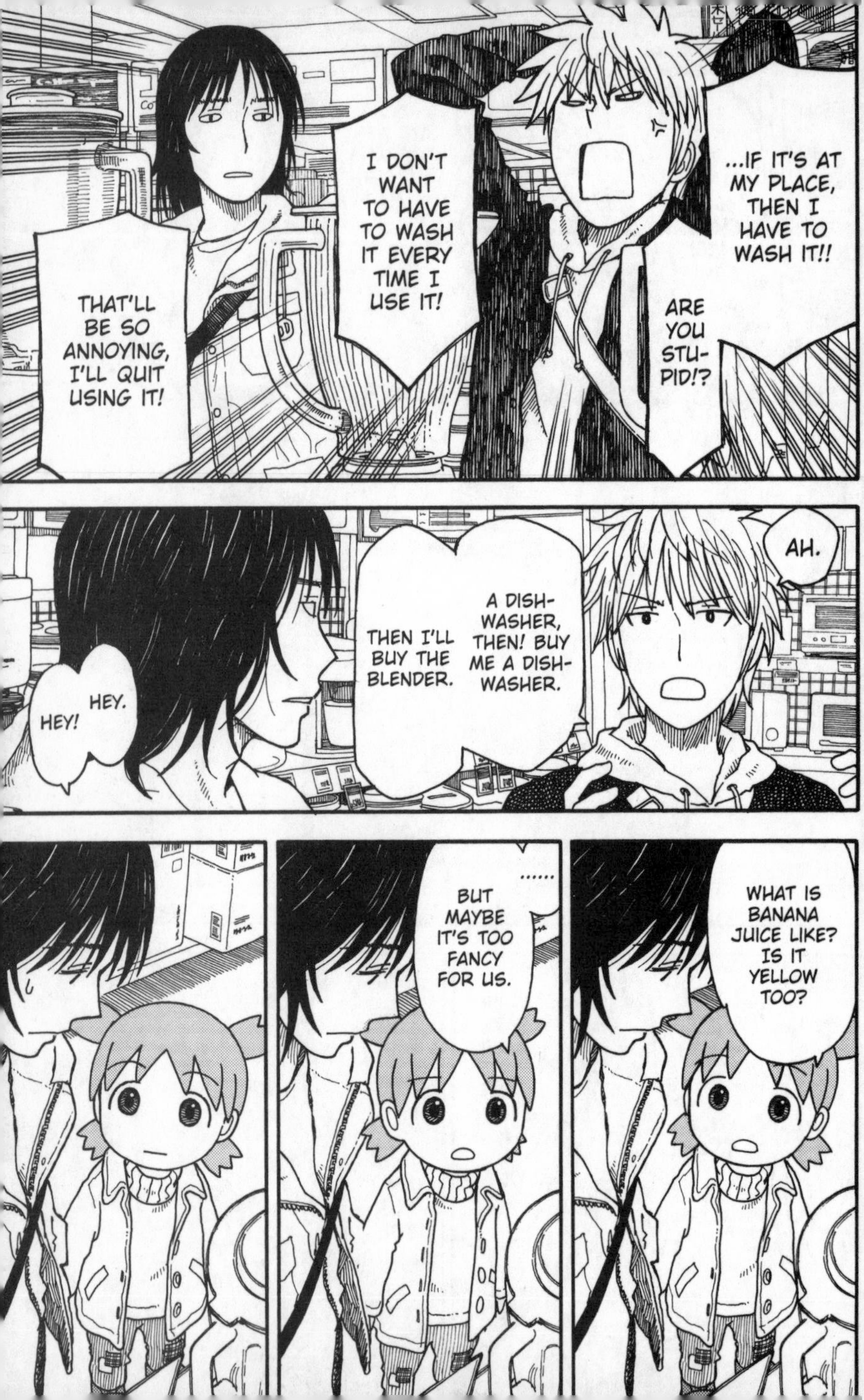
...IF IT'S AT MY PLACE, THEN I HAVE TO WASH IT!!
ARE YOU STU-PID!?
I DON'T WANT TO HAVE TO WASH IT EVERY TIME I USE IT!
THAT'LL BE SO ANNOYING, I'LL QUIT USING IT!
AH.
A DISH-WASHER, THEN! BUY ME A DISH-WASHER.
THEN I'LL BUY THE BLENDER.
HEY.
HEY!
WHAT IS BANANA JUICE LIKE? IS IT YELLOW TOO?
......
BUT MAYBE IT'S TOO FANCY FOR US.

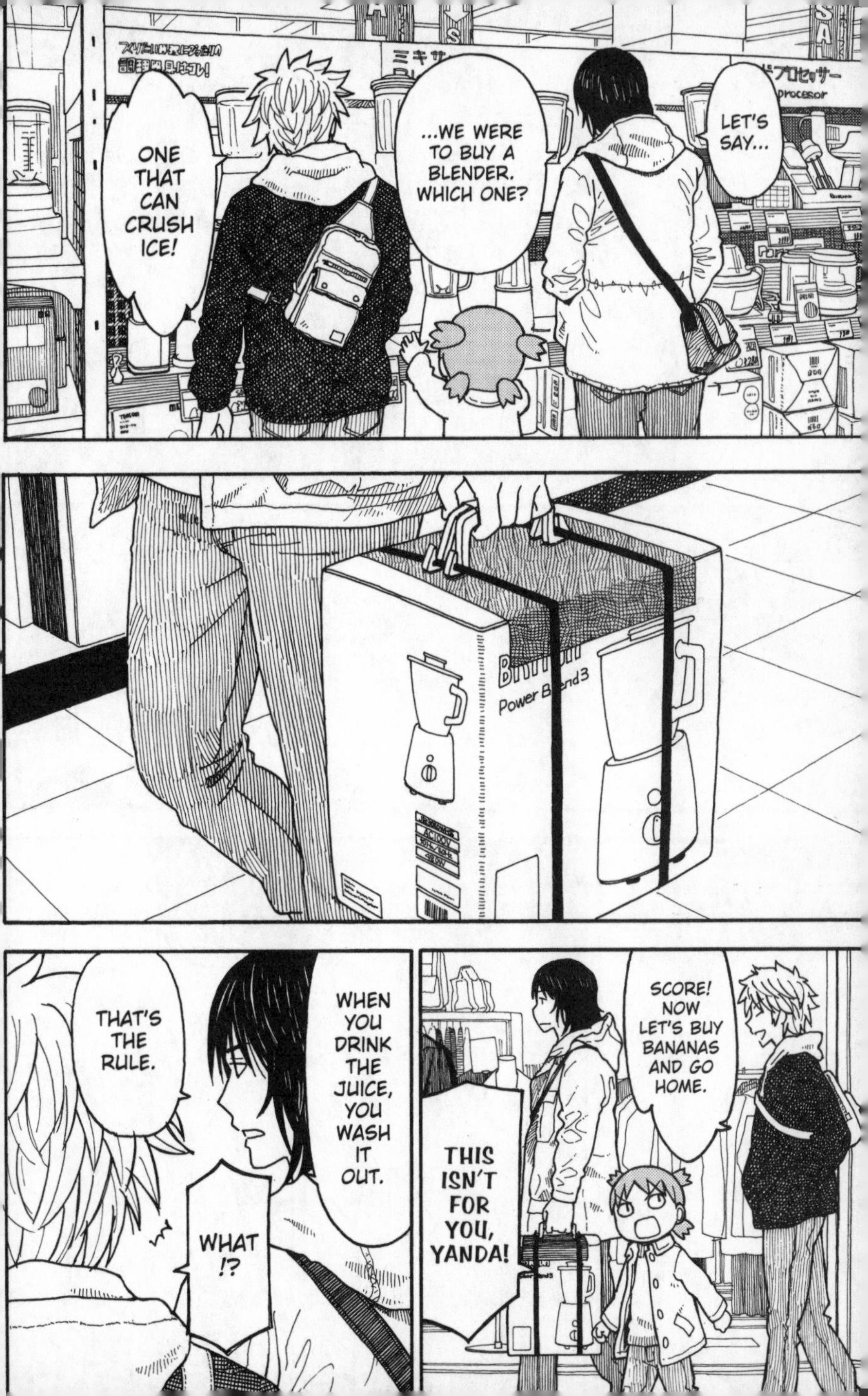
LET'S SAY...
...WE WERE TO BUY A BLENDER. WHICH ONE?
ONE THAT CAN CRUSH ICE!
Power Blend3
SCORE! NOW LET'S BUY BANANAS AND GO HOME.
THIS ISN'T FOR YOU, YANDA!
WHEN YOU DRINK THE JUICE, YOU WASH IT OUT.
THAT'S THE RULE.
WHAT!?

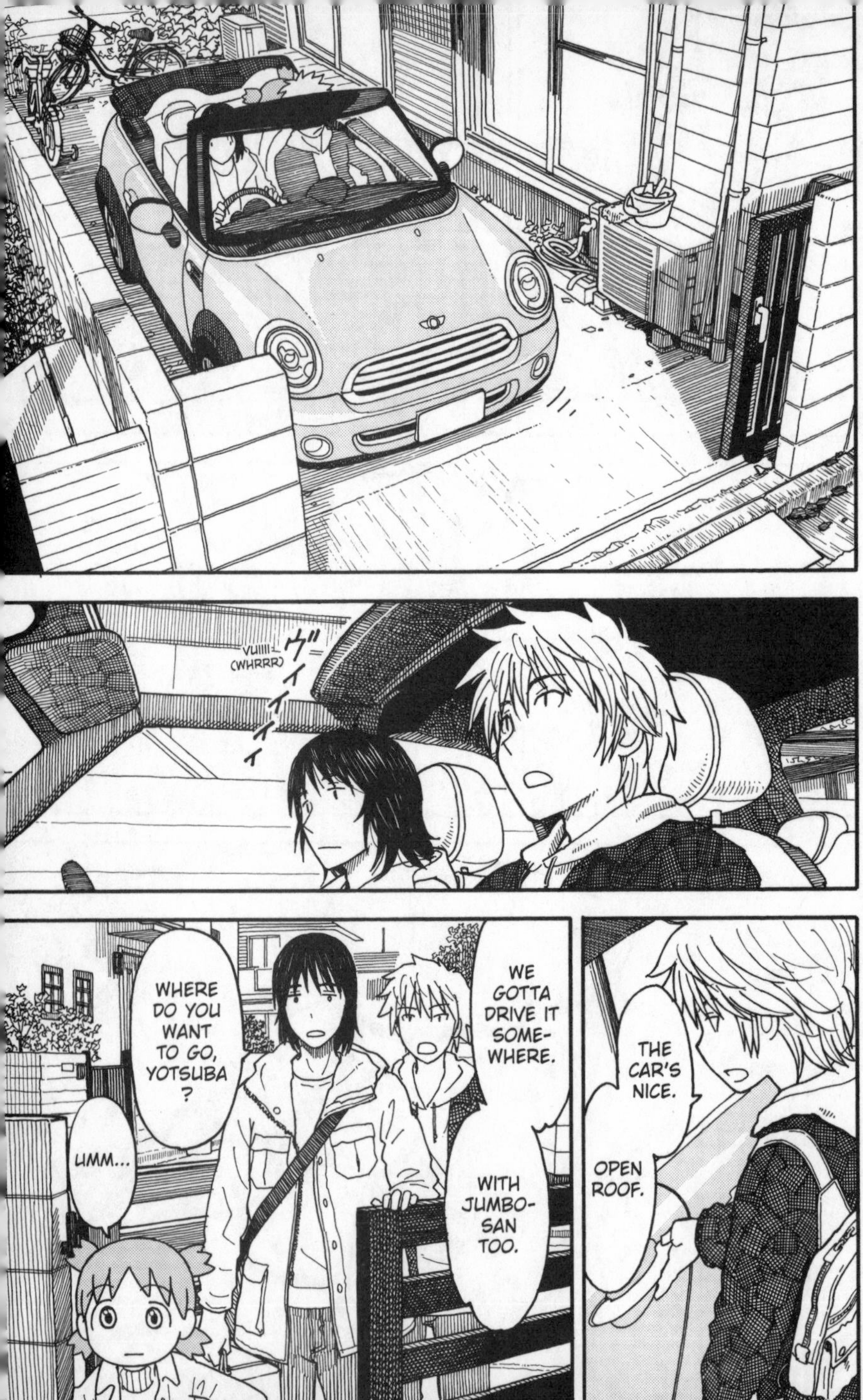
VUIIII (WHRRR)
ヴィイイイ
THE CAR'S NICE.
OPEN ROOF.
WE GOTTA DRIVE IT SOME-WHERE.
WITH JUMBO-SAN TOO.
WHERE DO YOU WANT TO GO, YOTSUBA?
UMM...

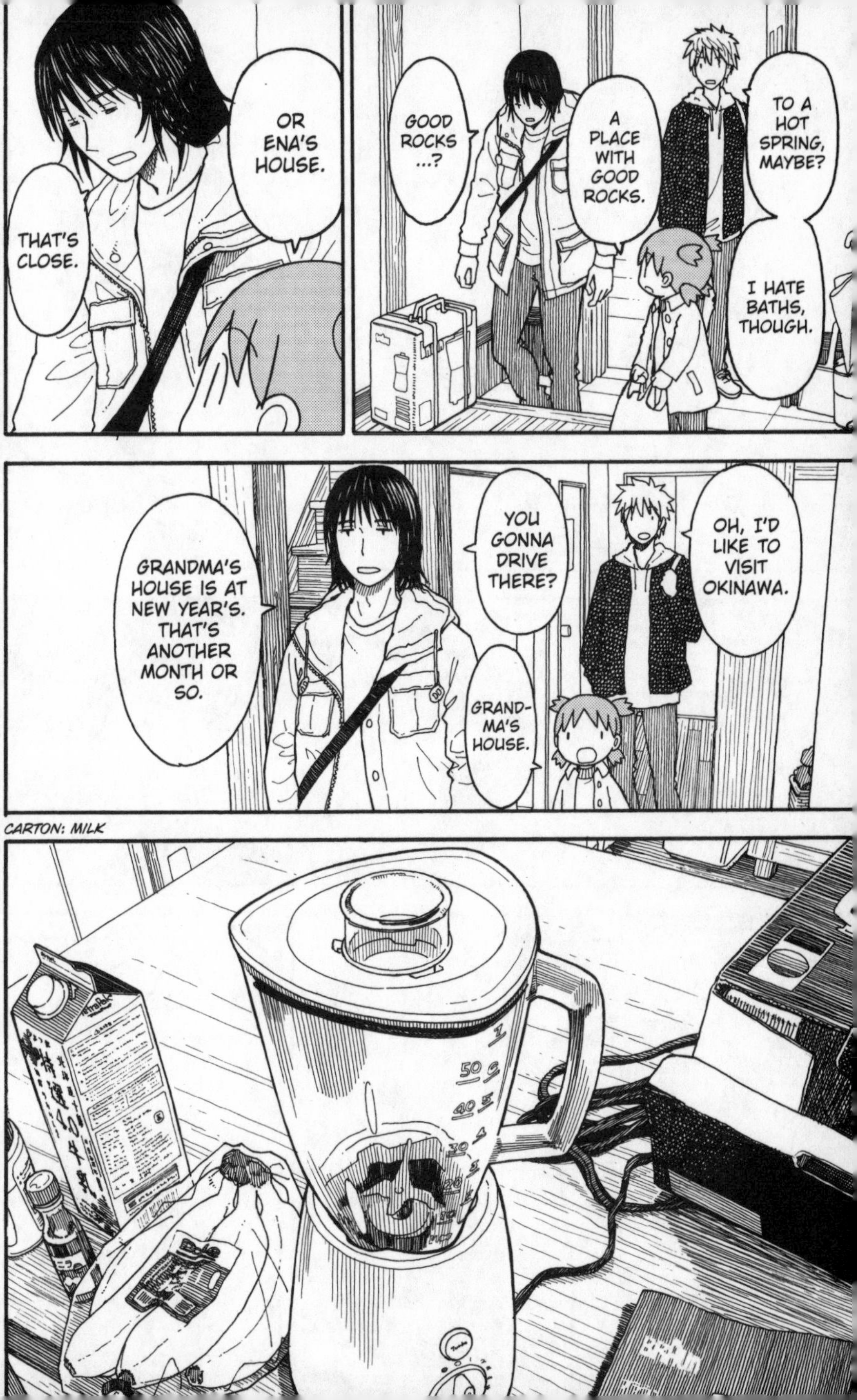
TO A HOT SPRING, MAYBE?
I HATE BATHS, THOUGH.
A PLACE WITH GOOD ROCKS.
GOOD ROCKS ...?
OR ENA'S HOUSE.
THAT'S CLOSE.
OH, I'D LIKE TO VISIT OKINAWA.
YOU GONNA DRIVE THERE?
GRAND-MA'S HOUSE.
GRANDMA'S HOUSE IS AT NEW YEAR'S. THAT'S ANOTHER MONTH OR SO.

CARTON: MILK

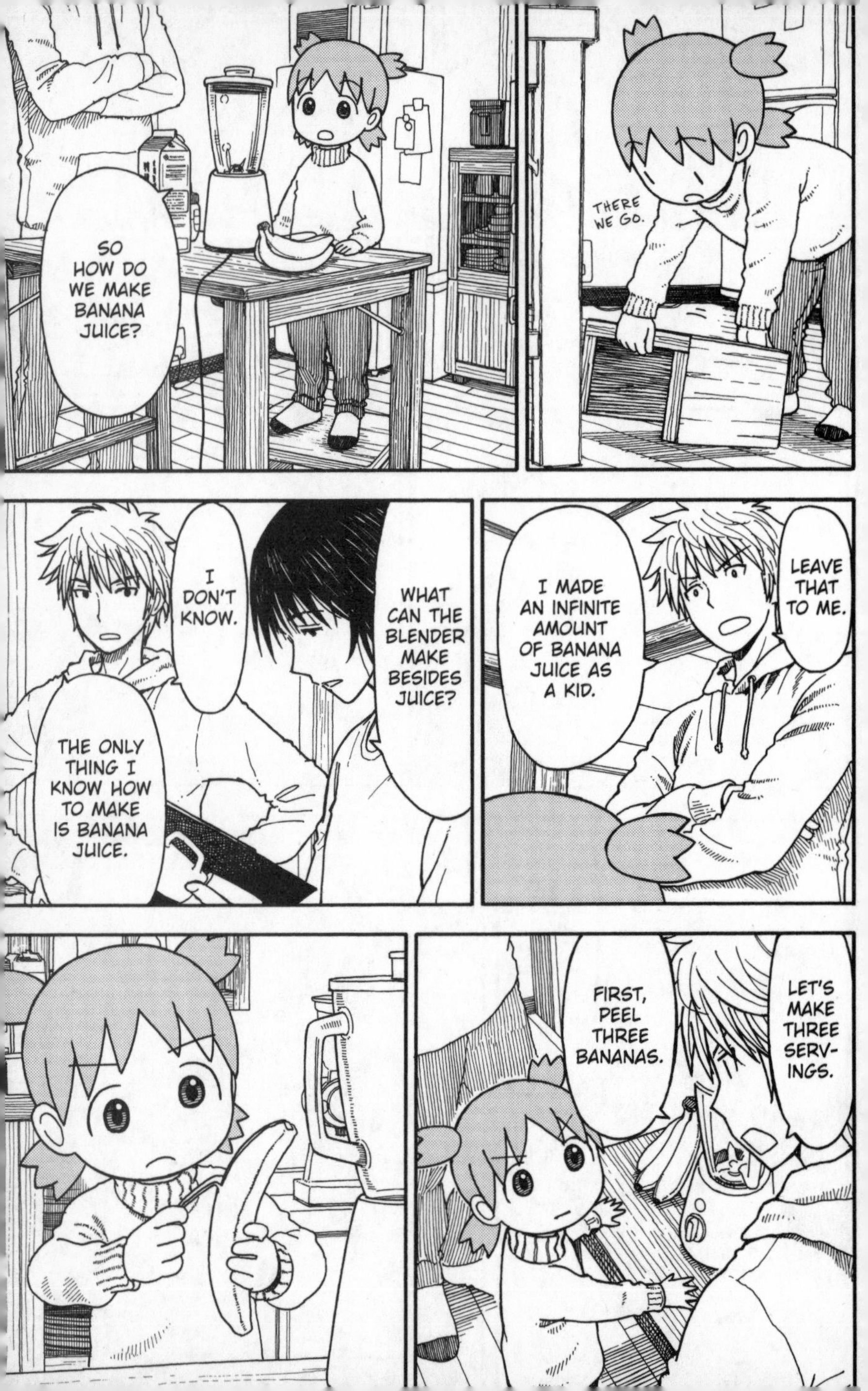
THERE WE GO.
SO HOW DO WE MAKE BANANA JUICE?
LEAVE THAT TO ME.
I MADE AN INFINITE AMOUNT OF BANANA JUICE AS A KID.
WHAT CAN THE BLENDER MAKE BESIDES JUICE?
I DON'T KNOW.
THE ONLY THING I KNOW HOW TO MAKE IS BANANA JUICE.
LET'S MAKE THREE SERV-INGS.
FIRST, PEEL THREE BANANAS.

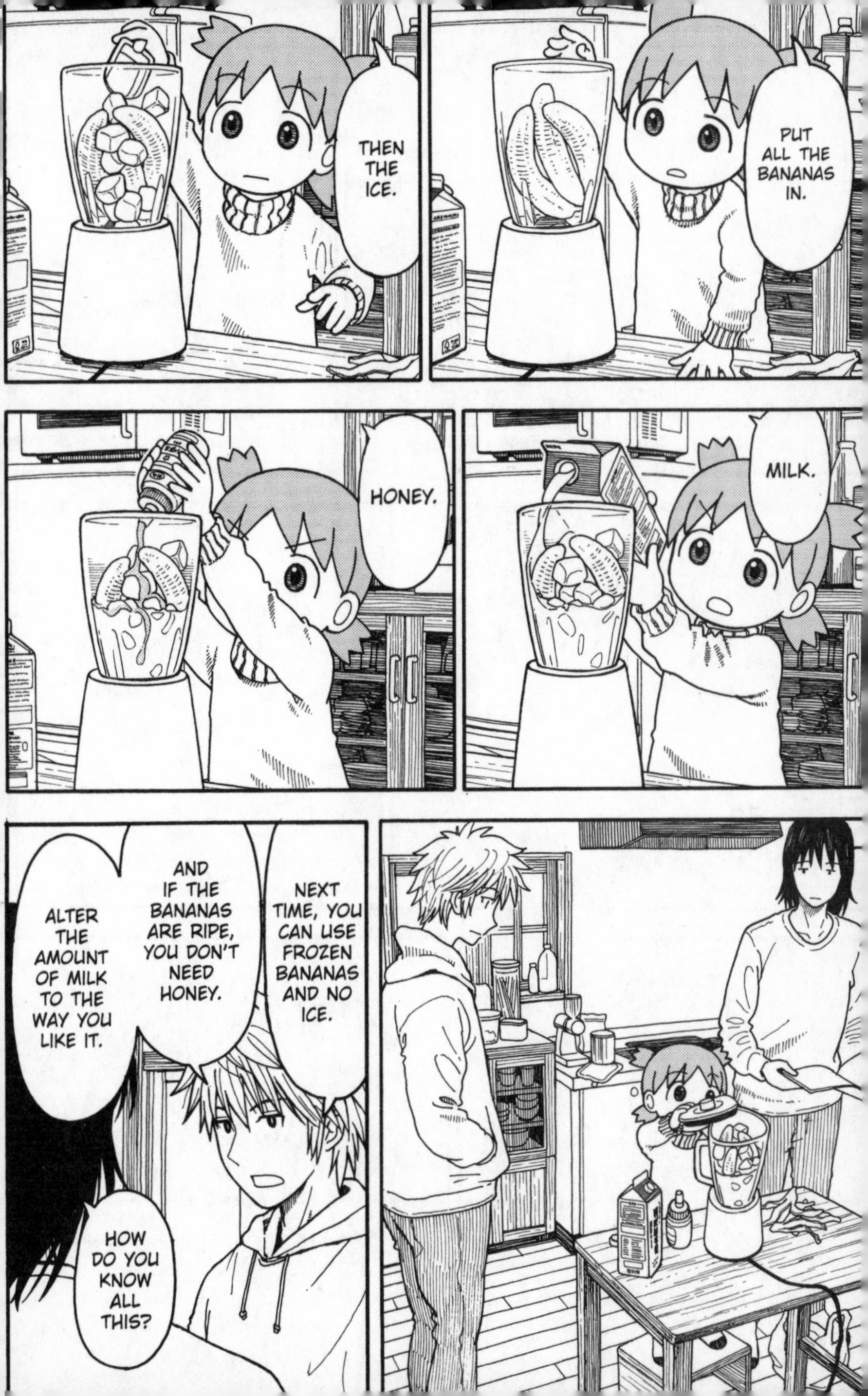
PUT ALL THE BANANAS IN.
THEN THE ICE.
MILK.
HONEY.
NEXT TIME, YOU CAN USE FROZEN BANANAS AND NO ICE.
AND IF THE BANANAS ARE RIPE, YOU DON'T NEED HONEY.
ALTER THE AMOUNT OF MILK TO THE WAY YOU LIKE IT.
HOW DO YOU KNOW ALL THIS?

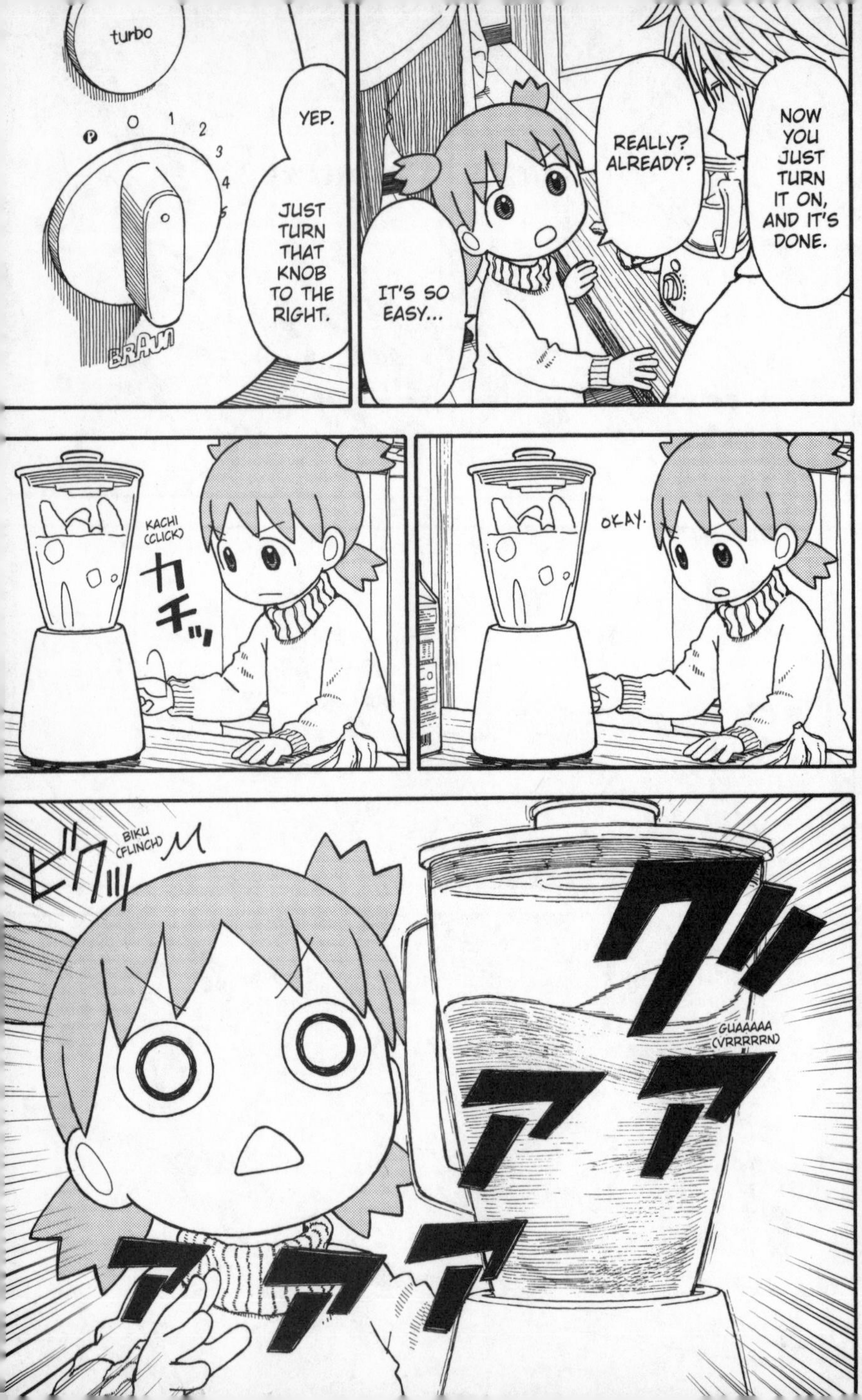
NOW YOU JUST TURN IT ON, AND IT'S DONE.
REALLY? ALREADY?
IT'S SO EASY...
YEP.
JUST TURN THAT KNOB TO THE RIGHT.
turbo
P O 1 2 3 4 5
BRAUN
OKAY.
KACHI (CLICK)
カチッ
GUAAAAA (VRRRRRN)
BIKU (FLINCH)
ビクッ

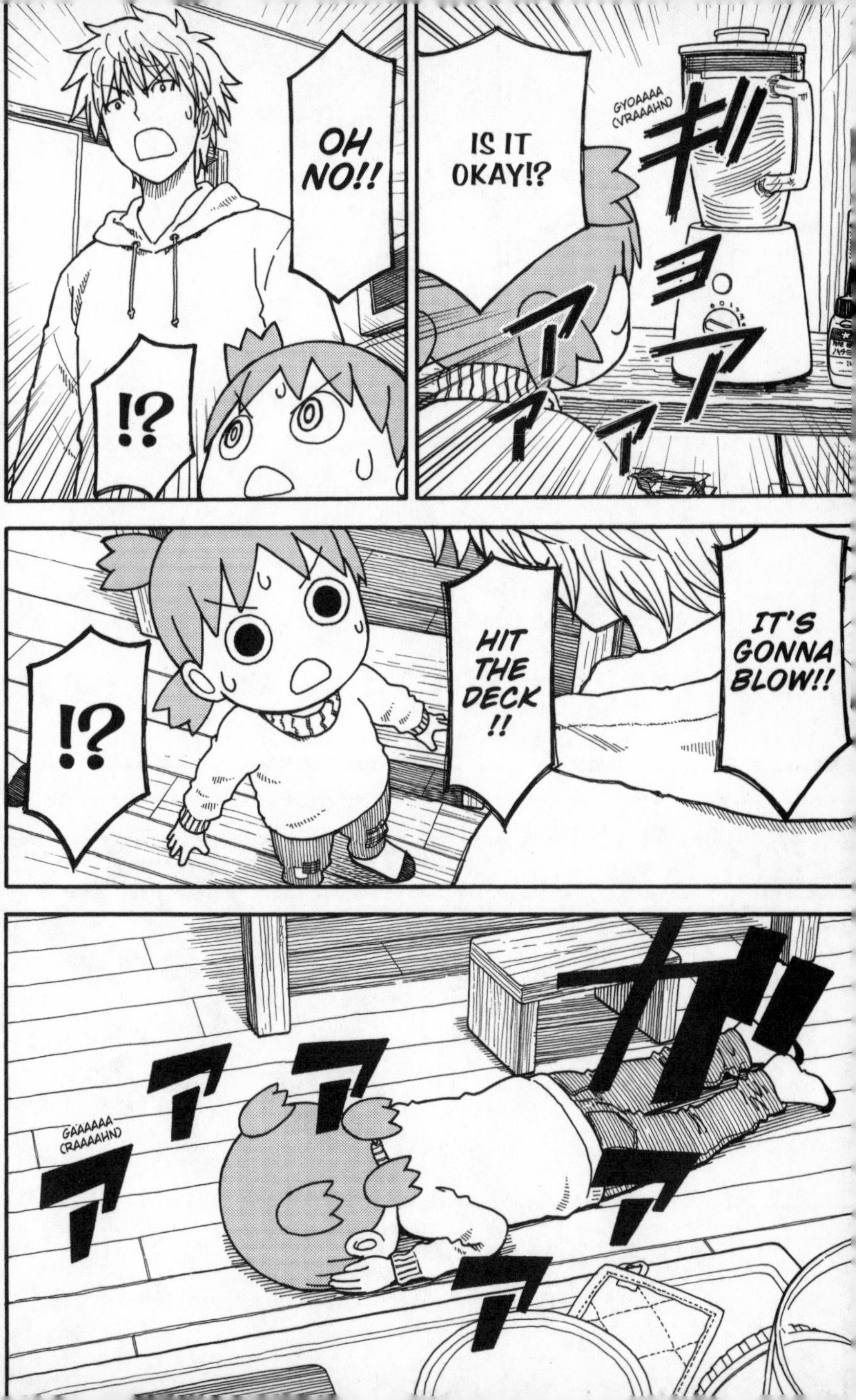
GYOAAAA (VRAAAHN)
IS IT OKAY!?
OH NO!!
!?
IT'S GONNA BLOW!!
HIT THE DECK!!
!?
GAAAAAA (RAAAAHN)

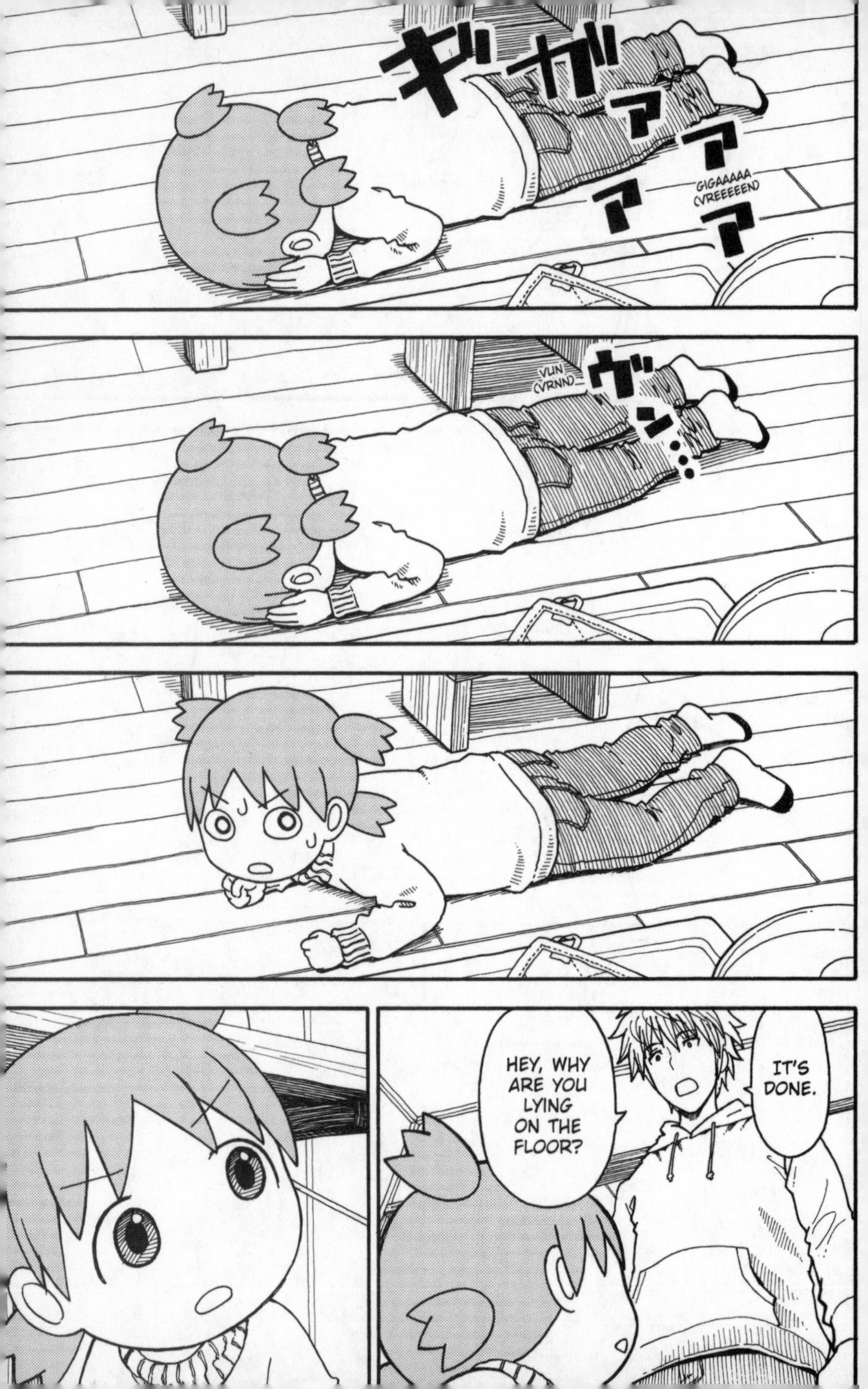
ギガアアアア
GIGAAAAA (VREEEEEN)
ヴン…
VUN (VRNNN)
IT'S DONE.
HEY, WHY ARE YOU LYING ON THE FLOOR?

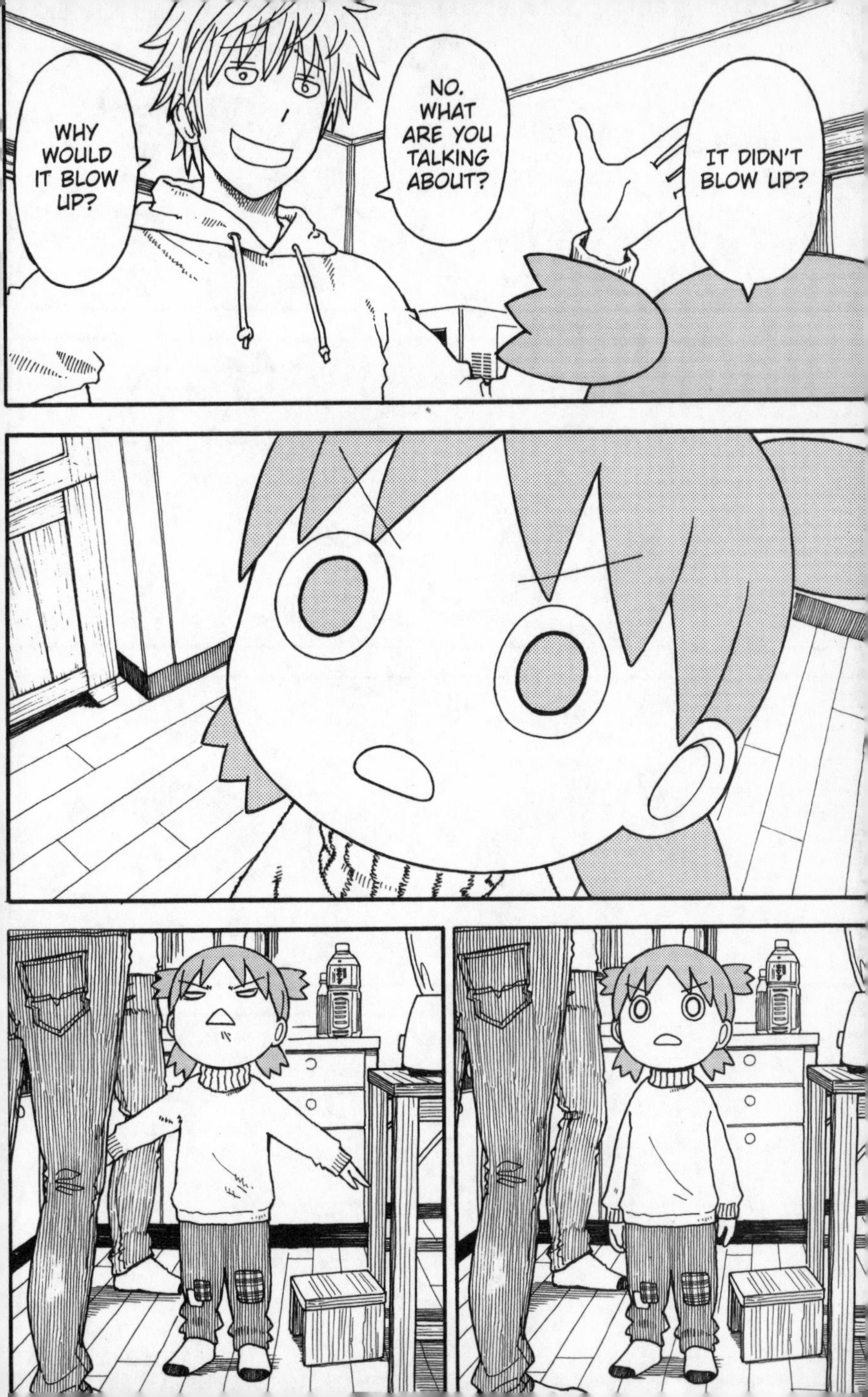
IT DIDN'T BLOW UP?
NO. WHAT ARE YOU TALKING ABOUT?
WHY WOULD IT BLOW UP?

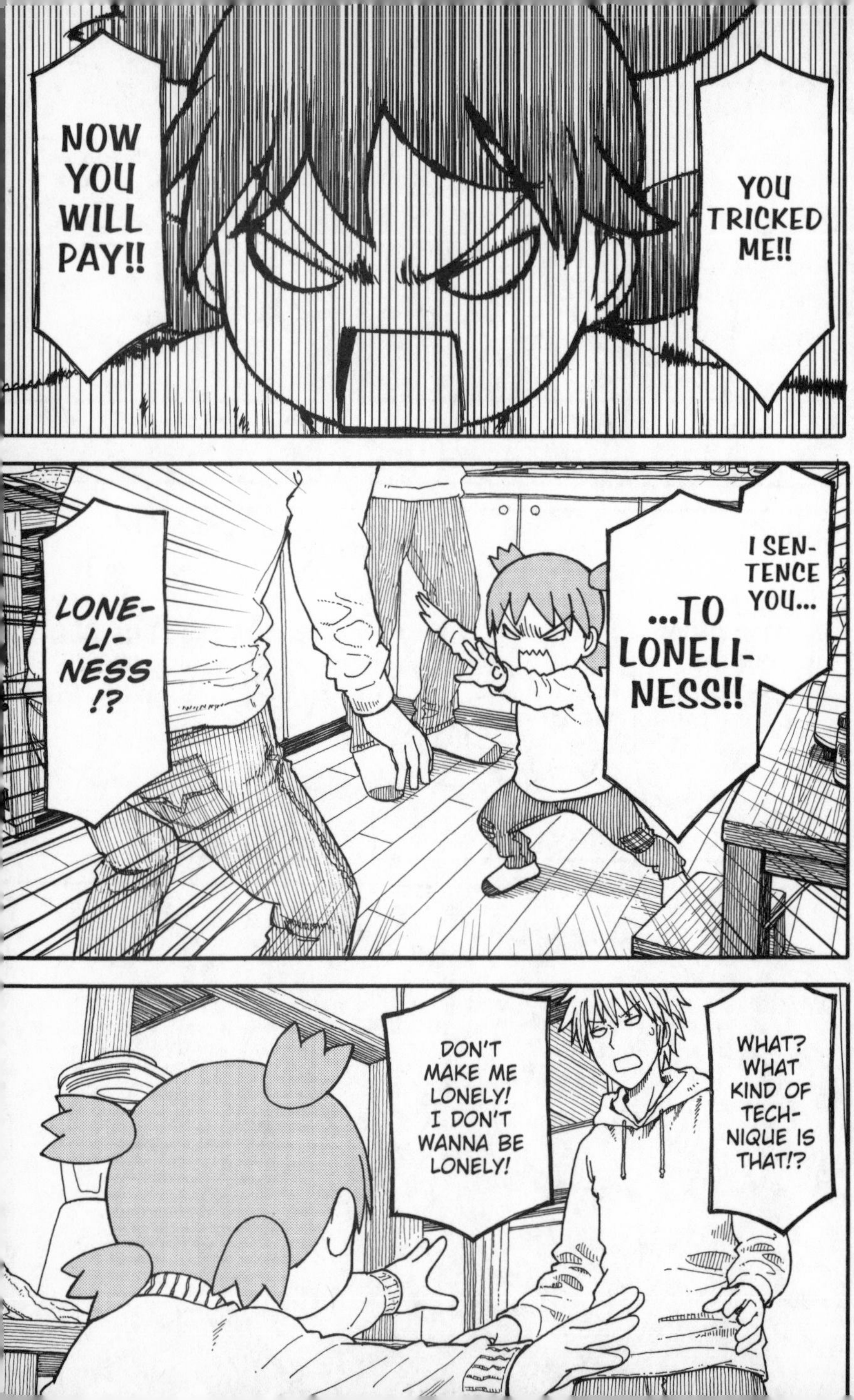
YOU TRICKED ME!!
NOW YOU WILL PAY!!
I SENTENCE YOU...
...TO LONELINESS!!
LONELINESS!?
WHAT? WHAT KIND OF TECHNIQUE IS THAT!?
DON'T MAKE ME LONELY! I DON'T WANNA BE LONELY!

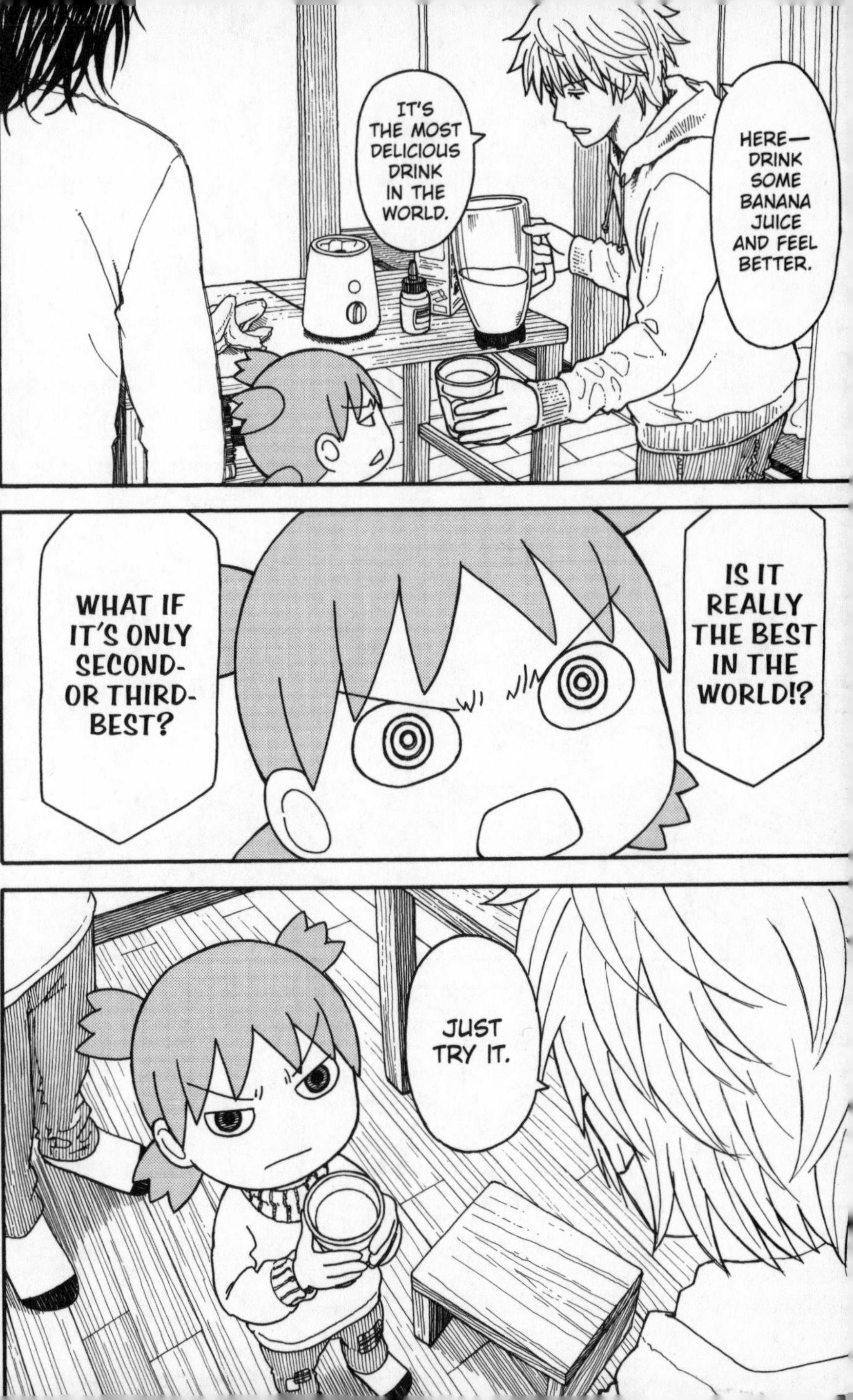
HERE—DRINK SOME BANANA JUICE AND FEEL BETTER.
IT'S THE MOST DELICIOUS DRINK IN THE WORLD.
IS IT REALLY THE BEST IN THE WORLD!?
WHAT IF IT'S ONLY SECOND- OR THIRD-BEST?
JUST TRY IT.

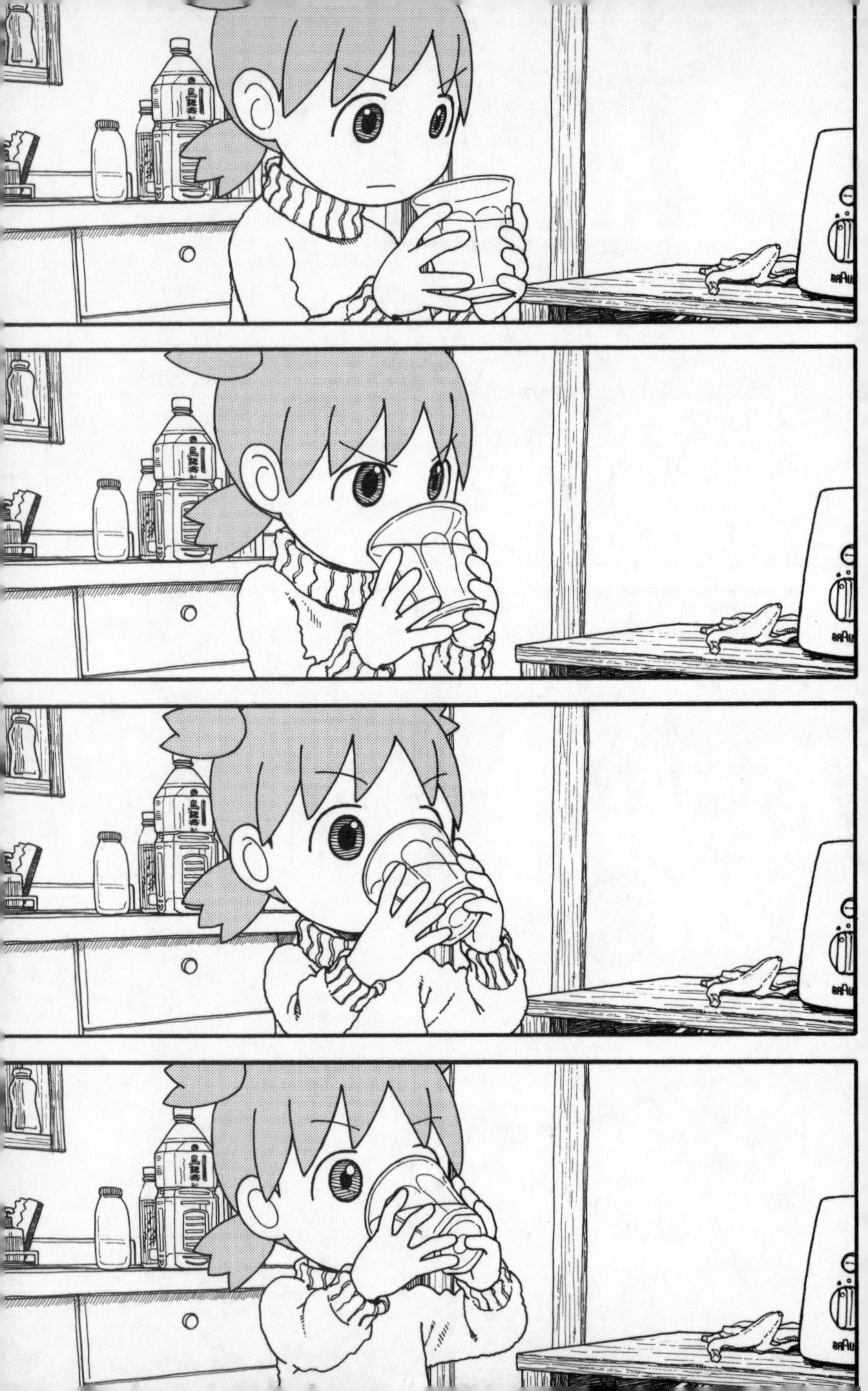

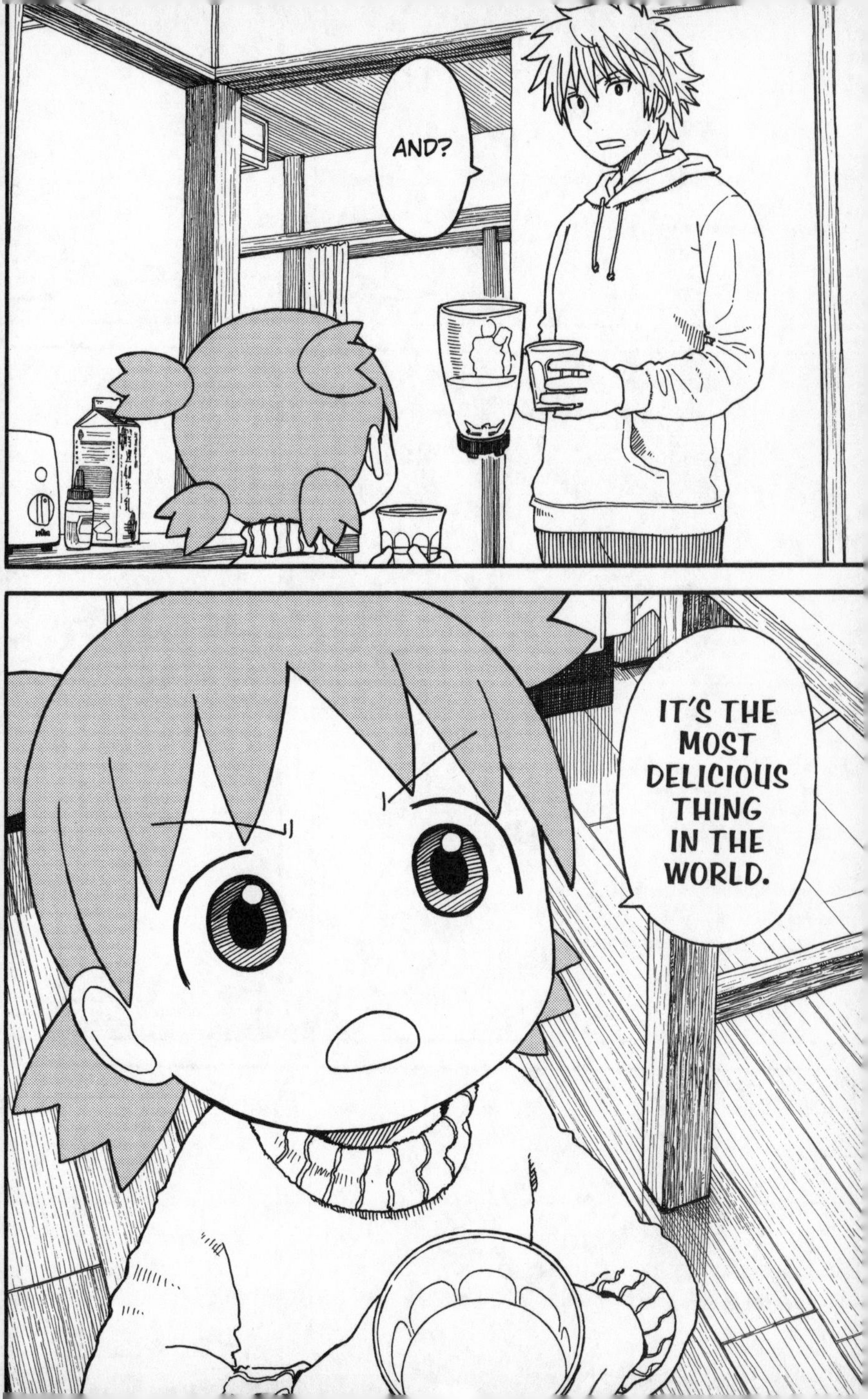
AND?
IT'S THE MOST DELICIOUS THING IN THE WORLD.

YOTSUBA&!

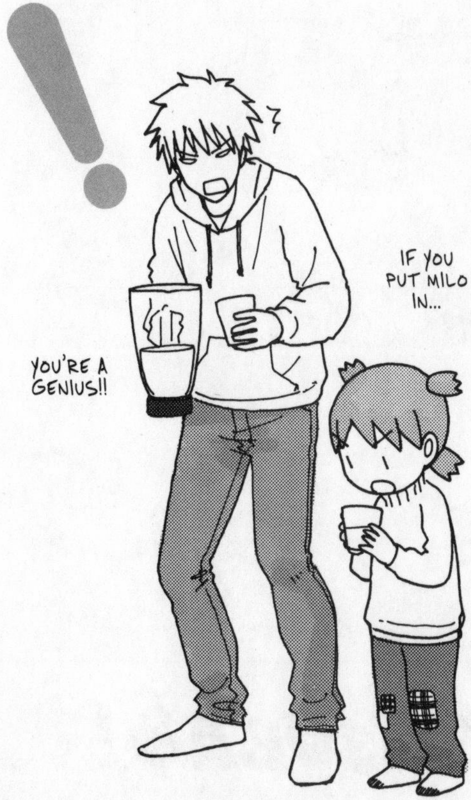
IF YOU PUT MILO IN...
YOU'RE A GENIUS!!

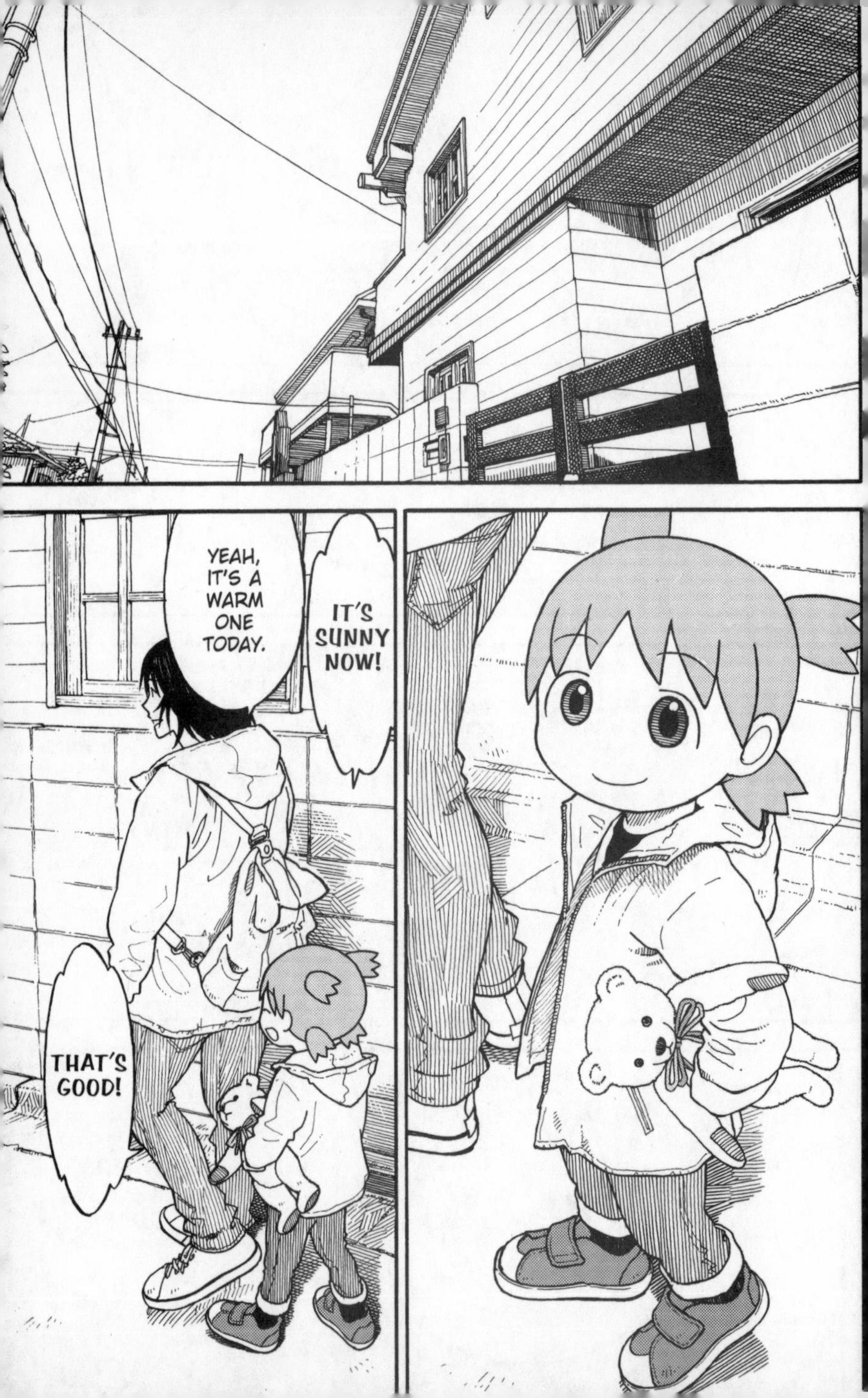
IT'S SUNNY NOW!
YEAH, IT'S A WARM ONE TODAY.
THAT'S GOOD!

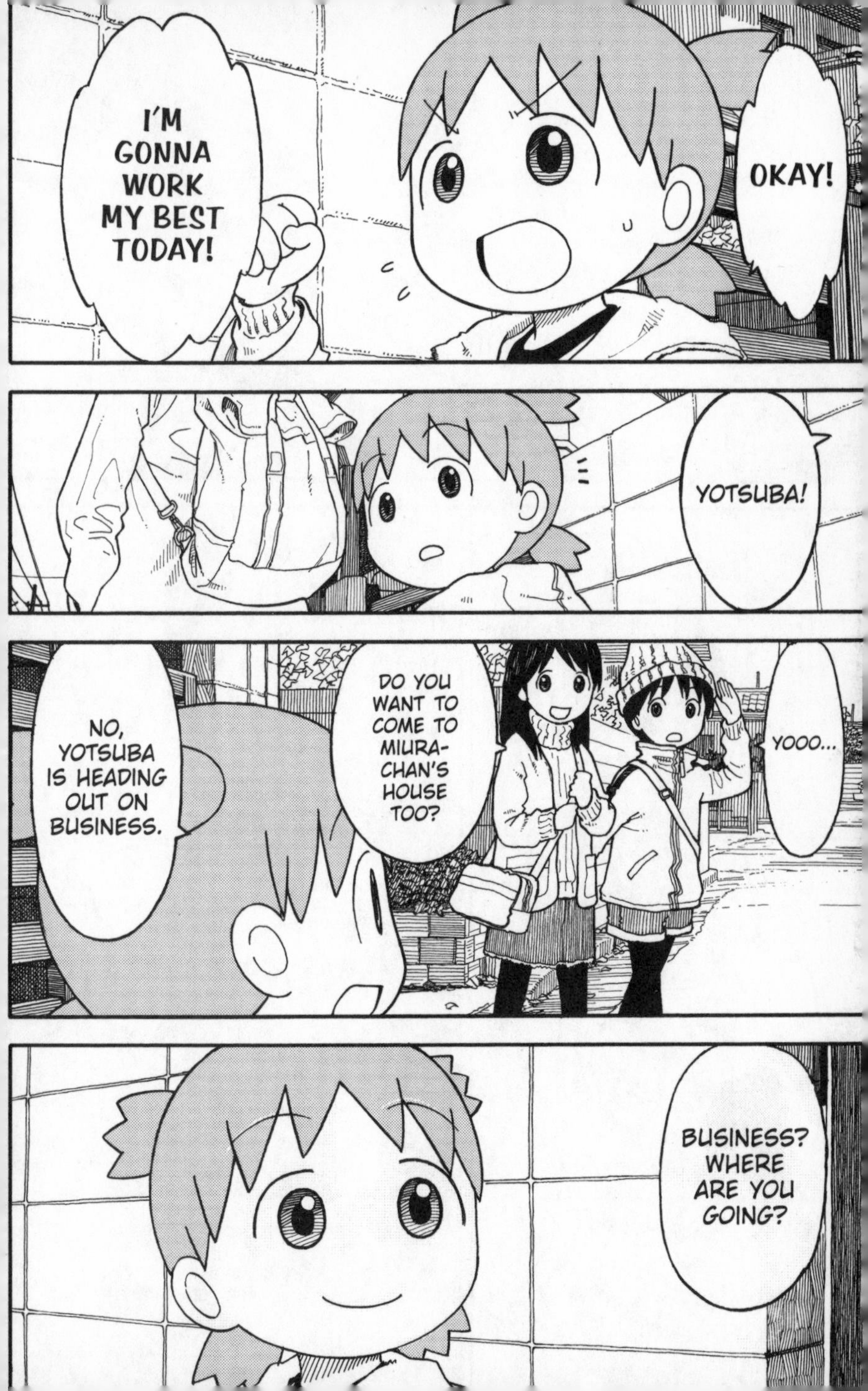
OKAY!
I'M GONNA WORK MY BEST TODAY!
YOTSUBA!
YOOO...
DO YOU WANT TO COME TO MIURA-CHAN'S HOUSE TOO?
NO, YOTSUBA IS HEADING OUT ON BUSINESS.
BUSINESS? WHERE ARE YOU GOING?

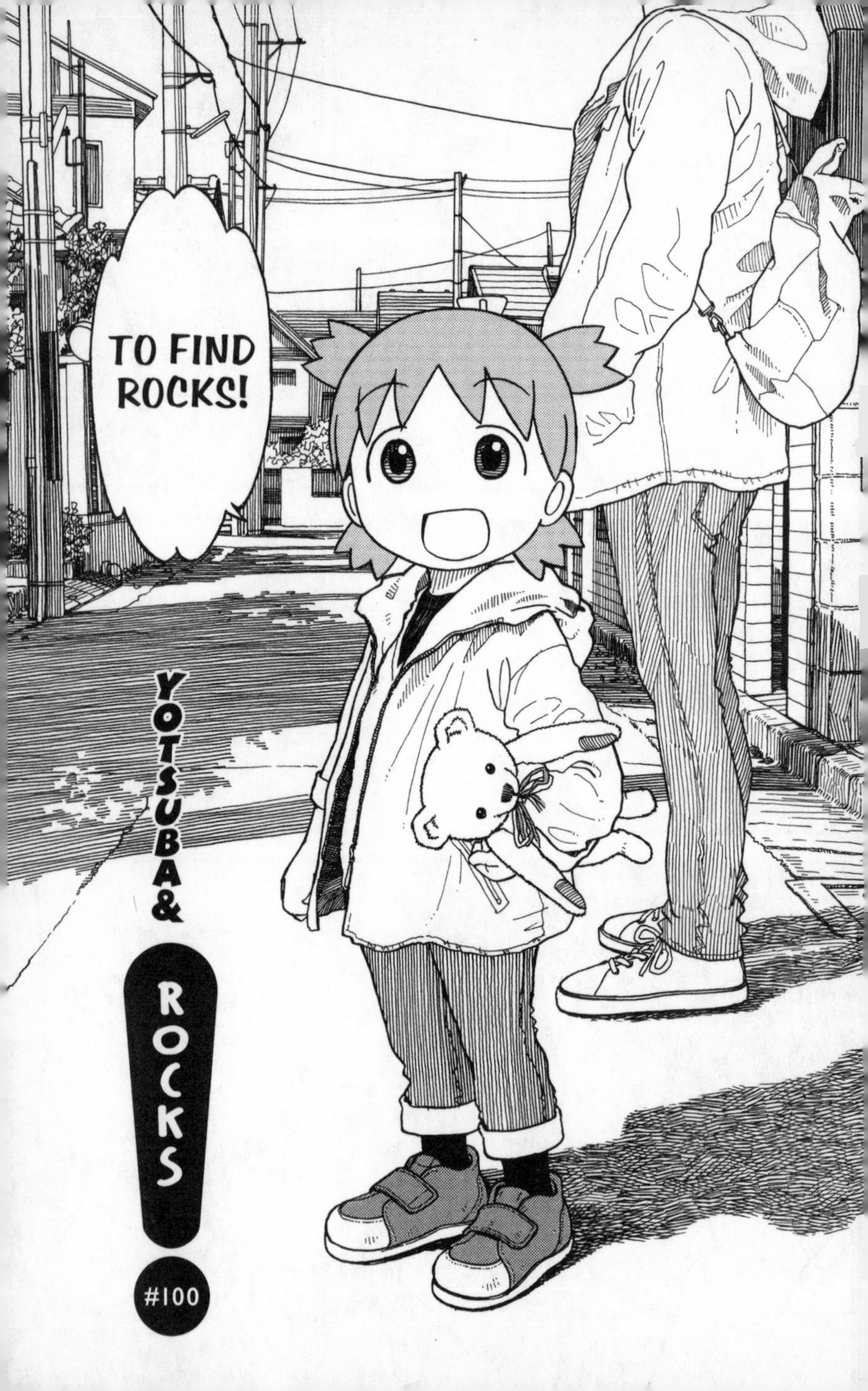
TO FIND ROCKS!
YOTSUBA&
ROCKS
#100

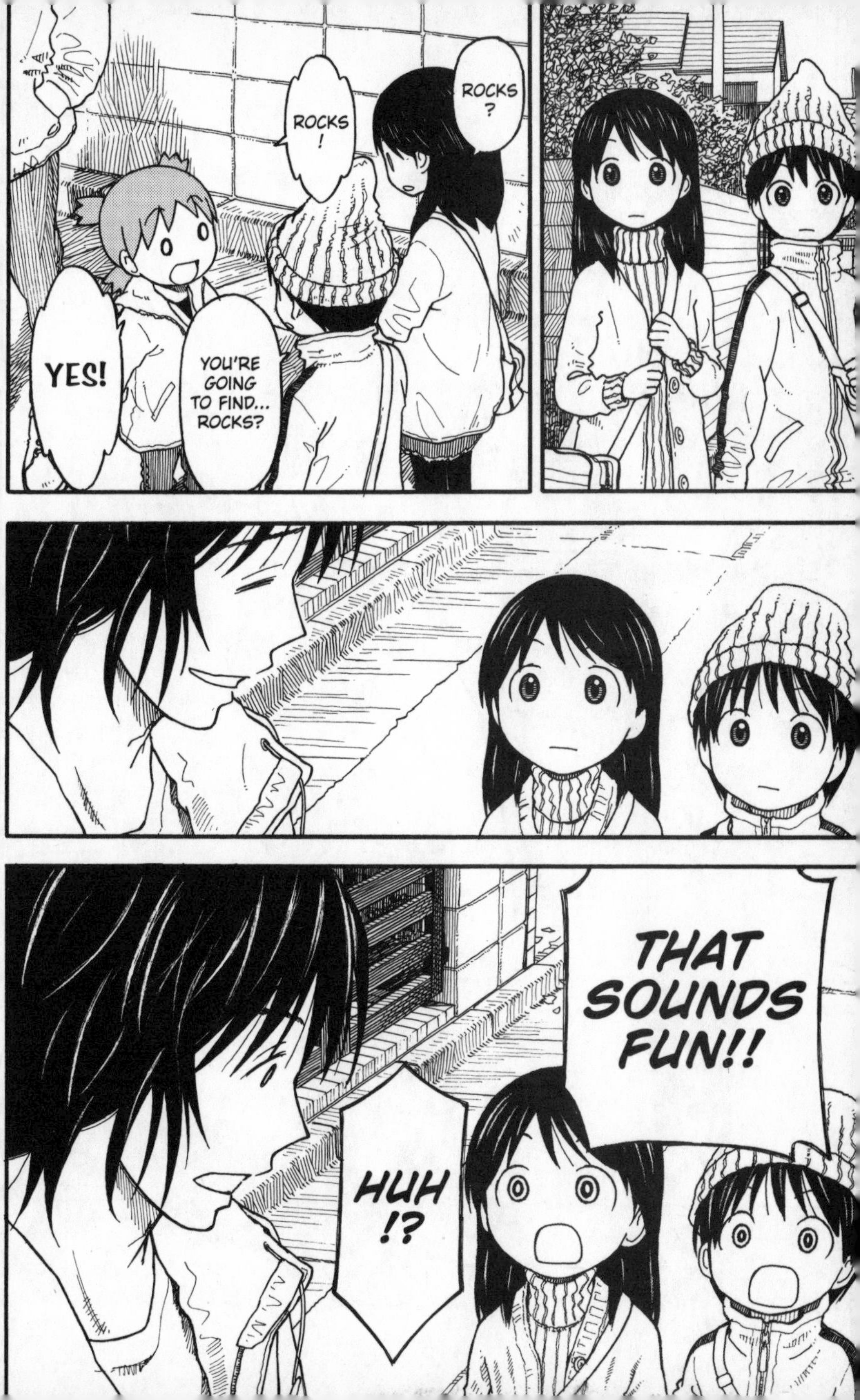
ROCKS?
ROCKS!
YOU'RE GOING TO FIND... ROCKS?
YES!
THAT SOUNDS FUN!!
HUH!?

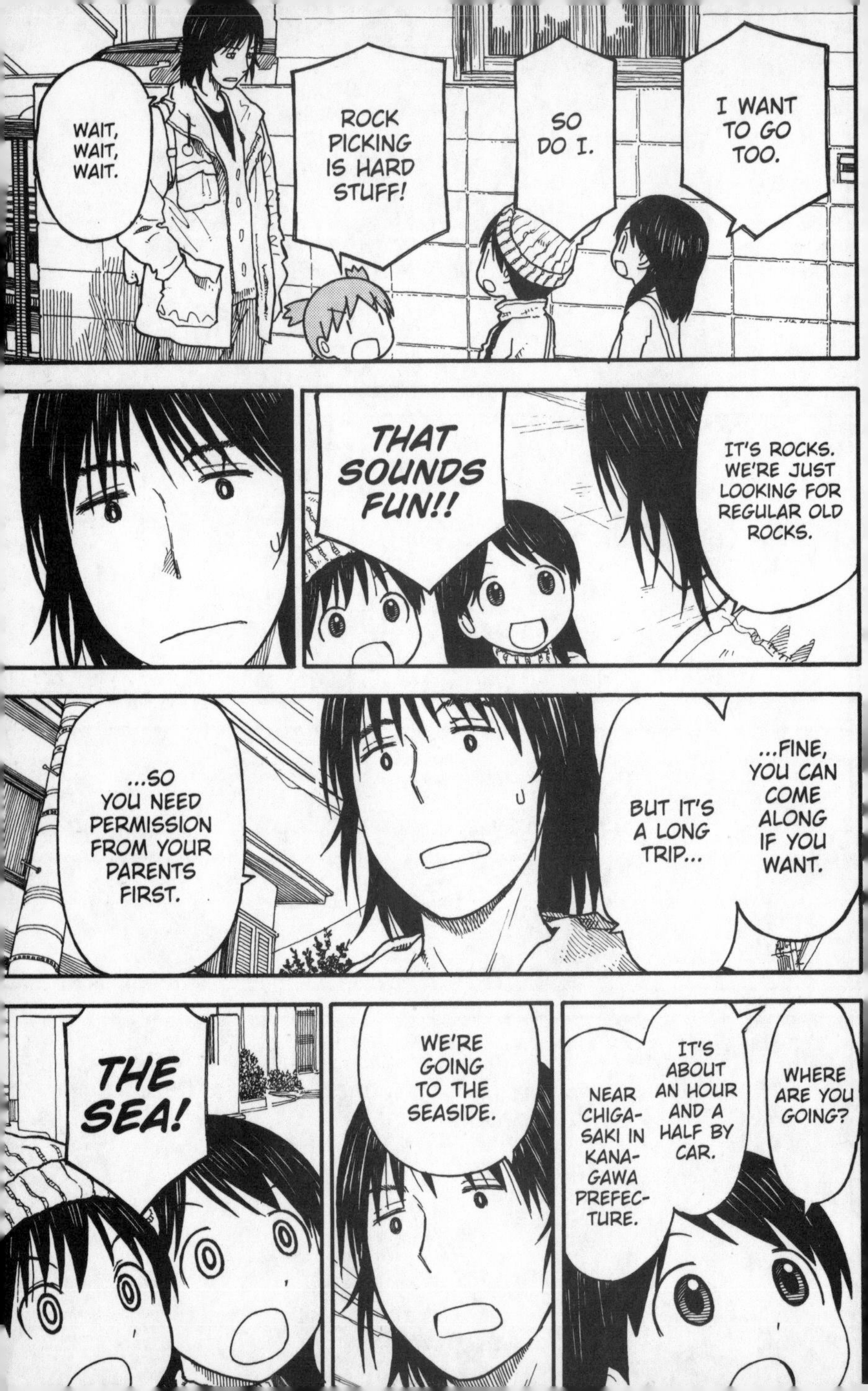
I WANT TO GO TOO.
SO DO I.
ROCK PICKING IS HARD STUFF!
WAIT, WAIT, WAIT.
IT'S ROCKS. WE'RE JUST LOOKING FOR REGULAR OLD ROCKS.
THAT SOUNDS FUN!!
...FINE, YOU CAN COME ALONG IF YOU WANT.
BUT IT'S A LONG TRIP...
...SO YOU NEED PERMISSION FROM YOUR PARENTS FIRST.
WHERE ARE YOU GOING?
IT'S ABOUT AN HOUR AND A HALF BY CAR.
NEAR CHIGASAKI IN KANAGAWA PREFECTURE.
WE'RE GOING TO THE SEASIDE.
THE SEA!

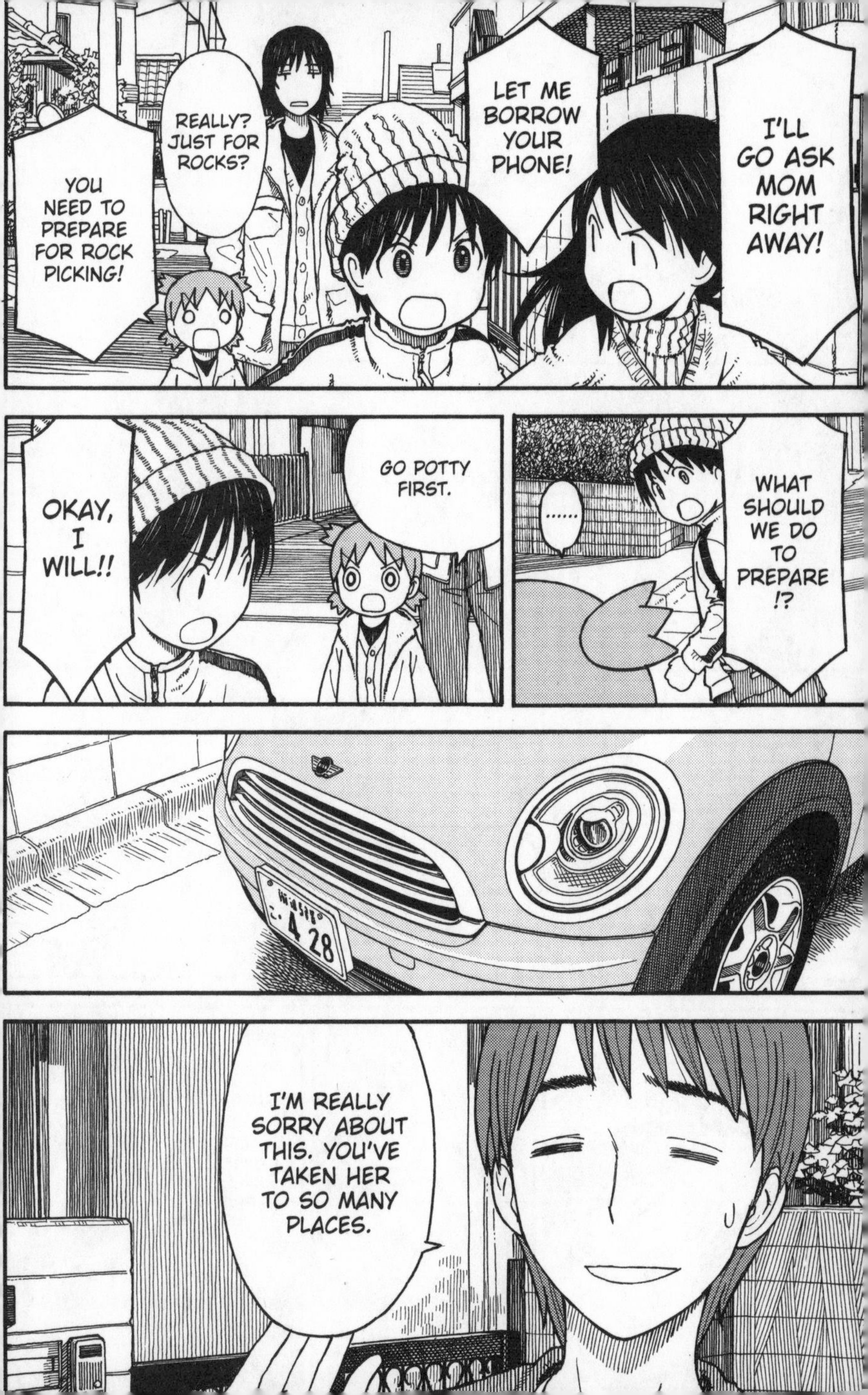
I'LL GO ASK MOM RIGHT AWAY!
LET ME BORROW YOUR PHONE!
REALLY? JUST FOR ROCKS?
YOU NEED TO PREPARE FOR ROCK PICKING!
WHAT SHOULD WE DO TO PREPARE!?
......
GO POTTY FIRST.
OKAY, I WILL!!
I'M REALLY SORRY ABOUT THIS. YOU'VE TAKEN HER TO SO MANY PLACES.

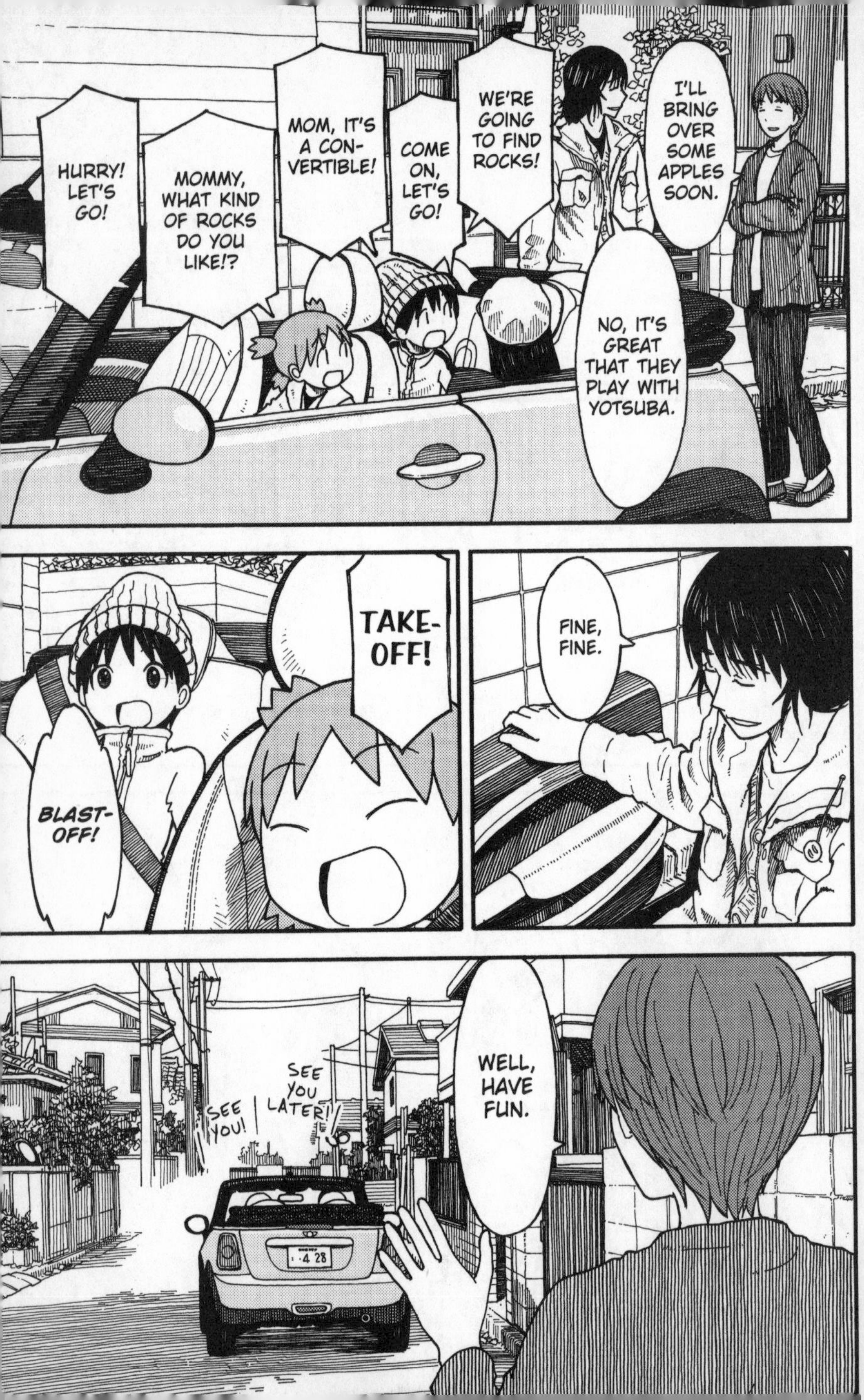
I'LL BRING OVER SOME APPLES SOON.
NO, IT'S GREAT THAT THEY PLAY WITH YOTSUBA.
WE'RE GOING TO FIND ROCKS!
COME ON, LET'S GO!
MOM, IT'S A CON-VERTIBLE!
MOMMY, WHAT KIND OF ROCKS DO YOU LIKE!?
HURRY! LET'S GO!
FINE, FINE.
TAKE-OFF!
BLAST-OFF!
WELL, HAVE FUN.
SEE YOU LATER!
SEE YOU!

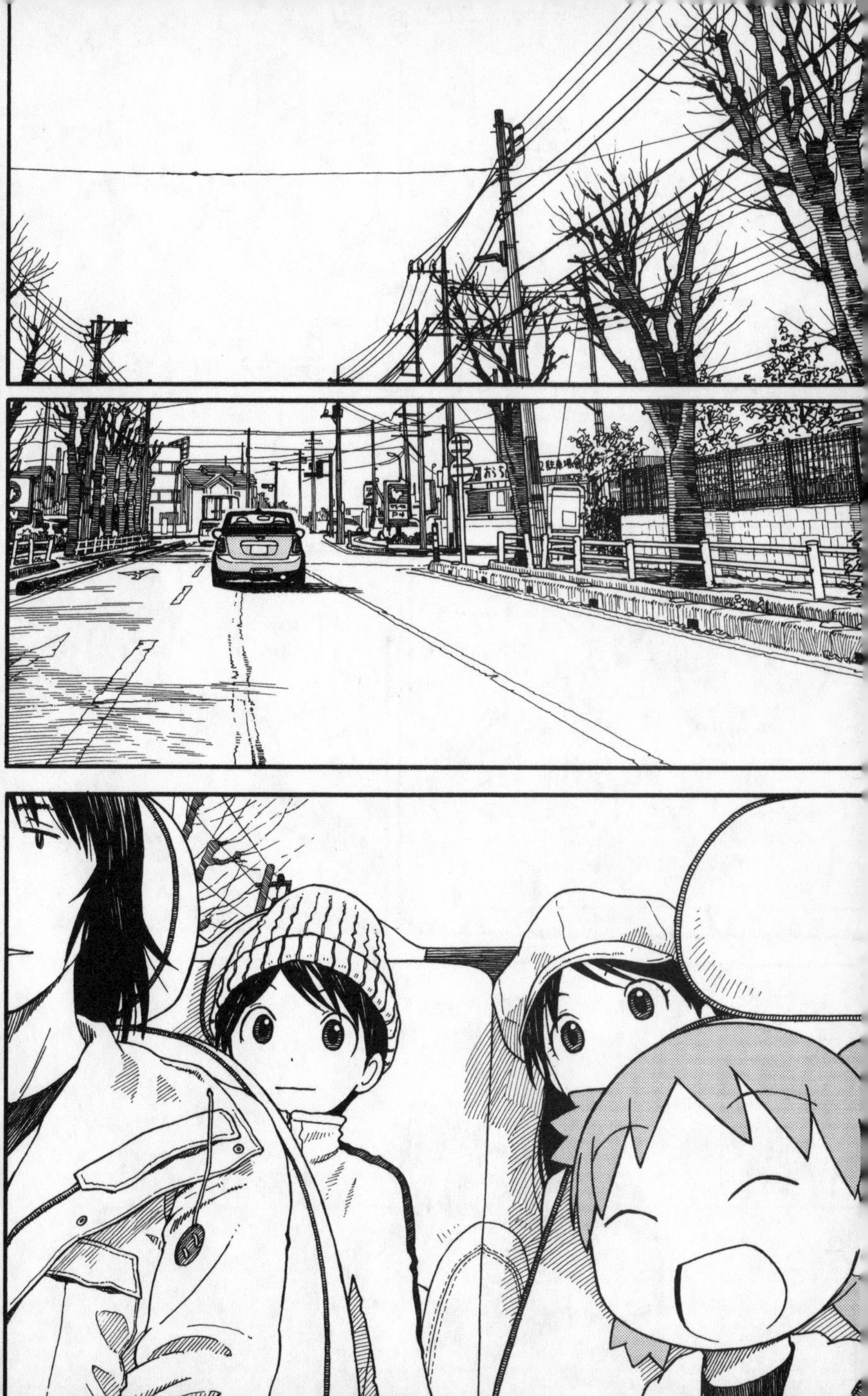
おうち
駐車場

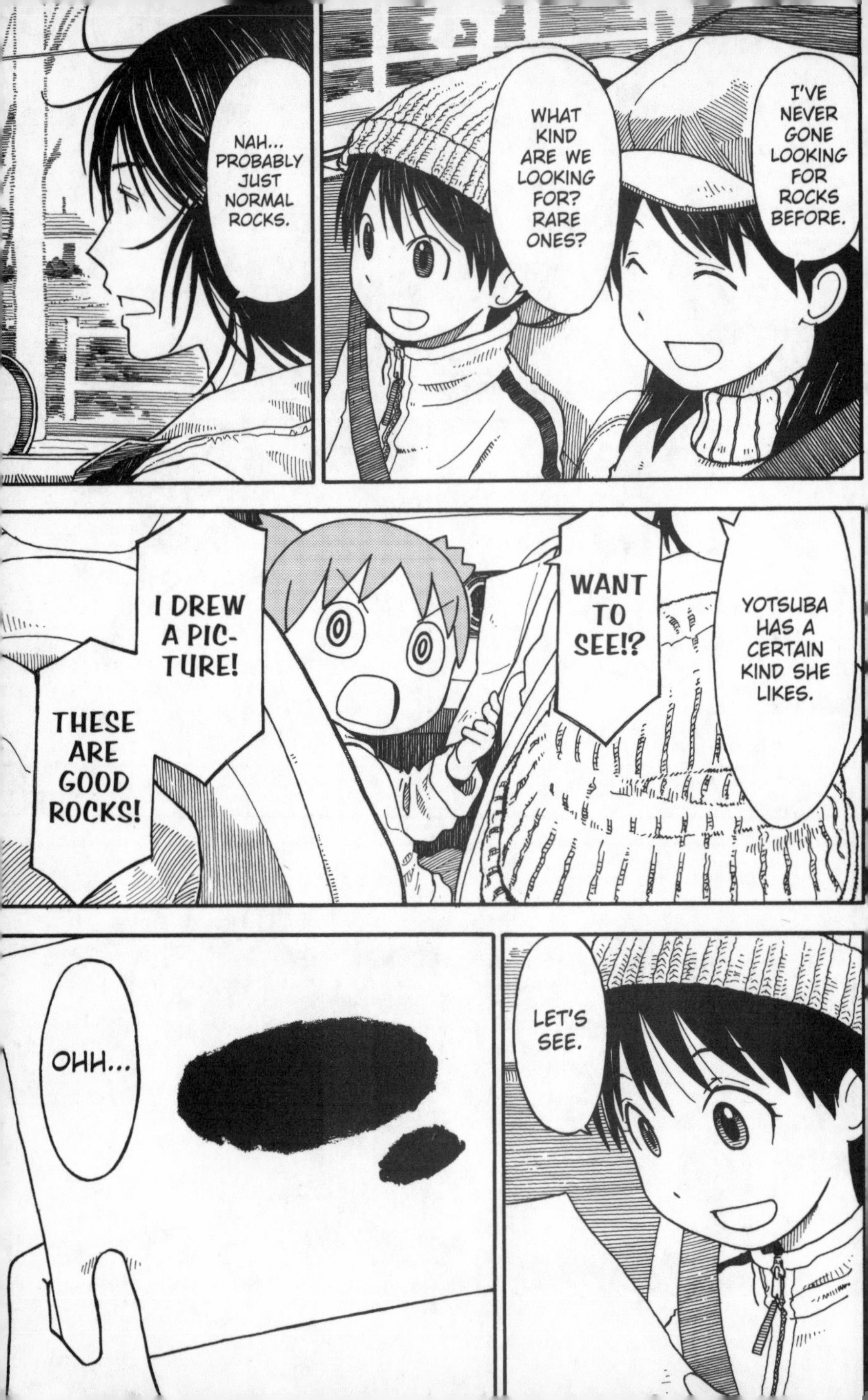
I'VE NEVER GONE LOOKING FOR ROCKS BEFORE.
WHAT KIND ARE WE LOOKING FOR? RARE ONES?
NAH... PROBABLY JUST NORMAL ROCKS.
YOTSUBA HAS A CERTAIN KIND SHE LIKES.
WANT TO SEE!?
I DREW A PIC-TURE!
THESE ARE GOOD ROCKS!
LET'S SEE.
OHH...

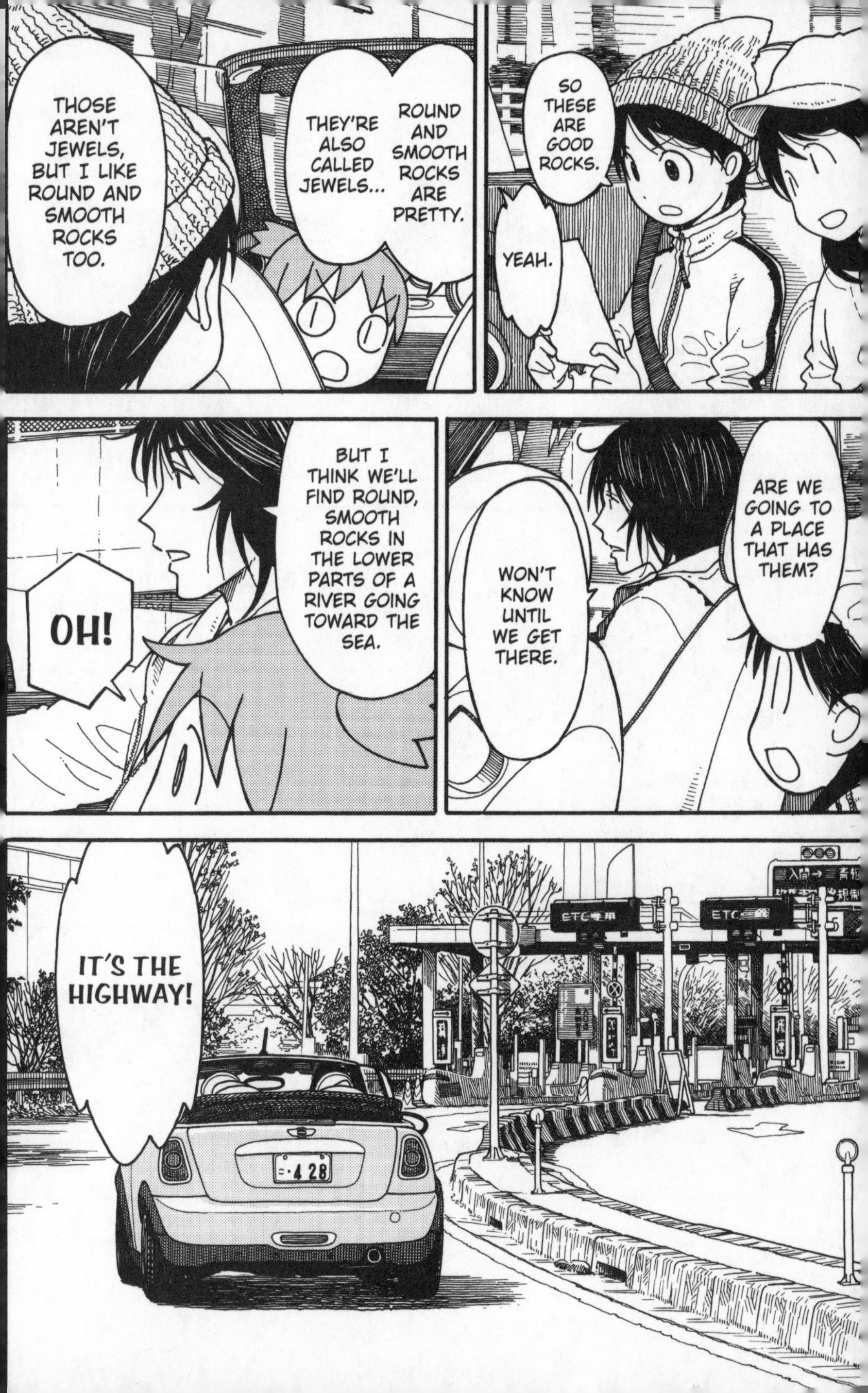
SO THESE ARE GOOD ROCKS.
YEAH.
ROUND AND SMOOTH ROCKS ARE PRETTY.
THEY'RE ALSO CALLED JEWELS...
THOSE AREN'T JEWELS, BUT I LIKE ROUND AND SMOOTH ROCKS TOO.
ARE WE GOING TO A PLACE THAT HAS THEM?
WON'T KNOW UNTIL WE GET THERE.
BUT I THINK WE'LL FIND ROUND, SMOOTH ROCKS IN THE LOWER PARTS OF A RIVER GOING TOWARD THE SEA.
OH!
IT'S THE HIGHWAY!

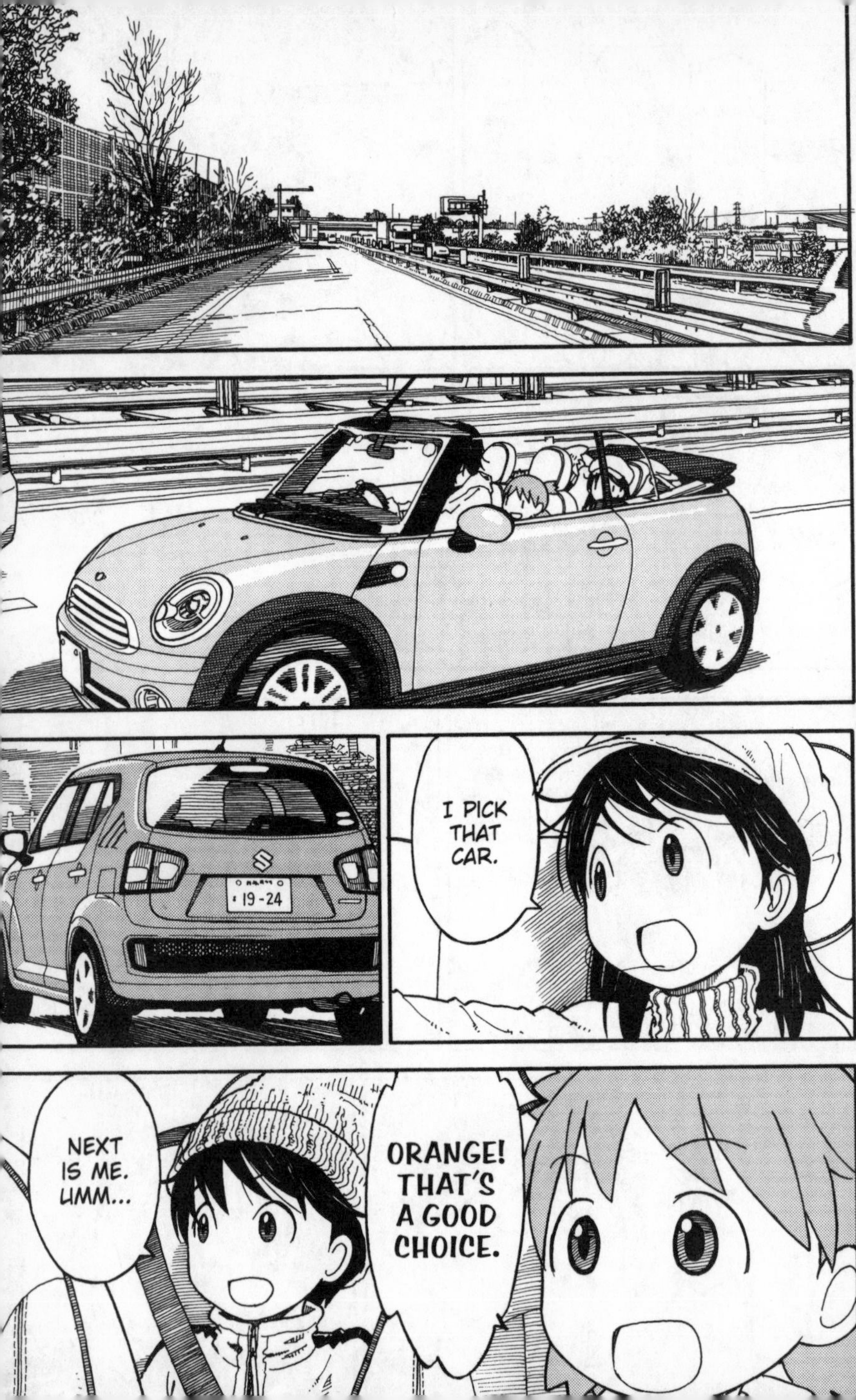
I PICK THAT CAR.
19-24
ORANGE! THAT'S A GOOD CHOICE.
NEXT IS ME. UMM...

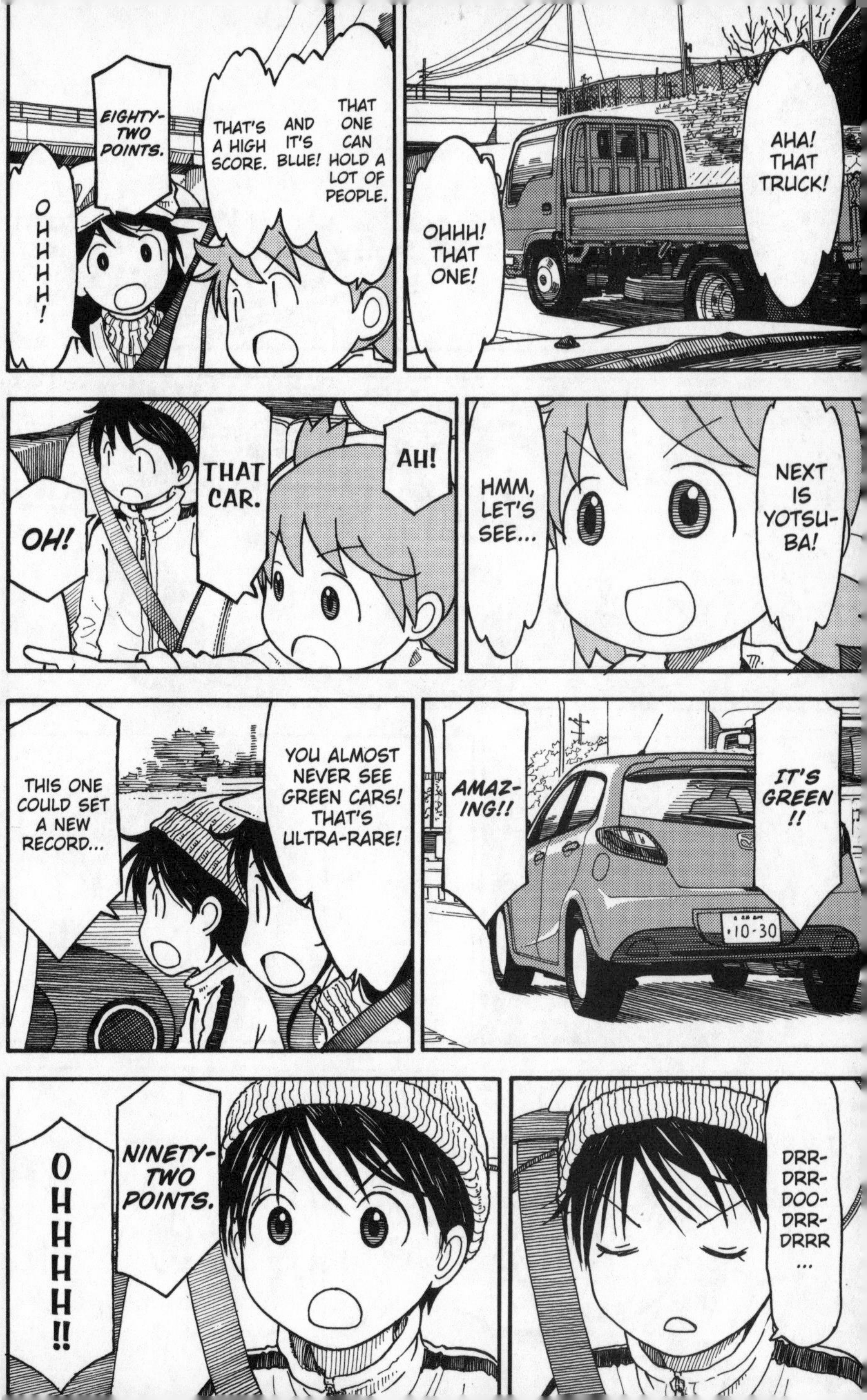
AHA! THAT TRUCK!
OHHH! THAT ONE!
THAT ONE CAN HOLD A LOT OF PEOPLE.
AND IT'S BLUE!
THAT'S A HIGH SCORE.
EIGHTY-TWO POINTS.
OHHHH!
NEXT IS YOTSUBA!
HMM, LET'S SEE...
AH!
THAT CAR.
OH!
IT'S GREEN!!
10-30
AMAZING!!
YOU ALMOST NEVER SEE GREEN CARS! THAT'S ULTRA-RARE!
THIS ONE COULD SET A NEW RECORD...
DRR-DRR-DOO-DRR-DRRR...
NINETY-TWO POINTS.
OHHHH!!

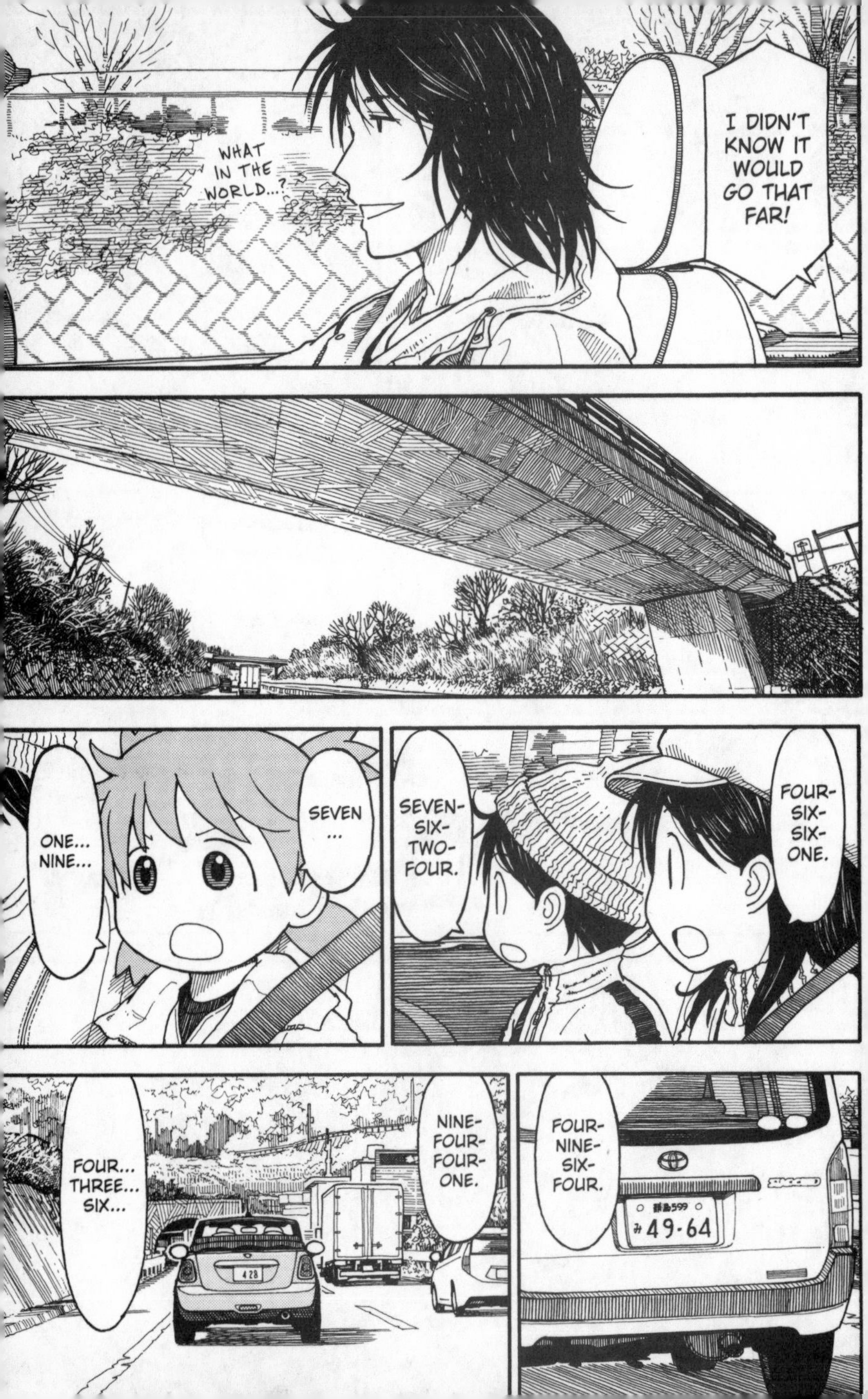
I DIDN'T KNOW IT WOULD GO THAT FAR!
WHAT IN THE WORLD...?
FOUR-SIX-SIX-ONE.
SEVEN-SIX-TWO-FOUR.
SEVEN ...
ONE... NINE...
FOUR-NINE-SIX-FOUR.
49-64
NINE-FOUR-FOUR-ONE.
FOUR... THREE... SIX...
428

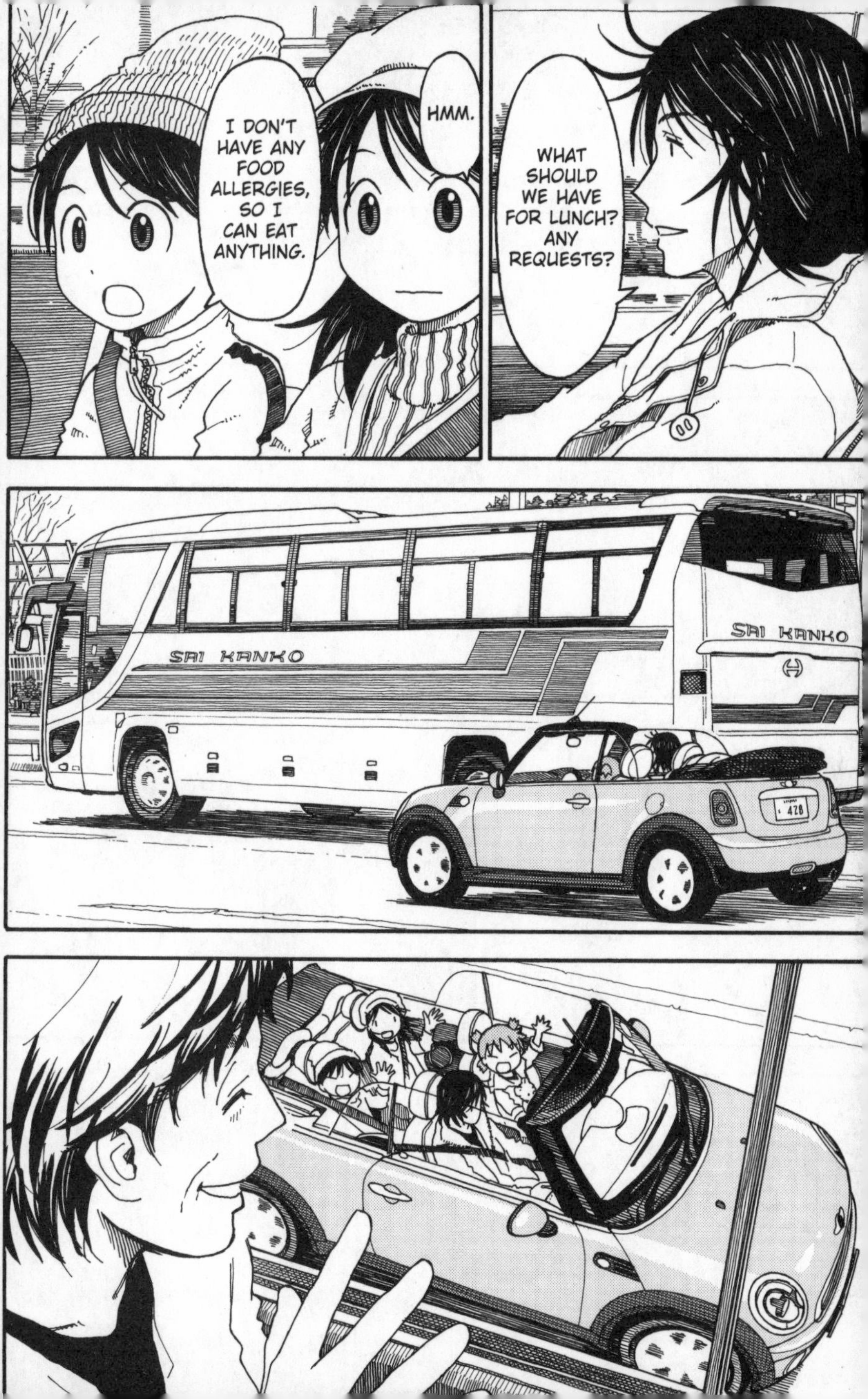
WHAT SHOULD WE HAVE FOR LUNCH? ANY REQUESTS?
HMM.
I DON'T HAVE ANY FOOD ALLERGIES, SO I CAN EAT ANYTHING.
SAI KANKO
SAI KANKO

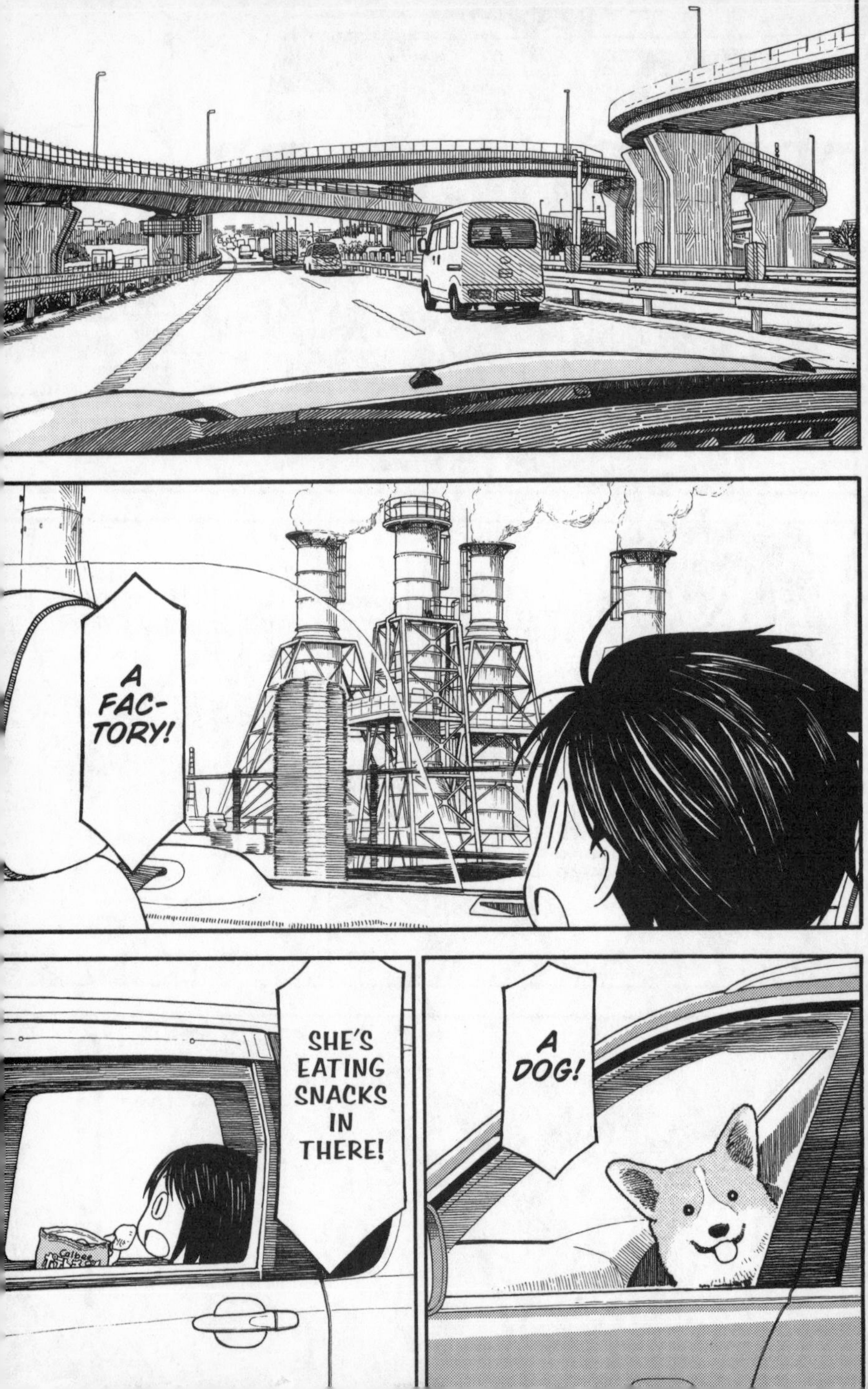
A FAC-TORY!
A DOG!
SHE'S EATING SNACKS IN THERE!

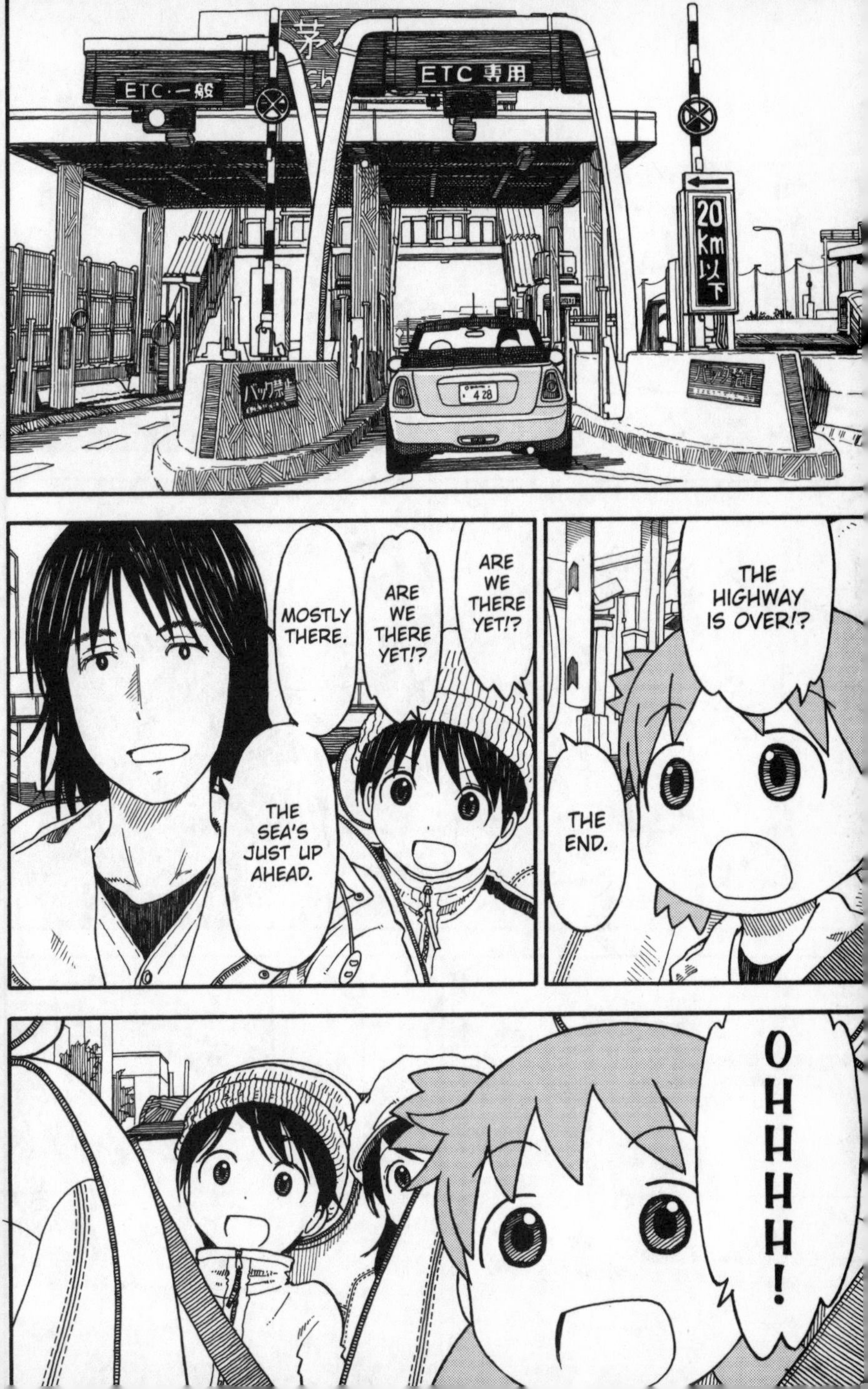
ETC 専用
ETC・一般
20km以下
バック禁止
バック禁止
THE HIGHWAY IS OVER!?
THE END.
ARE WE THERE YET!?
ARE WE THERE YET!?
MOSTLY THERE.
THE SEA'S JUST UP AHEAD.
OHHHH!

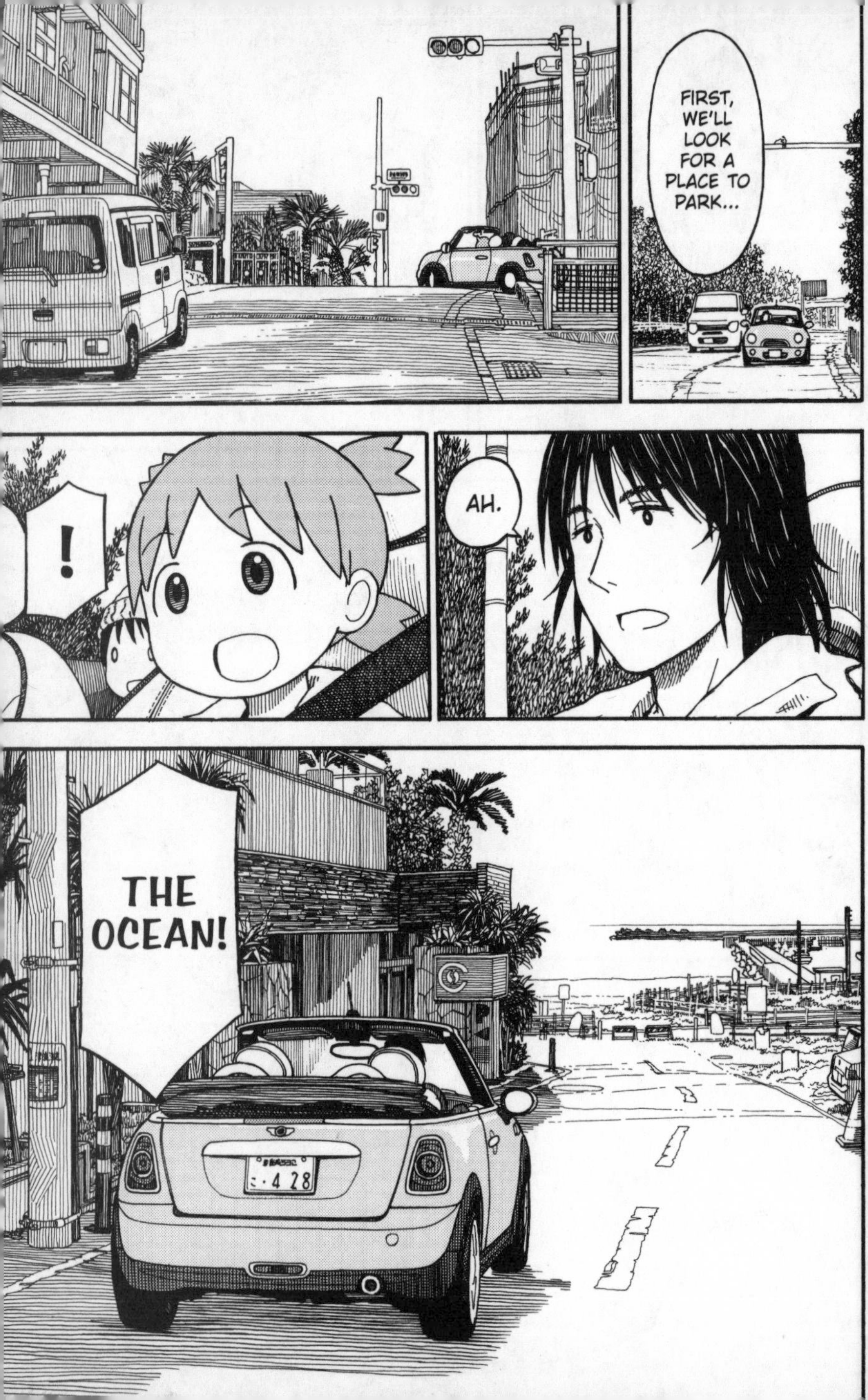
FIRST, WE'LL LOOK FOR A PLACE TO PARK...
AH.
!
THE OCEAN!

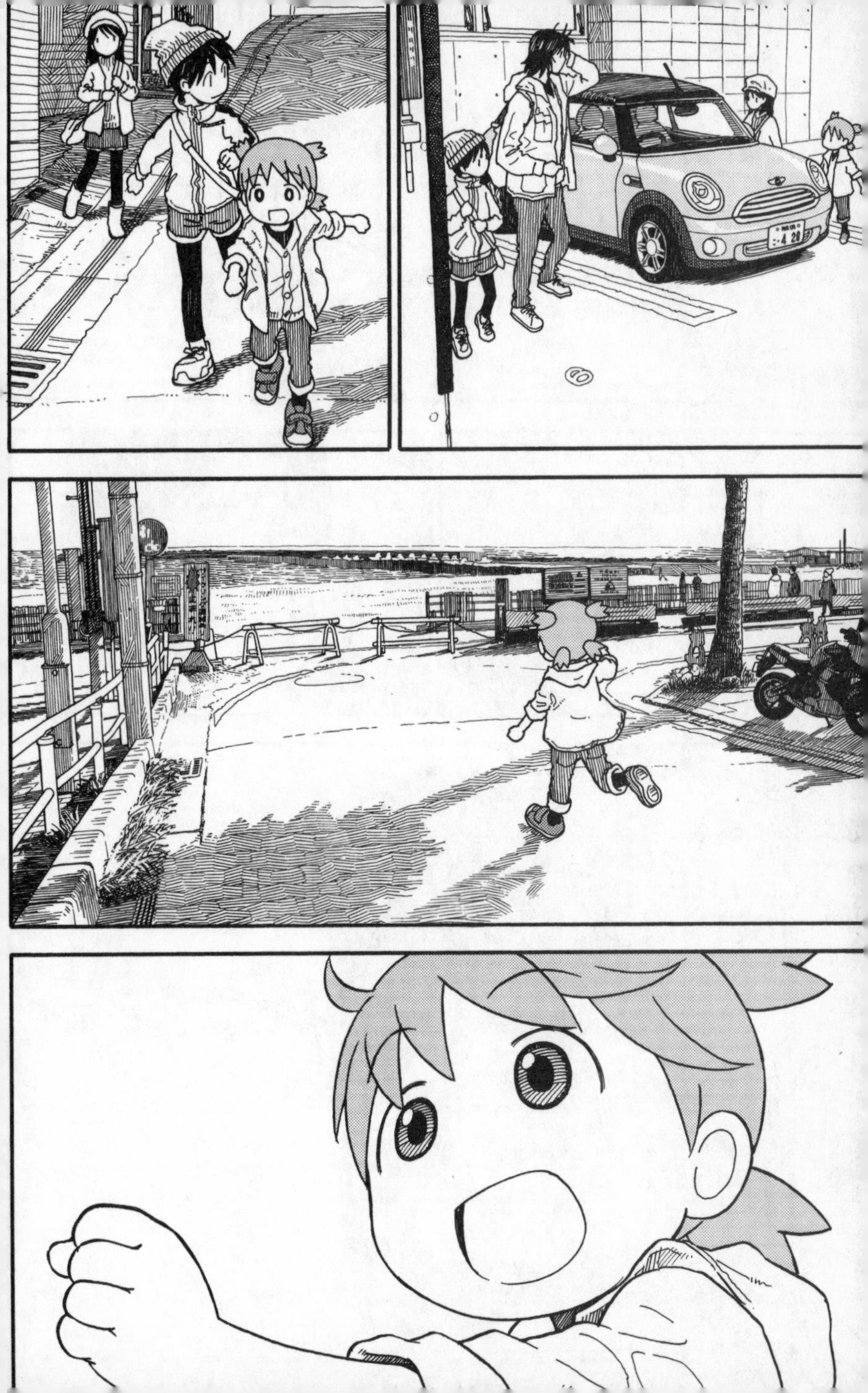

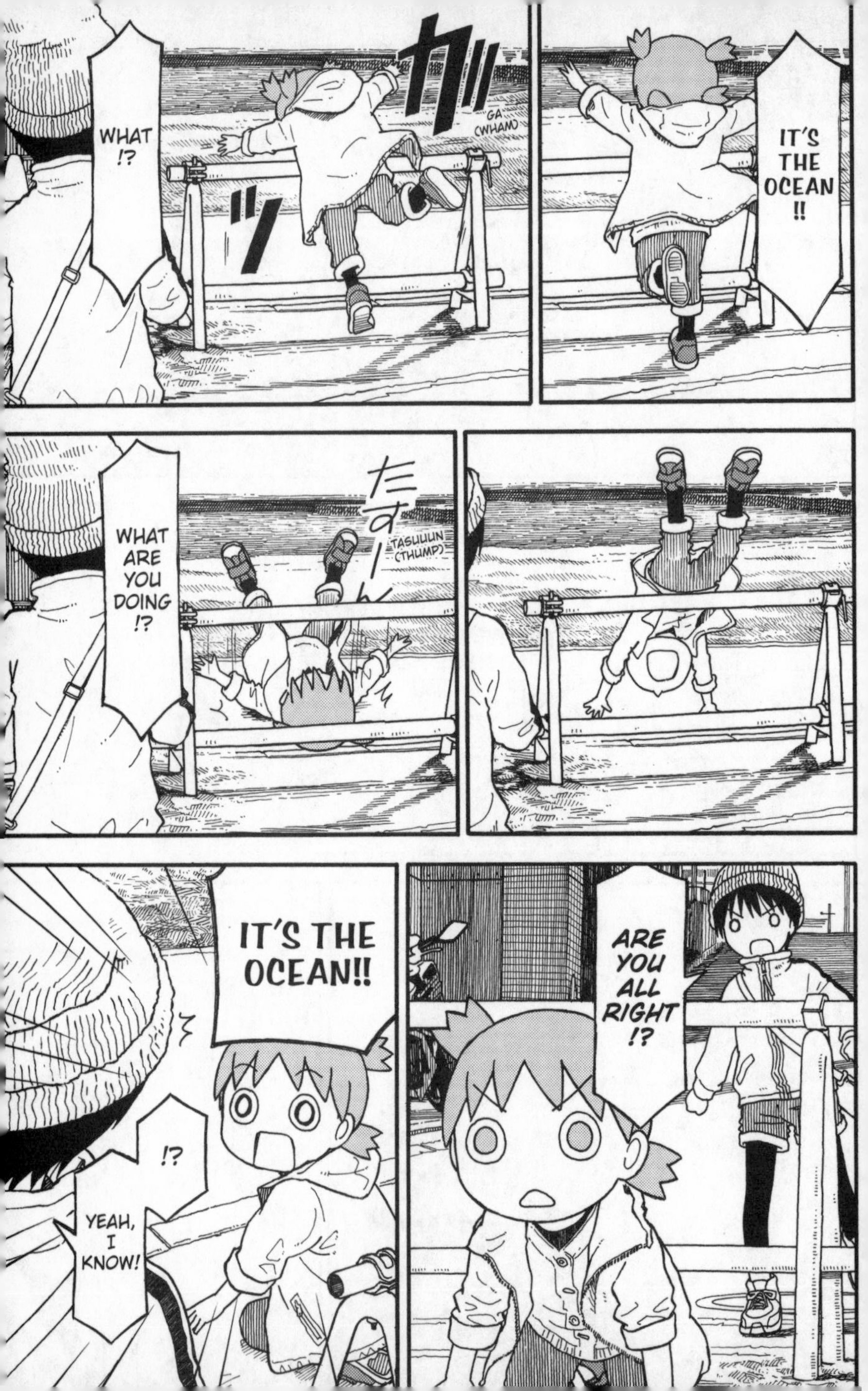
IT'S THE OCEAN !!
GA (WHAM)
WHAT !?
TASUUUN (THUMP)
WHAT ARE YOU DOING !?
ARE YOU ALL RIGHT !?
IT'S THE OCEAN!!
!?
YEAH, I KNOW!

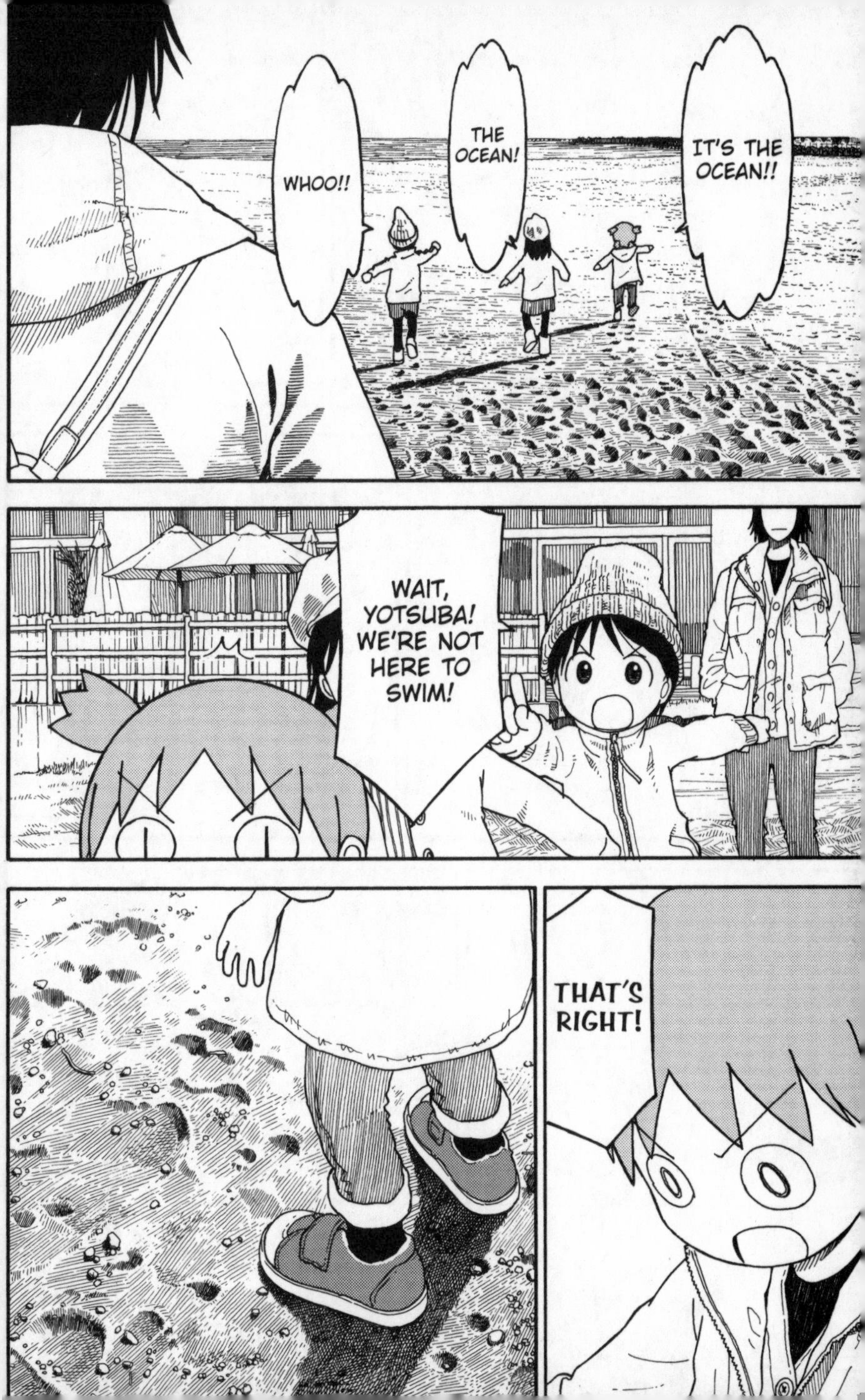
IT'S THE OCEAN!!
THE OCEAN!
WHOO!!
WAIT, YOTSUBA! WE'RE NOT HERE TO SWIM!
THAT'S RIGHT!

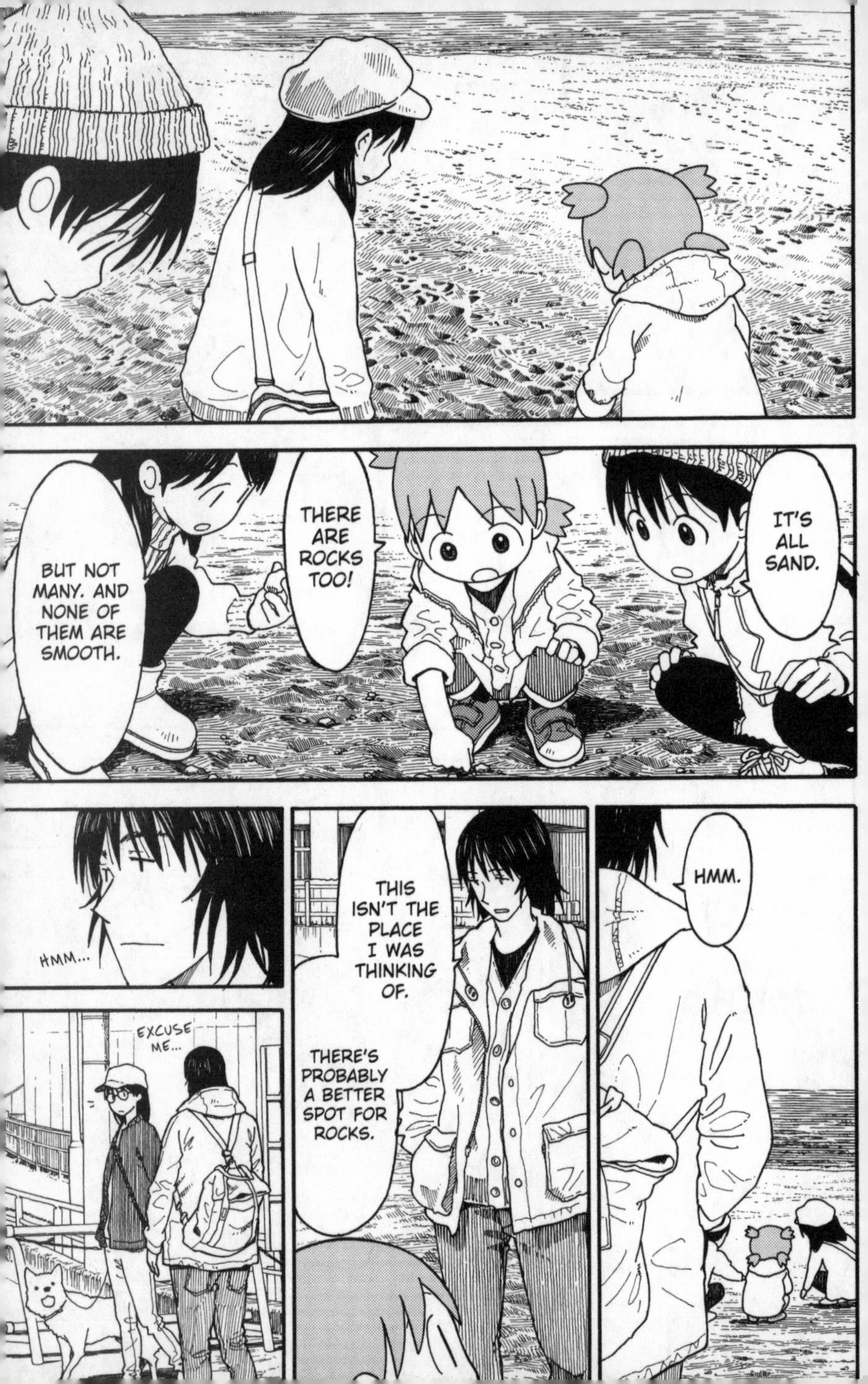
IT'S ALL SAND.
THERE ARE ROCKS TOO!
BUT NOT MANY. AND NONE OF THEM ARE SMOOTH.
HMM.
THIS ISN'T THE PLACE I WAS THINKING OF.
THERE'S PROBABLY A BETTER SPOT FOR ROCKS.
HMM...
EXCUSE ME...

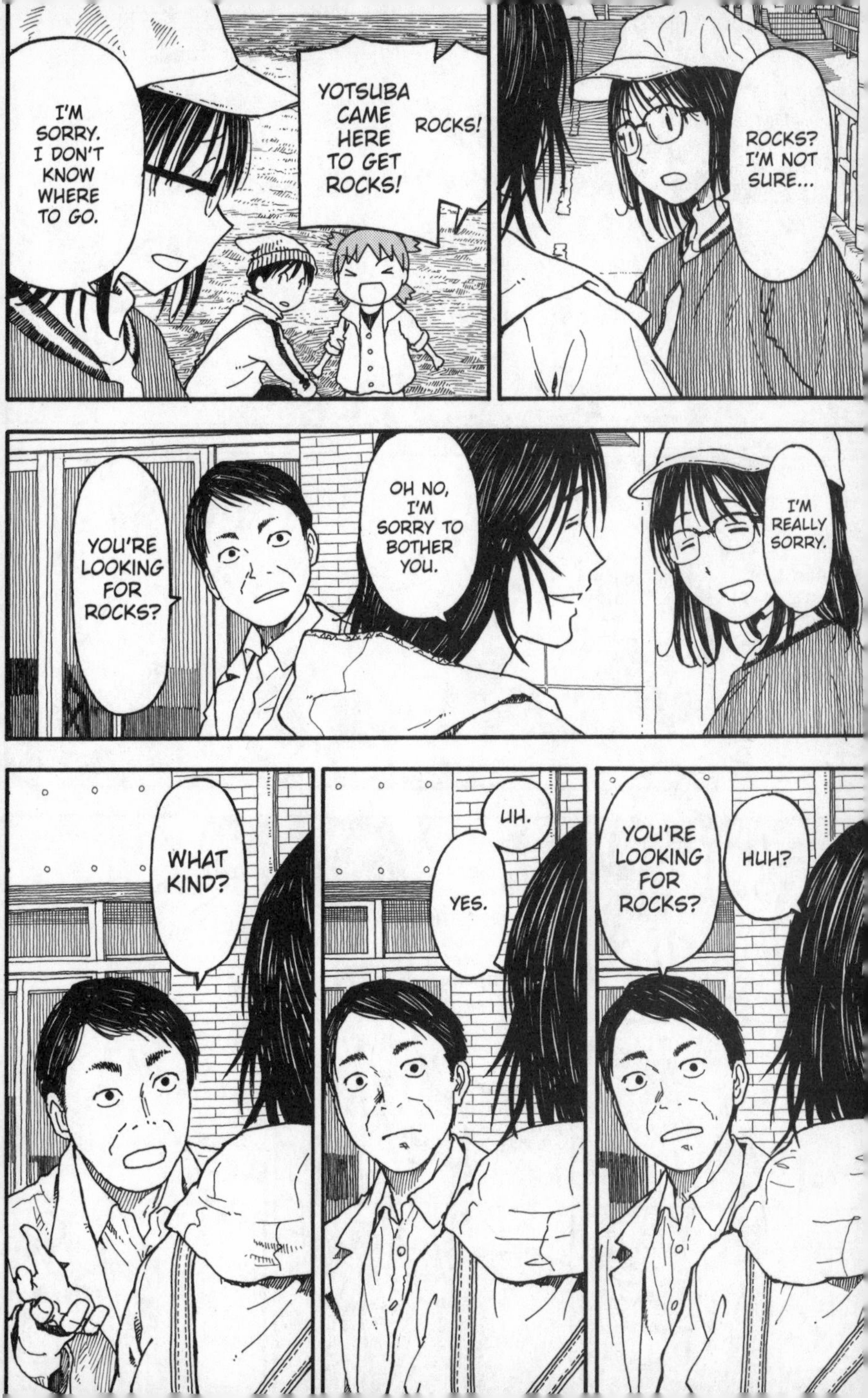
ROCKS? I'M NOT SURE...
ROCKS!
YOTSUBA CAME HERE TO GET ROCKS!
I'M SORRY. I DON'T KNOW WHERE TO GO.
I'M REALLY SORRY.
OH NO, I'M SORRY TO BOTHER YOU.
YOU'RE LOOKING FOR ROCKS?
HUH?
YOU'RE LOOKING FOR ROCKS?
UH.
YES.
WHAT KIND?

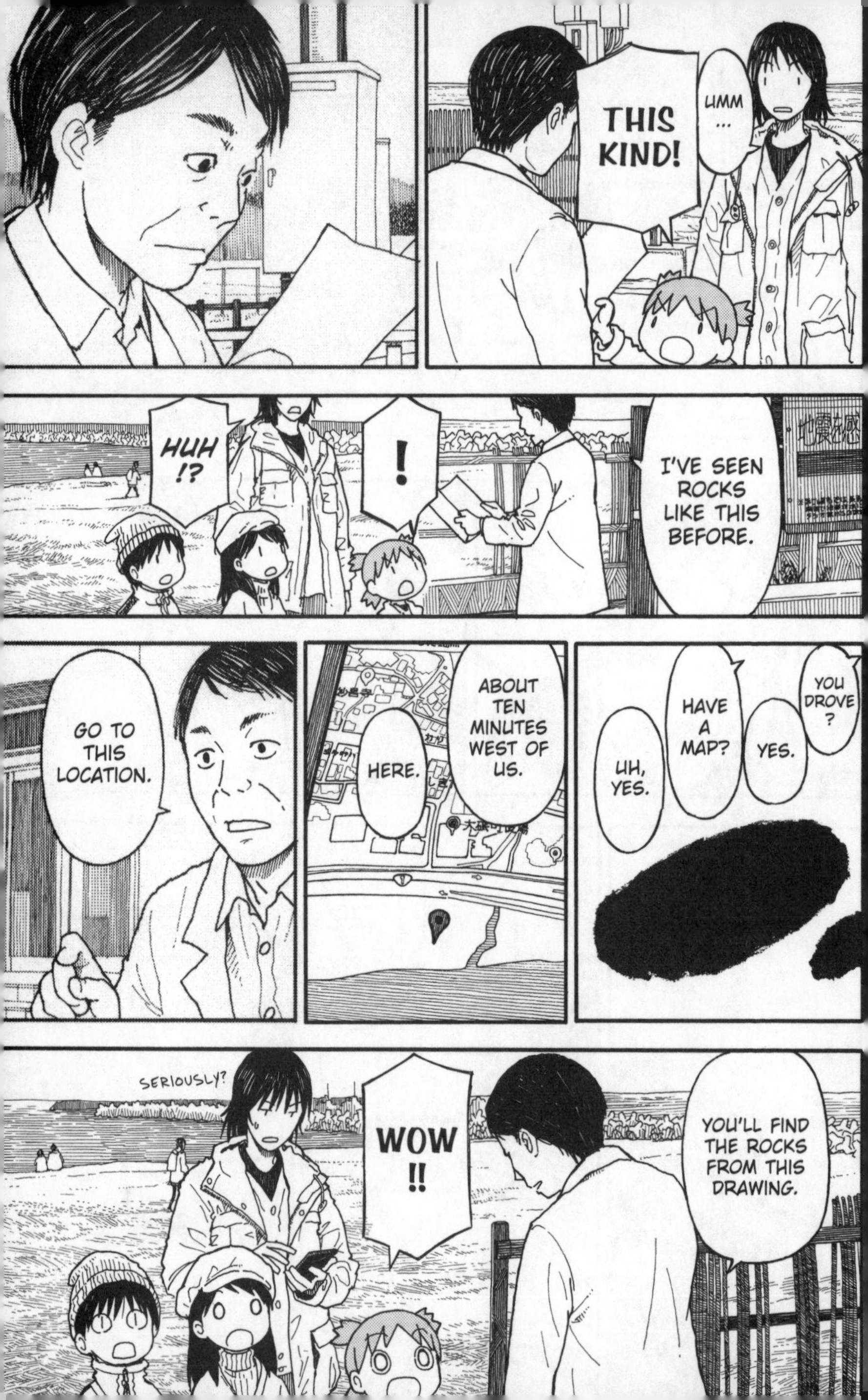
UMM ...
THIS KIND!
I'VE SEEN ROCKS LIKE THIS BEFORE.
!
HUH !?
YOU DROVE ?
YES.
HAVE A MAP?
UH, YES.
ABOUT TEN MINUTES WEST OF US.
HERE.
GO TO THIS LOCATION.
YOU'LL FIND THE ROCKS FROM THIS DRAWING.
WOW !!
SERIOUSLY?

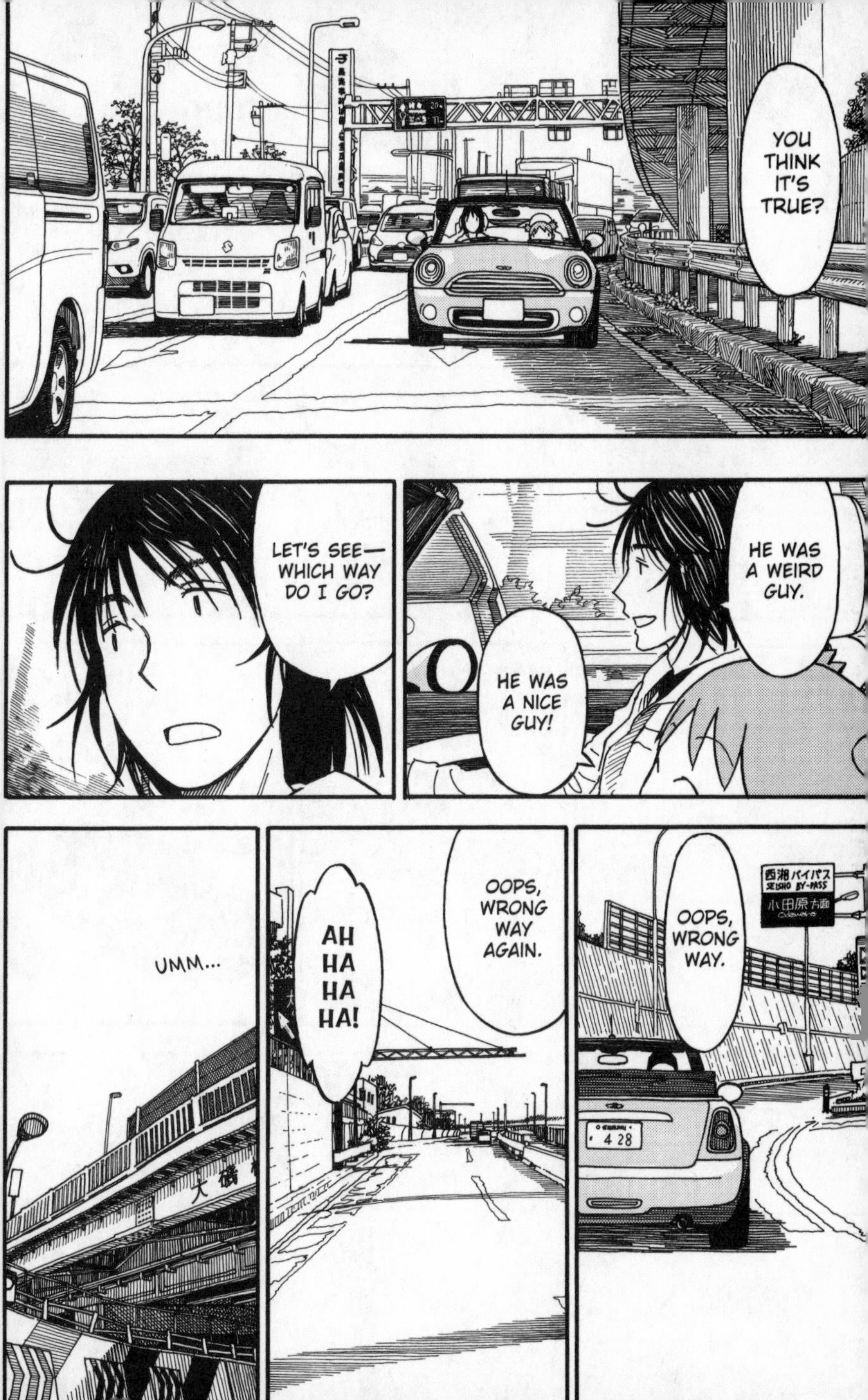
YOU THINK IT'S TRUE?
HE WAS A WEIRD GUY.
HE WAS A NICE GUY!
LET'S SEE— WHICH WAY DO I GO?
西湘バイパス
SEISHO BY-PASS
小田原方面
OOPS, WRONG WAY.
OOPS, WRONG WAY AGAIN.
AH HA HA HA!
UMM...

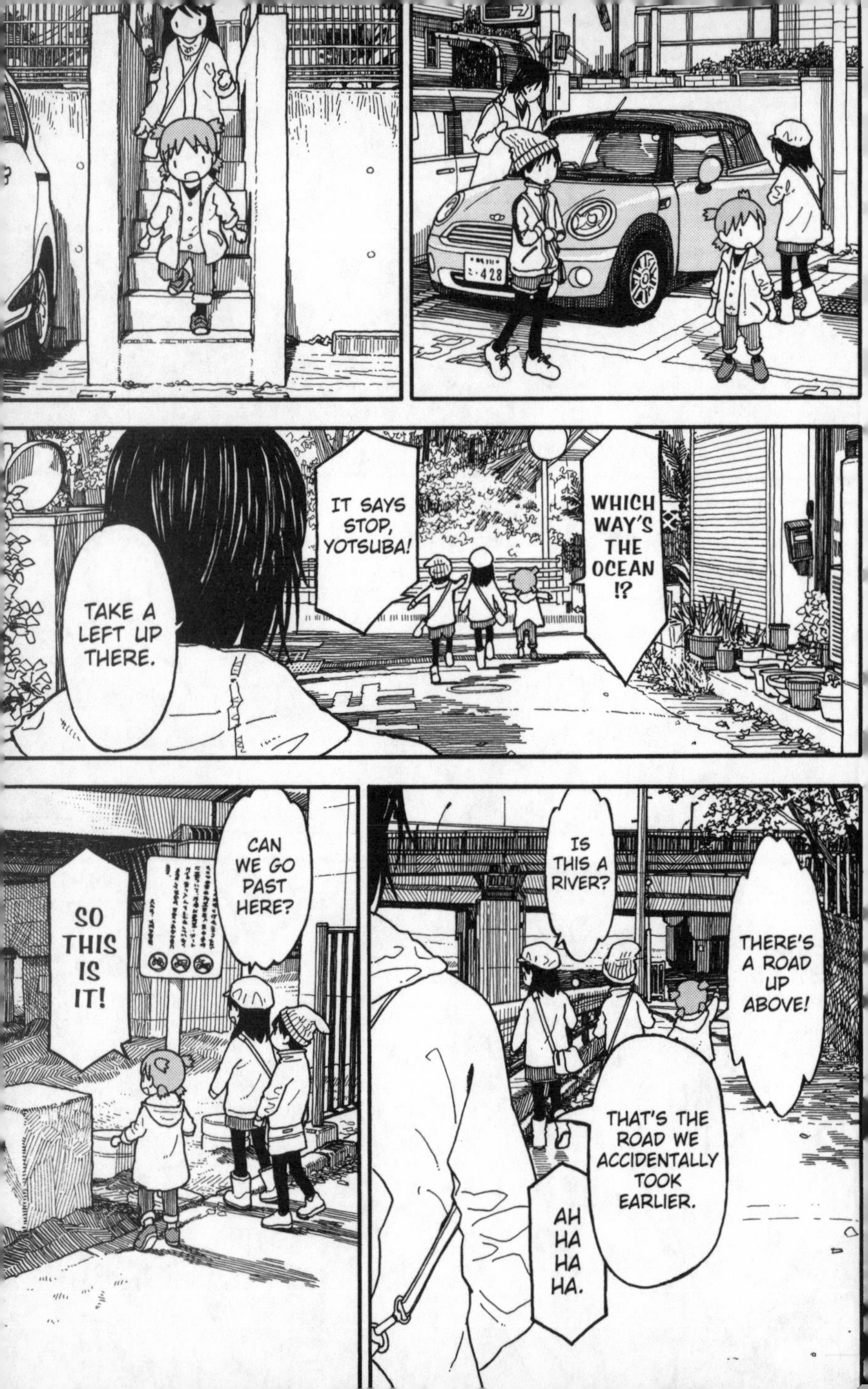
WHICH WAY'S THE OCEAN!?
IT SAYS STOP, YOTSUBA!
TAKE A LEFT UP THERE.
THERE'S A ROAD UP ABOVE!
IS THIS A RIVER?
THAT'S THE ROAD WE ACCIDENTALLY TOOK EARLIER.
AH HA HA HA.
CAN WE GO PAST HERE?
SO THIS IS IT!

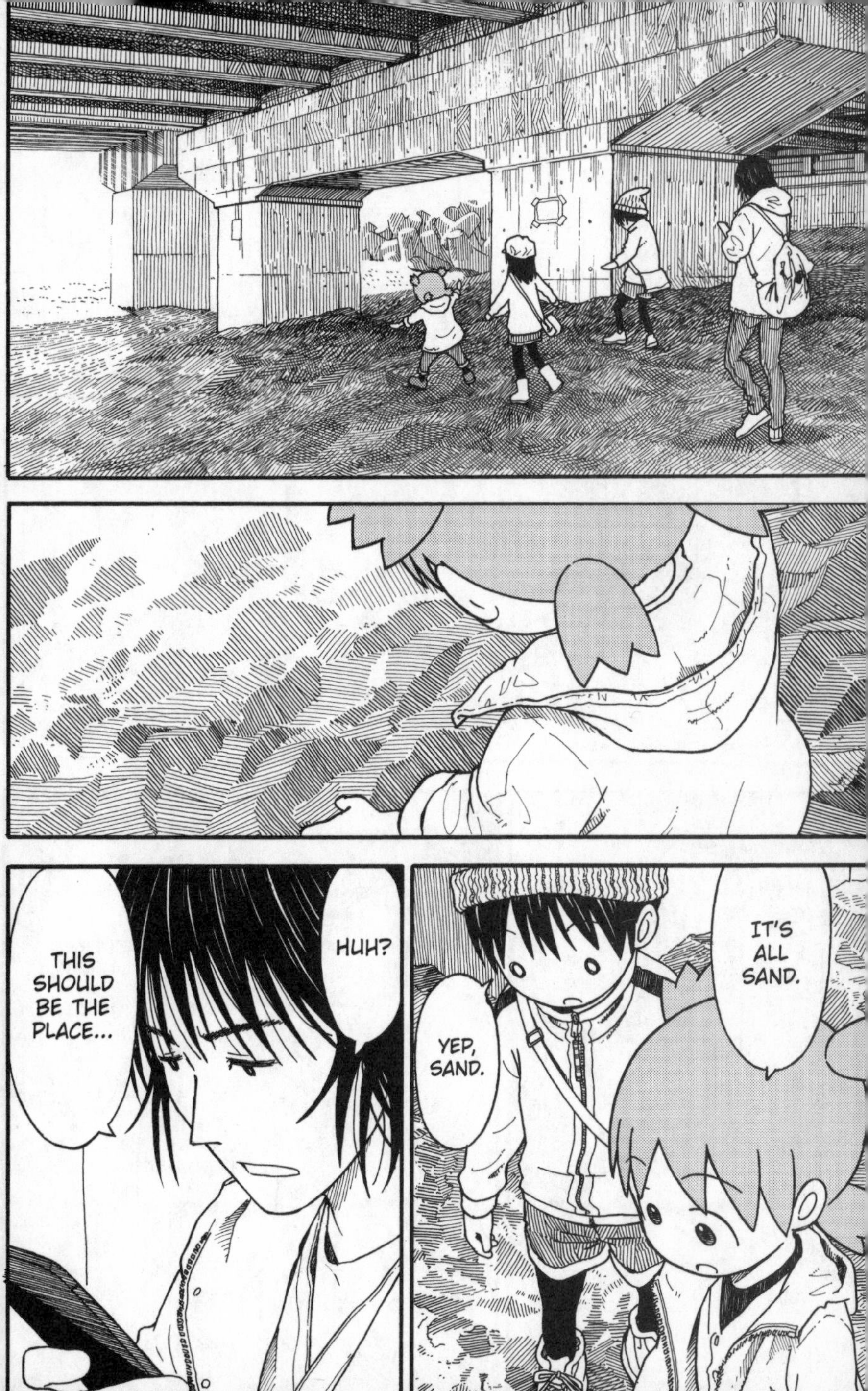
IT'S ALL SAND.
YEP, SAND.
HUH?
THIS SHOULD BE THE PLACE...

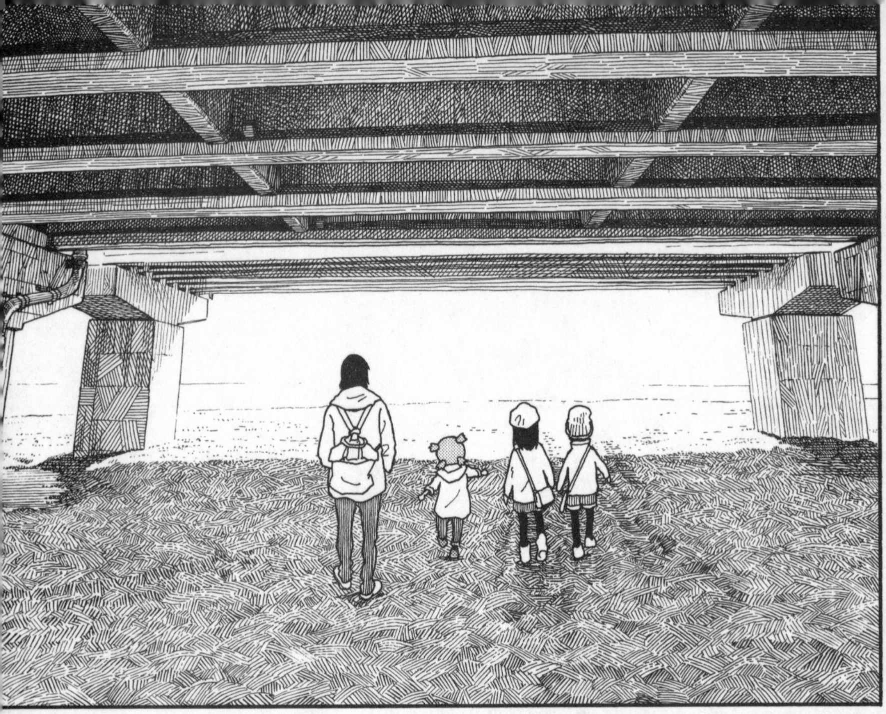

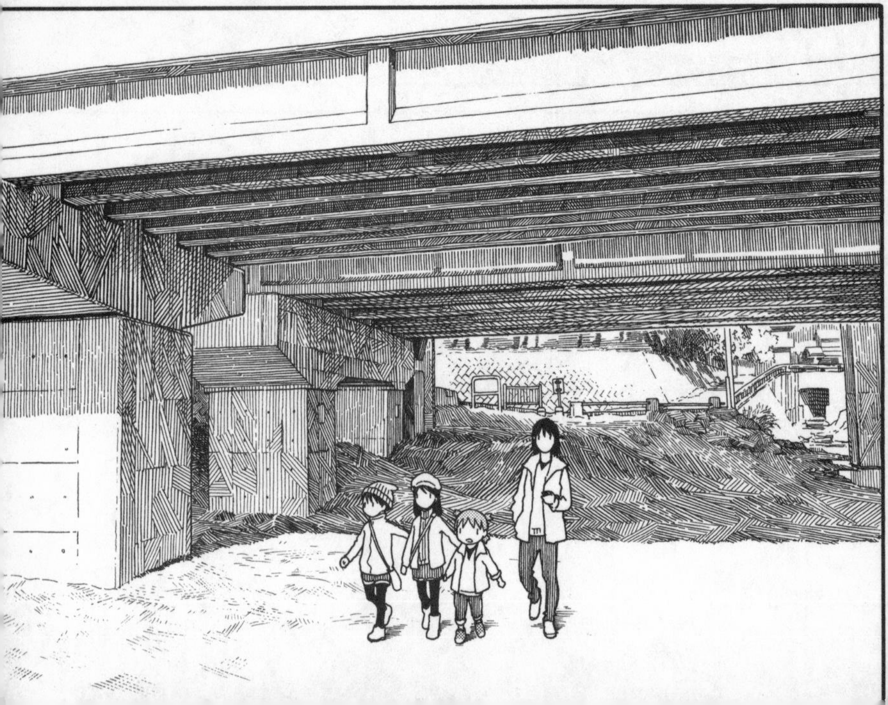

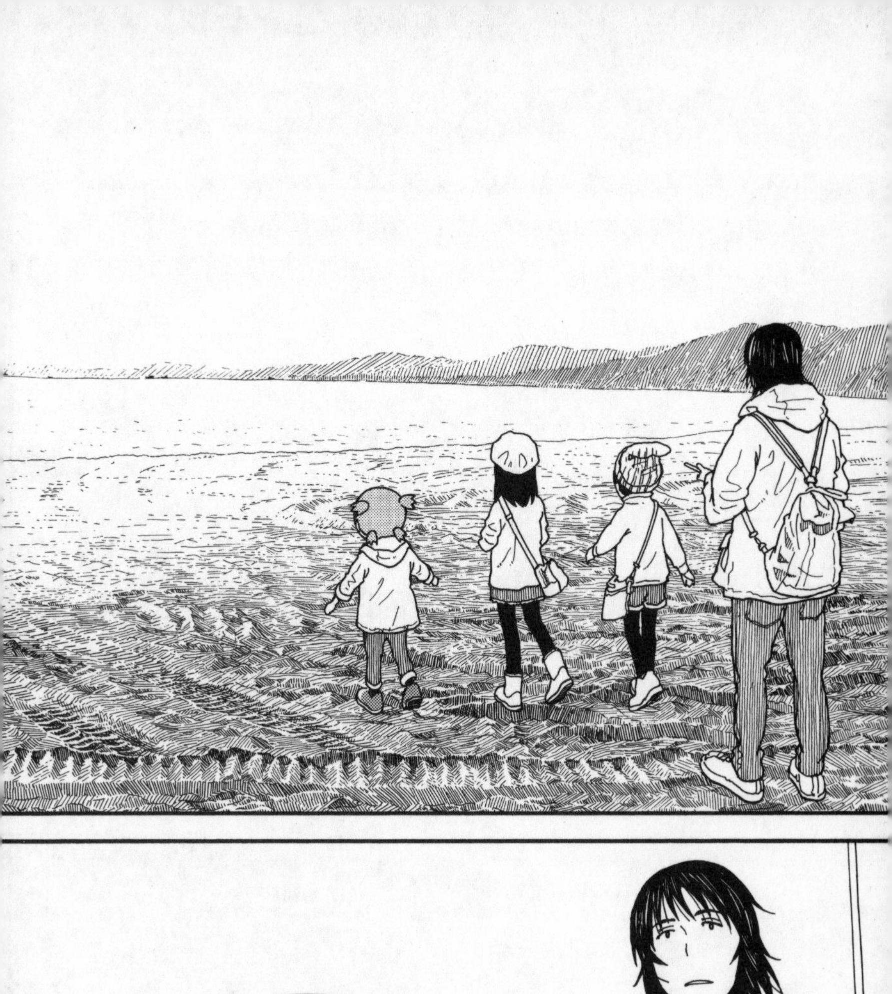
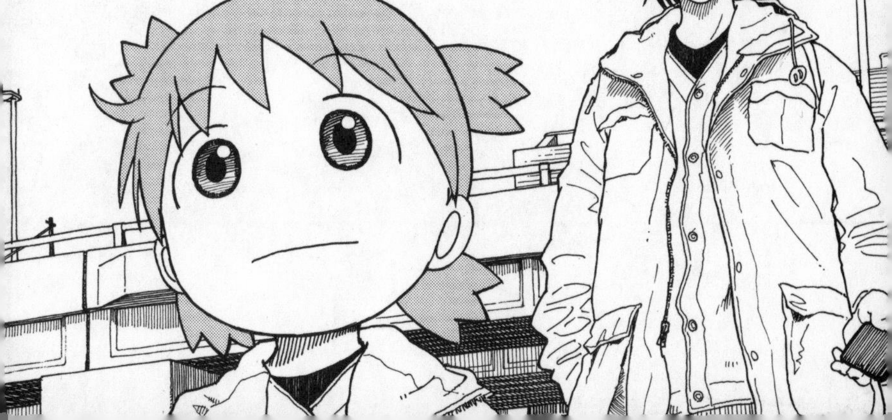

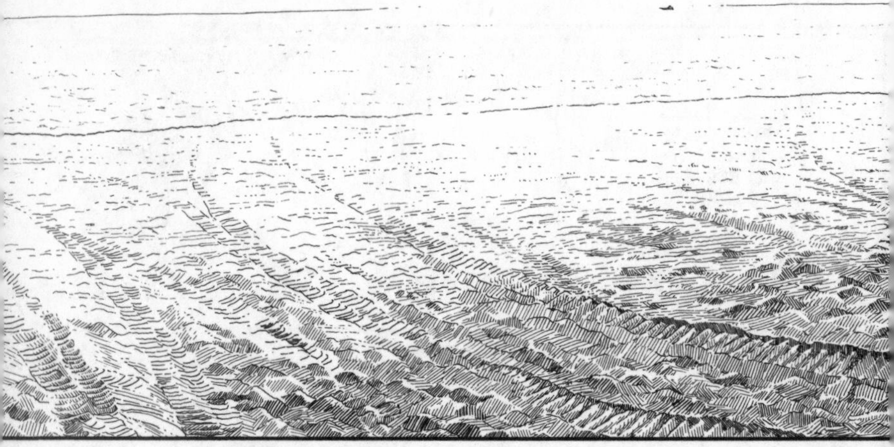
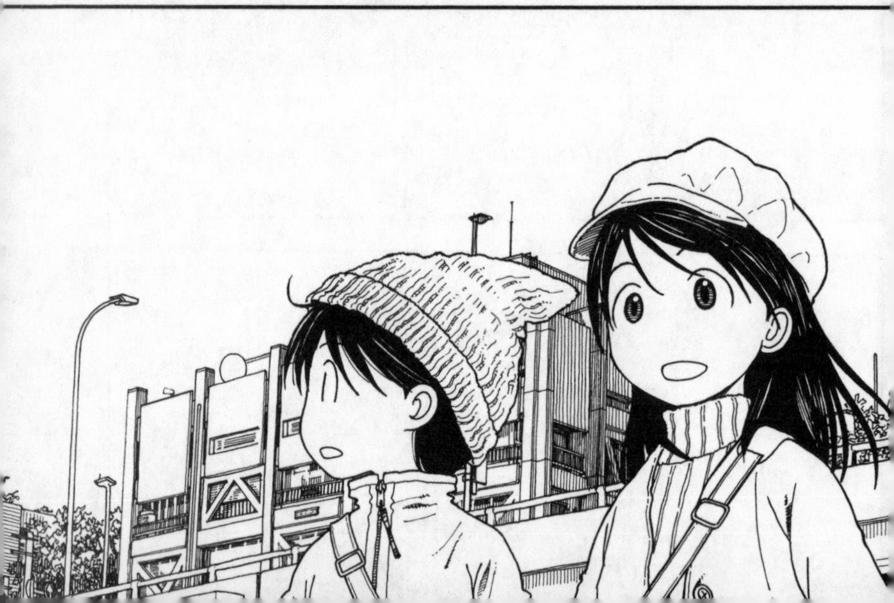

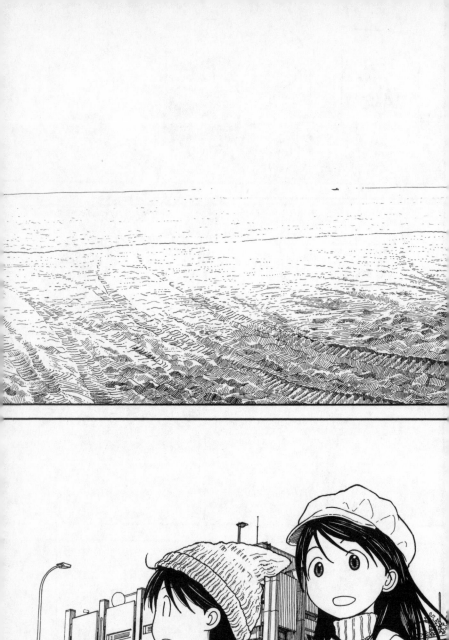

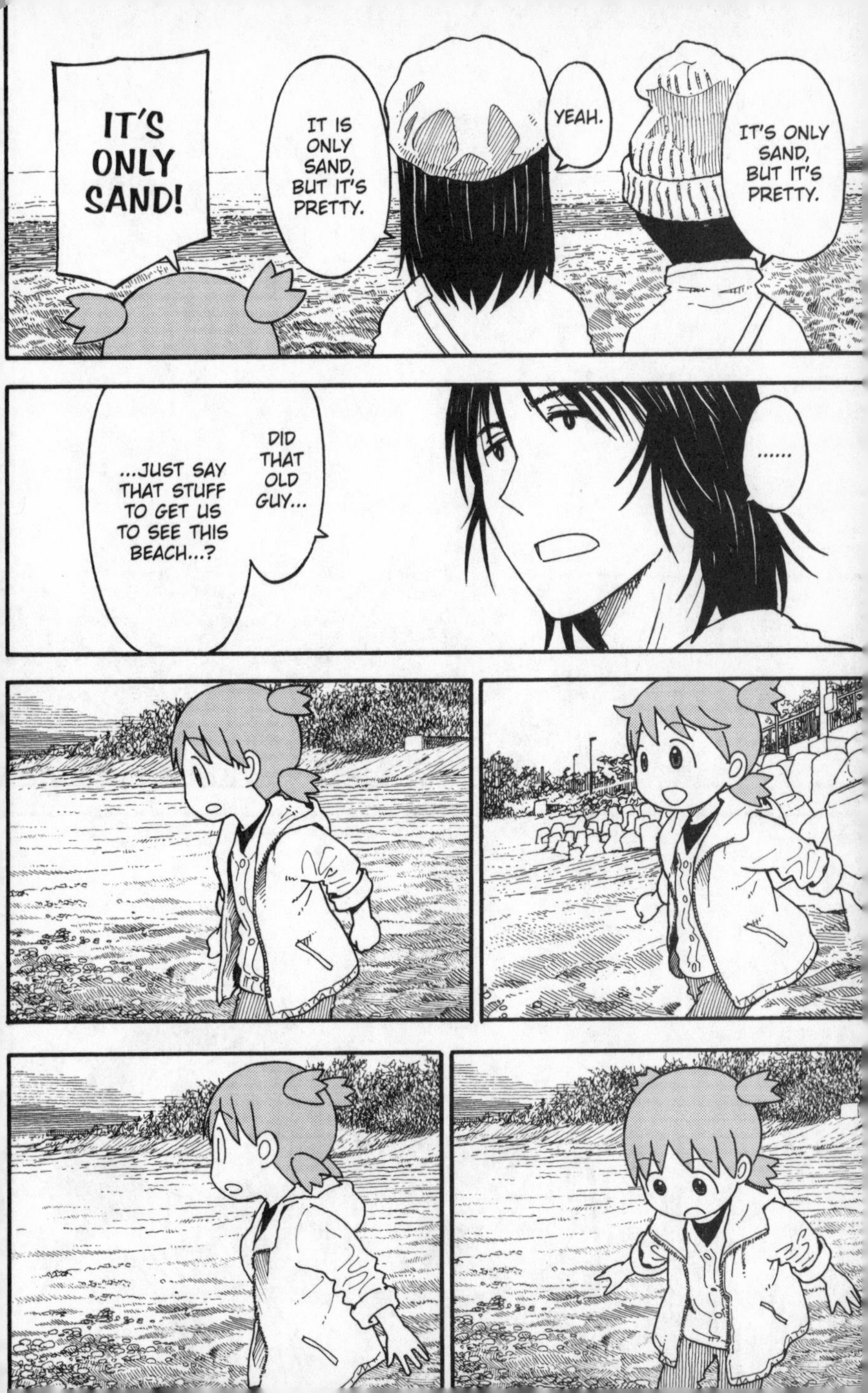
IT'S ONLY SAND, BUT IT'S PRETTY.
YEAH.
IT IS ONLY SAND, BUT IT'S PRETTY.
IT'S ONLY SAND!
......
DID THAT OLD GUY...
...JUST SAY THAT STUFF TO GET US TO SEE THIS BEACH...?

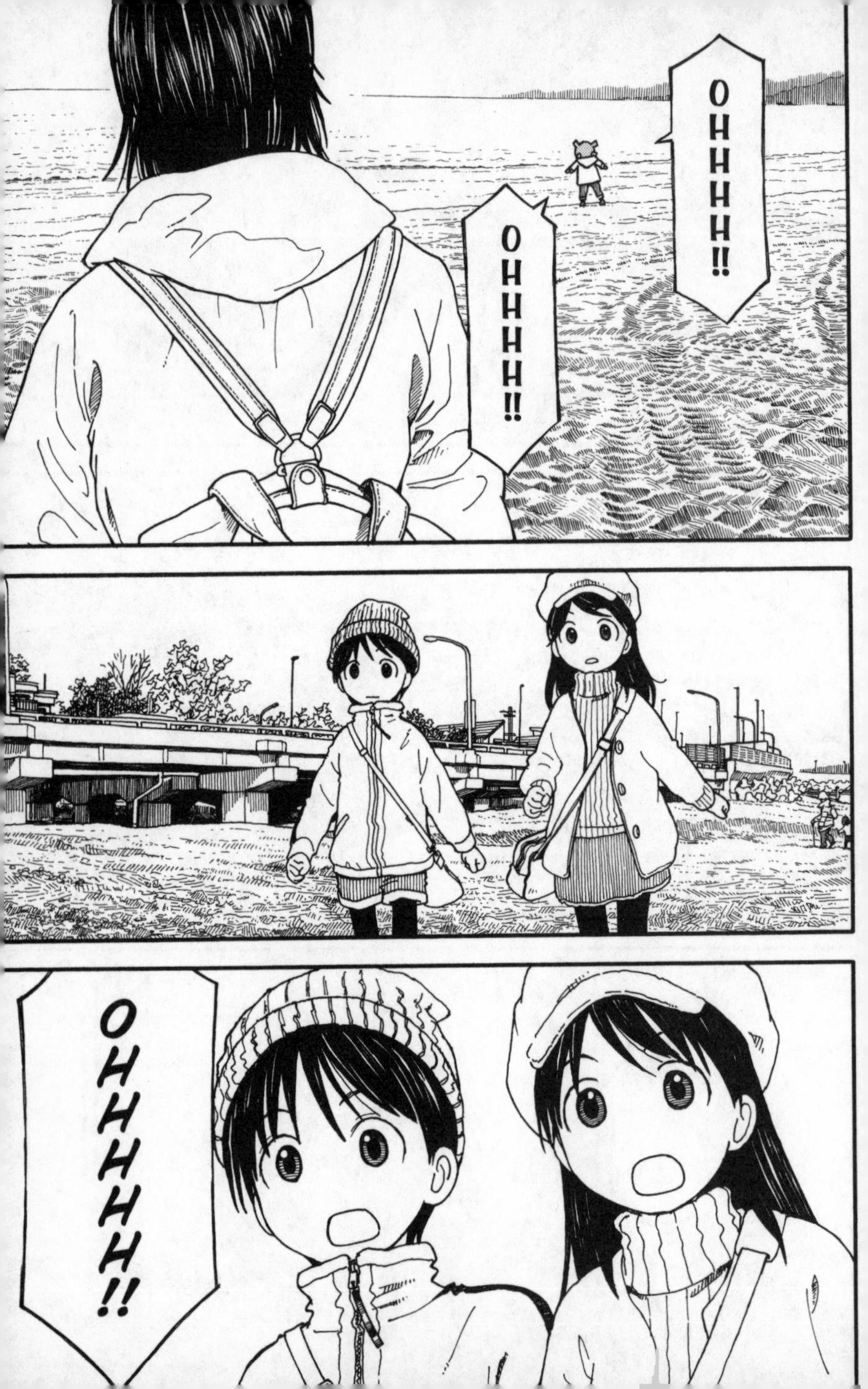
OHHHH!!
OHHHH!!
OHHHHHH!!

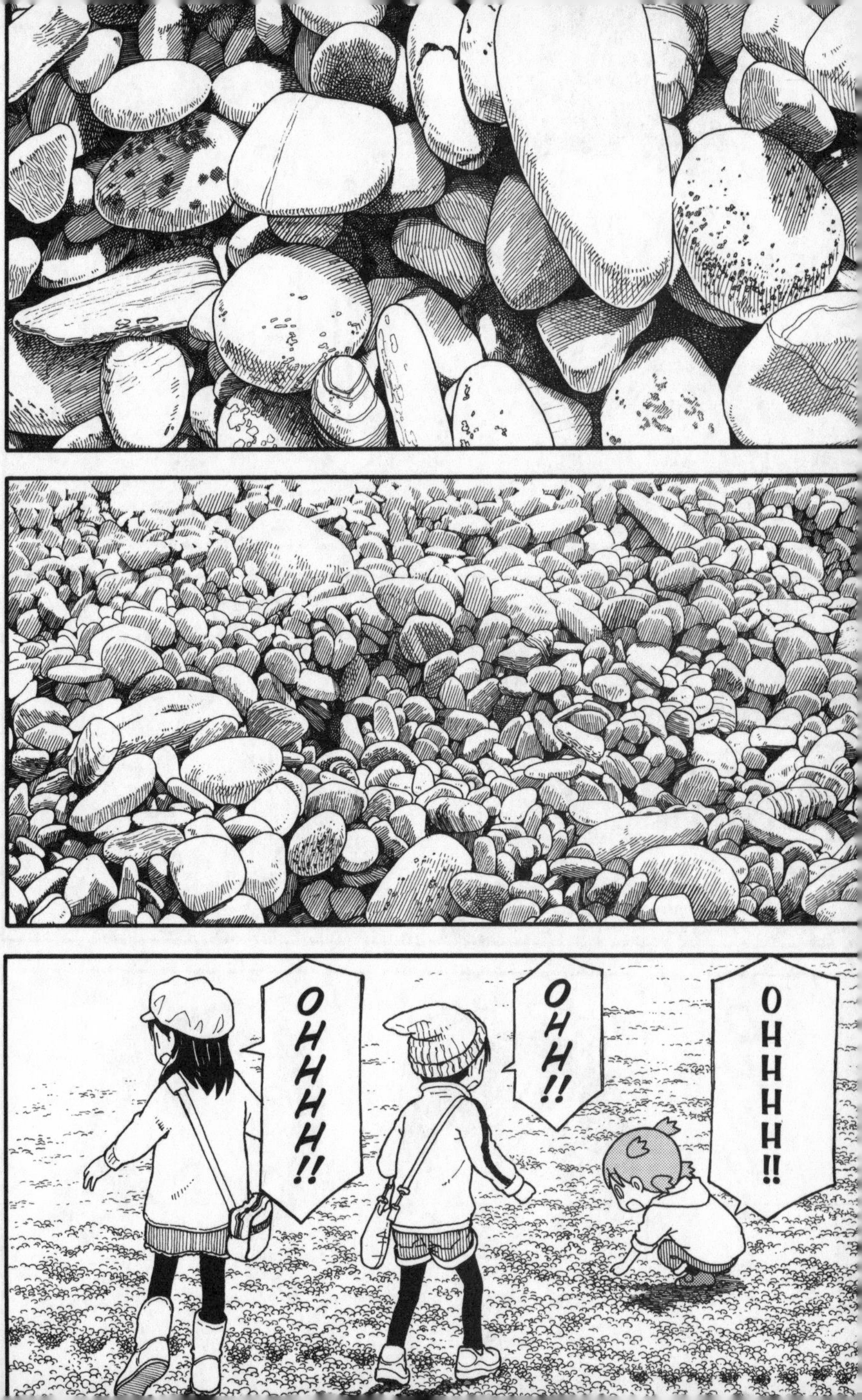
OHHHHH!!
OHH!!
OHHHHH!!

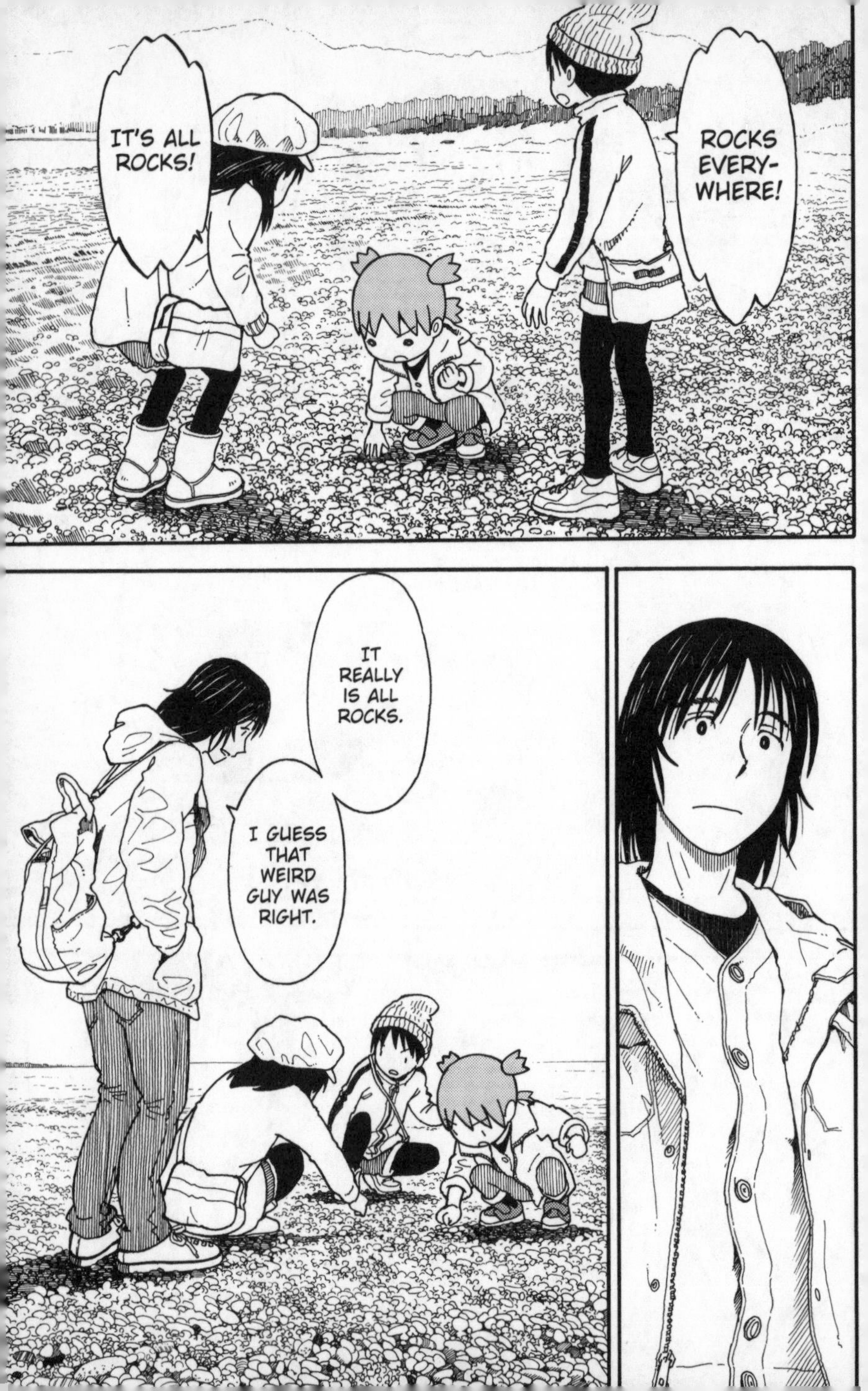
ROCKS EVERY-WHERE!
IT'S ALL ROCKS!
IT REALLY IS ALL ROCKS.
I GUESS THAT WEIRD GUY WAS RIGHT.

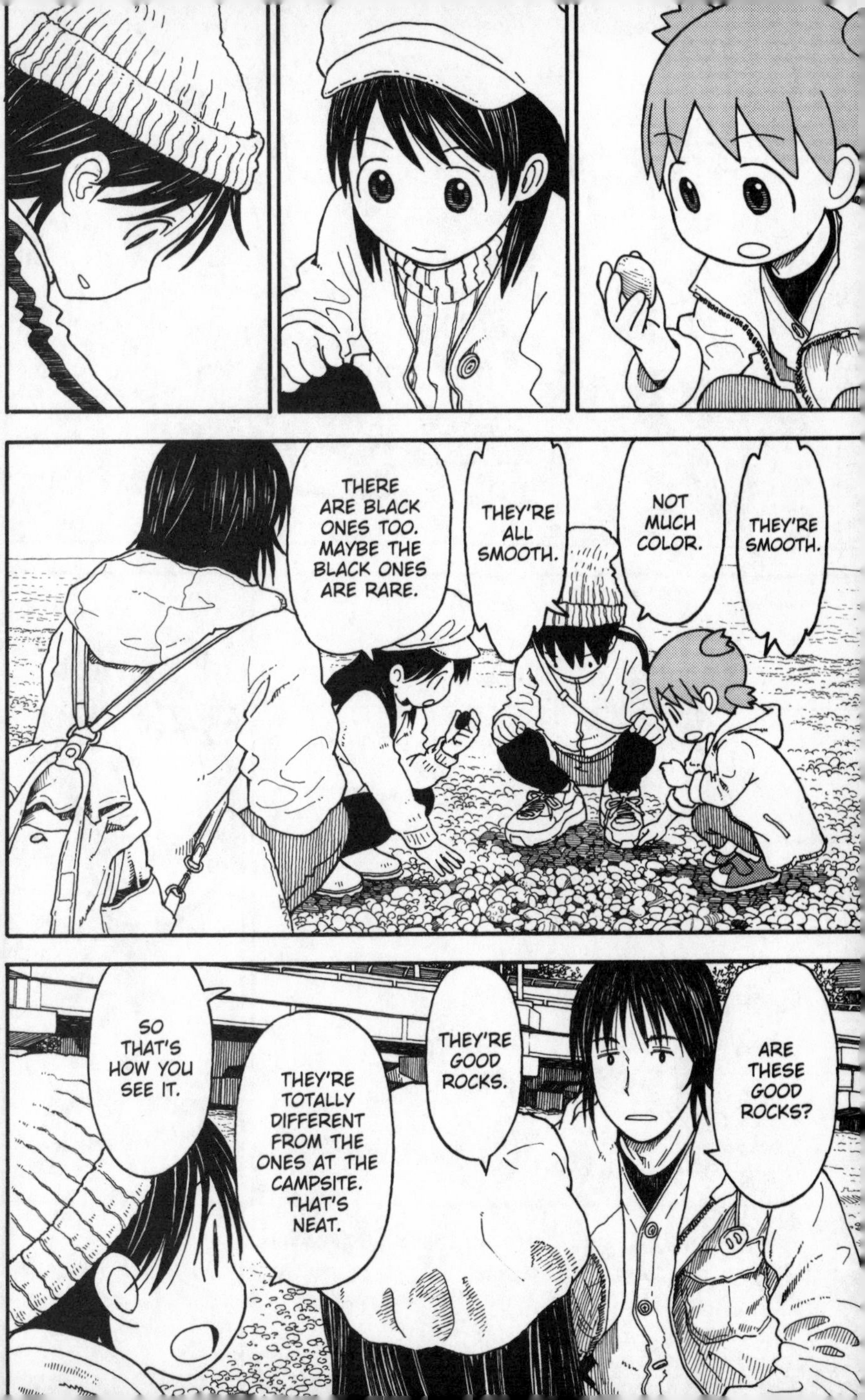
THEY'RE SMOOTH.
NOT MUCH COLOR.
THEY'RE ALL SMOOTH.
THERE ARE BLACK ONES TOO. MAYBE THE BLACK ONES ARE RARE.
ARE THESE GOOD ROCKS?
THEY'RE GOOD ROCKS.
THEY'RE TOTALLY DIFFERENT FROM THE ONES AT THE CAMPSITE. THAT'S NEAT.
SO THAT'S HOW YOU SEE IT.

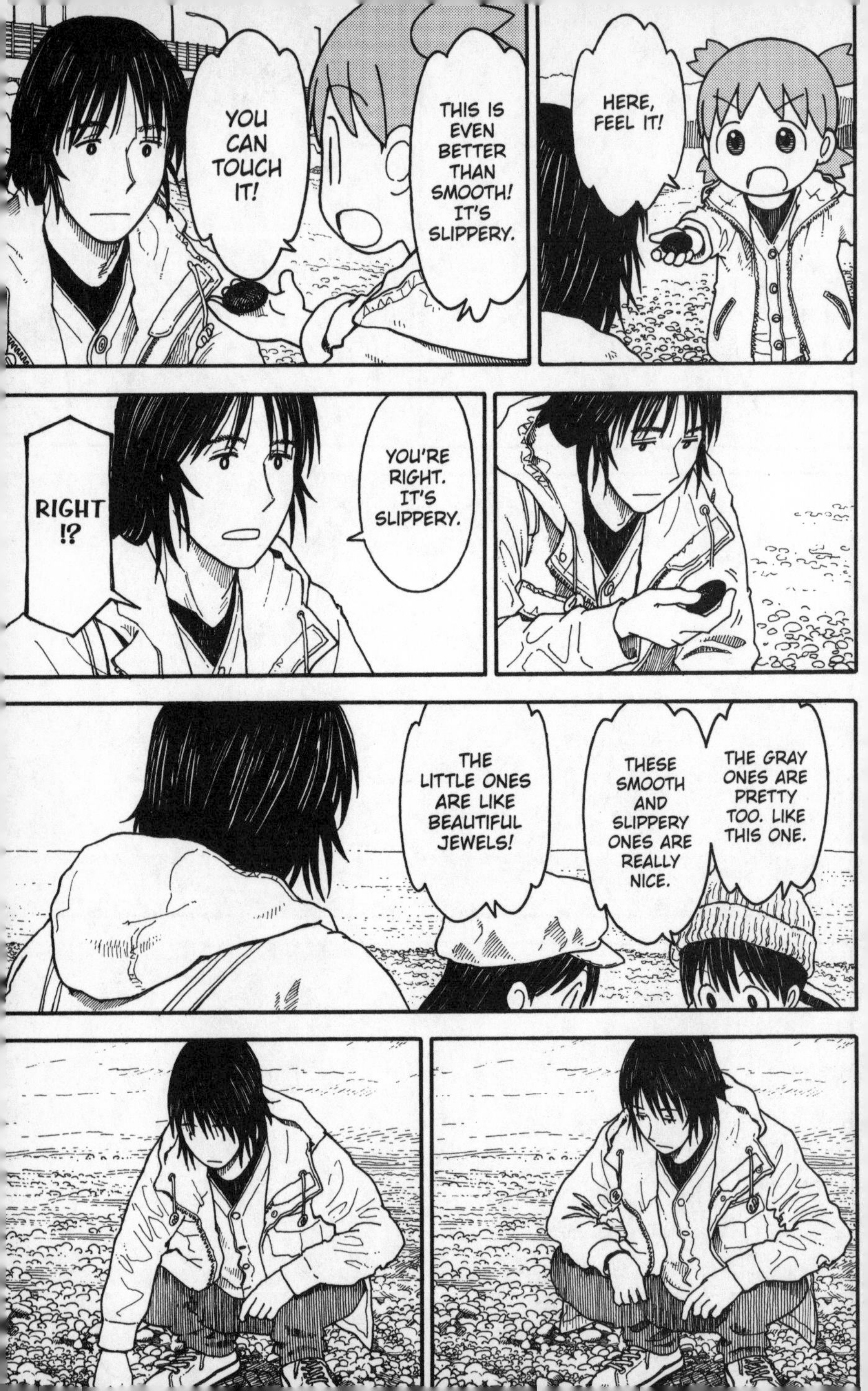
HERE, FEEL IT!
THIS IS EVEN BETTER THAN SMOOTH! IT'S SLIPPERY.
YOU CAN TOUCH IT!
YOU'RE RIGHT. IT'S SLIPPERY.
RIGHT !?
THE GRAY ONES ARE PRETTY TOO. LIKE THIS ONE.
THESE SMOOTH AND SLIPPERY ONES ARE REALLY NICE.
THE LITTLE ONES ARE LIKE BEAUTIFUL JEWELS!

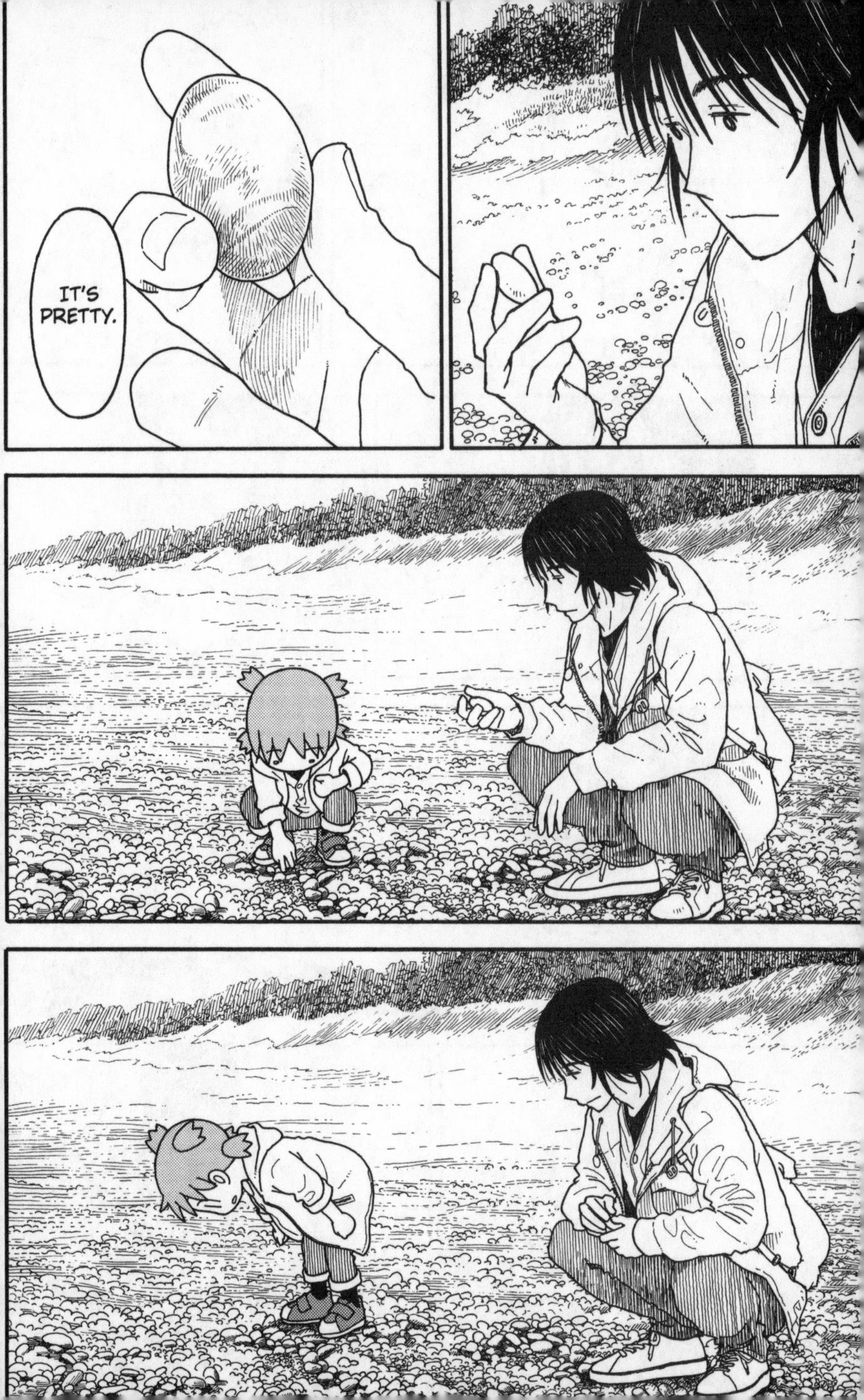
IT'S PRETTY.

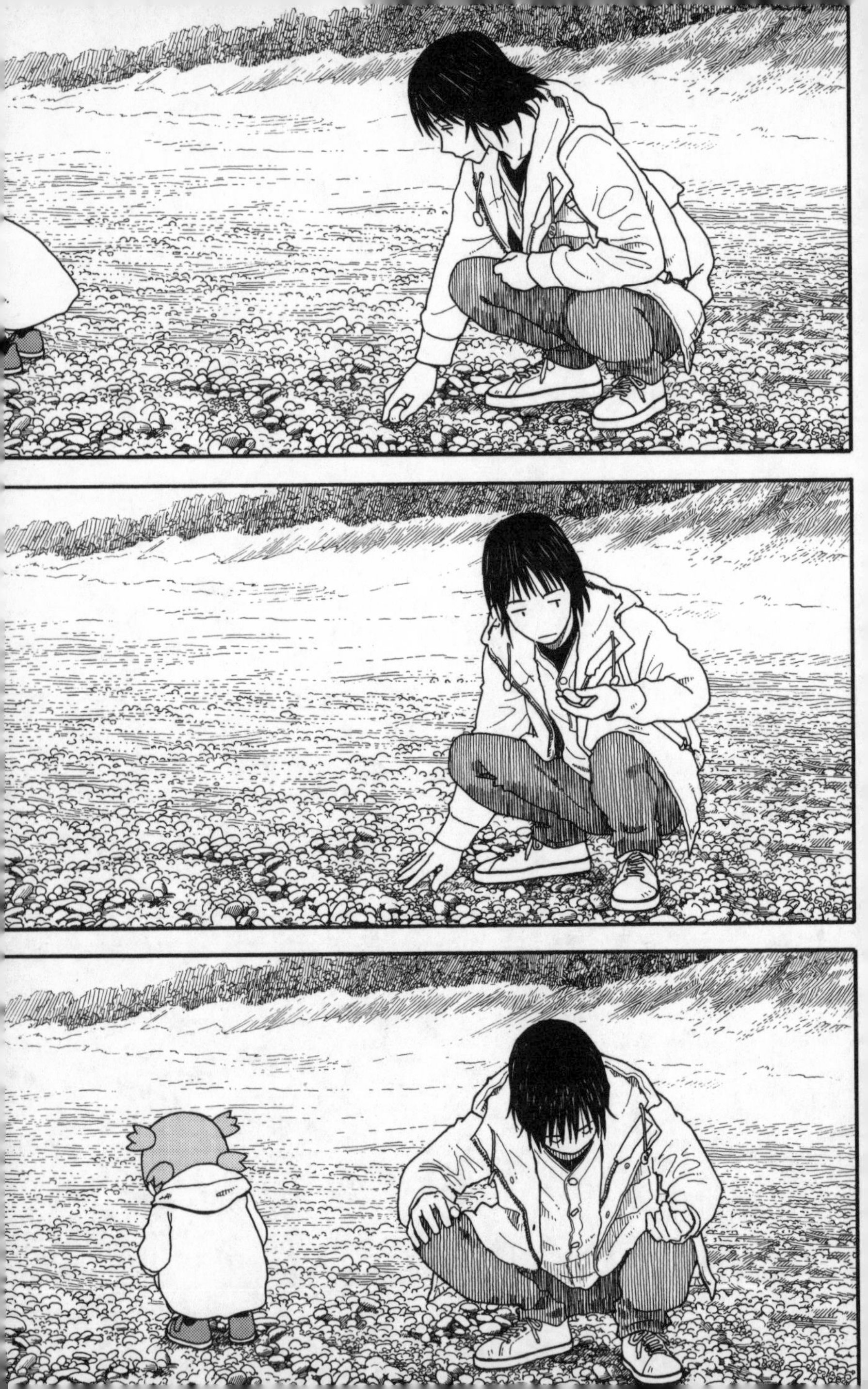

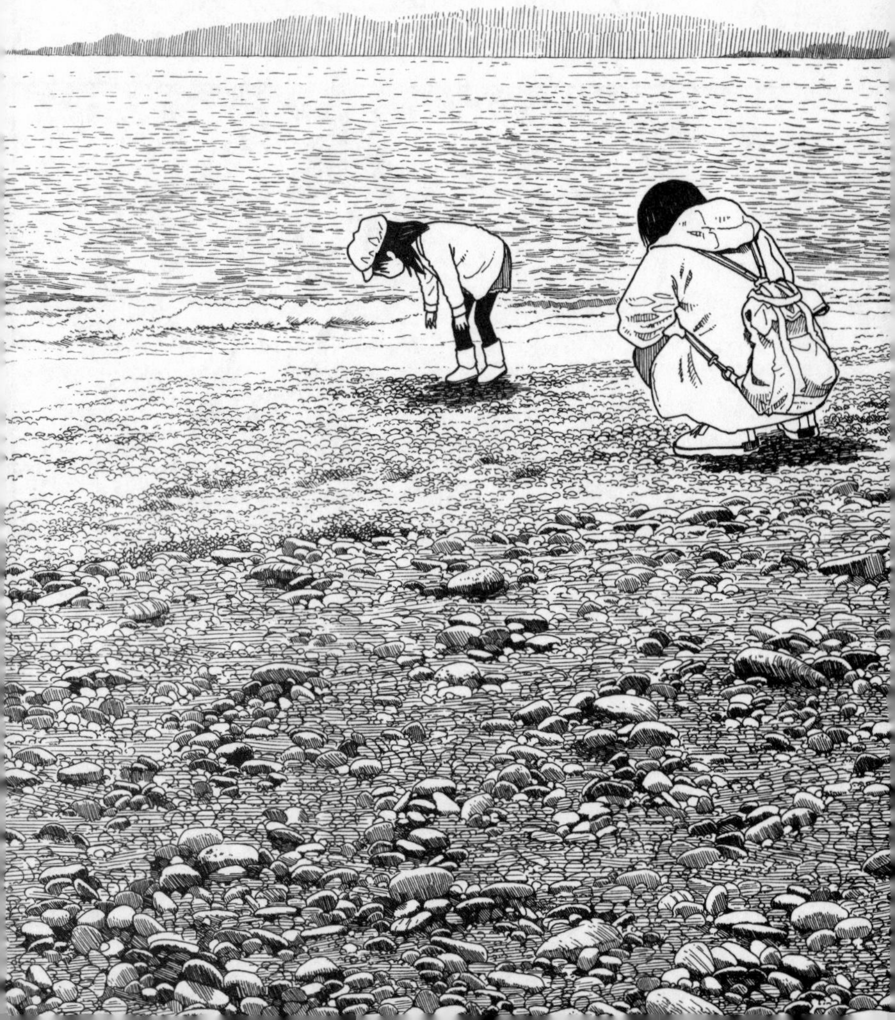

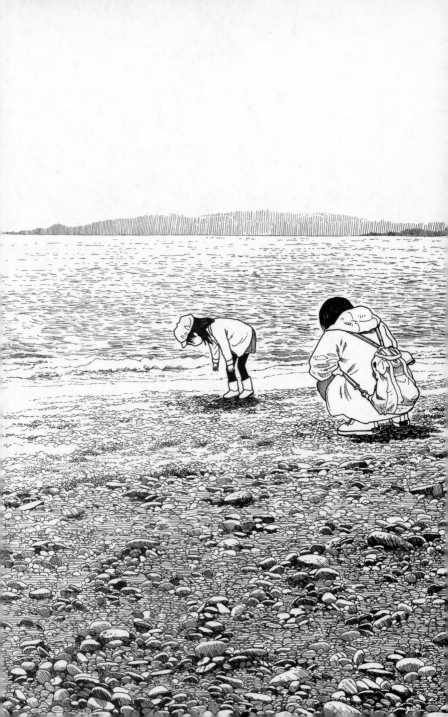

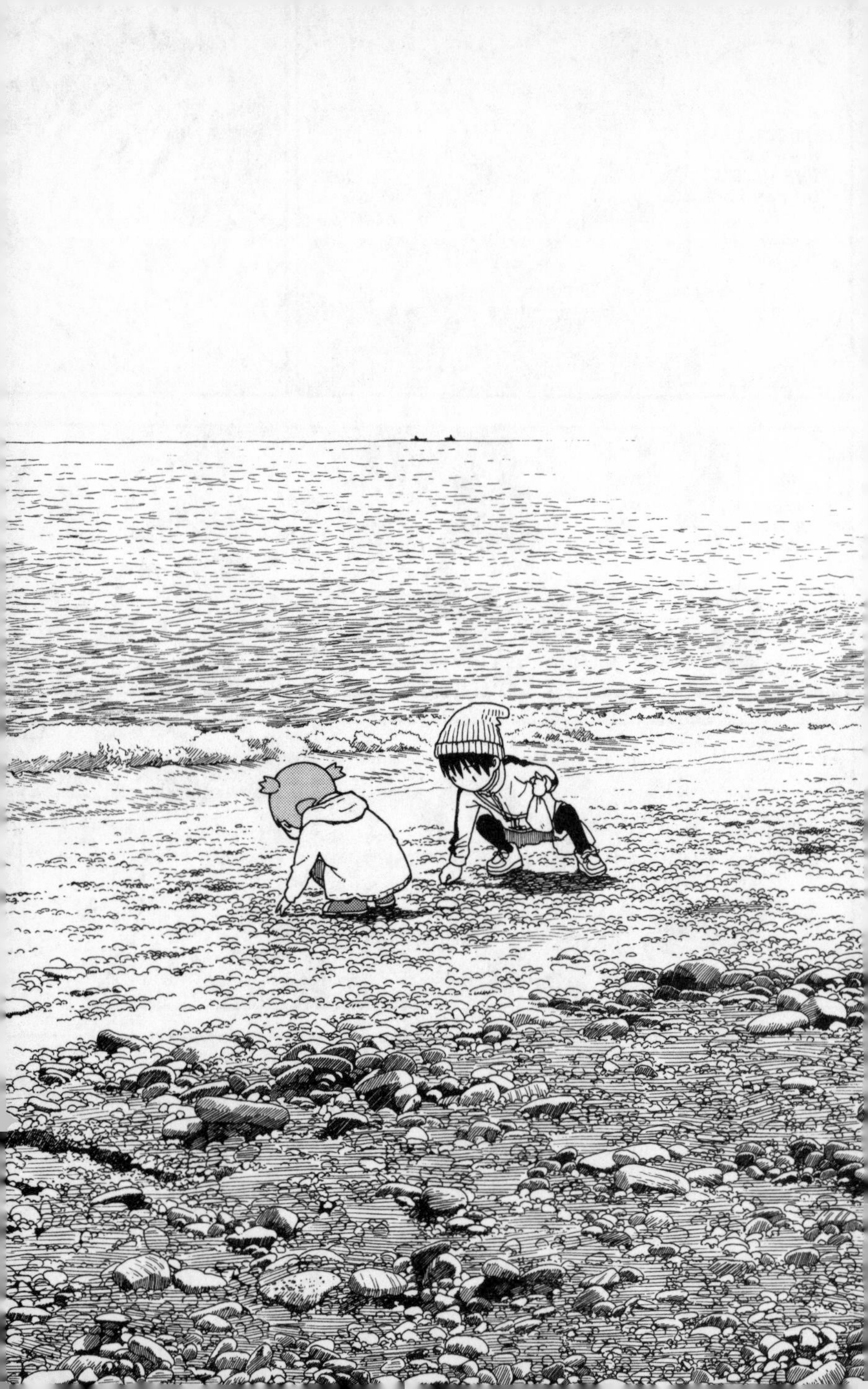

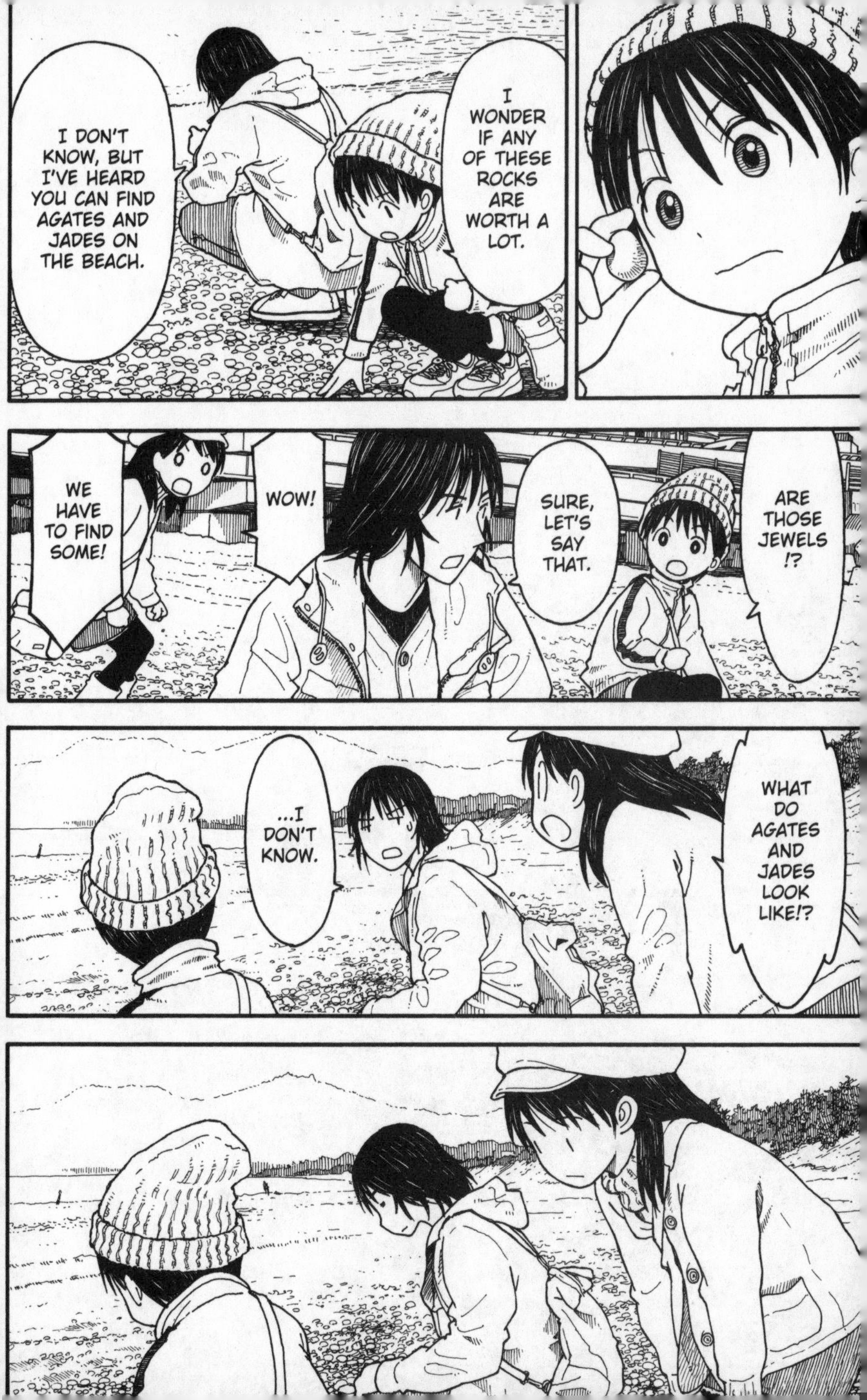
I WONDER IF ANY OF THESE ROCKS ARE WORTH A LOT.
I DON'T KNOW, BUT I'VE HEARD YOU CAN FIND AGATES AND JADES ON THE BEACH.
ARE THOSE JEWELS!?
SURE, LET'S SAY THAT.
WOW!
WE HAVE TO FIND SOME!
WHAT DO AGATES AND JADES LOOK LIKE!?
...I DON'T KNOW.

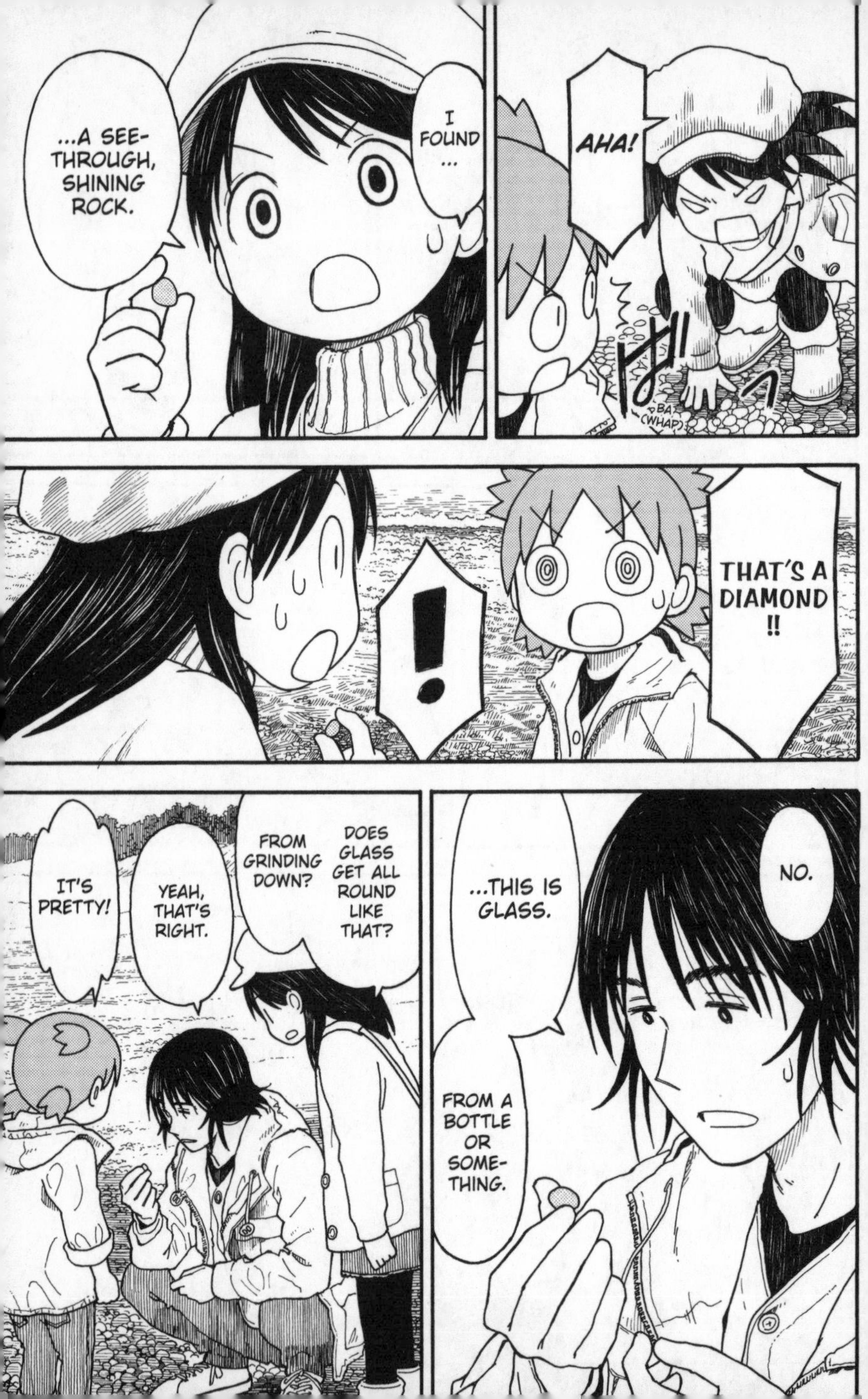
AHA!
BA (WHAP)
I FOUND ...
...A SEE-THROUGH, SHINING ROCK.
THAT'S A DIAMOND !!
!
NO.
...THIS IS GLASS.
FROM A BOTTLE OR SOME-THING.
DOES GLASS GET ALL ROUND LIKE THAT?
FROM GRINDING DOWN?
YEAH, THAT'S RIGHT.
IT'S PRETTY!

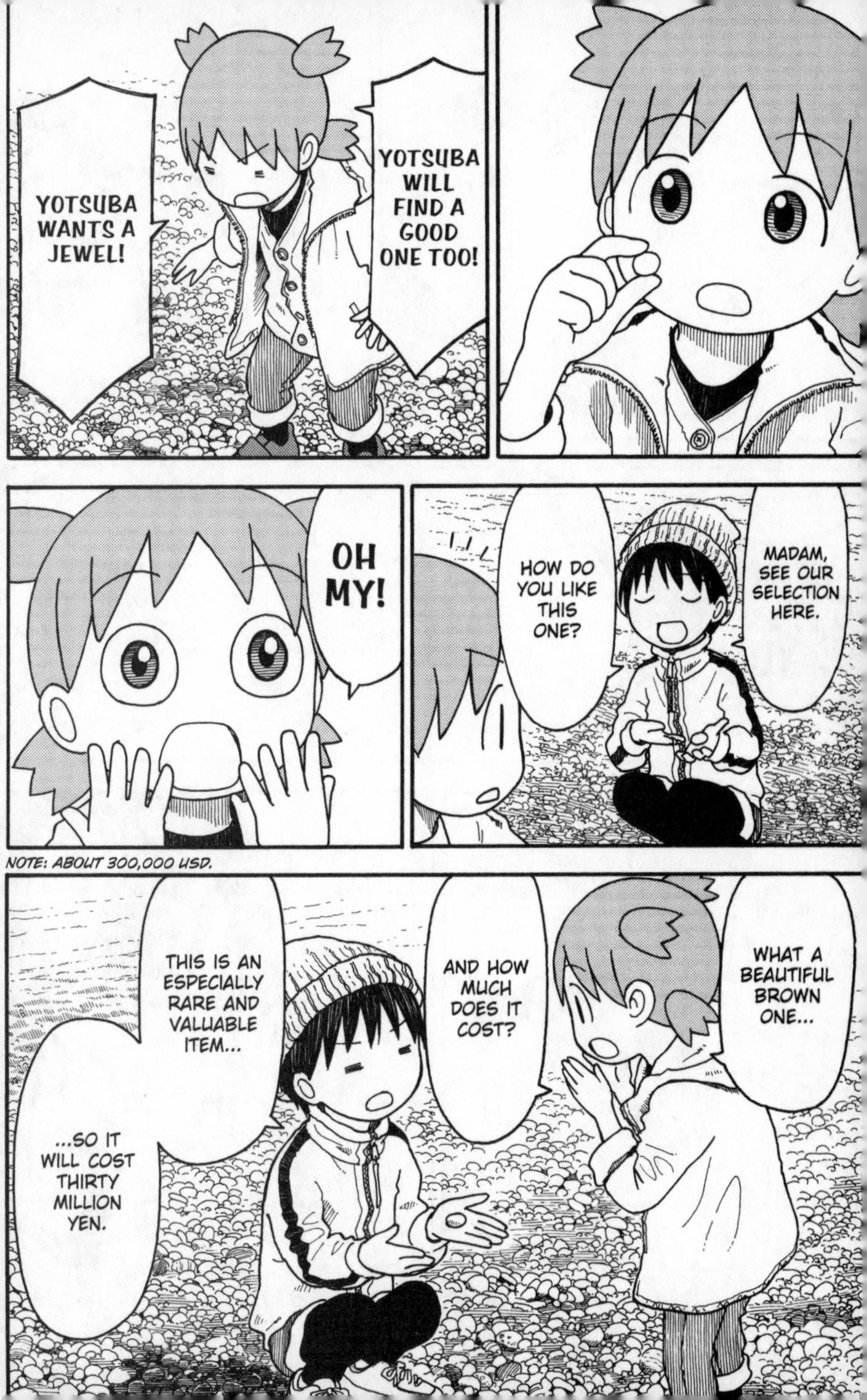
YOTSUBA WILL FIND A GOOD ONE TOO!
YOTSUBA WANTS A JEWEL!
MADAM, SEE OUR SELECTION HERE.
HOW DO YOU LIKE THIS ONE?
OH MY!
WHAT A BEAUTIFUL BROWN ONE...
AND HOW MUCH DOES IT COST?
THIS IS AN ESPECIALLY RARE AND VALUABLE ITEM...
...SO IT WILL COST THIRTY MILLION YEN.

NOTE: ABOUT 300,000 USD.

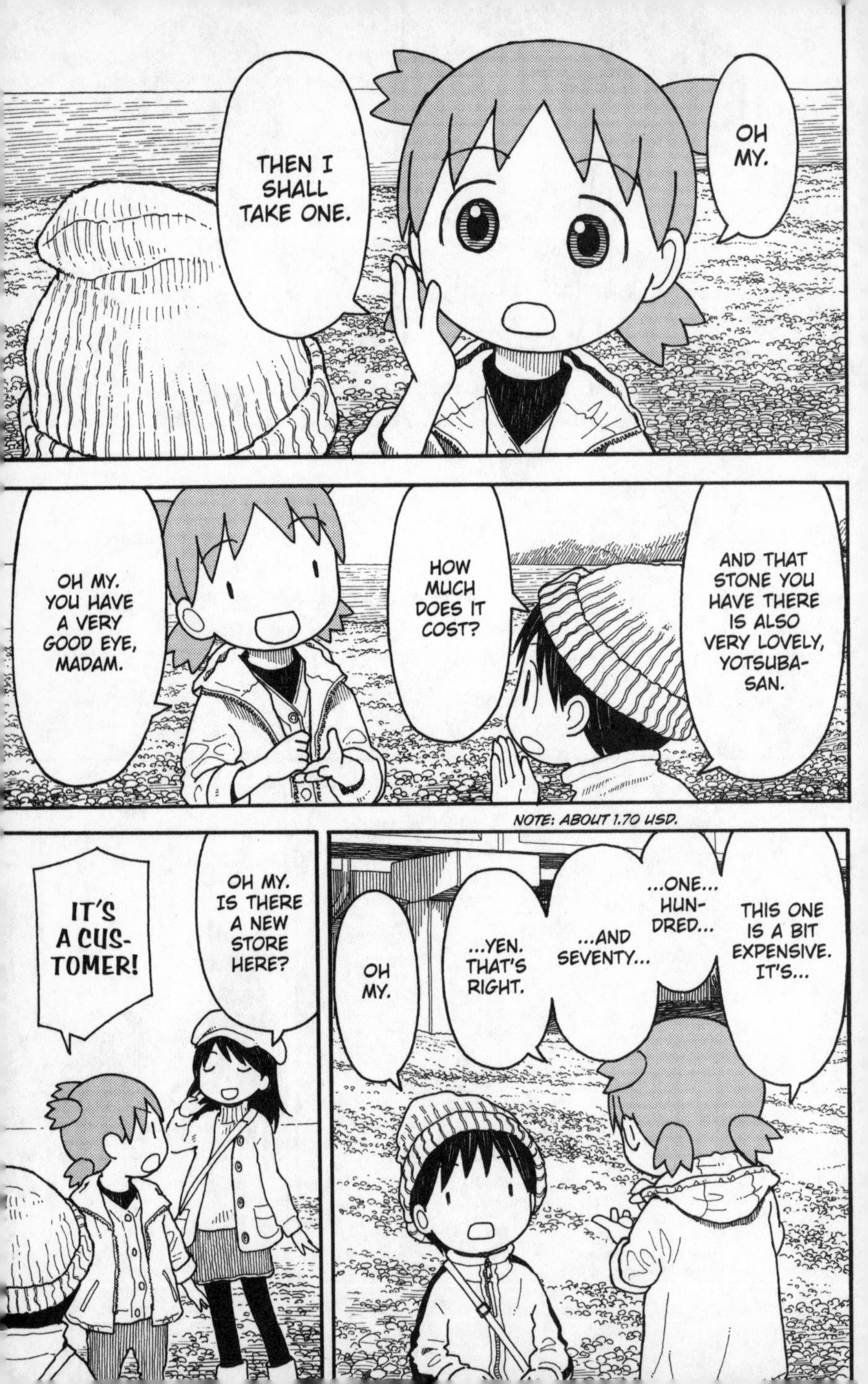
OH MY.
THEN I SHALL TAKE ONE.
AND THAT STONE YOU HAVE THERE IS ALSO VERY LOVELY, YOTSUBA-SAN.
HOW MUCH DOES IT COST?
OH MY. YOU HAVE A VERY GOOD EYE, MADAM.
NOTE: ABOUT 1.70 USD.
THIS ONE IS A BIT EXPENSIVE. IT'S...
...ONE... HUNDRED...
...AND SEVENTY...
...YEN. THAT'S RIGHT.
OH MY.
OH MY. IS THERE A NEW STORE HERE?
IT'S A CUSTOMER!

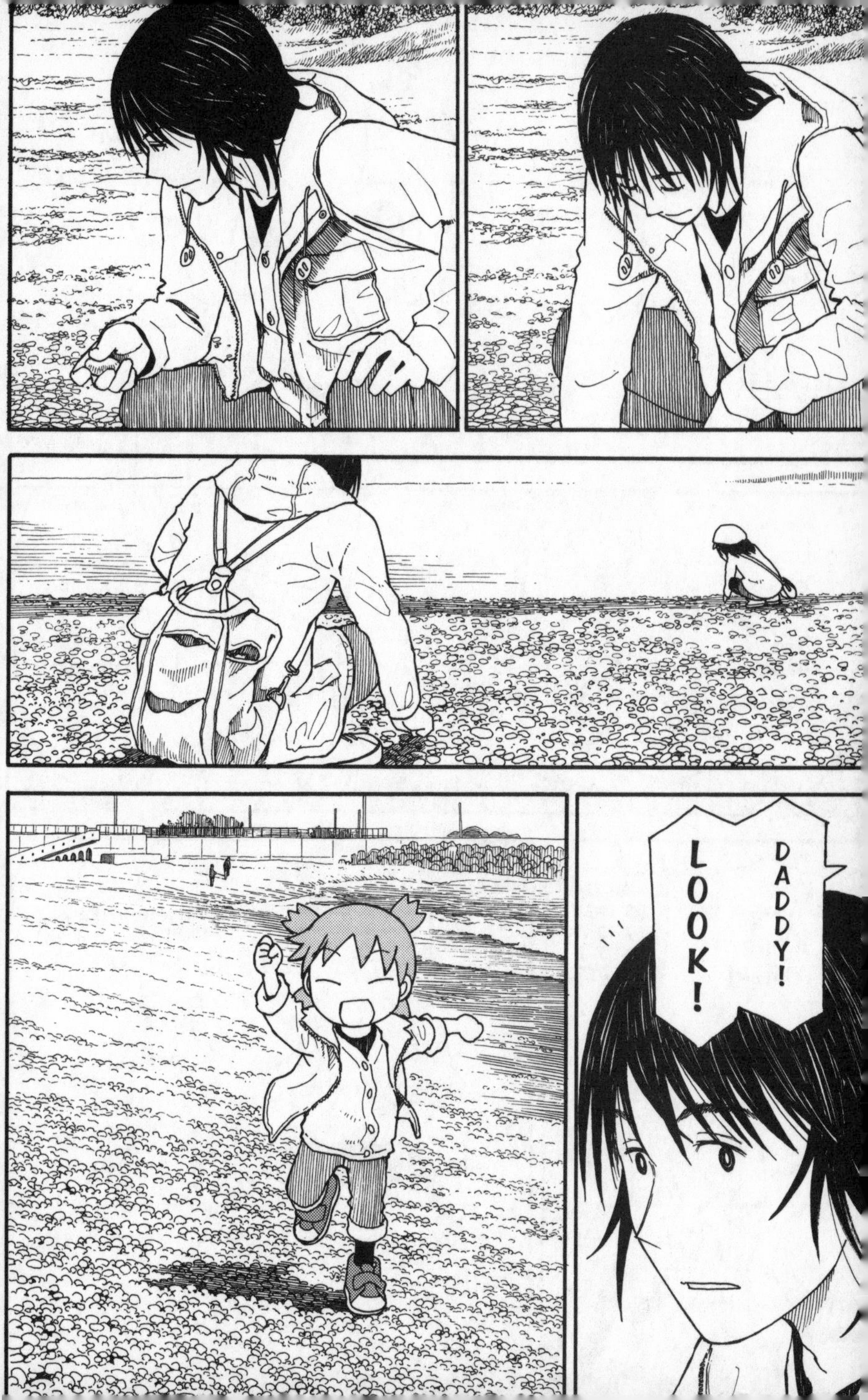
DADDY! LOOK!

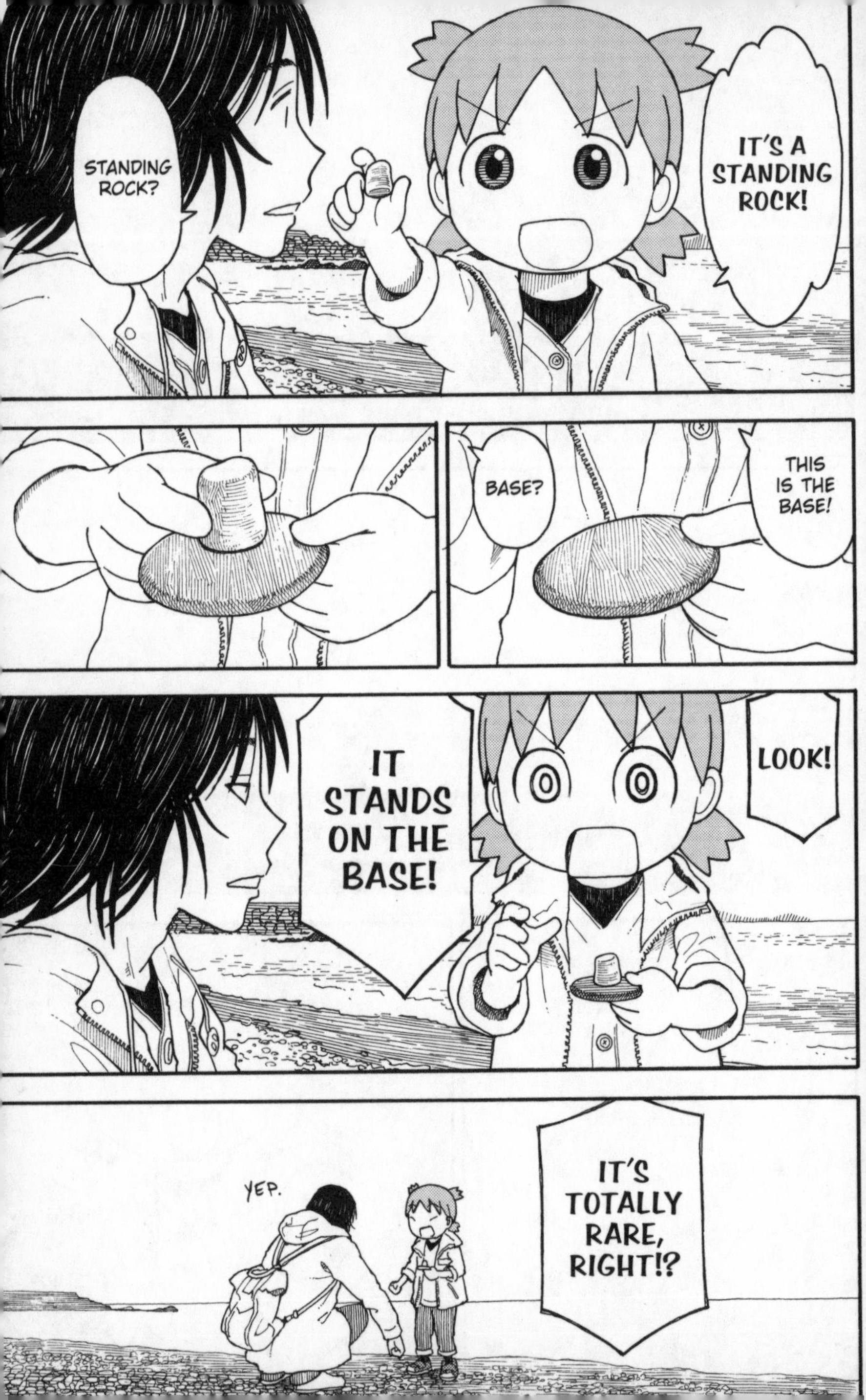
IT'S A STANDING ROCK!
STANDING ROCK?
THIS IS THE BASE!
BASE?
LOOK!
IT STANDS ON THE BASE!
IT'S TOTALLY RARE, RIGHT!?
YEP.

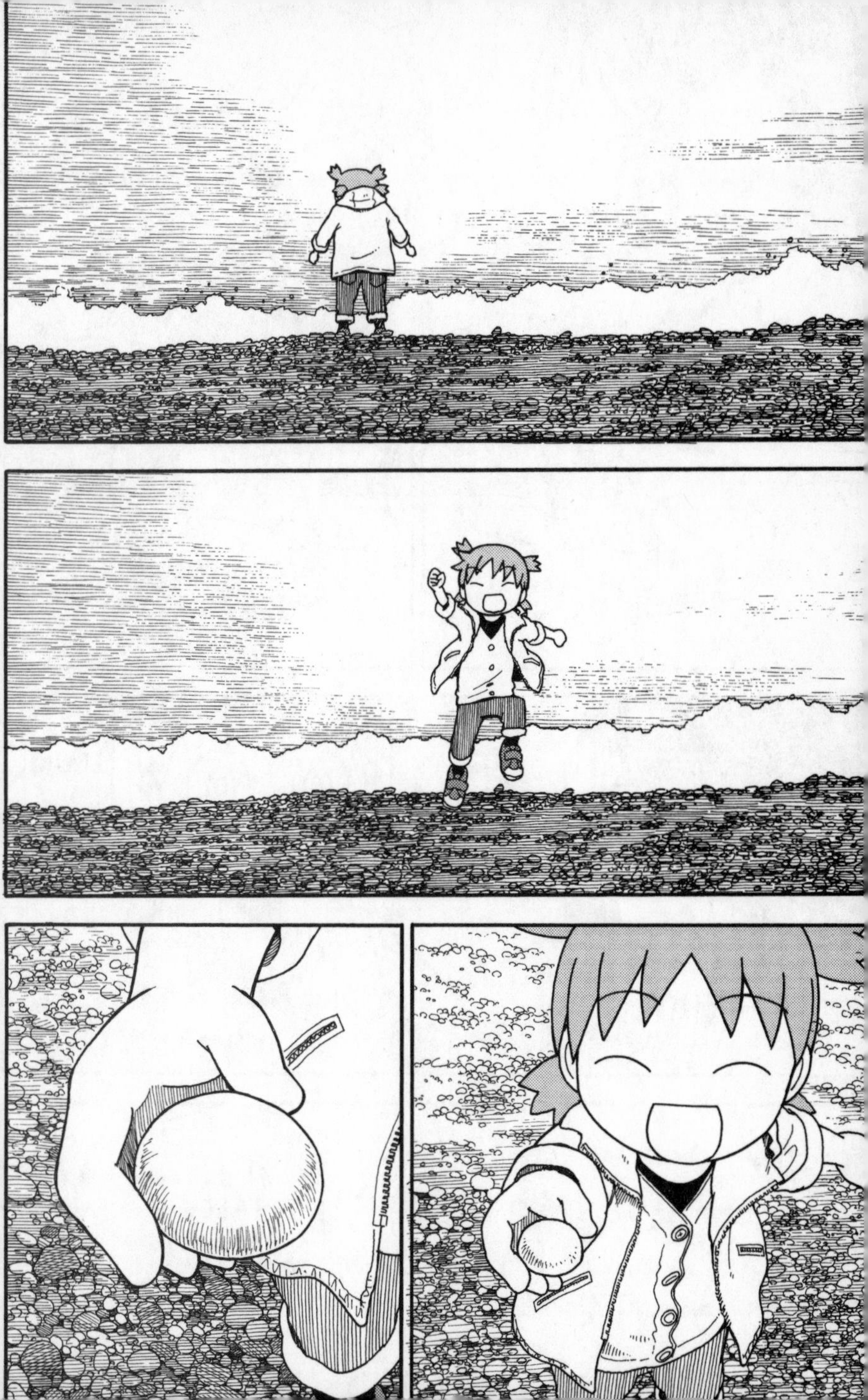

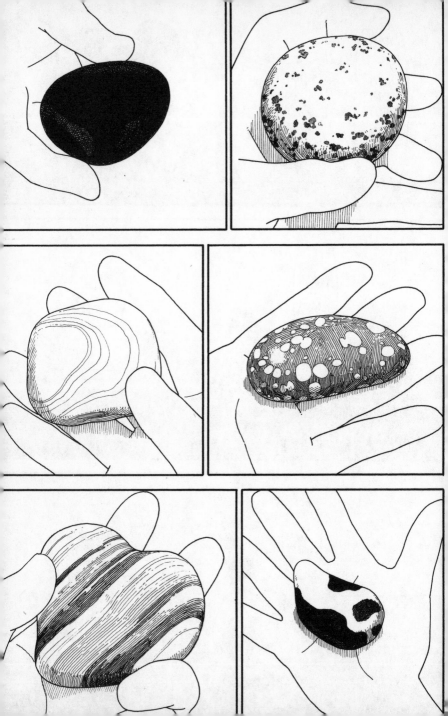

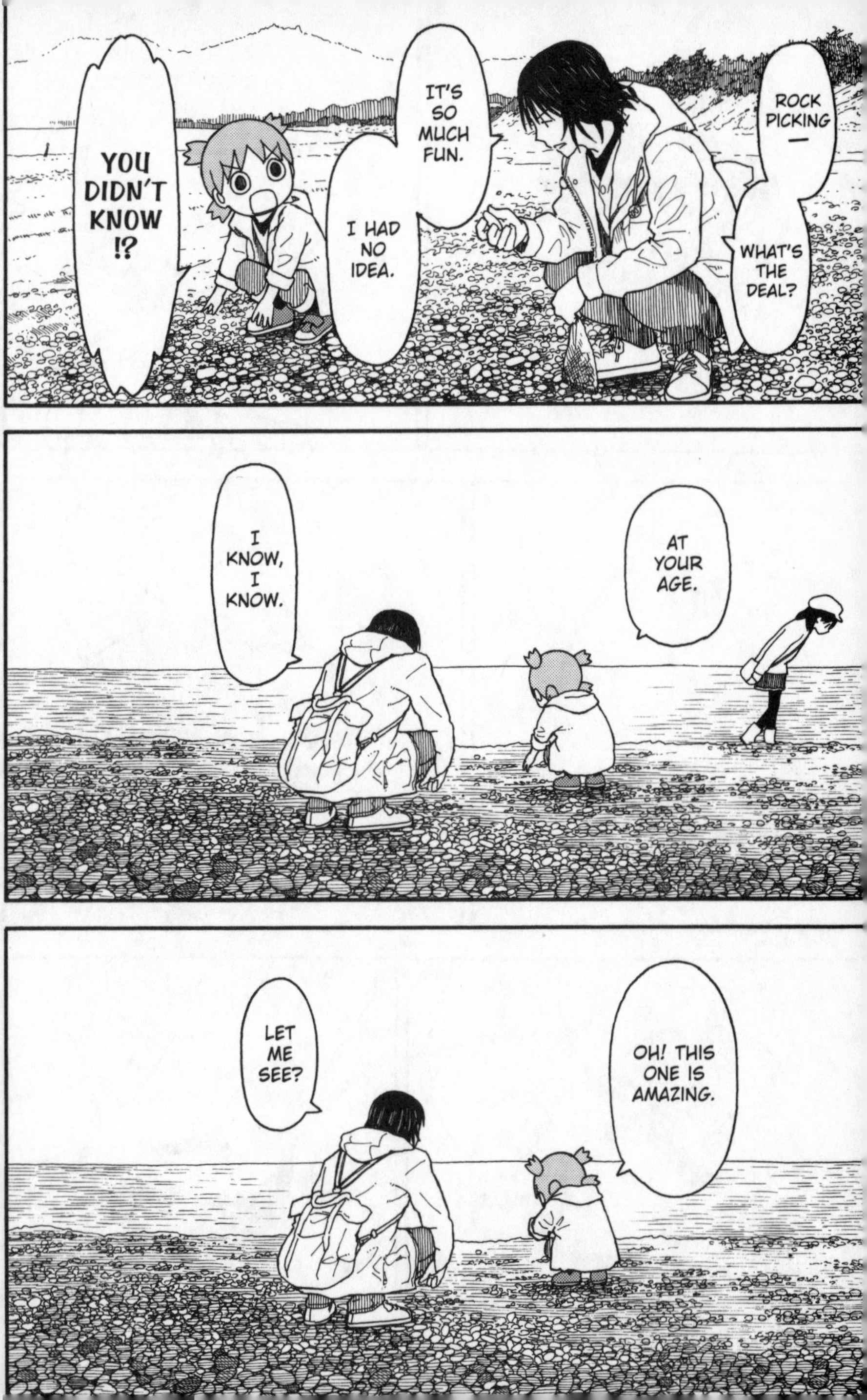
ROCK PICKING — WHAT'S THE DEAL?
IT'S SO MUCH FUN.
I HAD NO IDEA.
YOU DIDN'T KNOW !?
AT YOUR AGE.
I KNOW, I KNOW.
OH! THIS ONE IS AMAZING.
LET ME SEE?

YOTSUBA&!

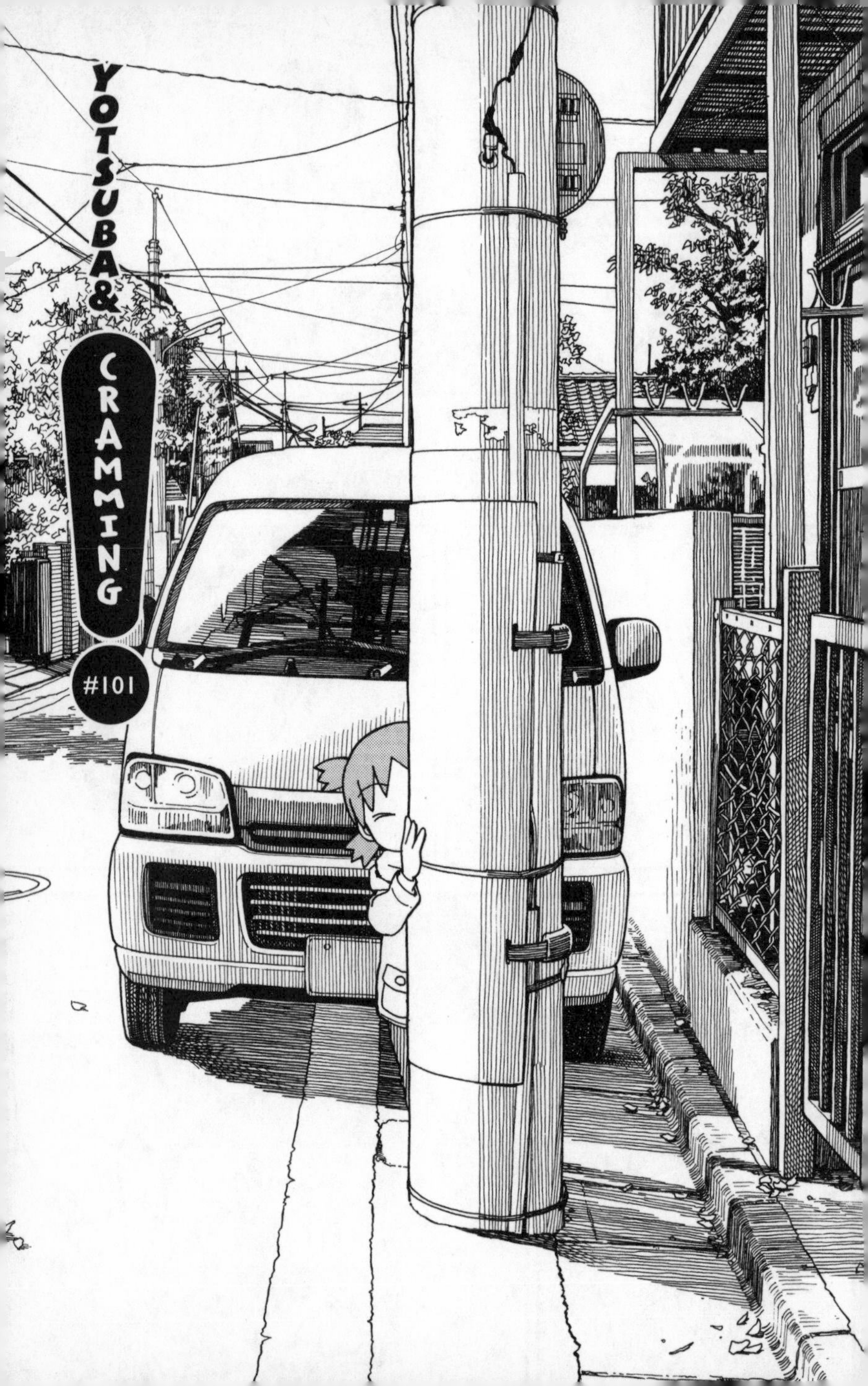
YOTSUBA&
CRAMMING
#101

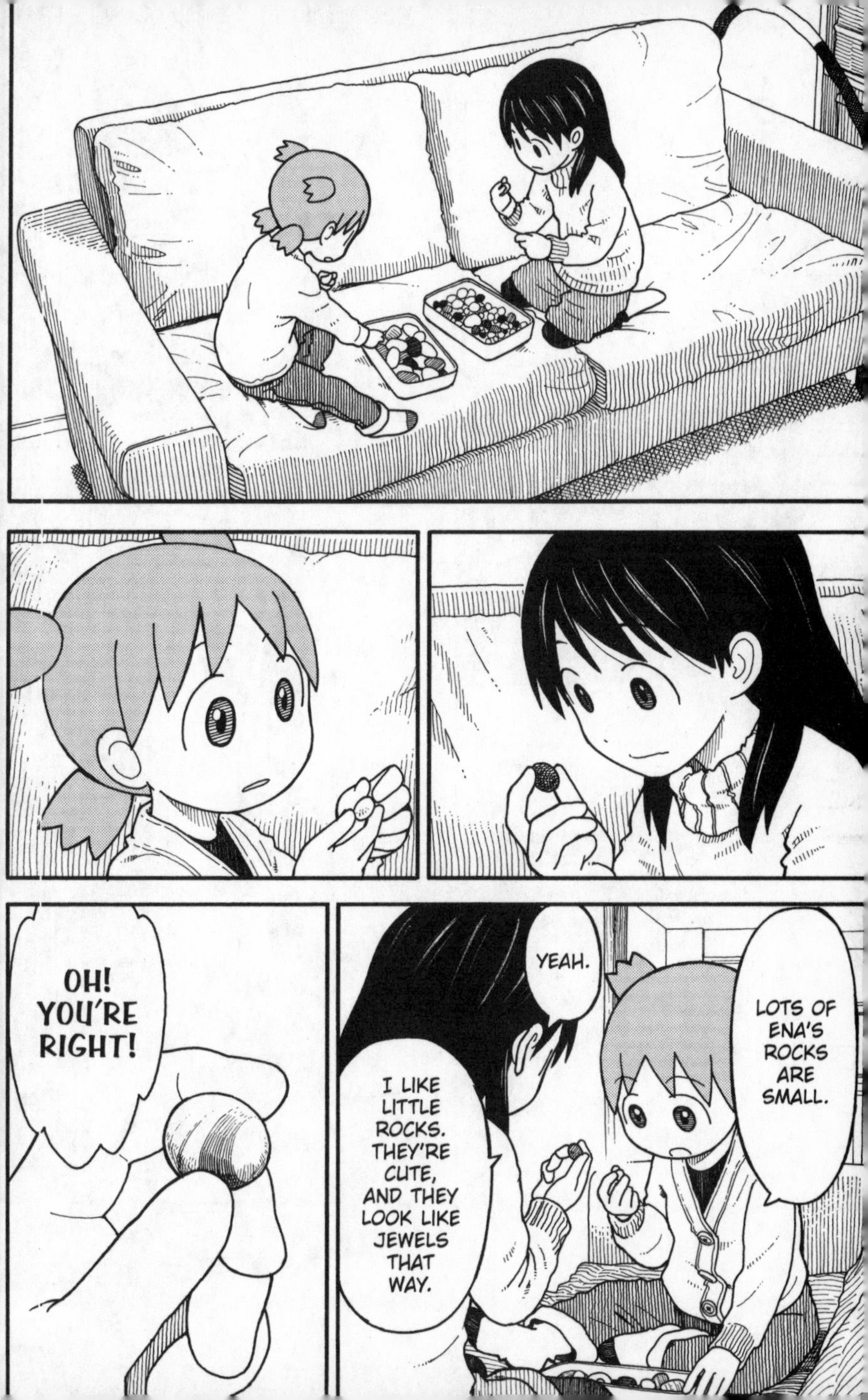
LOTS OF ENA'S ROCKS ARE SMALL.
YEAH.
I LIKE LITTLE ROCKS. THEY'RE CUTE, AND THEY LOOK LIKE JEWELS THAT WAY.
OH! YOU'RE RIGHT!

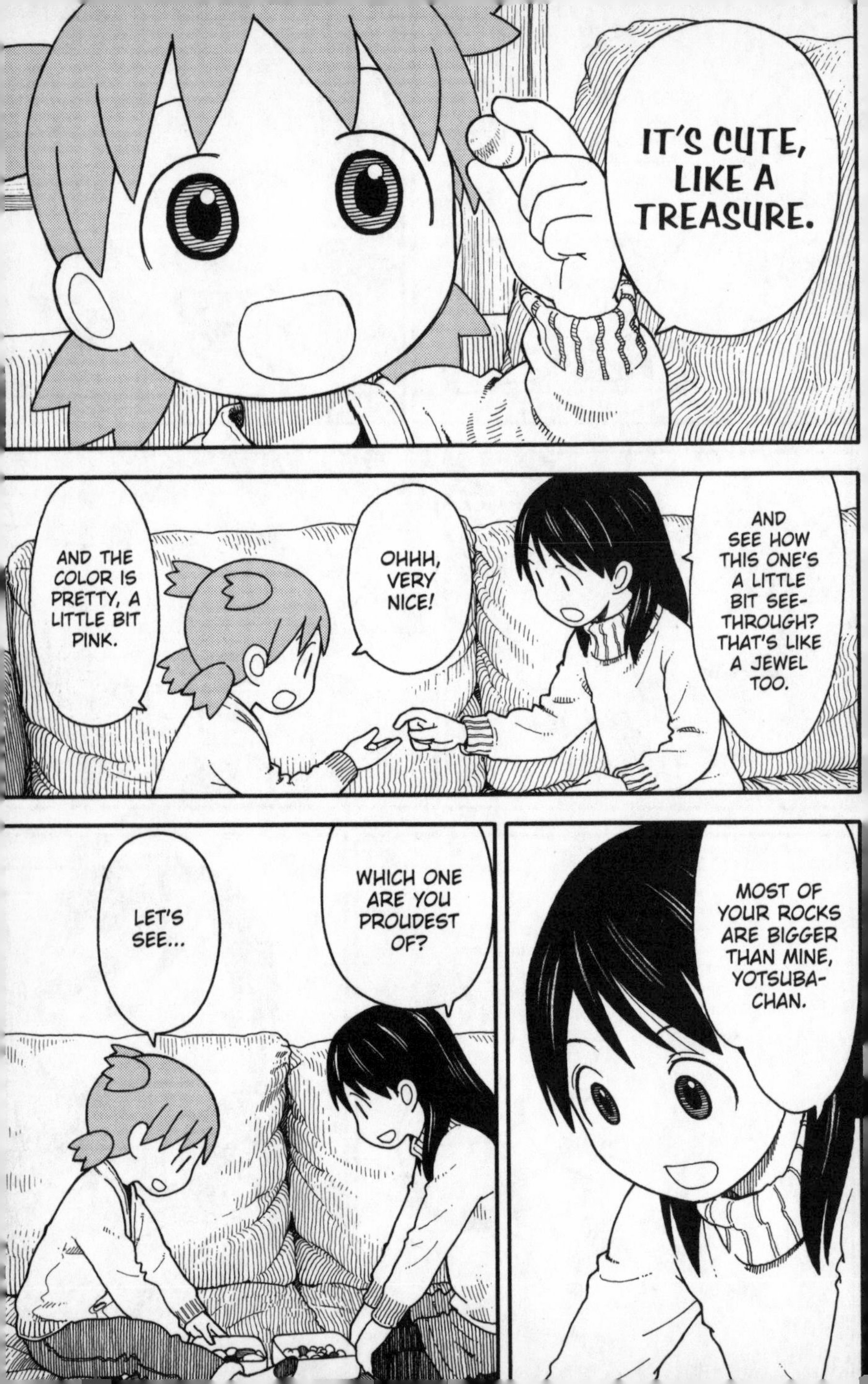
IT'S CUTE, LIKE A TREASURE.
AND SEE HOW THIS ONE'S A LITTLE BIT SEE-THROUGH? THAT'S LIKE A JEWEL TOO.
OHHH, VERY NICE!
AND THE COLOR IS PRETTY, A LITTLE BIT PINK.
MOST OF YOUR ROCKS ARE BIGGER THAN MINE, YOTSUBA-CHAN.
WHICH ONE ARE YOU PROUDEST OF?
LET'S SEE...

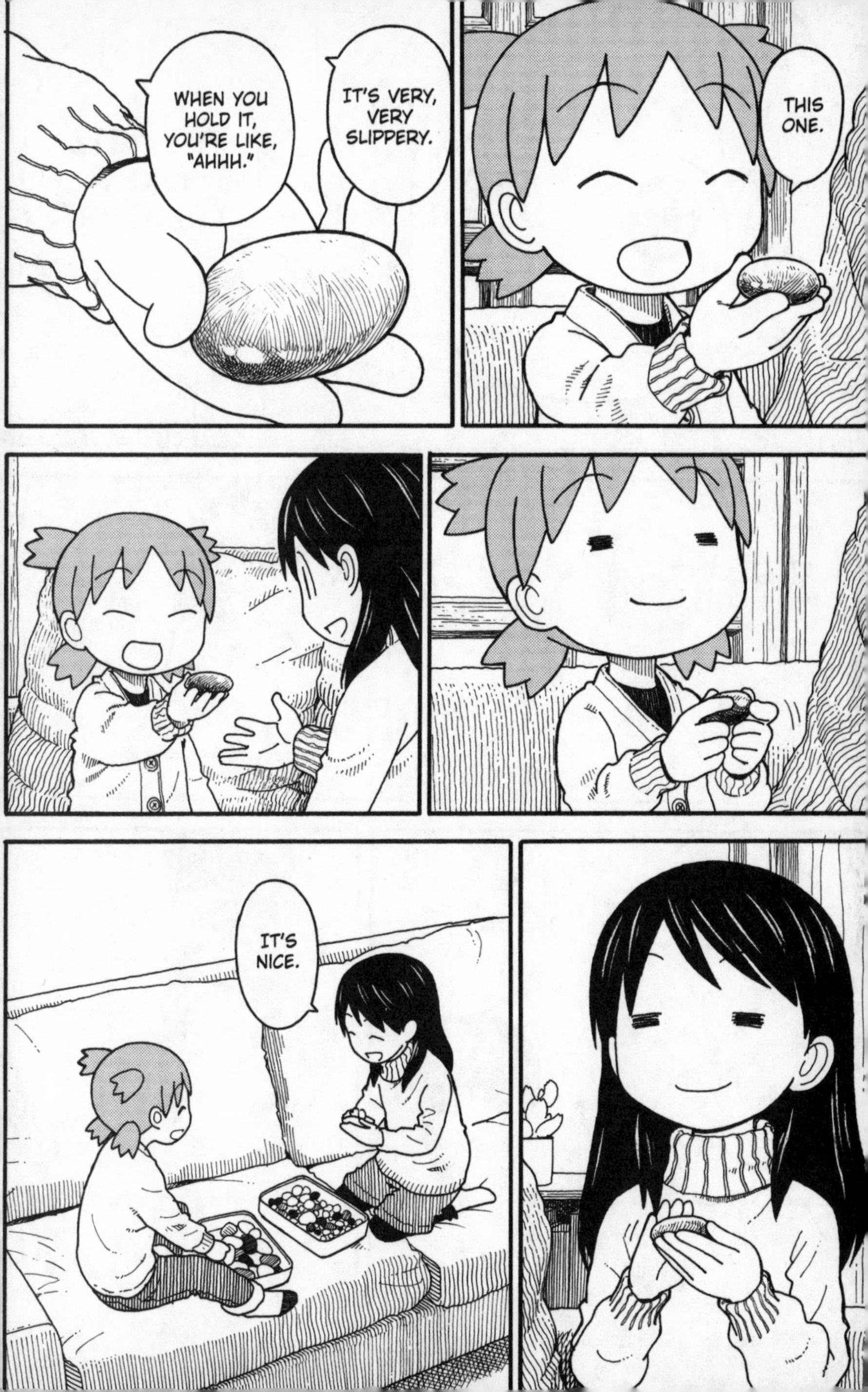
THIS ONE.
IT'S VERY, VERY SLIPPERY.
WHEN YOU HOLD IT, YOU'RE LIKE, "AHHH."
IT'S NICE.

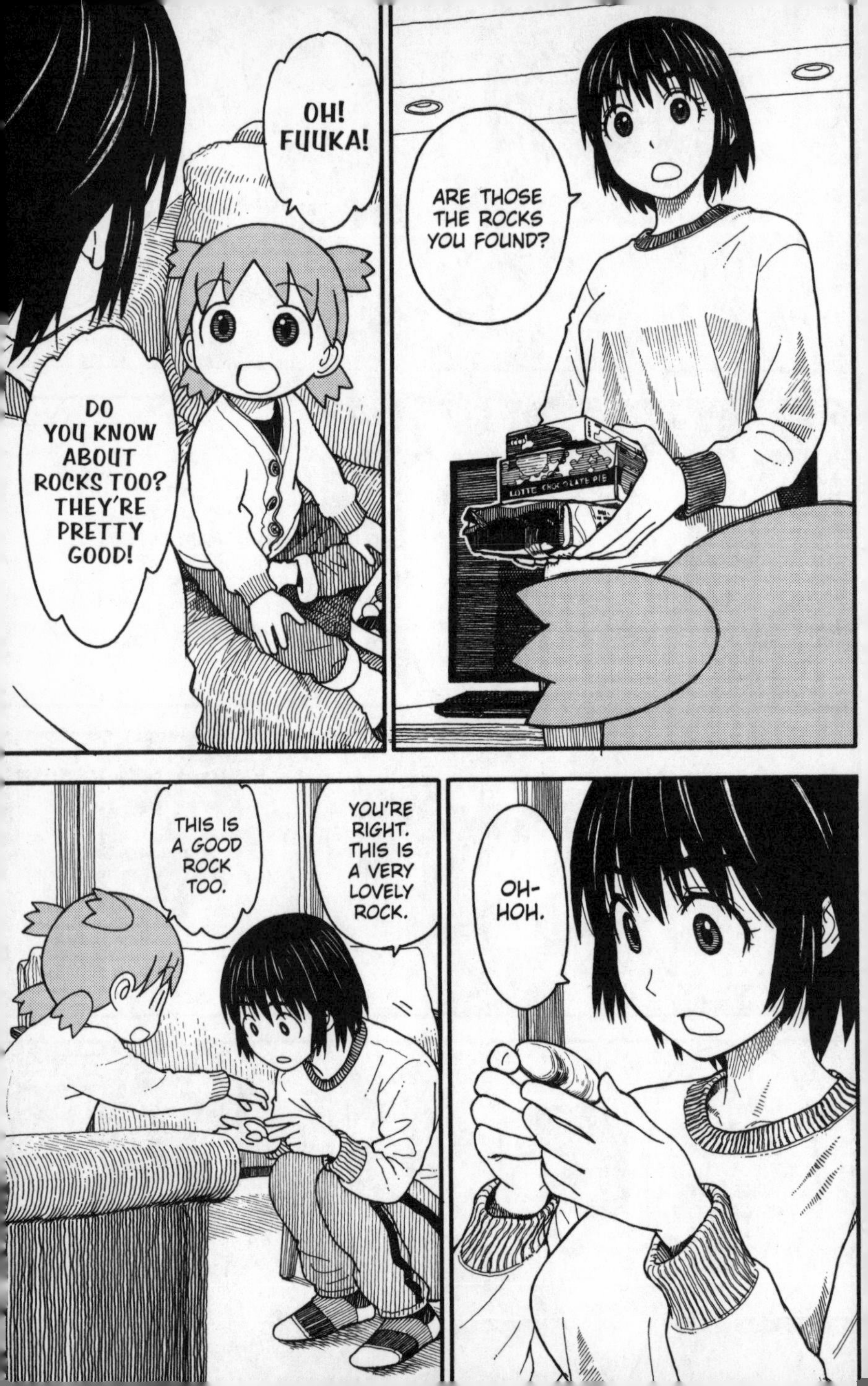
ARE THOSE THE ROCKS YOU FOUND?
LOTTE CHOCOLATE PIE
OH! FUUKA!
DO YOU KNOW ABOUT ROCKS TOO? THEY'RE PRETTY GOOD!
OH-HOH.
YOU'RE RIGHT. THIS IS A VERY LOVELY ROCK.
THIS IS A GOOD ROCK TOO.

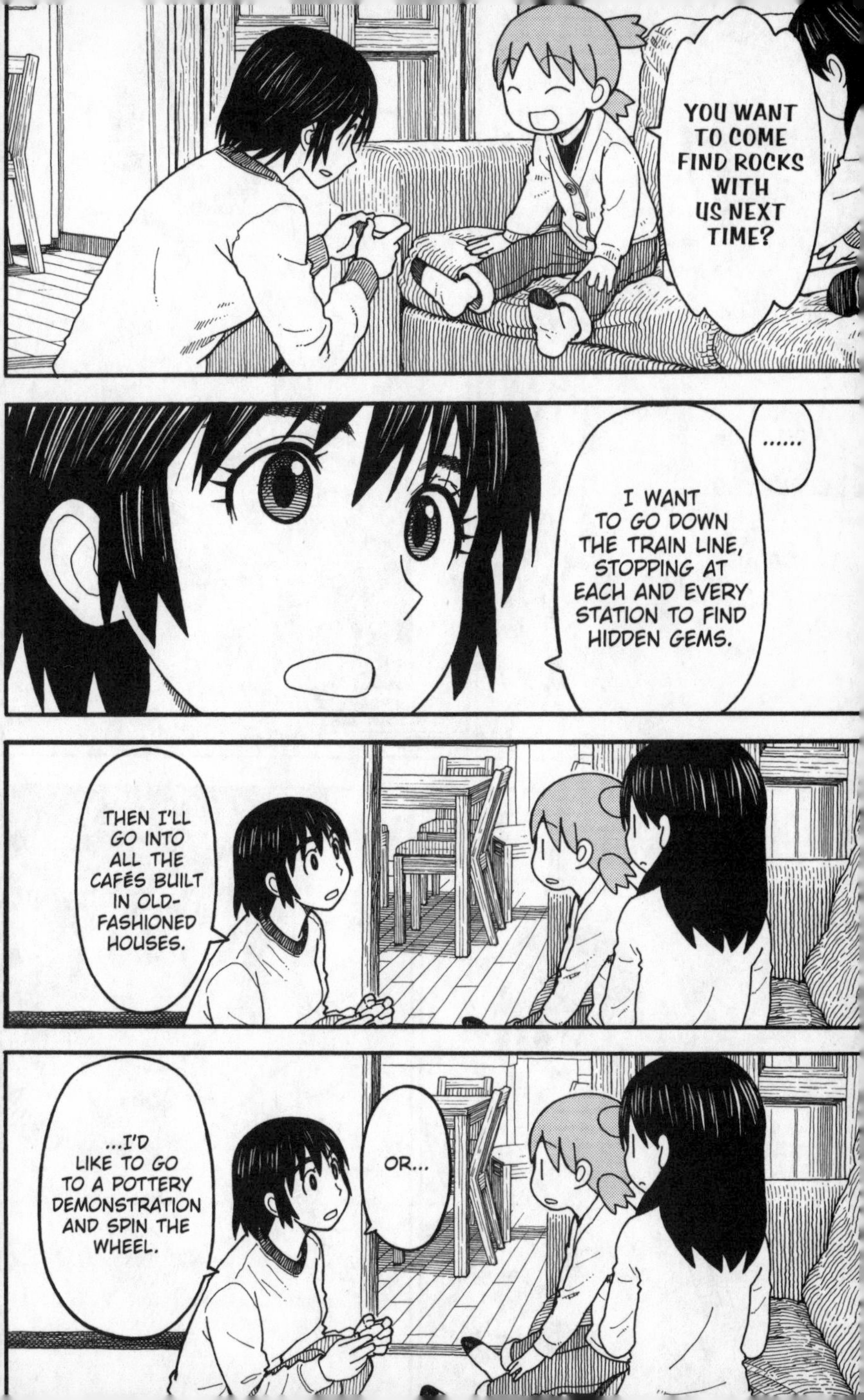
YOU WANT TO COME FIND ROCKS WITH US NEXT TIME?
......
I WANT TO GO DOWN THE TRAIN LINE, STOPPING AT EACH AND EVERY STATION TO FIND HIDDEN GEMS.
THEN I'LL GO INTO ALL THE CAFÉS BUILT IN OLD-FASHIONED HOUSES.
OR...
...I'D LIKE TO GO TO A POTTERY DEMONSTRATION AND SPIN THE WHEEL.

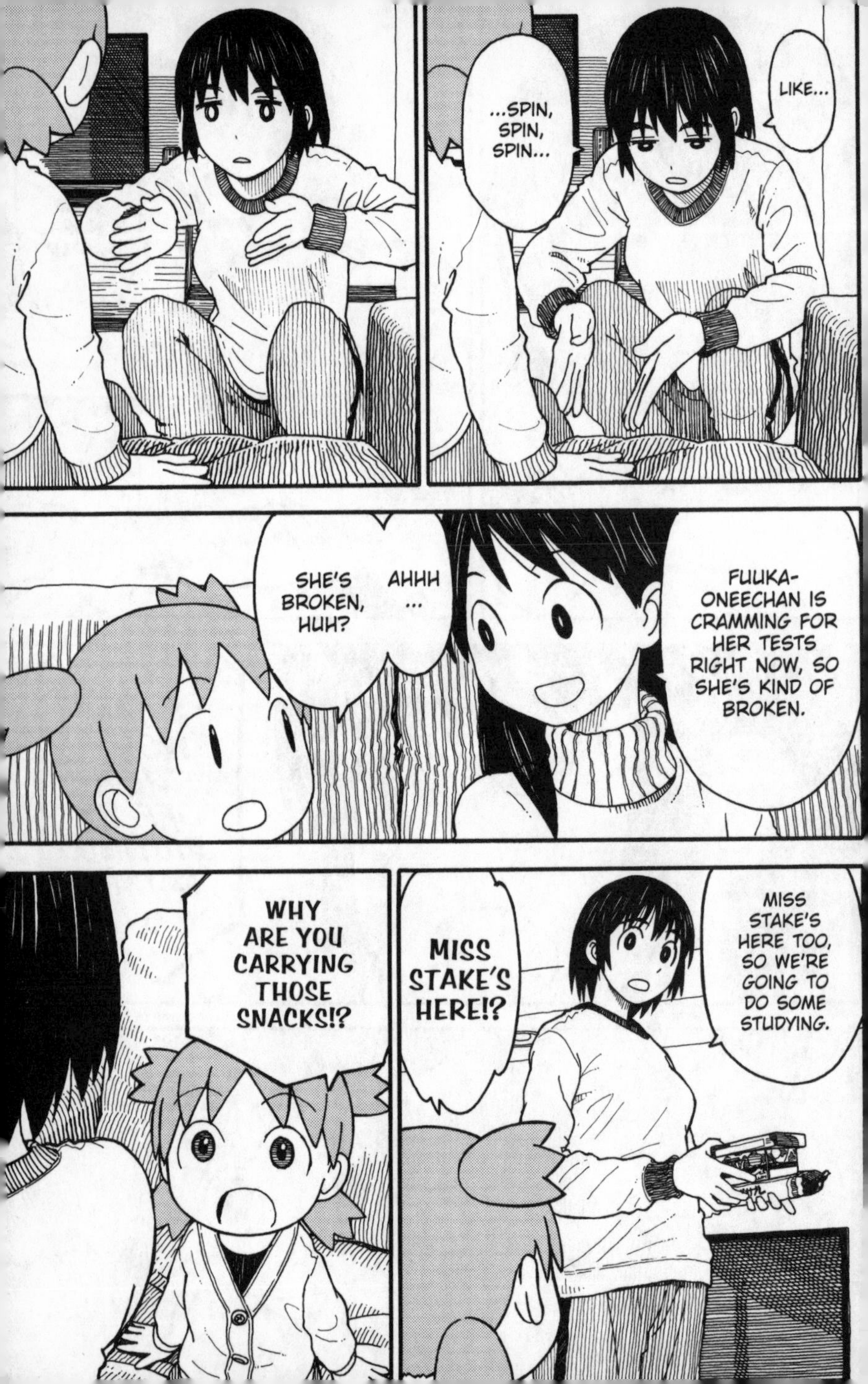
LIKE...
...SPIN, SPIN, SPIN...
FUUKA-ONEECHAN IS CRAMMING FOR HER TESTS RIGHT NOW, SO SHE'S KIND OF BROKEN.
AHHH ...
SHE'S BROKEN, HUH?
MISS STAKE'S HERE TOO, SO WE'RE GOING TO DO SOME STUDYING.
MISS STAKE'S HERE!?
WHY ARE YOU CARRYING THOSE SNACKS!?

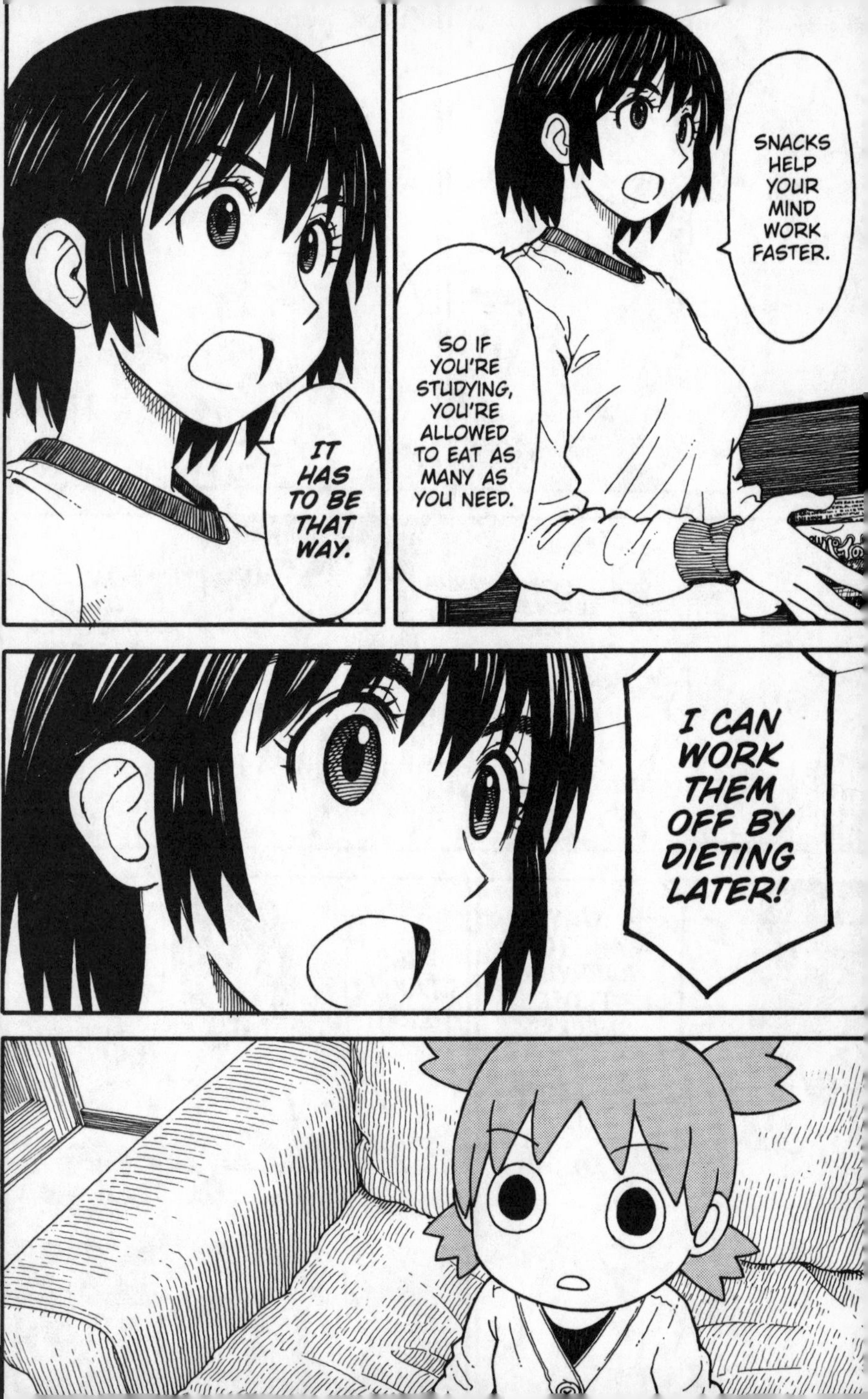
SNACKS HELP YOUR MIND WORK FASTER.
SO IF YOU'RE STUDYING, YOU'RE ALLOWED TO EAT AS MANY AS YOU NEED.
IT HAS TO BE THAT WAY.
I CAN WORK THEM OFF BY DIETING LATER!

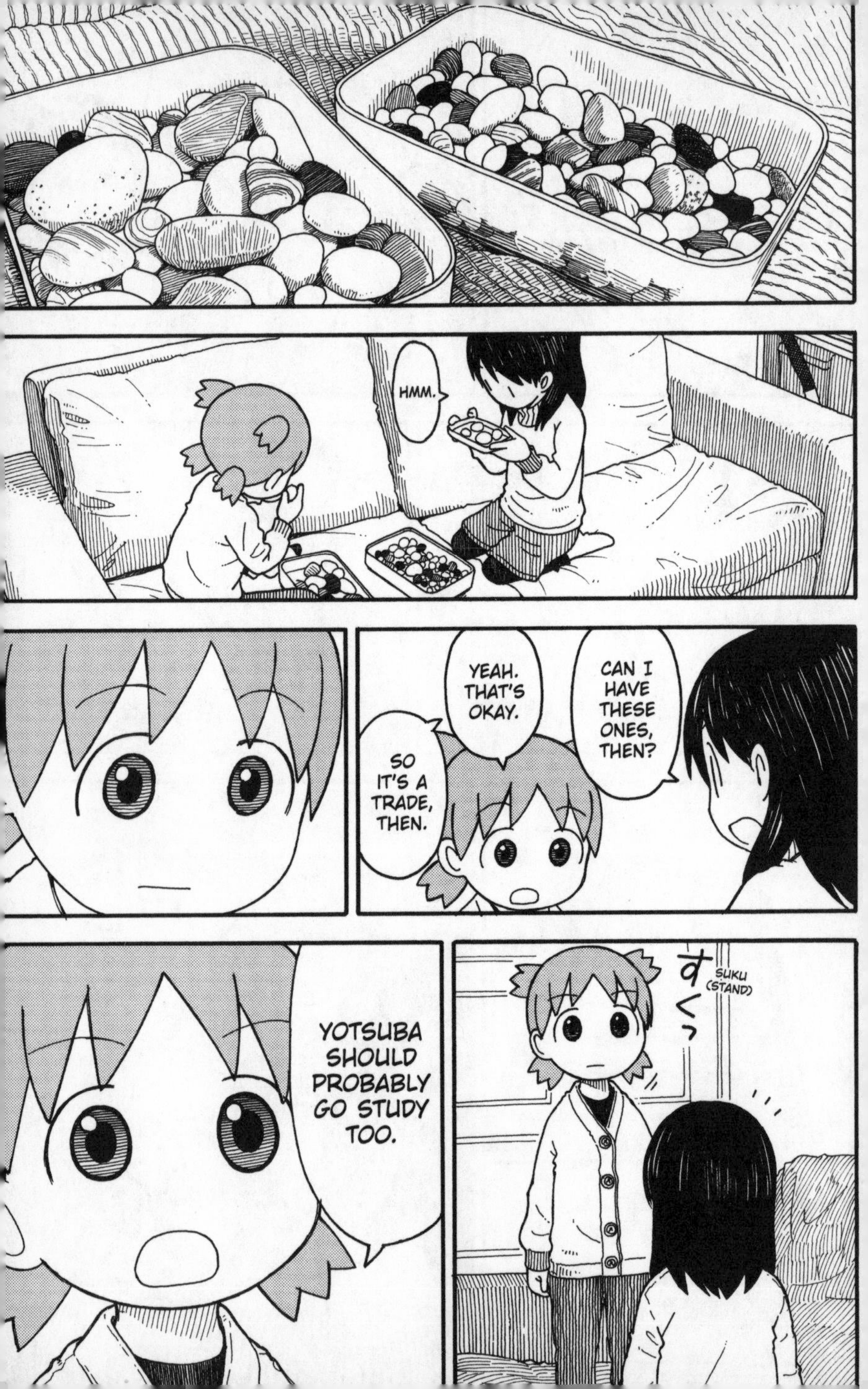
HMM.
CAN I HAVE THESE ONES, THEN?
YEAH. THAT'S OKAY.
SO IT'S A TRADE, THEN.
すくっ
SUKU (STAND)
YOTSUBA SHOULD PROBABLY GO STUDY TOO.

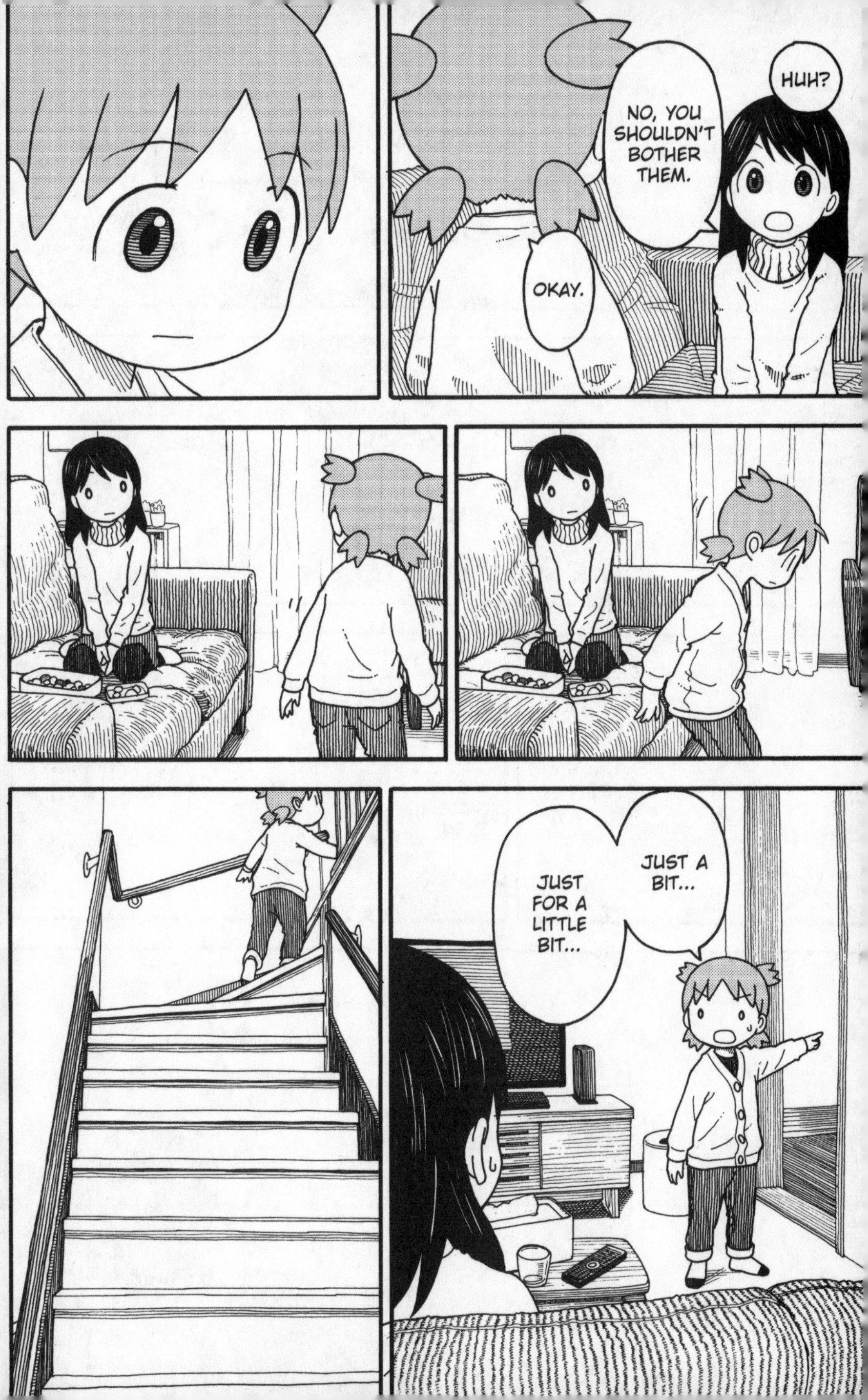
HUH?
NO, YOU SHOULDN'T BOTHER THEM.
OKAY.
JUST A BIT...
JUST FOR A LITTLE BIT...

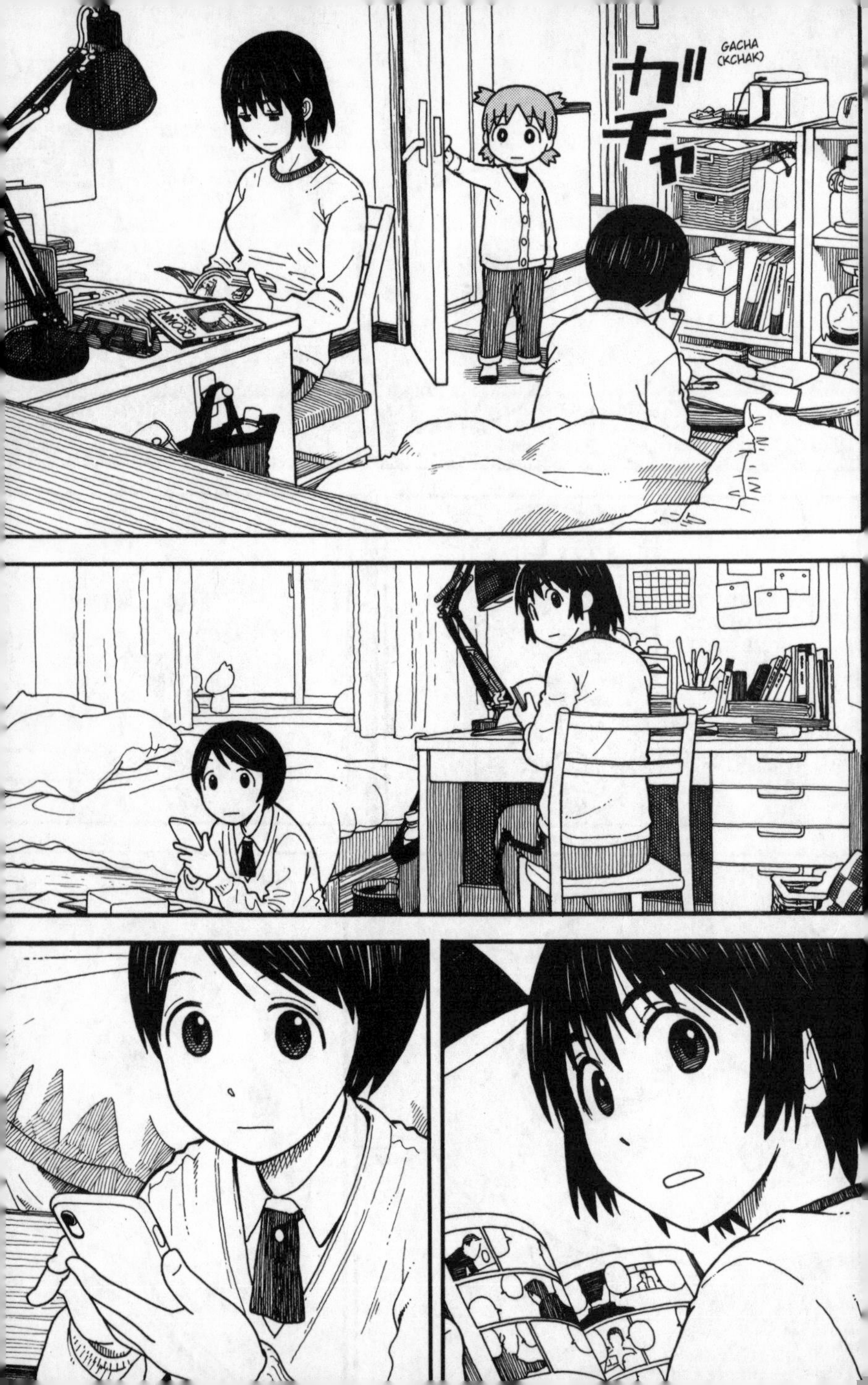

ガチャ
GACHA
(KCHAK)

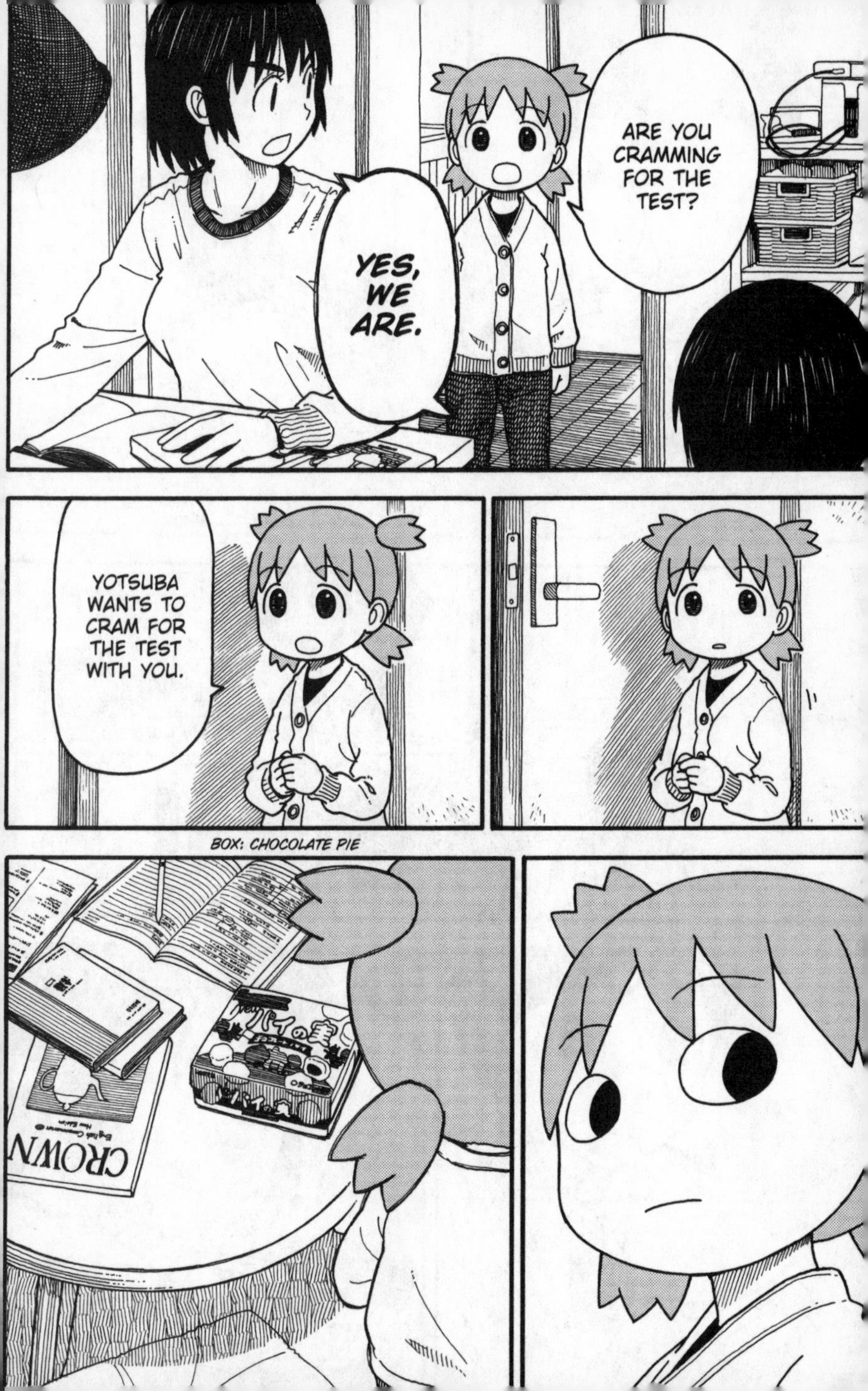
ARE YOU CRAMMING FOR THE TEST?
YES, WE ARE.
YOTSUBA WANTS TO CRAM FOR THE TEST WITH YOU.
BOX: CHOCOLATE PIE
CROWN

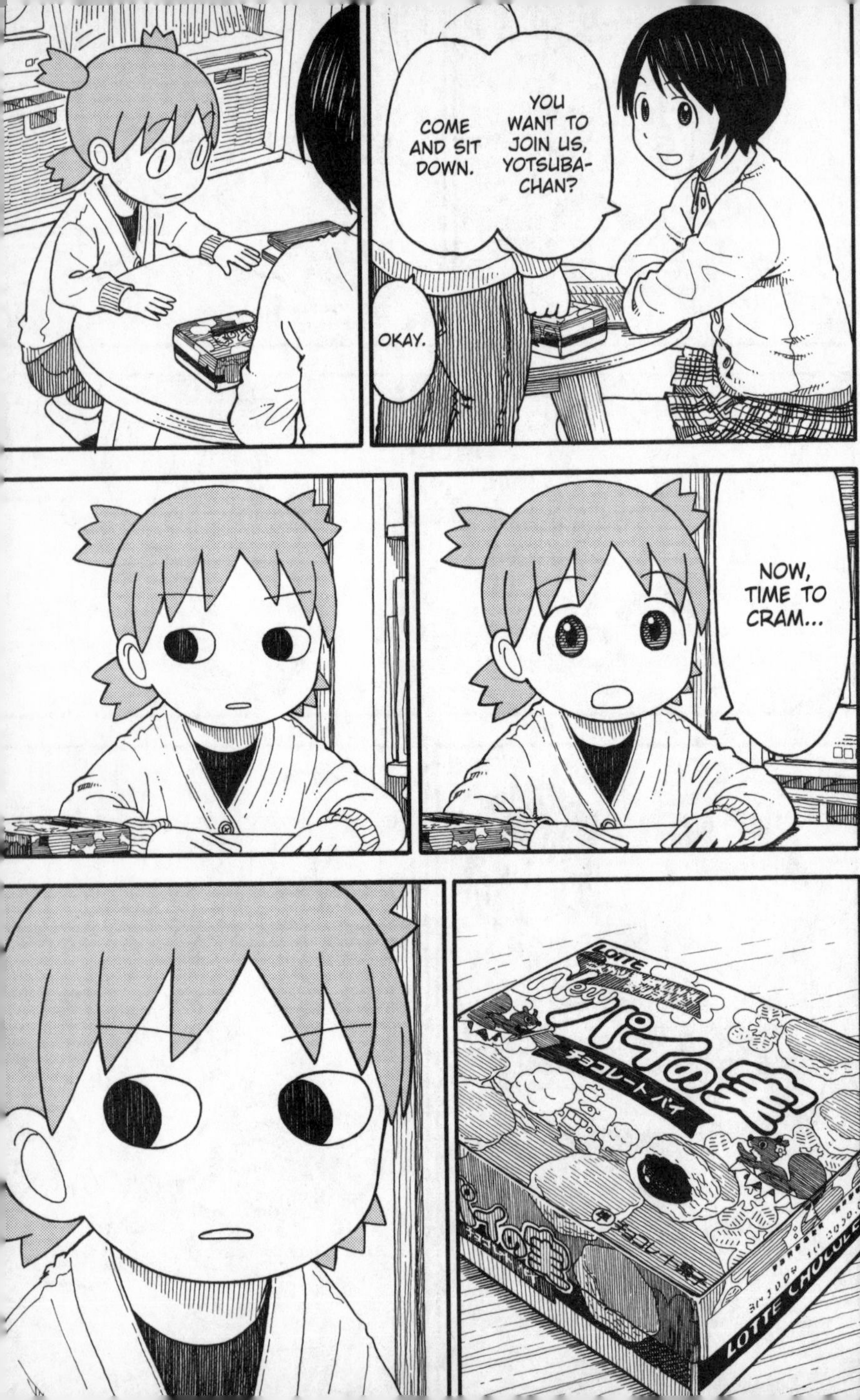
YOU WANT TO JOIN US, YOTSUBA-CHAN?
COME AND SIT DOWN.
OKAY.
NOW, TIME TO CRAM...
LOTTE
New
パイの実
チョコレートパイ

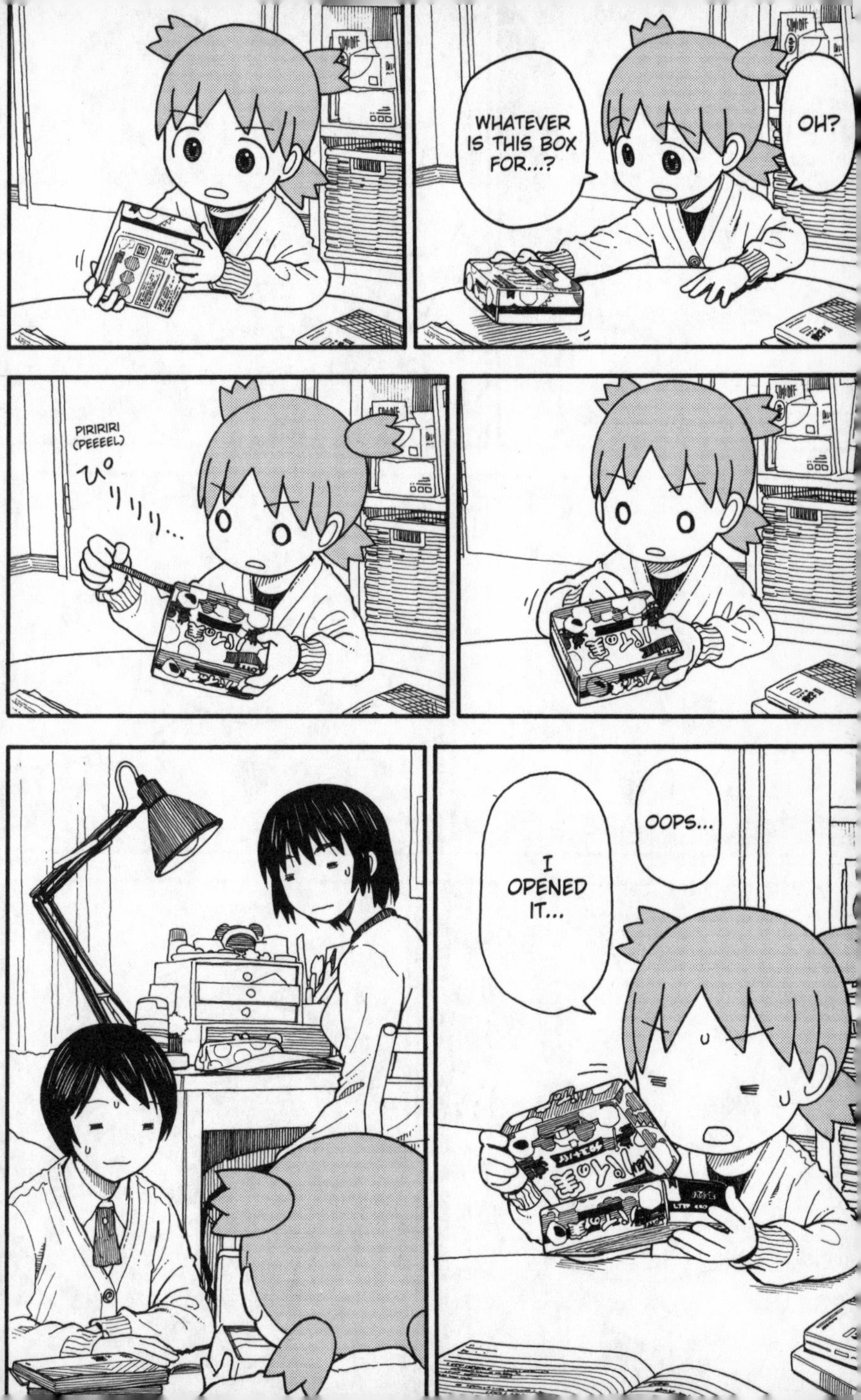
OH?
WHATEVER IS THIS BOX FOR...?
PIRIRIRI (PEEEEL)
ぴりりり…
OOPS...
I OPENED IT...

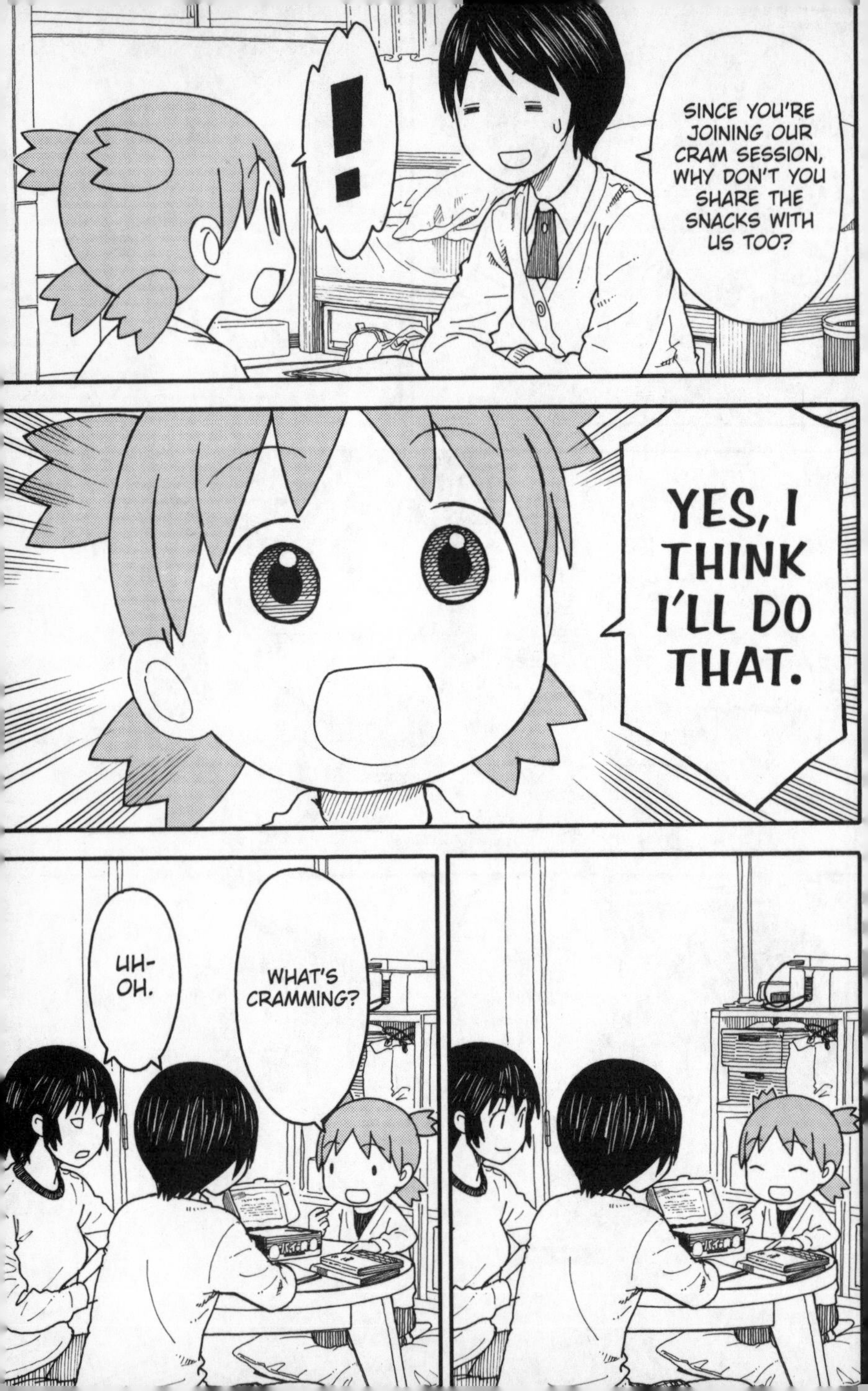
SINCE YOU'RE JOINING OUR CRAM SESSION, WHY DON'T YOU SHARE THE SNACKS WITH US TOO?
!
YES, I THINK I'LL DO THAT.
WHAT'S CRAMMING?
UH-OH.

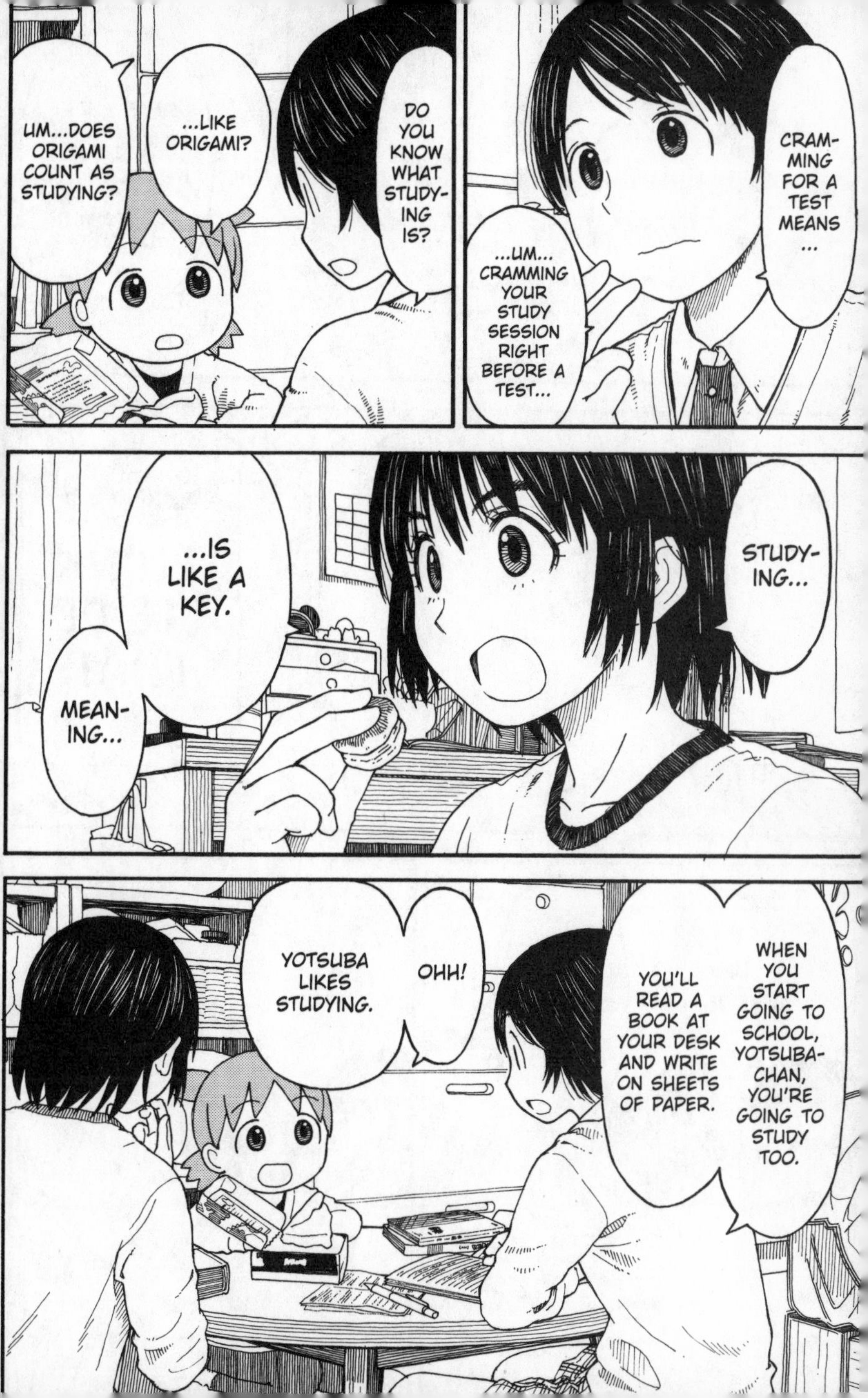
CRAM-MING FOR A TEST MEANS...
...UM... CRAMMING YOUR STUDY SESSION RIGHT BEFORE A TEST...
DO YOU KNOW WHAT STUDY-ING IS?
...LIKE ORIGAMI?
UM...DOES ORIGAMI COUNT AS STUDYING?
STUDY-ING...
...IS LIKE A KEY.
MEAN-ING...
WHEN YOU START GOING TO SCHOOL, YOTSUBA-CHAN, YOU'RE GOING TO STUDY TOO.
YOU'LL READ A BOOK AT YOUR DESK AND WRITE ON SHEETS OF PAPER.
OHH!
YOTSUBA LIKES STUDYING.

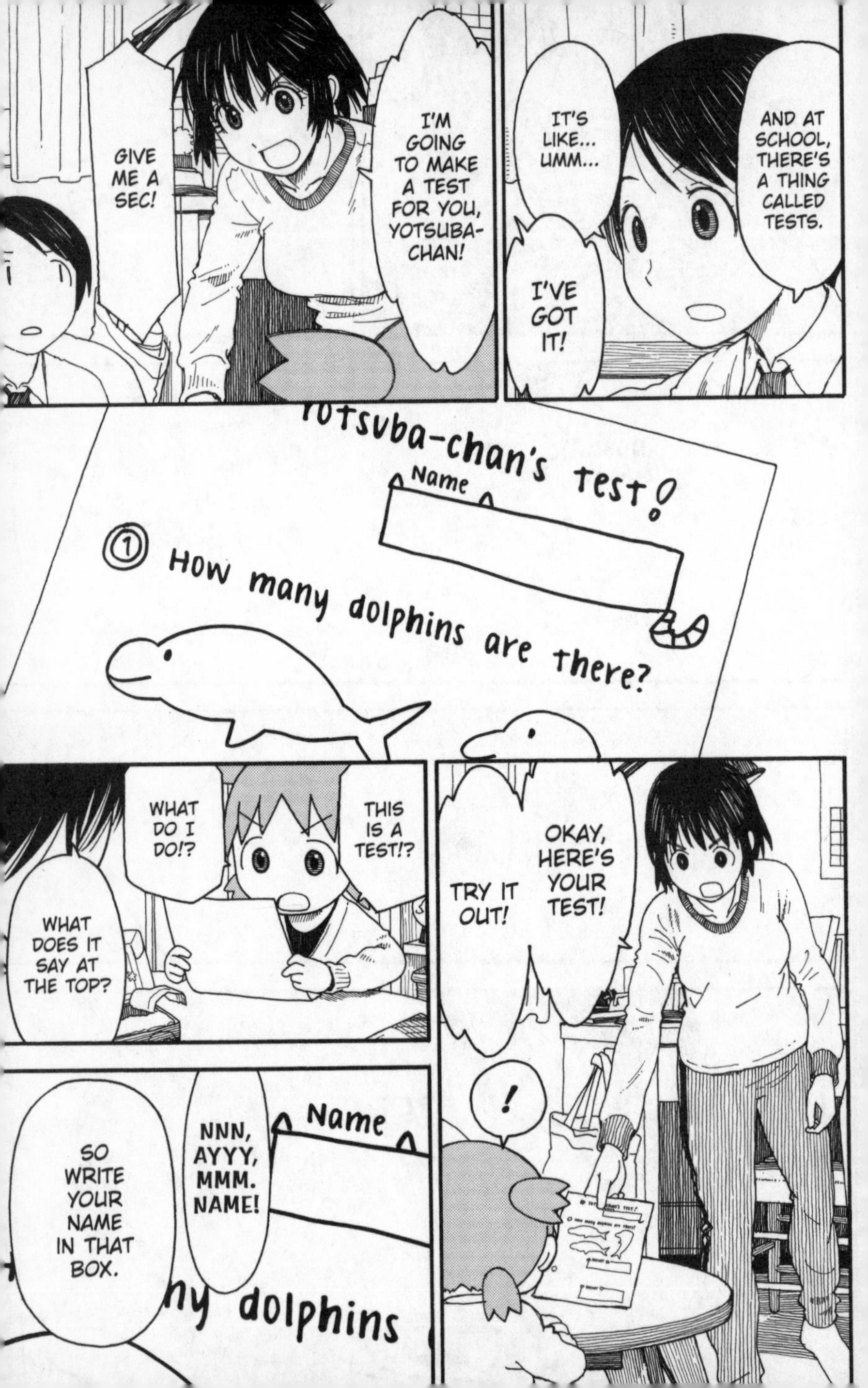
AND AT SCHOOL, THERE'S A THING CALLED TESTS.
IT'S LIKE... UMM...
I'VE GOT IT!
I'M GOING TO MAKE A TEST FOR YOU, YOTSUBA-CHAN!
GIVE ME A SEC!
Yotsuba-chan's test!
Name
① How many dolphins are there?
OKAY, HERE'S YOUR TEST!
TRY IT OUT!
THIS IS A TEST!?
WHAT DO I DO!?
WHAT DOES IT SAY AT THE TOP?
!
Name
NNN, AYYY, MMM. NAME!
SO WRITE YOUR NAME IN THAT BOX.
ny dolphins

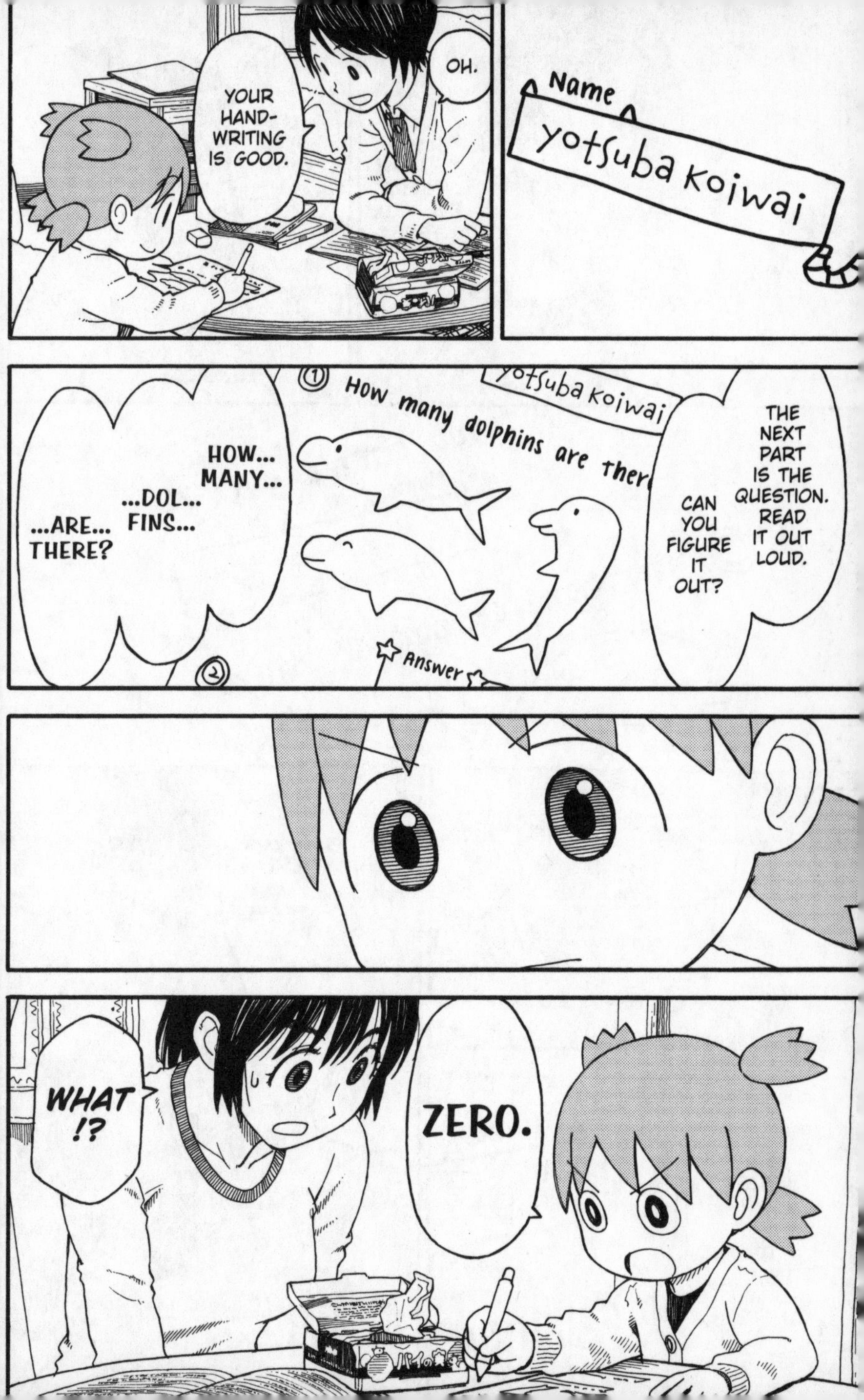

Name
yotsuba koiwai
OH.
YOUR HAND-WRITING IS GOOD.
THE NEXT PART IS THE QUESTION. READ IT OUT LOUD.
CAN YOU FIGURE IT OUT?
yotsuba koiwai
① How many dolphins are ther
Answer
②
HOW... MANY...
...DOL... FINS...
...ARE... THERE?
ZERO.
WHAT!?

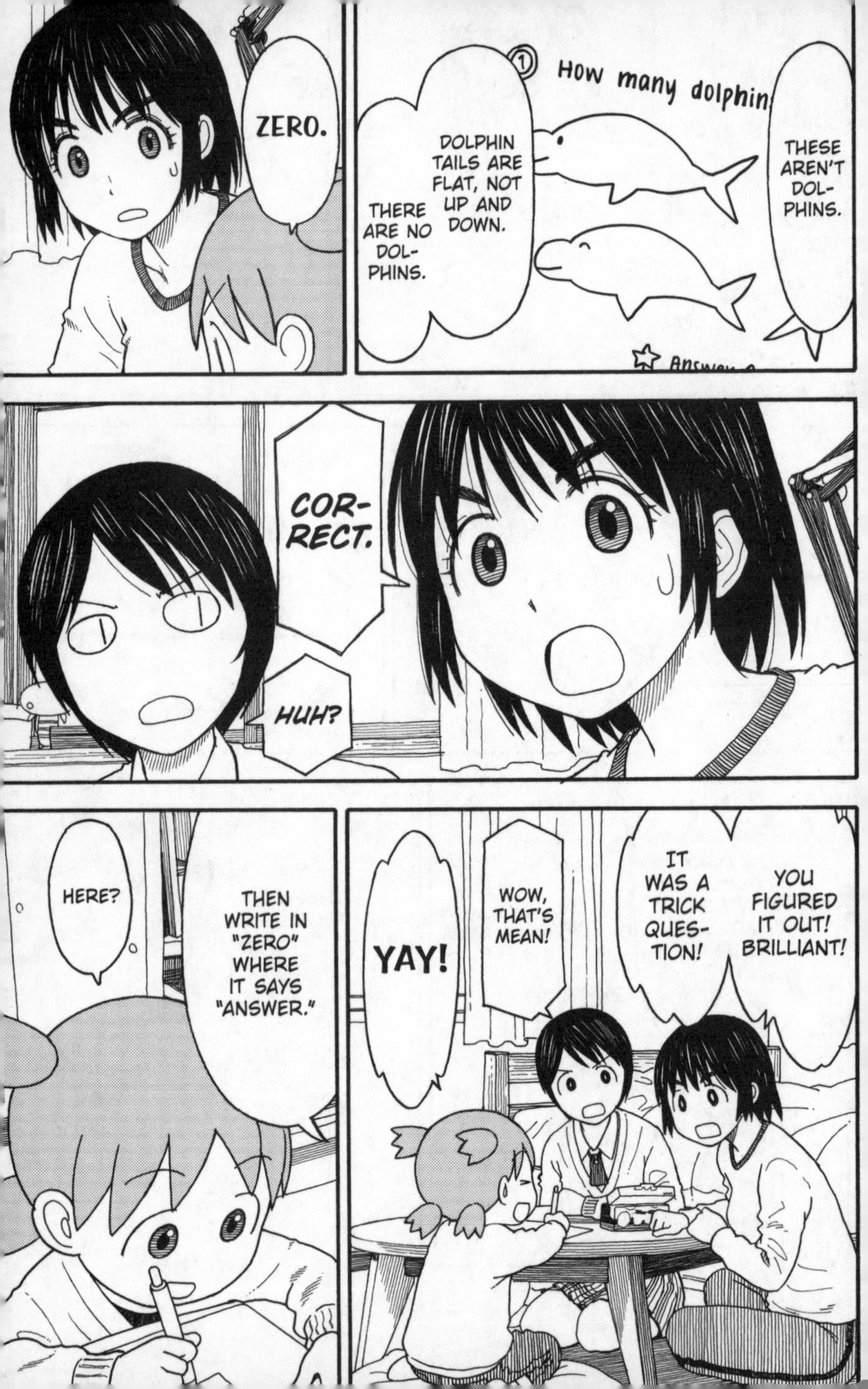
How many dolphin
THESE AREN'T DOL-PHINS.
DOLPHIN TAILS ARE FLAT, NOT UP AND DOWN.
THERE ARE NO DOL-PHINS.
ZERO.
COR-RECT.
HUH?
YOU FIGURED IT OUT! BRILLIANT!
IT WAS A TRICK QUES-TION!
WOW, THAT'S MEAN!
YAY!
THEN WRITE IN "ZERO" WHERE IT SAYS "ANSWER."
HERE?

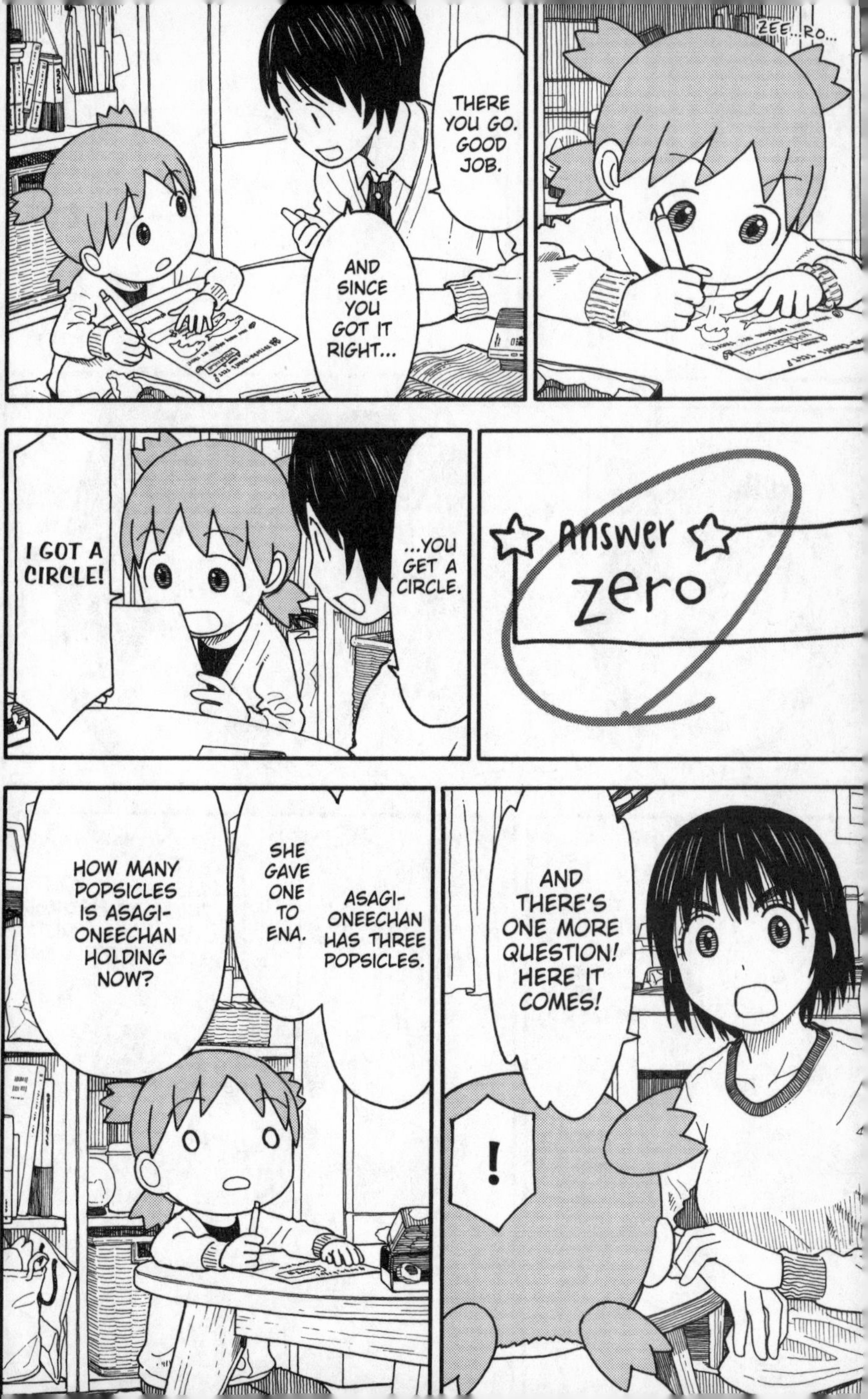
ZEE...RO...
THERE YOU GO. GOOD JOB.
AND SINCE YOU GOT IT RIGHT...
Answer
zero
...YOU GET A CIRCLE.
I GOT A CIRCLE!
AND THERE'S ONE MORE QUESTION! HERE IT COMES!
!
ASAGI-ONEECHAN HAS THREE POPSICLES.
SHE GAVE ONE TO ENA.
HOW MANY POPSICLES IS ASAGI-ONEECHAN HOLDING NOW?

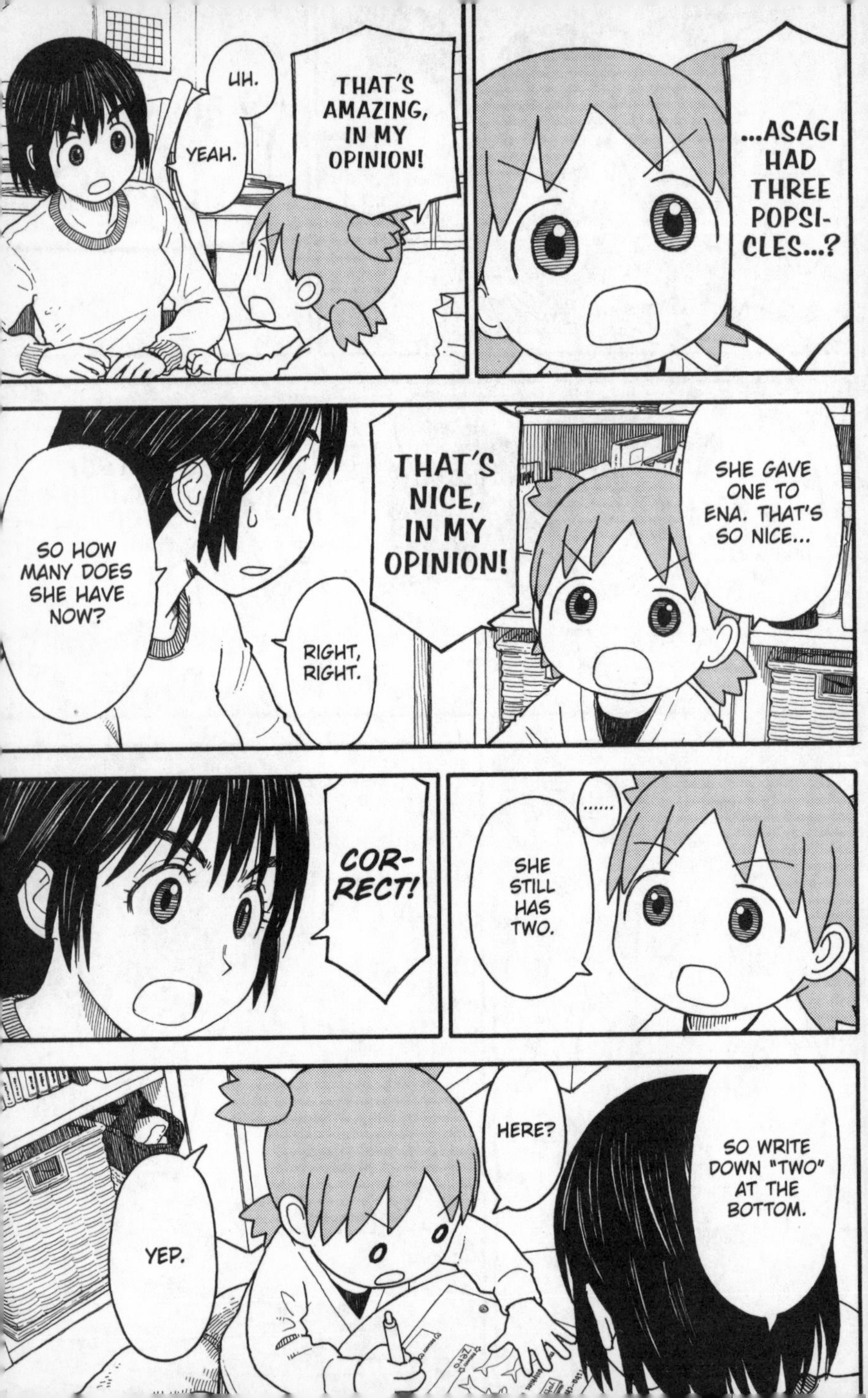
...ASAGI HAD THREE POPSI-CLES...?
THAT'S AMAZING, IN MY OPINION!
UH.
YEAH.
SHE GAVE ONE TO ENA. THAT'S SO NICE...
THAT'S NICE, IN MY OPINION!
RIGHT, RIGHT.
SO HOW MANY DOES SHE HAVE NOW?
......
SHE STILL HAS TWO.
COR-RECT!
SO WRITE DOWN "TWO" AT THE BOTTOM.
HERE?
YEP.

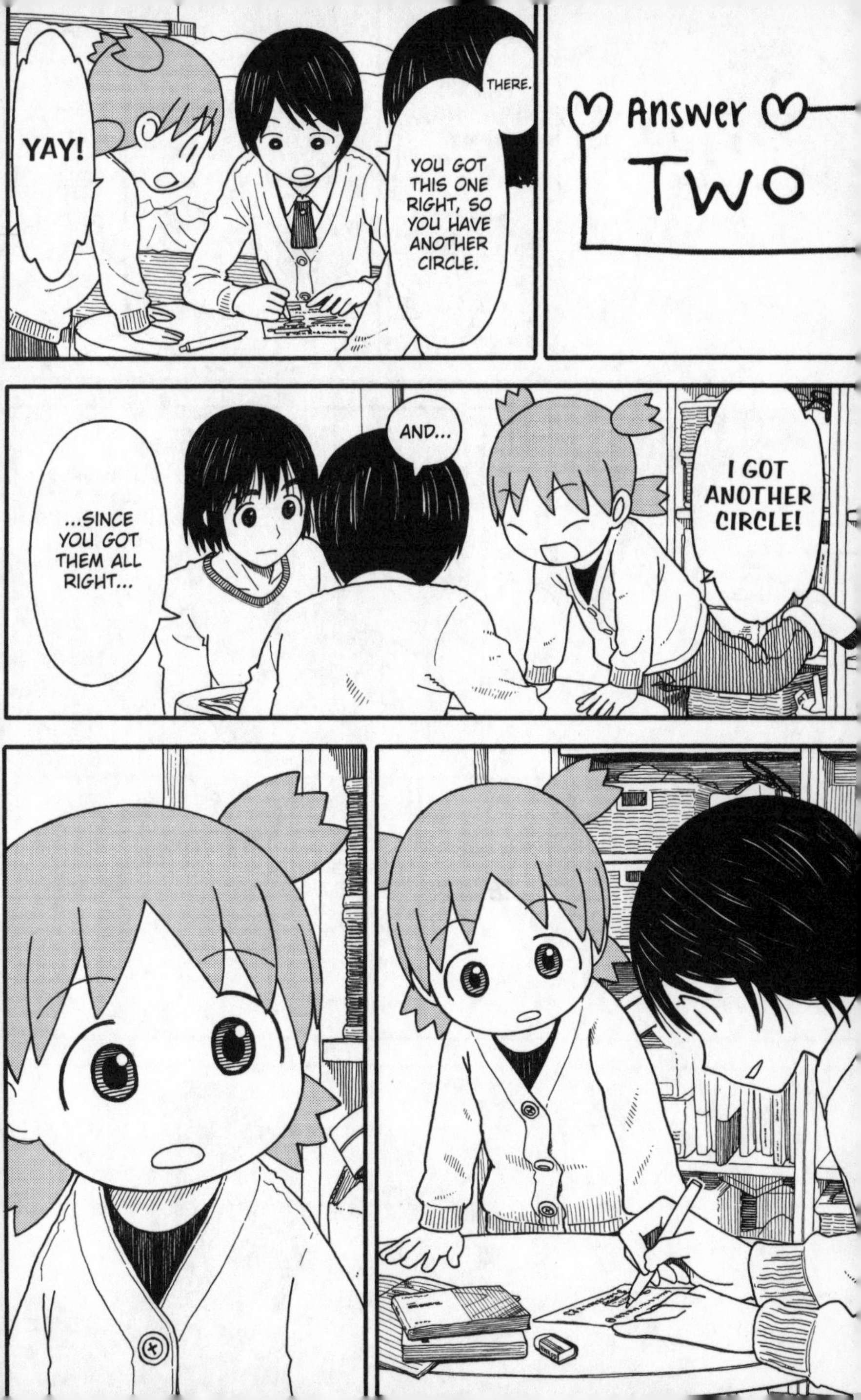
Answer
Two
THERE.
YOU GOT THIS ONE RIGHT, SO YOU HAVE ANOTHER CIRCLE.
YAY!
I GOT ANOTHER CIRCLE!
AND...
...SINCE YOU GOT THEM ALL RIGHT...

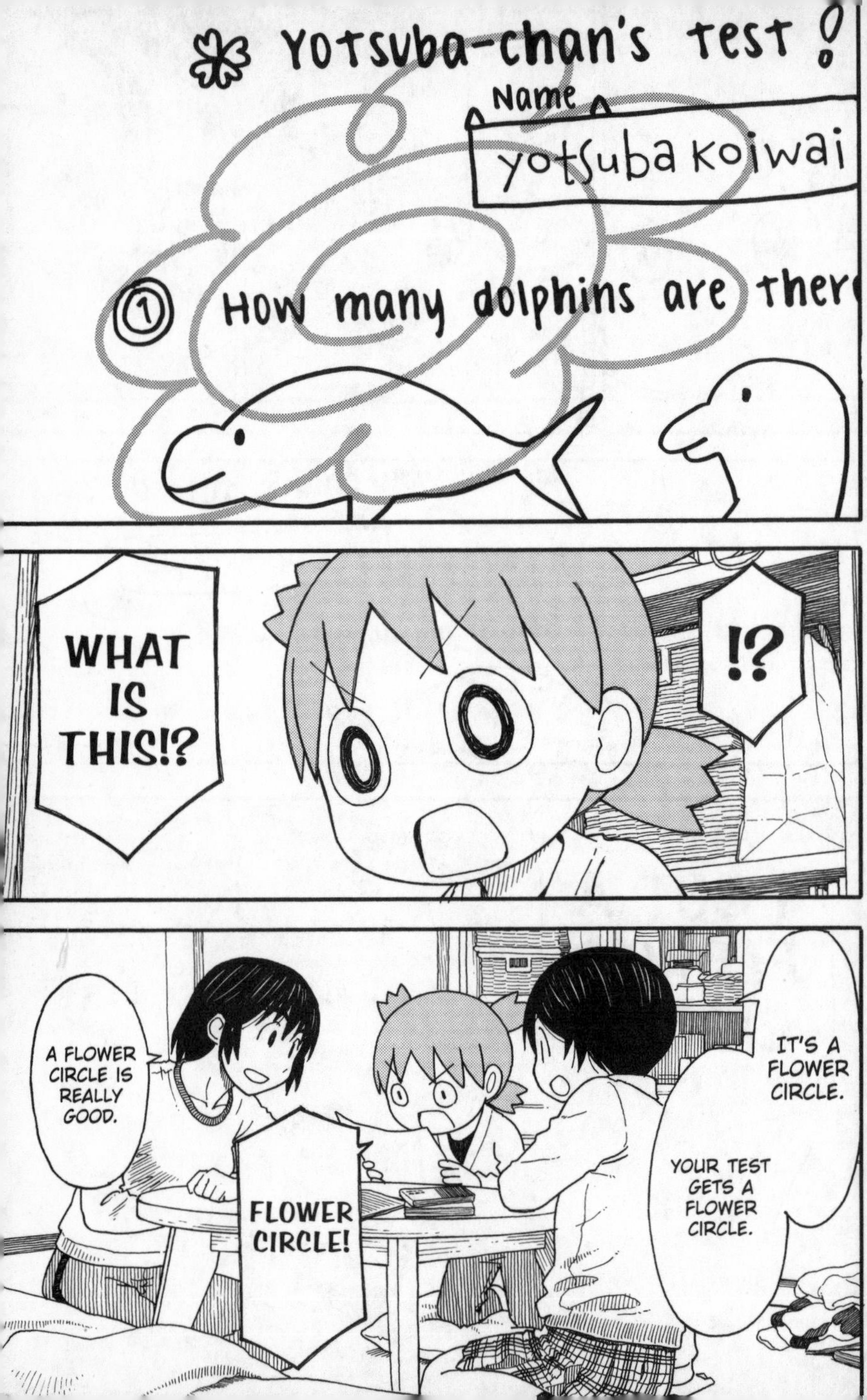
Yotsuba-chan's test!
Name
yotsuba koiwai
① How many dolphins are ther
!?
WHAT IS THIS!?
IT'S A FLOWER CIRCLE.
YOUR TEST GETS A FLOWER CIRCLE.
FLOWER CIRCLE!
A FLOWER CIRCLE IS REALLY GOOD.

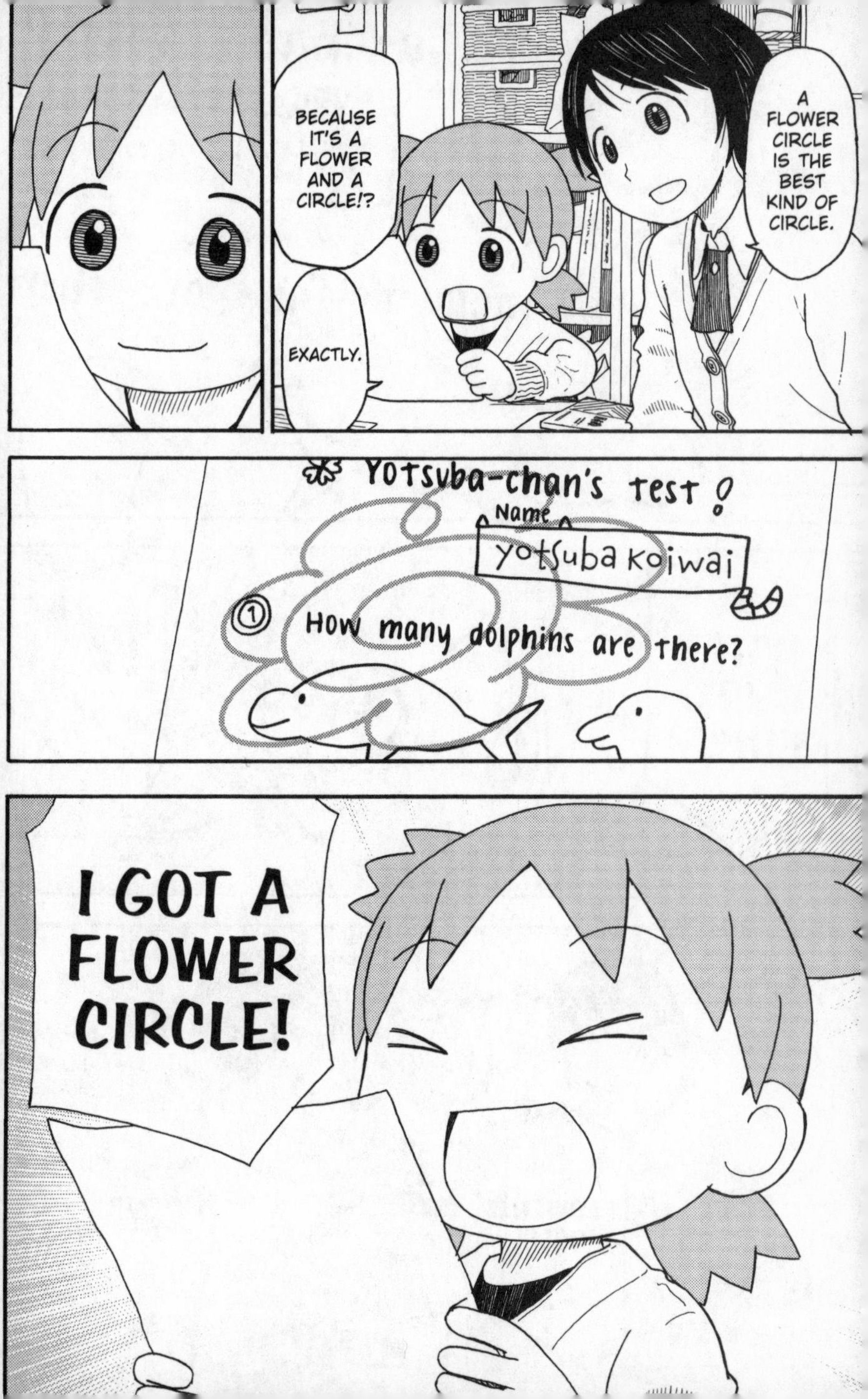
A FLOWER CIRCLE IS THE BEST KIND OF CIRCLE.
BECAUSE IT'S A FLOWER AND A CIRCLE!?
EXACTLY.
Yotsuba-chan's test
Name
yotsuba koiwai
① How many dolphins are there?
I GOT A FLOWER CIRCLE!

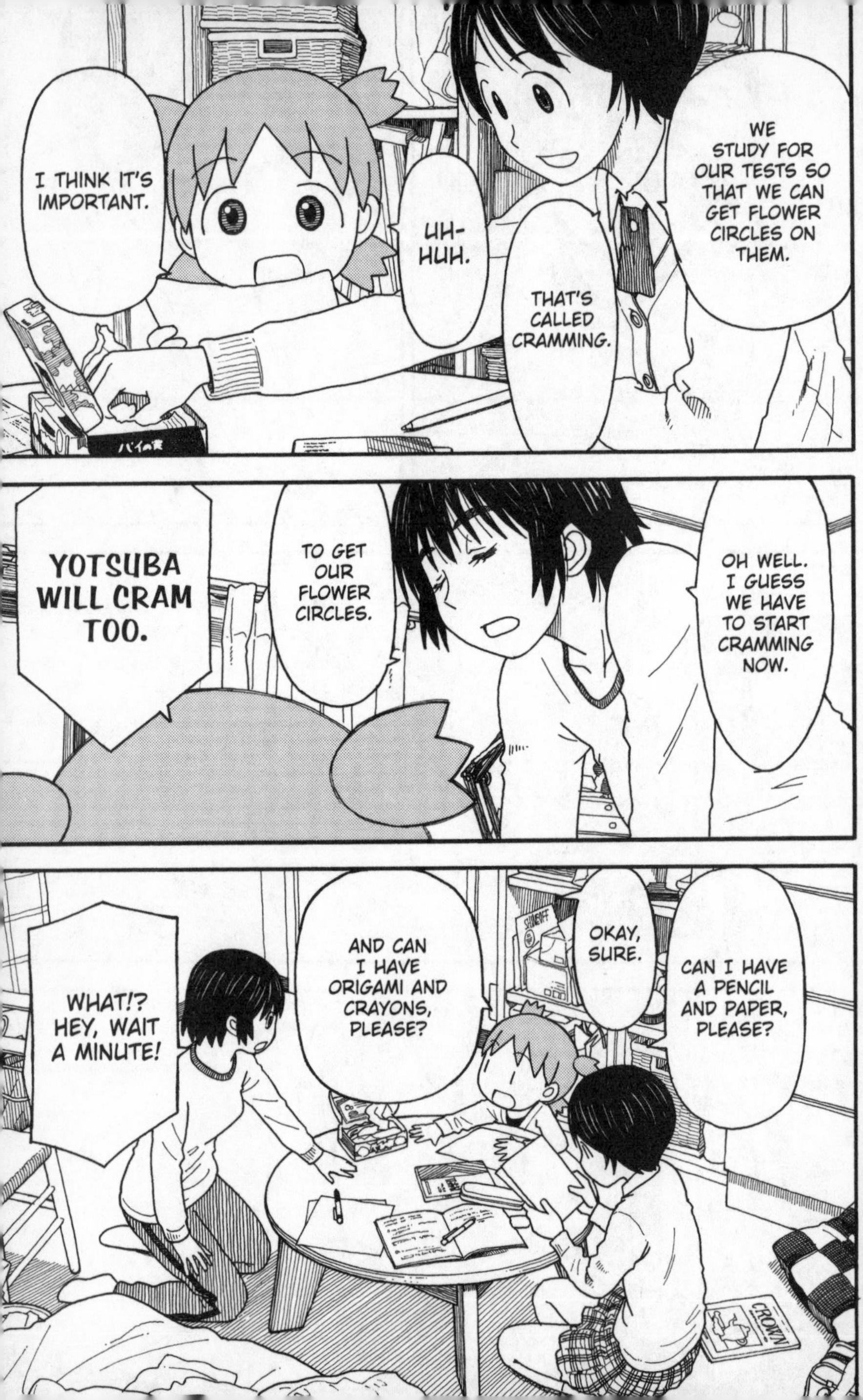
WE STUDY FOR OUR TESTS SO THAT WE CAN GET FLOWER CIRCLES ON THEM.
THAT'S CALLED CRAMMING.
UH-HUH.
I THINK IT'S IMPORTANT.
OH WELL. I GUESS WE HAVE TO START CRAMMING NOW.
TO GET OUR FLOWER CIRCLES.
YOTSUBA WILL CRAM TOO.
CAN I HAVE A PENCIL AND PAPER, PLEASE?
OKAY, SURE.
AND CAN I HAVE ORIGAMI AND CRAYONS, PLEASE?
WHAT!? HEY, WAIT A MINUTE!

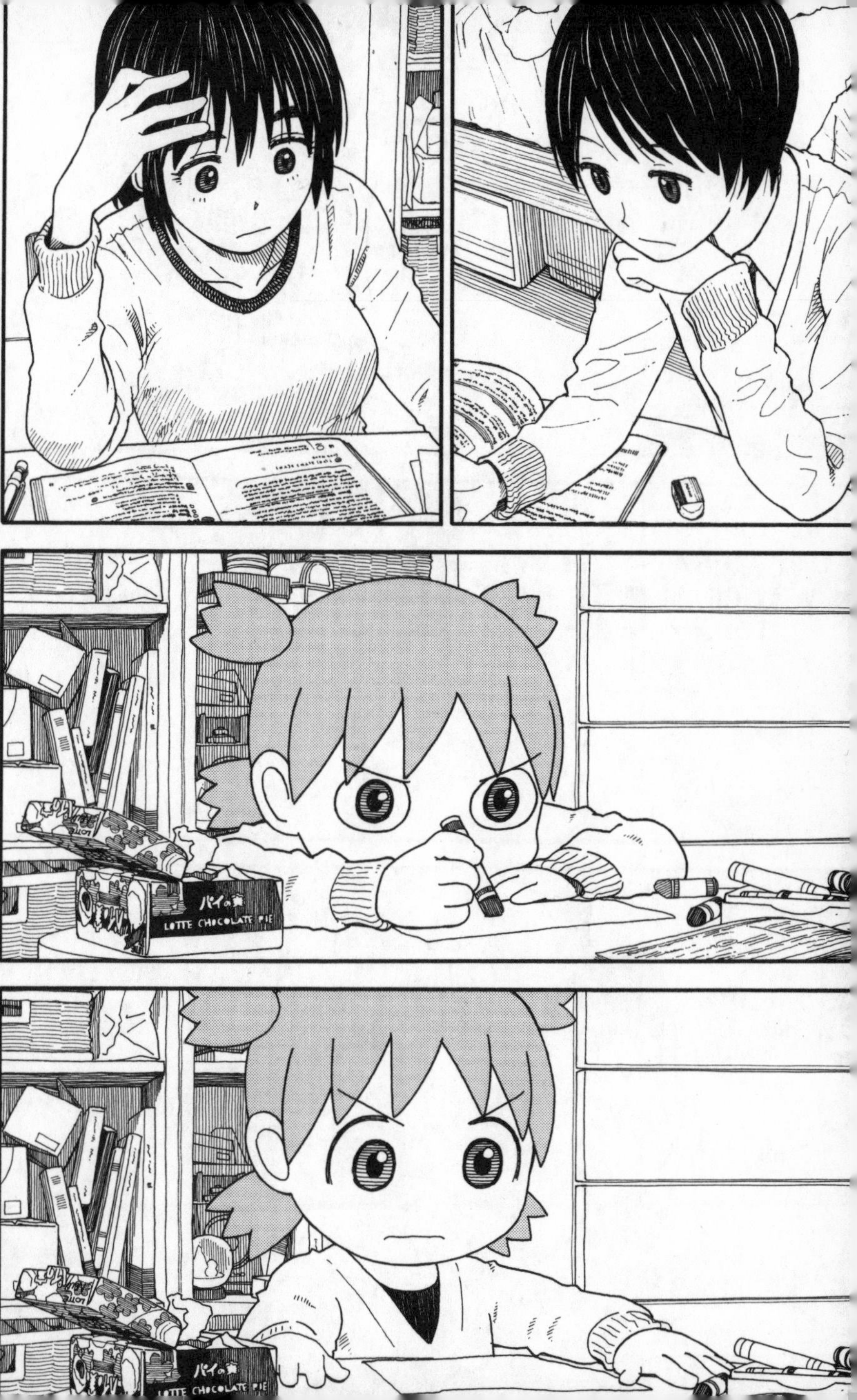
パイの實
LOTTE CHOCOLATE PIE
パイの實
LOTTE CHOCOLATE PIE

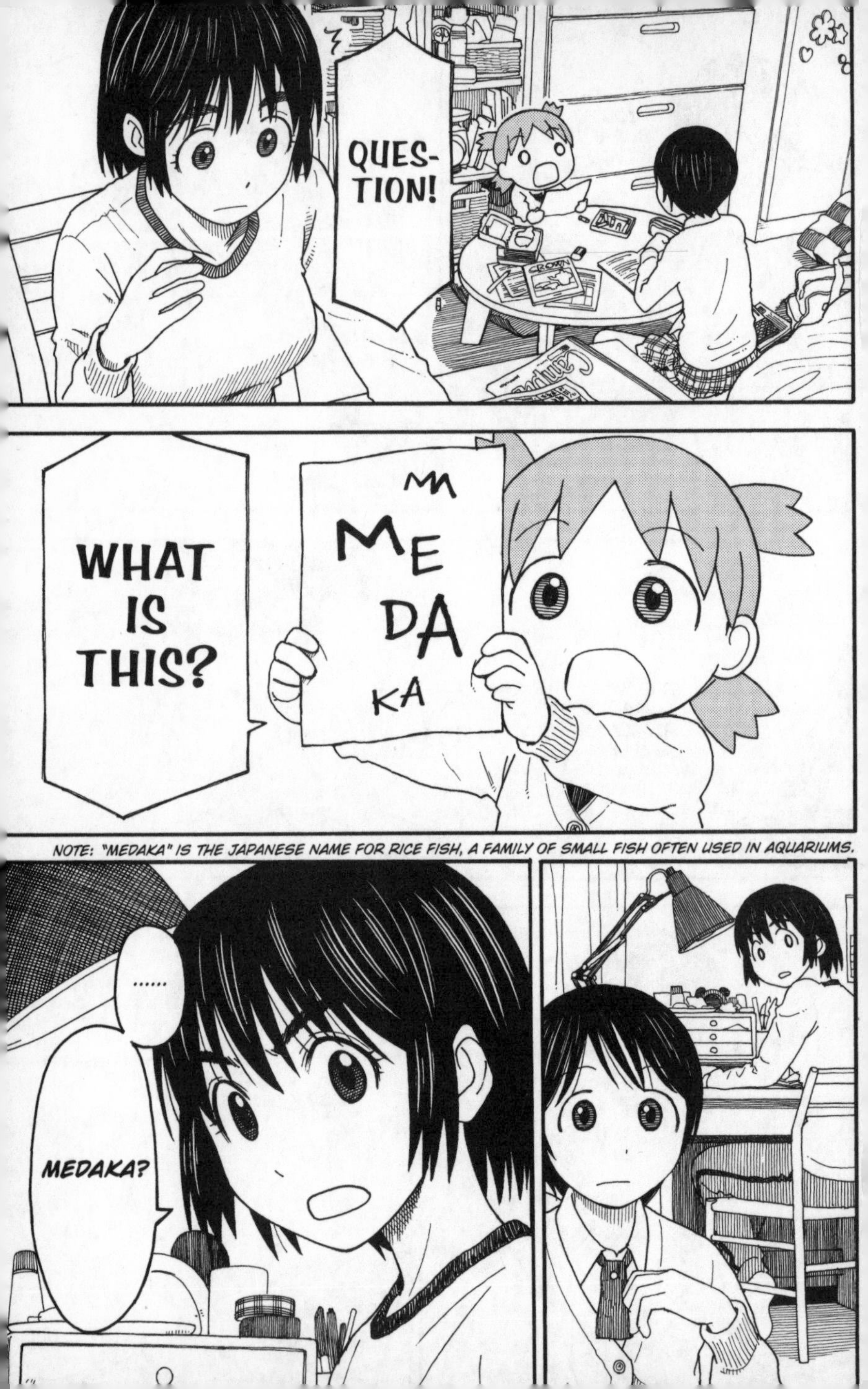
QUES-TION!
WHAT IS THIS?
ME DA KA
NOTE: "MEDAKA" IS THE JAPANESE NAME FOR RICE FISH, A FAMILY OF SMALL FISH OFTEN USED IN AQUARIUMS.
......
MEDAKA?

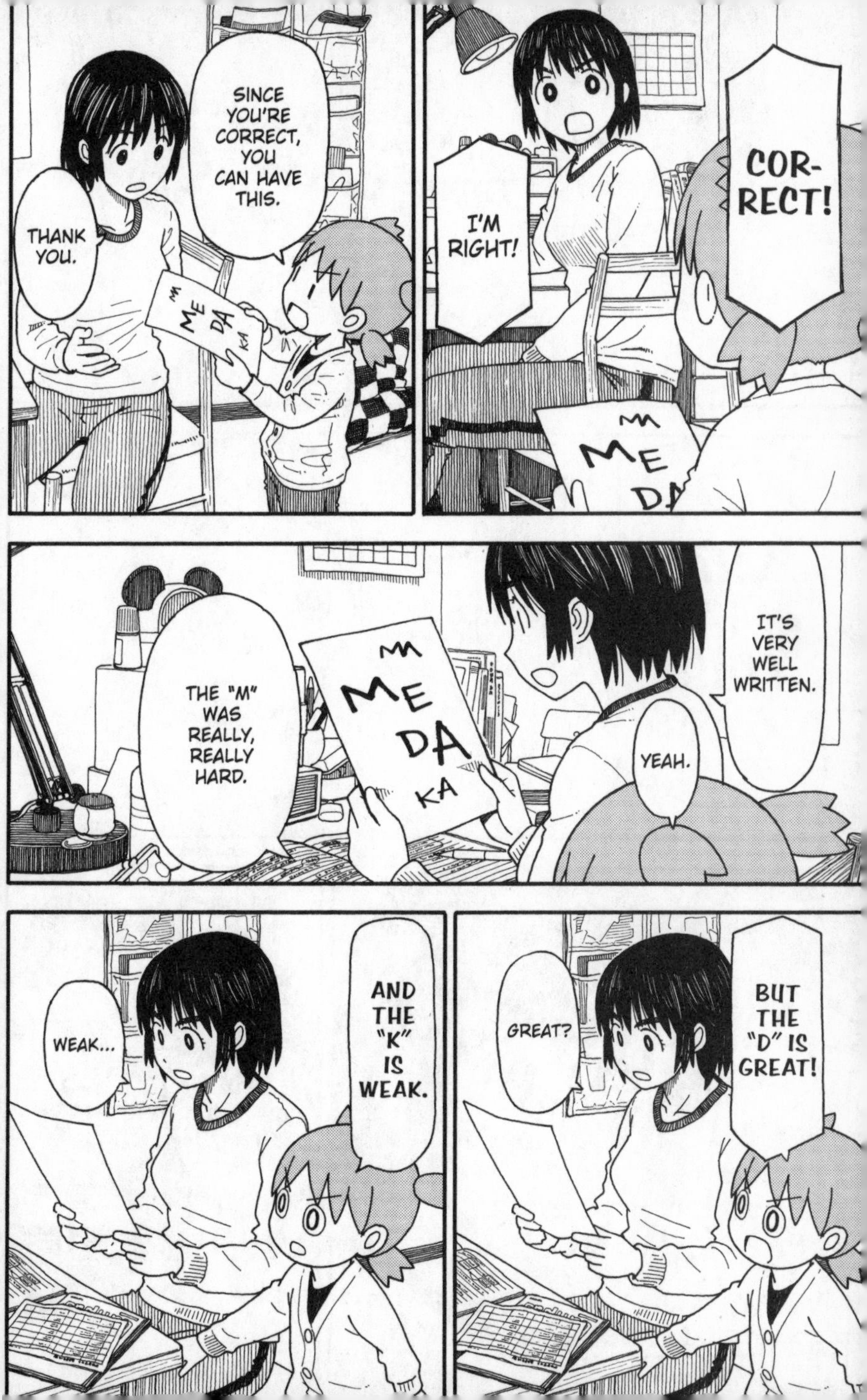
CORRECT!
I'M RIGHT!
SINCE YOU'RE CORRECT, YOU CAN HAVE THIS.
THANK YOU.
M
ME
DA
KA
IT'S VERY WELL WRITTEN.
YEAH.
THE "M" WAS REALLY, REALLY HARD.
M
ME
DA
KA
BUT THE "D" IS GREAT!
GREAT?
AND THE "K" IS WEAK.
WEAK...

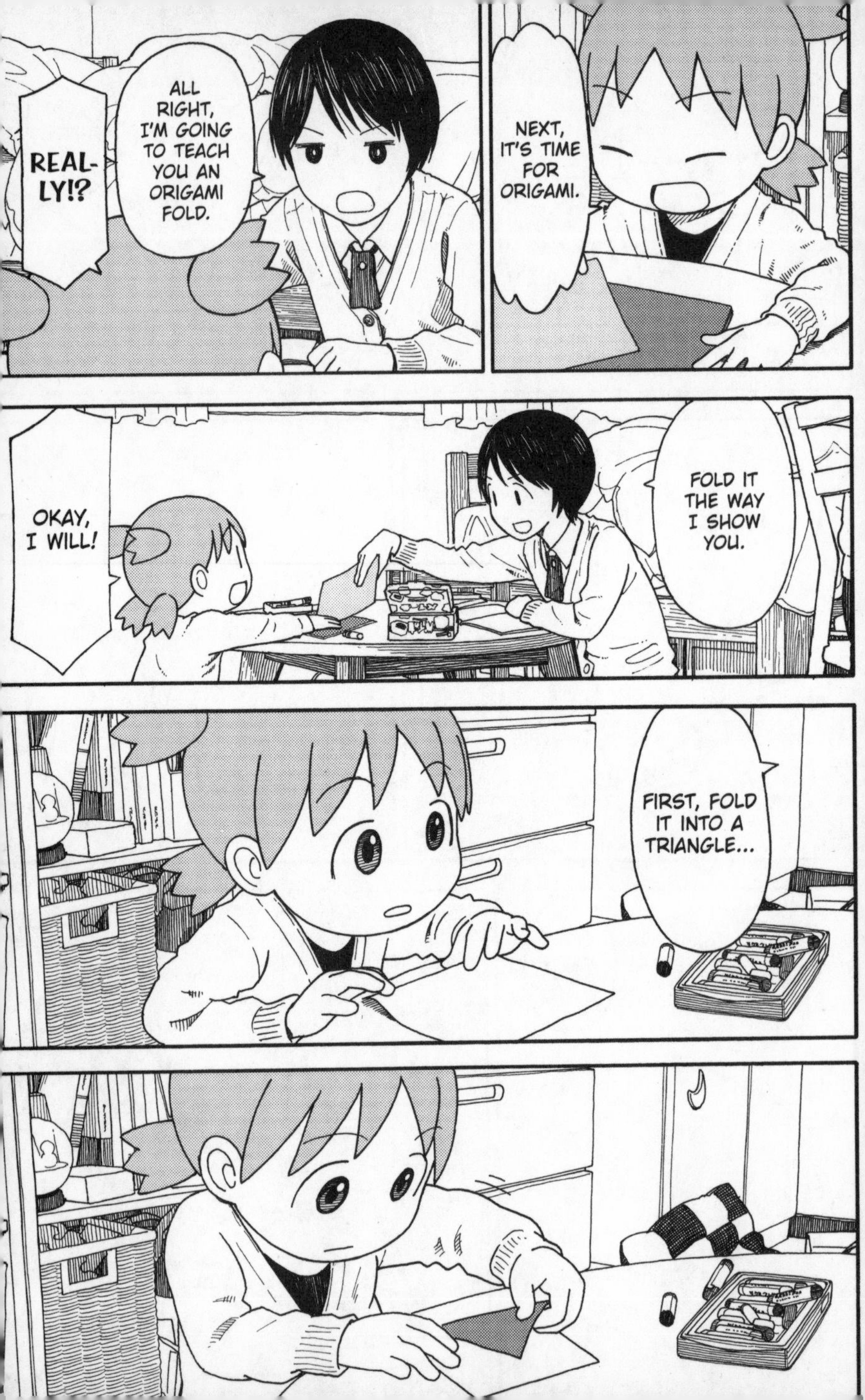
NEXT, IT'S TIME FOR ORIGAMI.
ALL RIGHT, I'M GOING TO TEACH YOU AN ORIGAMI FOLD.
REAL-LY!?
FOLD IT THE WAY I SHOW YOU.
OKAY, I WILL!
FIRST, FOLD IT INTO A TRIANGLE...

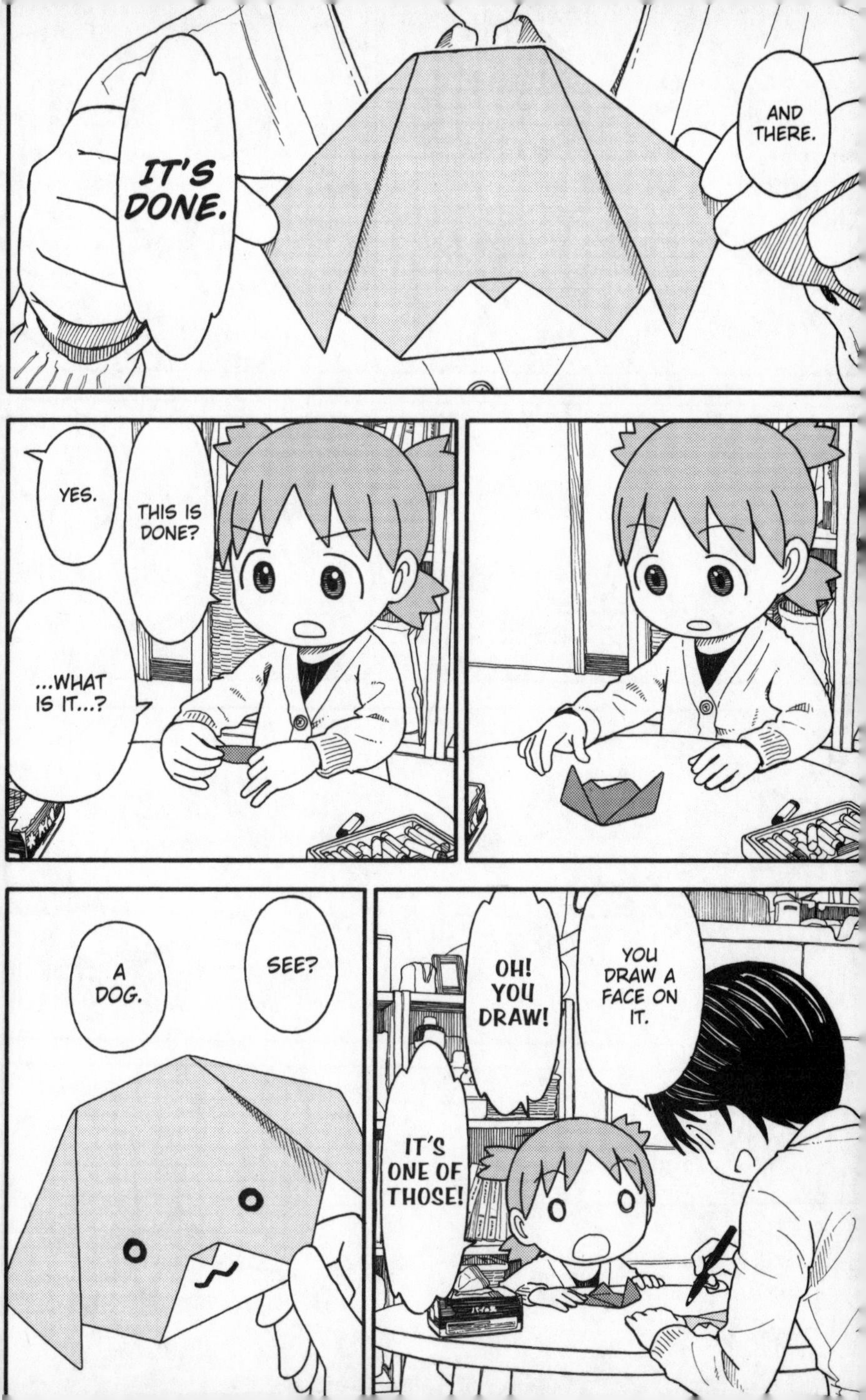
AND THERE.
IT'S DONE.
THIS IS DONE?
YES.
...WHAT IS IT...?
YOU DRAW A FACE ON IT.
OH! YOU DRAW!
IT'S ONE OF THOSE!
SEE?
A DOG.

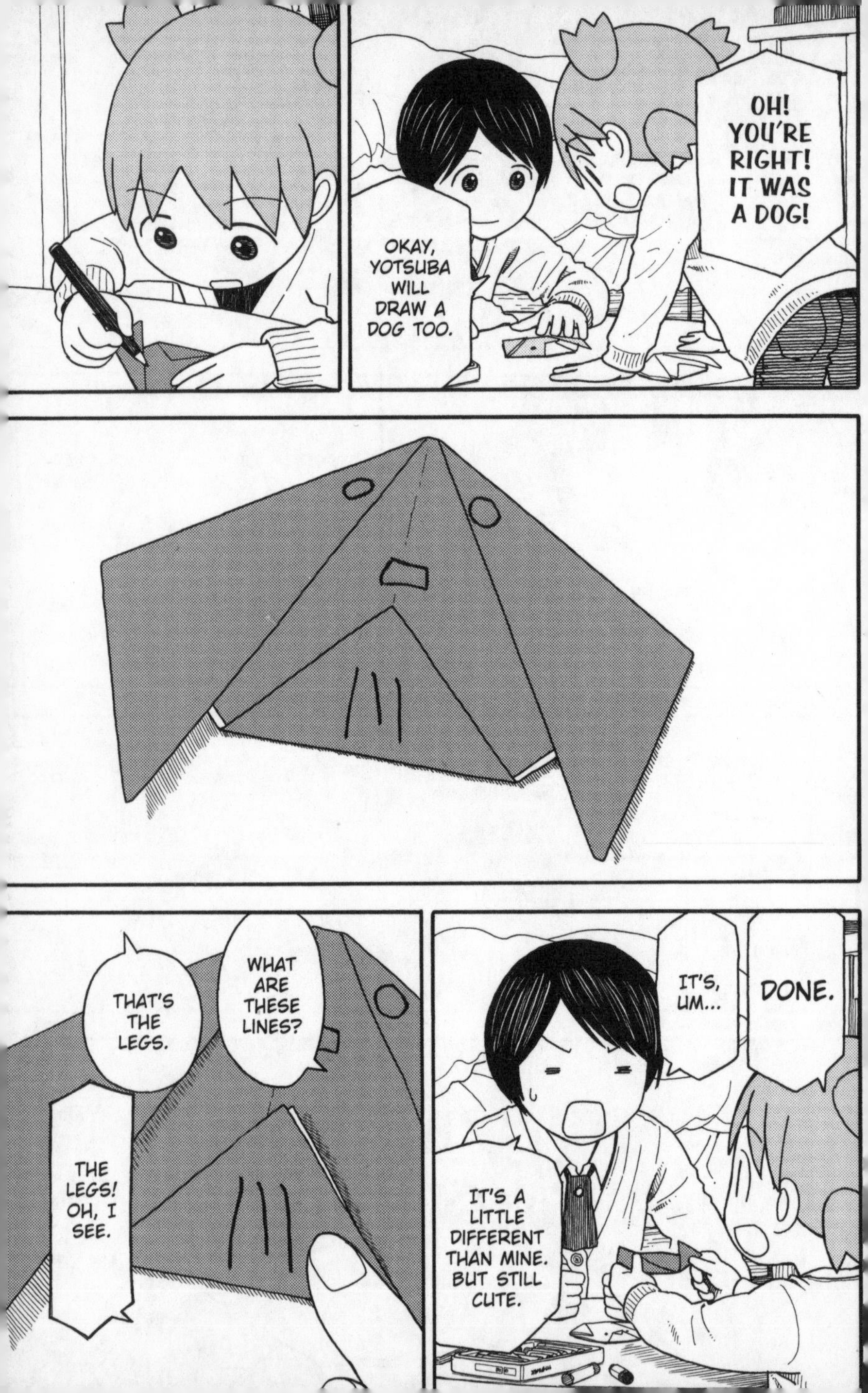
OH! YOU'RE RIGHT! IT WAS A DOG!
OKAY, YOTSUBA WILL DRAW A DOG TOO.
DONE.
IT'S, UM...
IT'S A LITTLE DIFFERENT THAN MINE. BUT STILL CUTE.
WHAT ARE THESE LINES?
THAT'S THE LEGS.
THE LEGS! OH, I SEE.

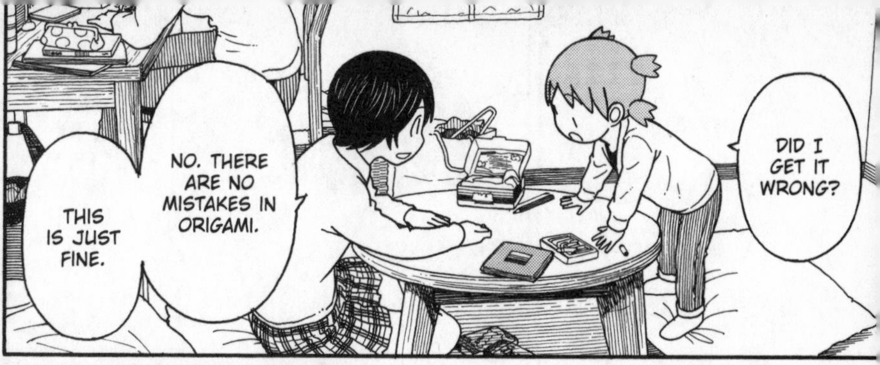
DID I GET IT WRONG?
NO. THERE ARE NO MISTAKES IN ORIGAMI.
THIS IS JUST FINE.

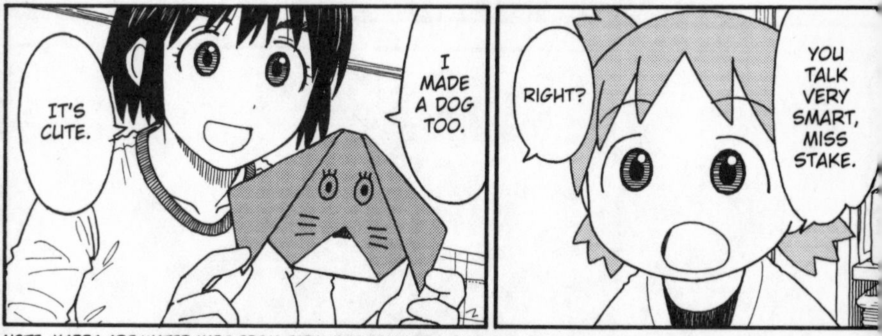
YOU TALK VERY SMART, MISS STAKE.
RIGHT?
I MADE A DOG TOO.
IT'S CUTE.

NOTE: KAPPA ARE WATER IMPS FROM JAPANESE FOLKLORE THAT ARE GREEN AND HUMANOID.

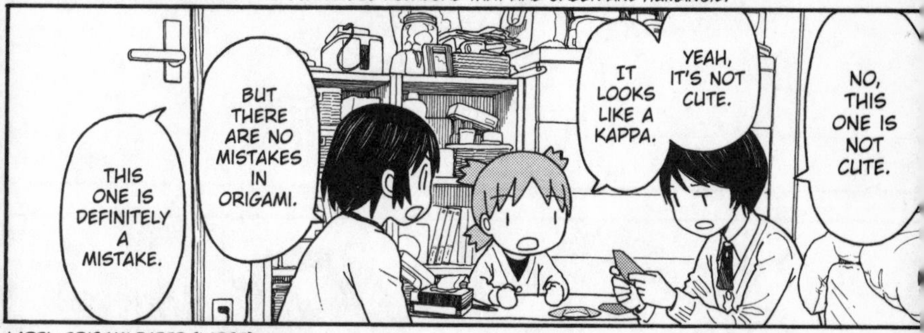
NO, THIS ONE IS NOT CUTE.
YEAH, IT'S NOT CUTE.
IT LOOKS LIKE A KAPPA.
BUT THERE ARE NO MISTAKES IN ORIGAMI.
THIS ONE IS DEFINITELY A MISTAKE.

LABEL: ORIGAMI PAPER (LARGE)

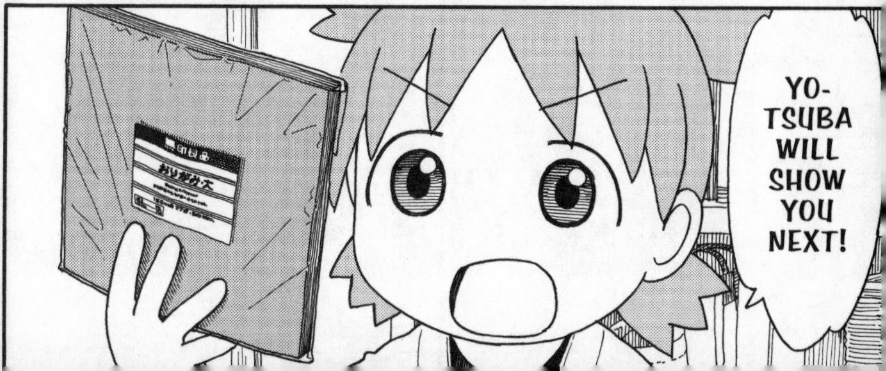
YO-TSUBA WILL SHOW YOU NEXT!

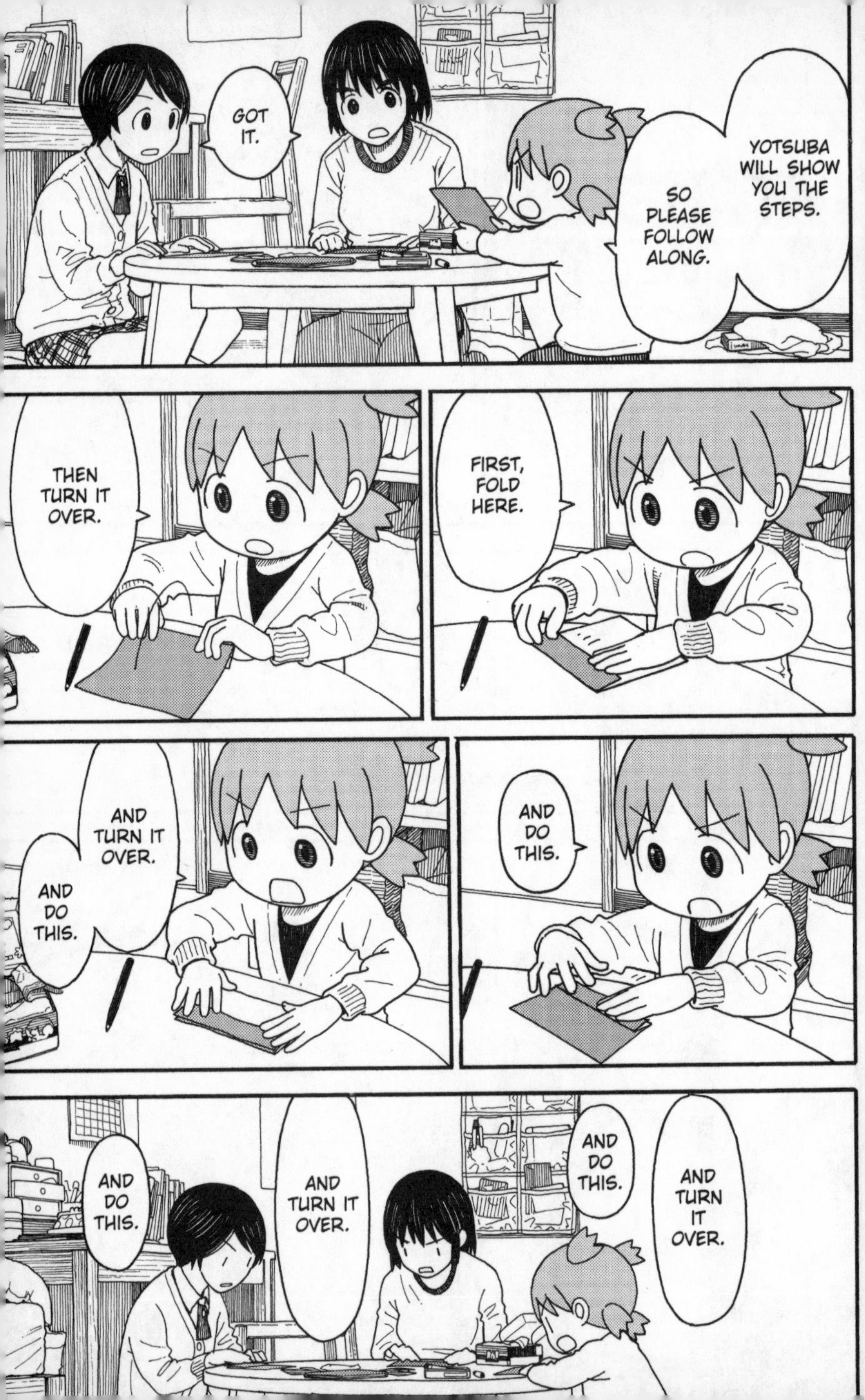
YOTSUBA WILL SHOW YOU THE STEPS.
SO PLEASE FOLLOW ALONG.
GOT IT.
FIRST, FOLD HERE.
THEN TURN IT OVER.
AND DO THIS.
AND TURN IT OVER.
AND DO THIS.
AND TURN IT OVER.
AND DO THIS.
AND TURN IT OVER.
AND DO THIS.

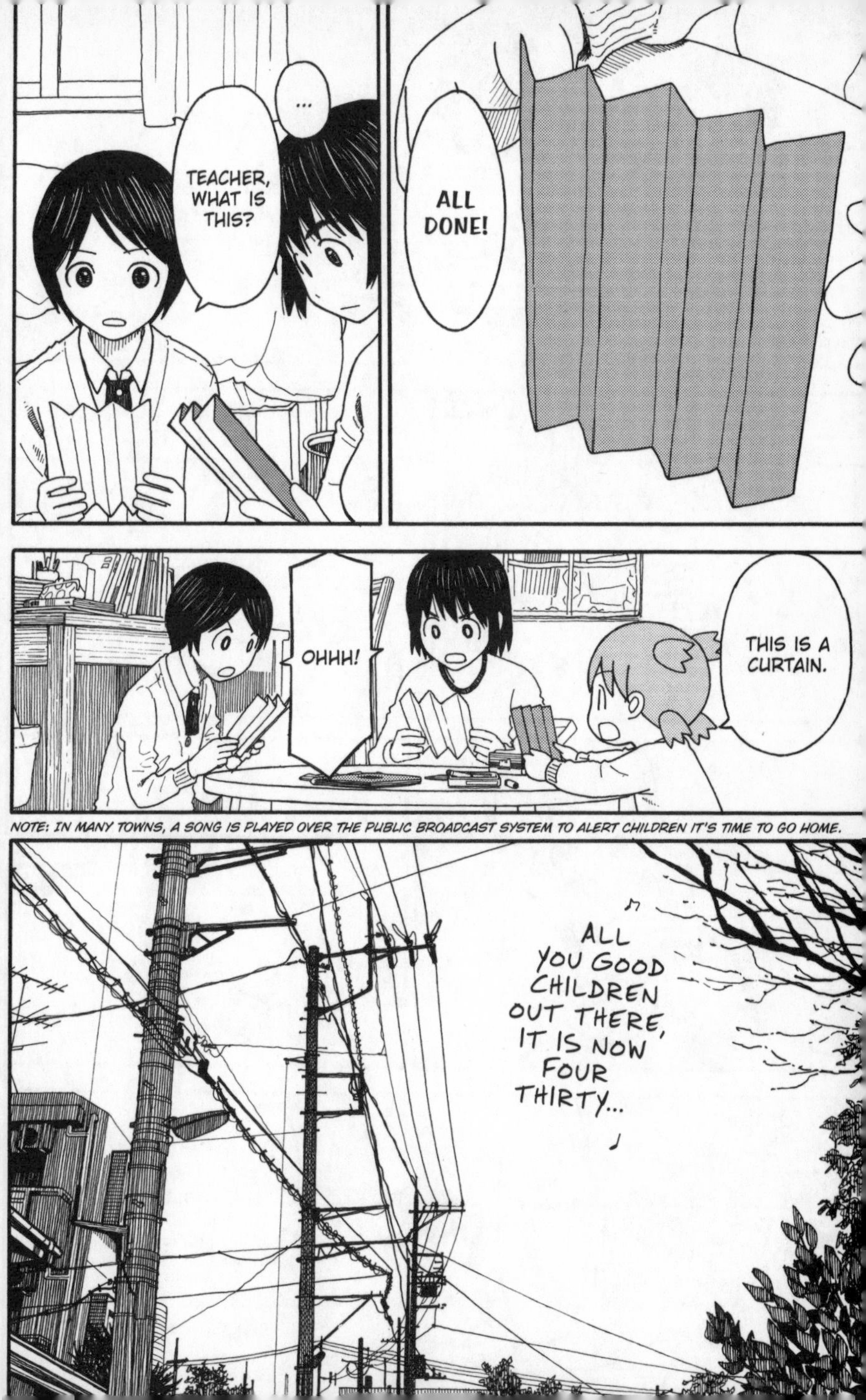
ALL DONE!
...
TEACHER, WHAT IS THIS?
THIS IS A CURTAIN.
OHHH!
♪ ALL YOU GOOD CHILDREN OUT THERE, IT IS NOW FOUR THIRTY... ♪
NOTE: IN MANY TOWNS, A SONG IS PLAYED OVER THE PUBLIC BROADCAST SYSTEM TO ALERT CHILDREN IT'S TIME TO GO HOME.

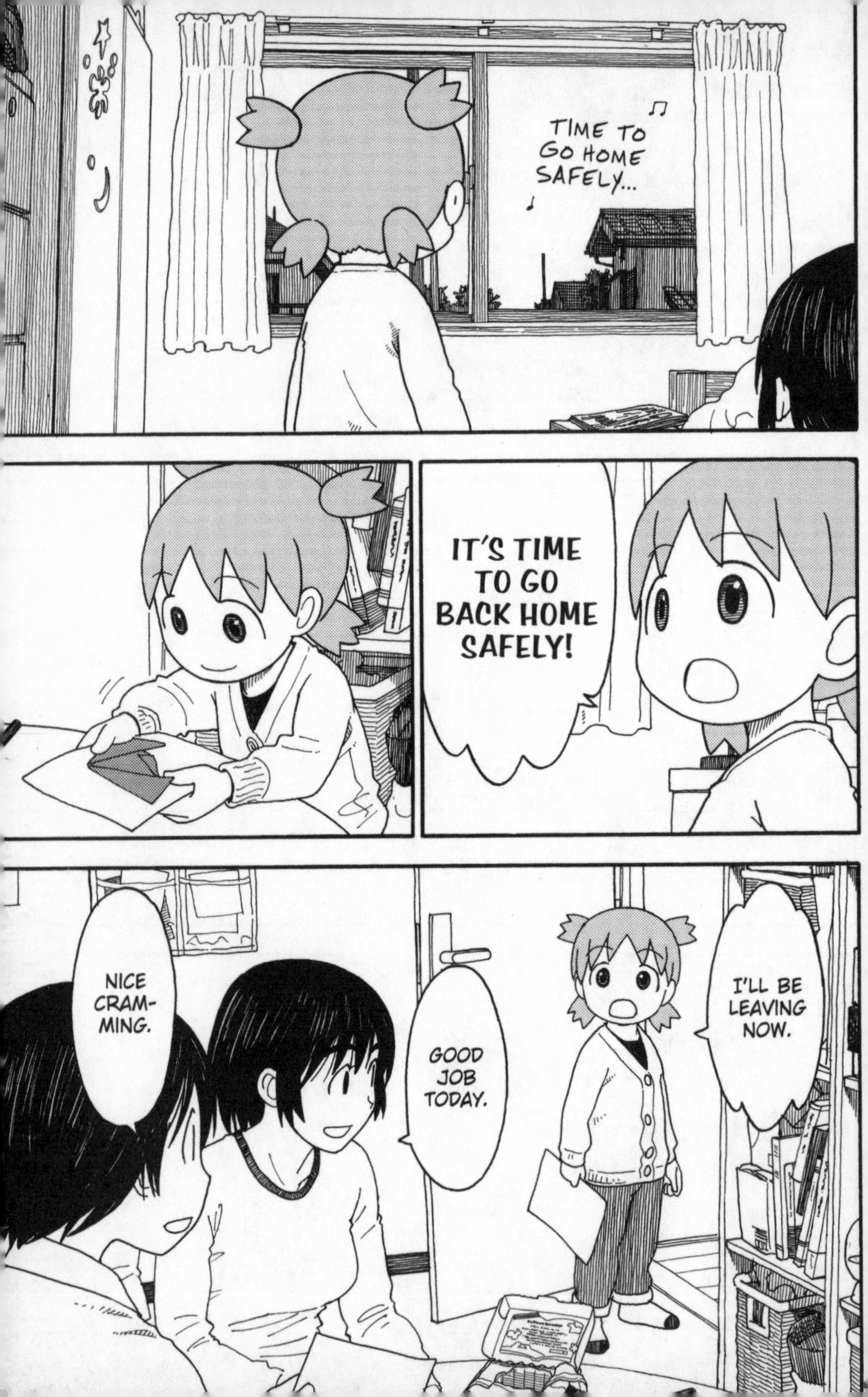
TIME TO GO HOME SAFELY...
IT'S TIME TO GO BACK HOME SAFELY!
I'LL BE LEAVING NOW.
GOOD JOB TODAY.
NICE CRAM-MING.

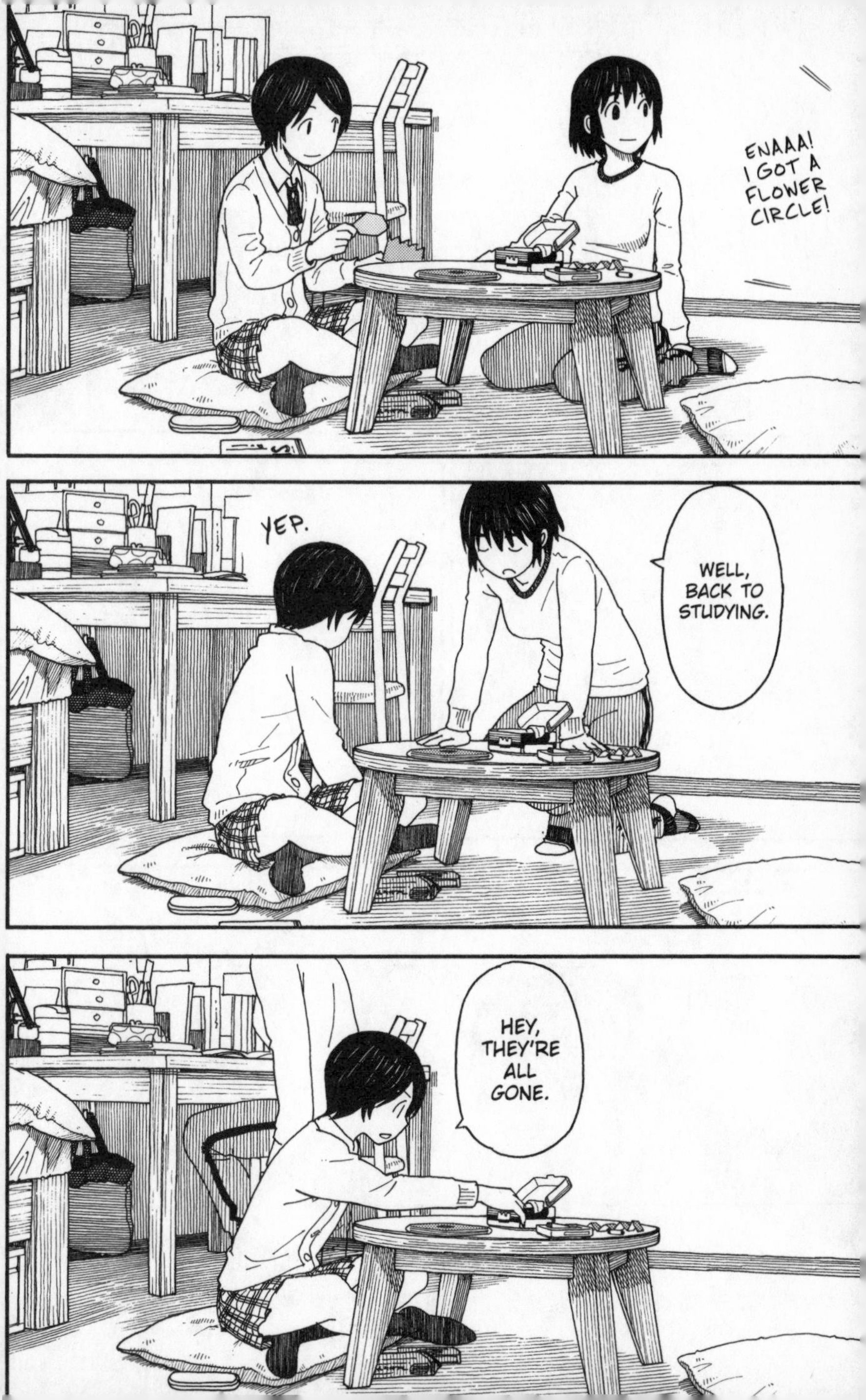
ENAAA! I GOT A FLOWER CIRCLE!
WELL, BACK TO STUDYING.
YEP.
HEY, THEY'RE ALL GONE.

YOTSUBA&!

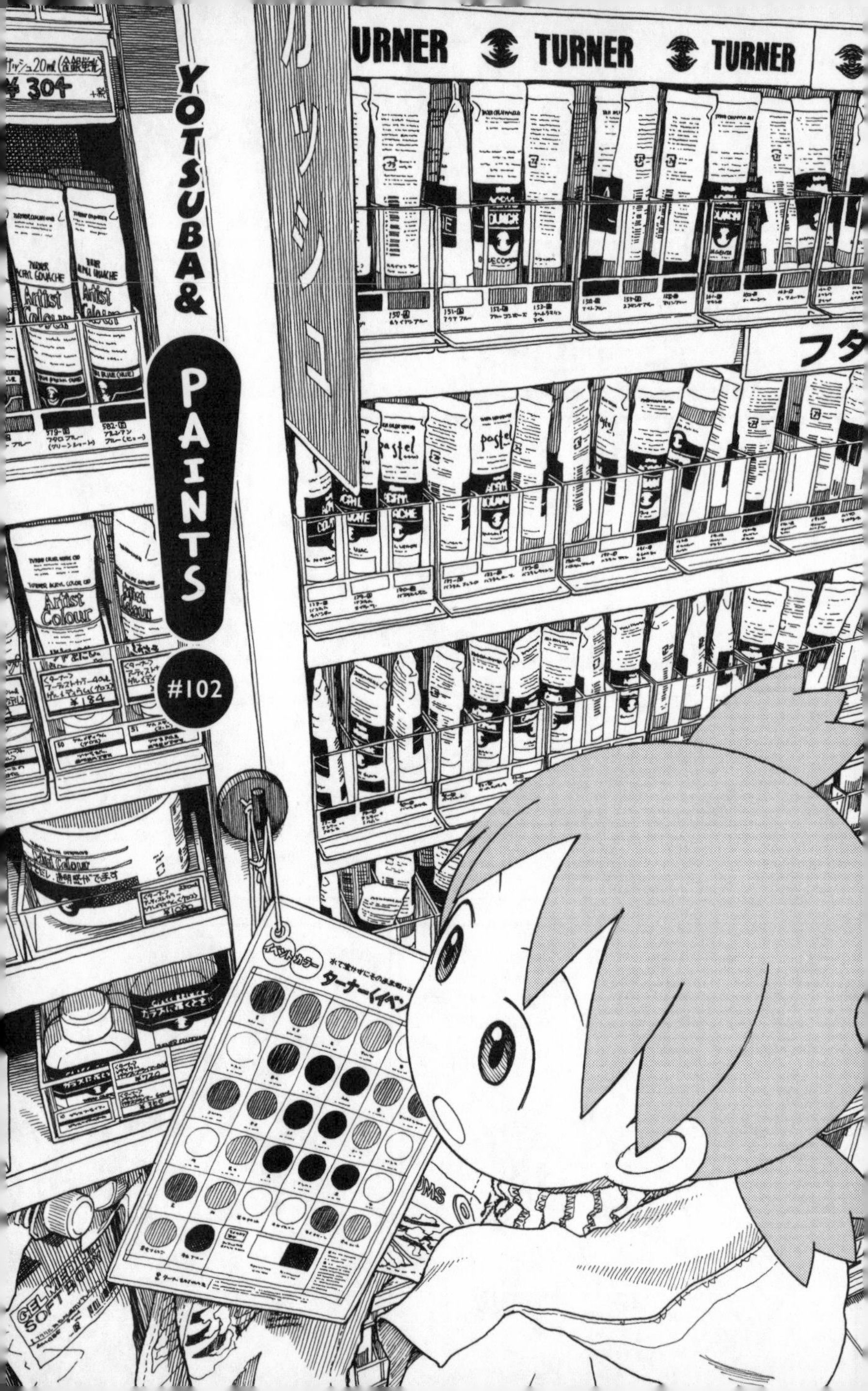
YOTSUBA&
PAINTS
#102
TURNER TURNER TURNER

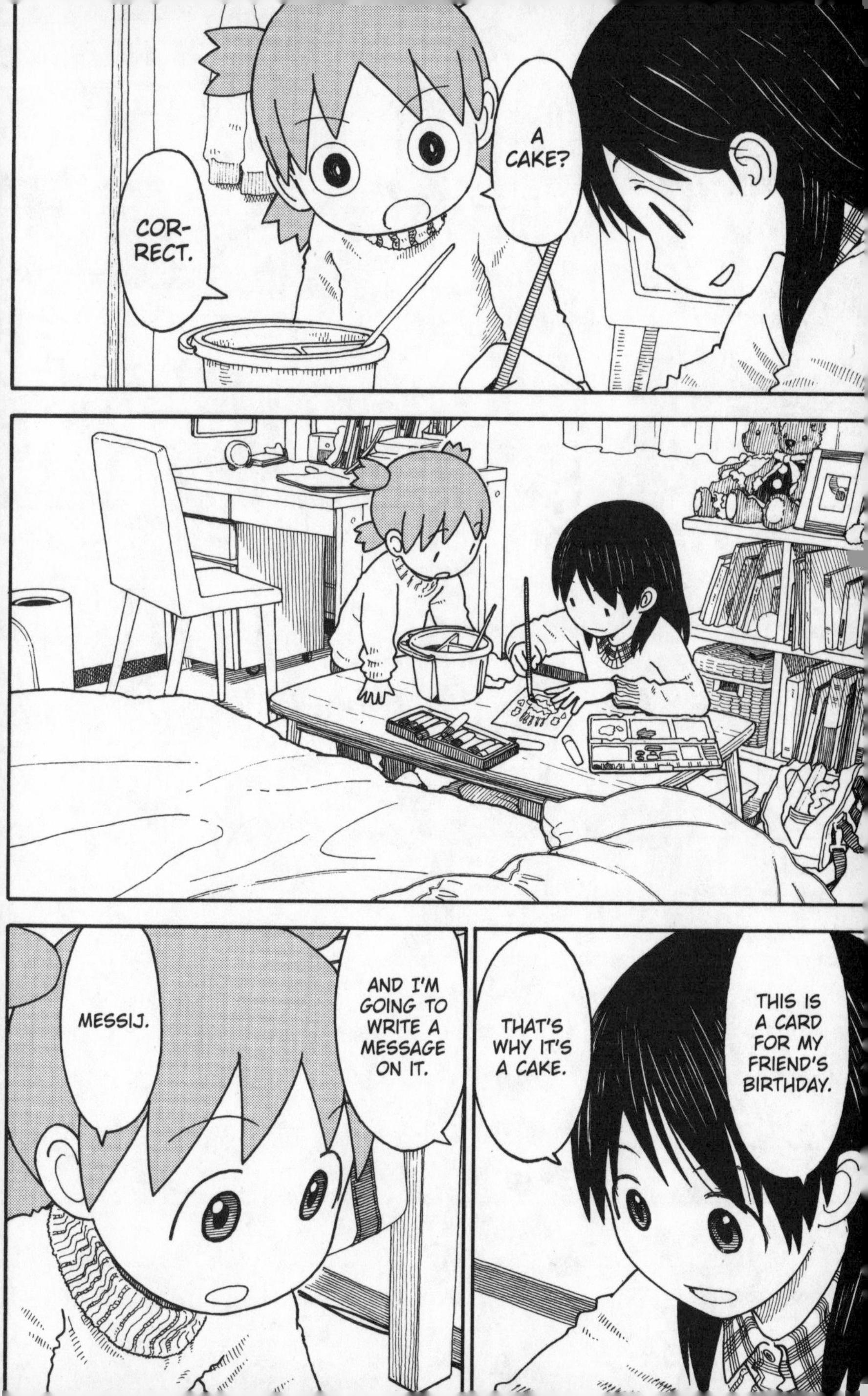
A CAKE?
COR-RECT.
THIS IS A CARD FOR MY FRIEND'S BIRTHDAY.
THAT'S WHY IT'S A CAKE.
AND I'M GOING TO WRITE A MESSAGE ON IT.
MESSIJ.

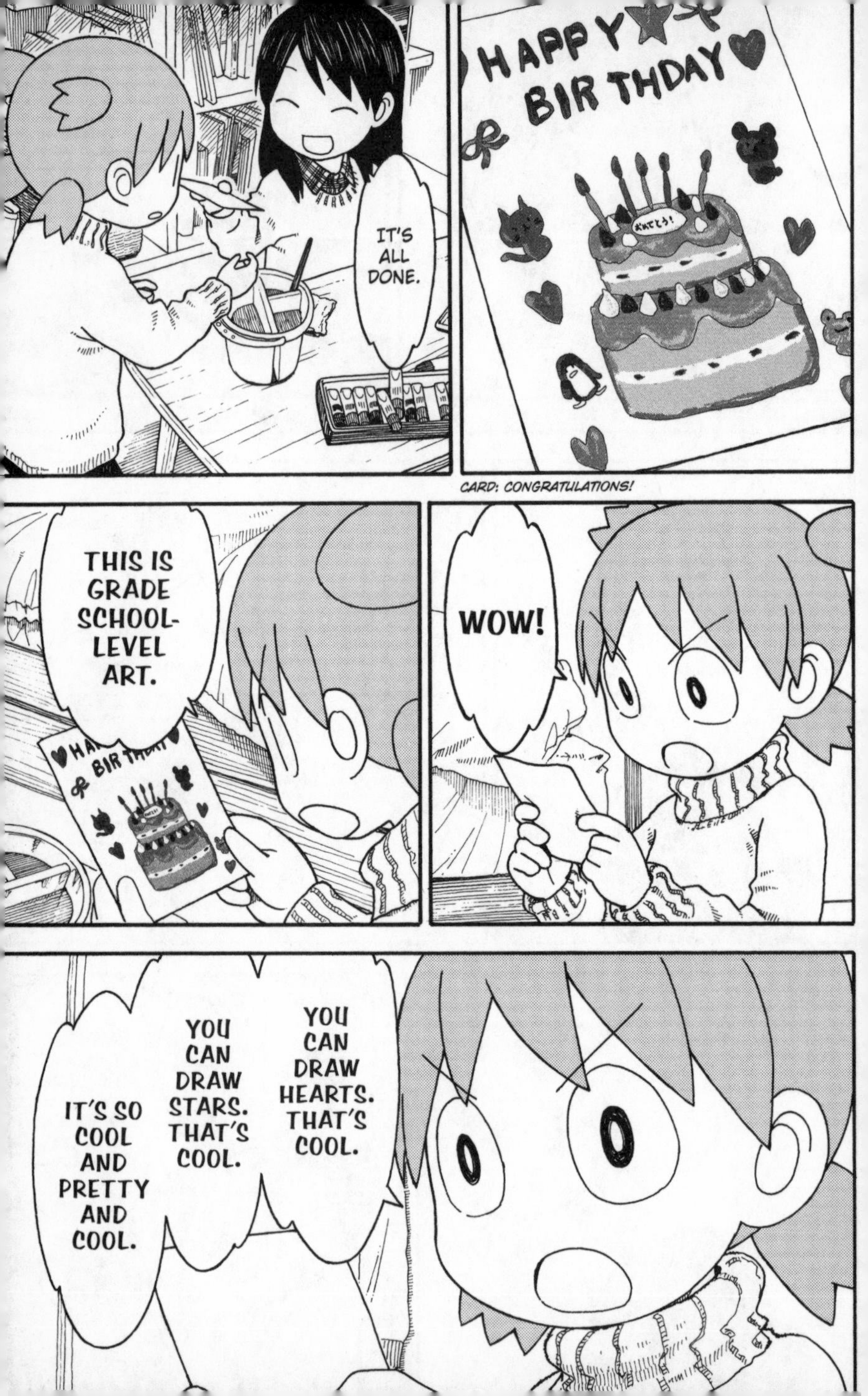
HAPPY BIRTHDAY
CARD: CONGRATULATIONS!
IT'S ALL DONE.
WOW!
THIS IS GRADE SCHOOL-LEVEL ART.
YOU CAN DRAW HEARTS. THAT'S COOL.
YOU CAN DRAW STARS. THAT'S COOL.
IT'S SO COOL AND PRETTY AND COOL.

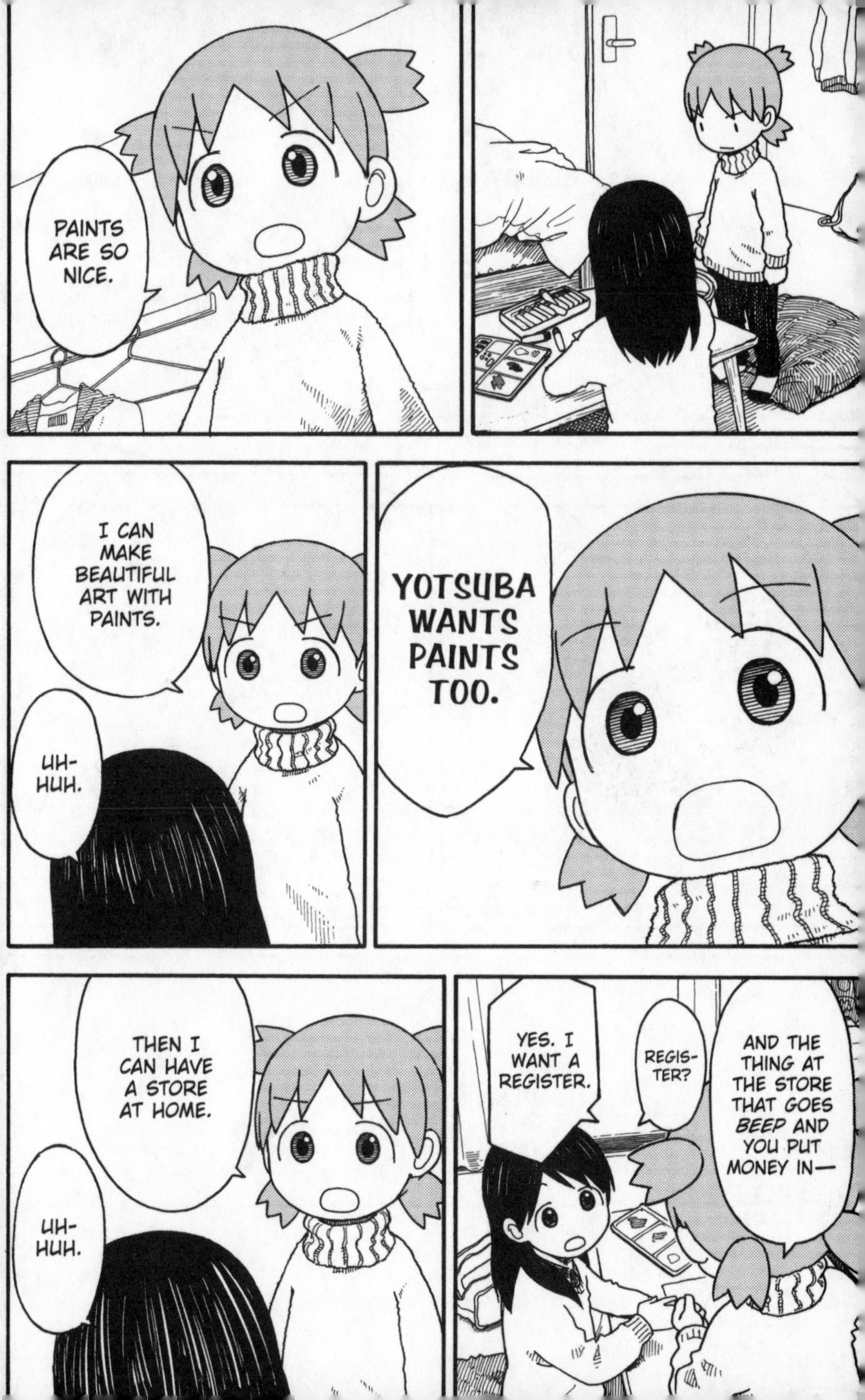
PAINTS ARE SO NICE.
YOTSUBA WANTS PAINTS TOO.
I CAN MAKE BEAUTIFUL ART WITH PAINTS.
UH-HUH.
AND THE THING AT THE STORE THAT GOES *BEEP* AND YOU PUT MONEY IN—
REGIS-TER?
YES. I WANT A REGISTER.
THEN I CAN HAVE A STORE AT HOME.
UH-HUH.

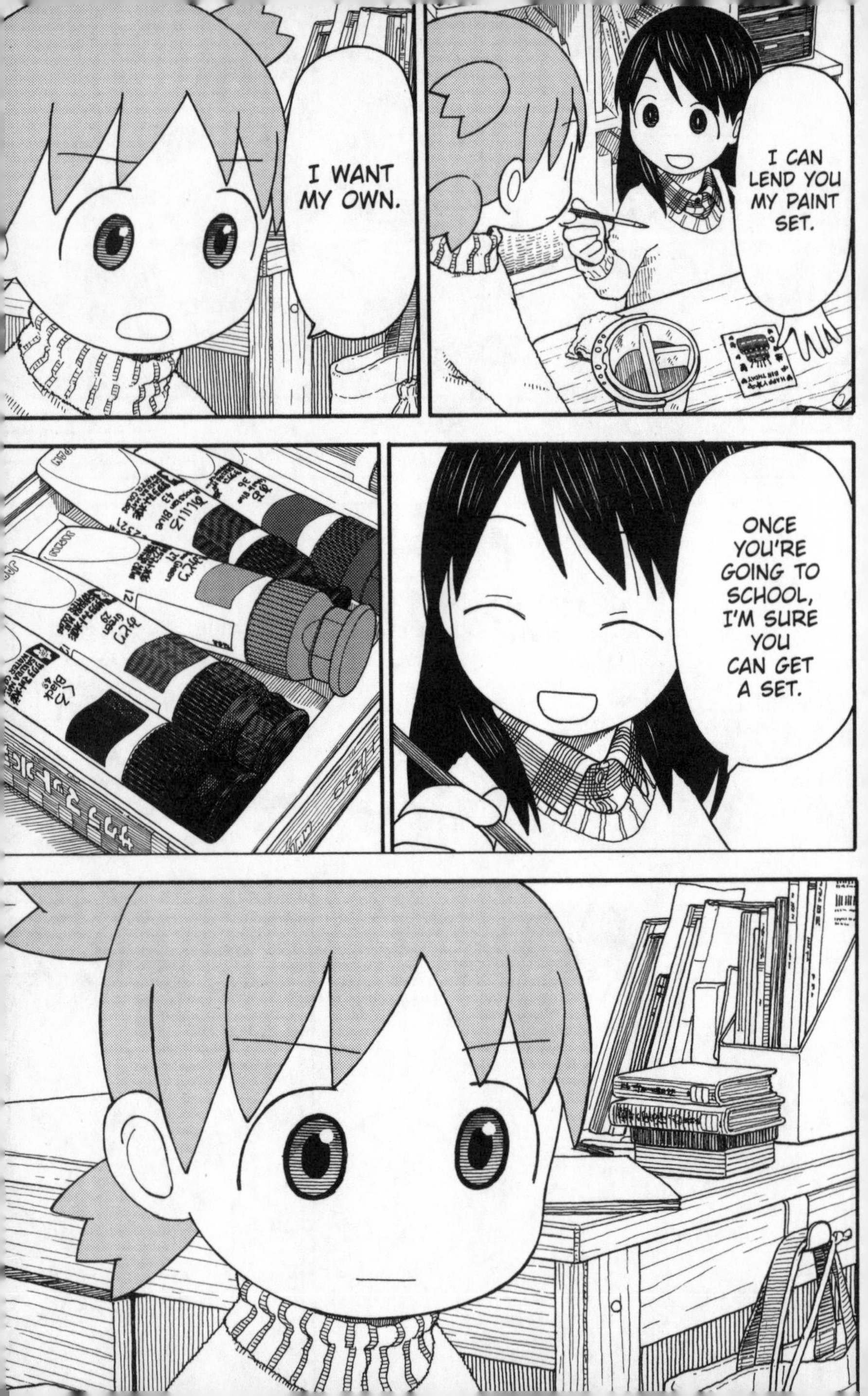
I CAN LEND YOU MY PAINT SET.
I WANT MY OWN.
ONCE YOU'RE GOING TO SCHOOL, I'M SURE YOU CAN GET A SET.

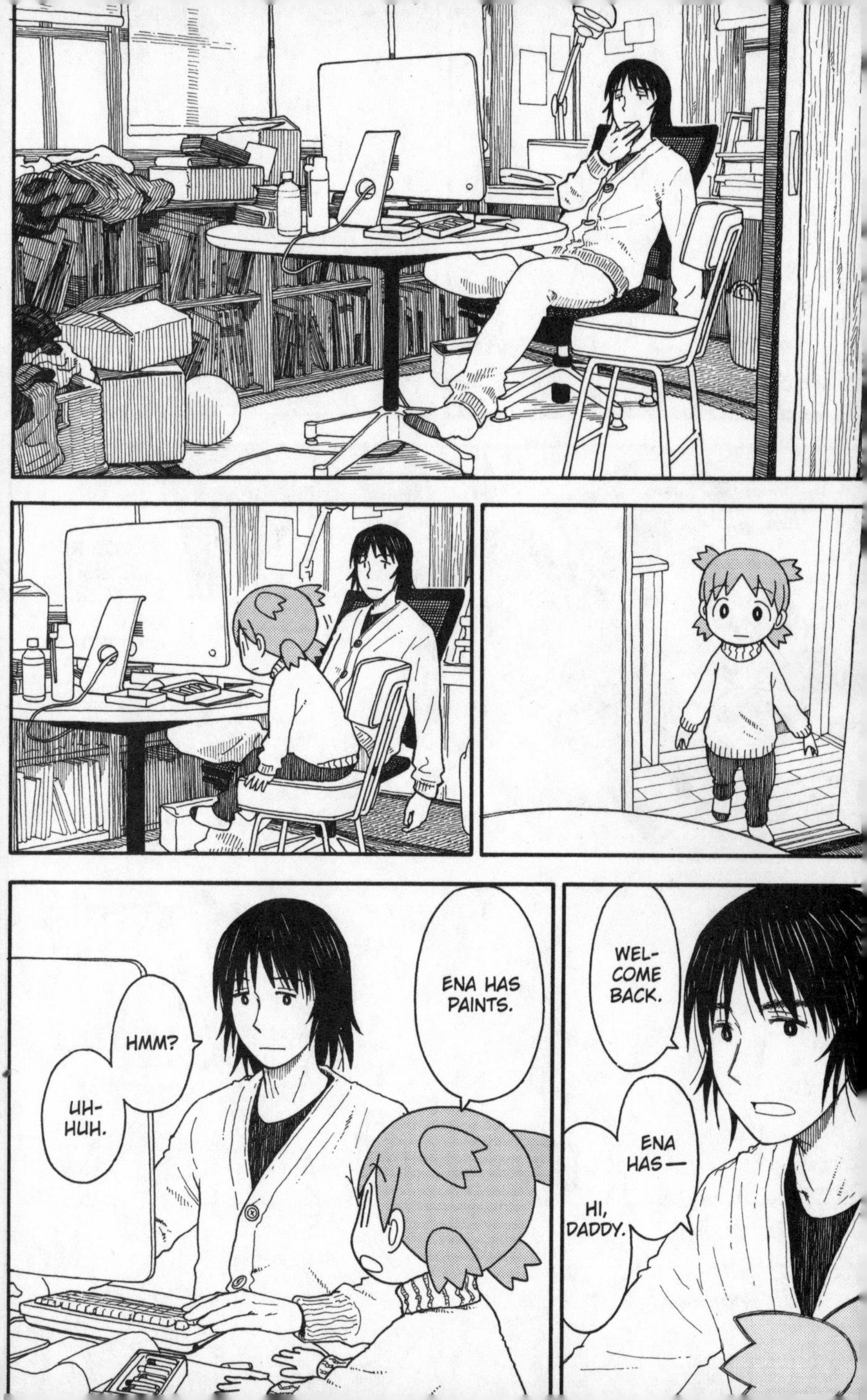
WEL-
COME
BACK.
ENA
HAS—
HI,
DADDY.
ENA HAS
PAINTS.
HMM?
UH-
HUH.

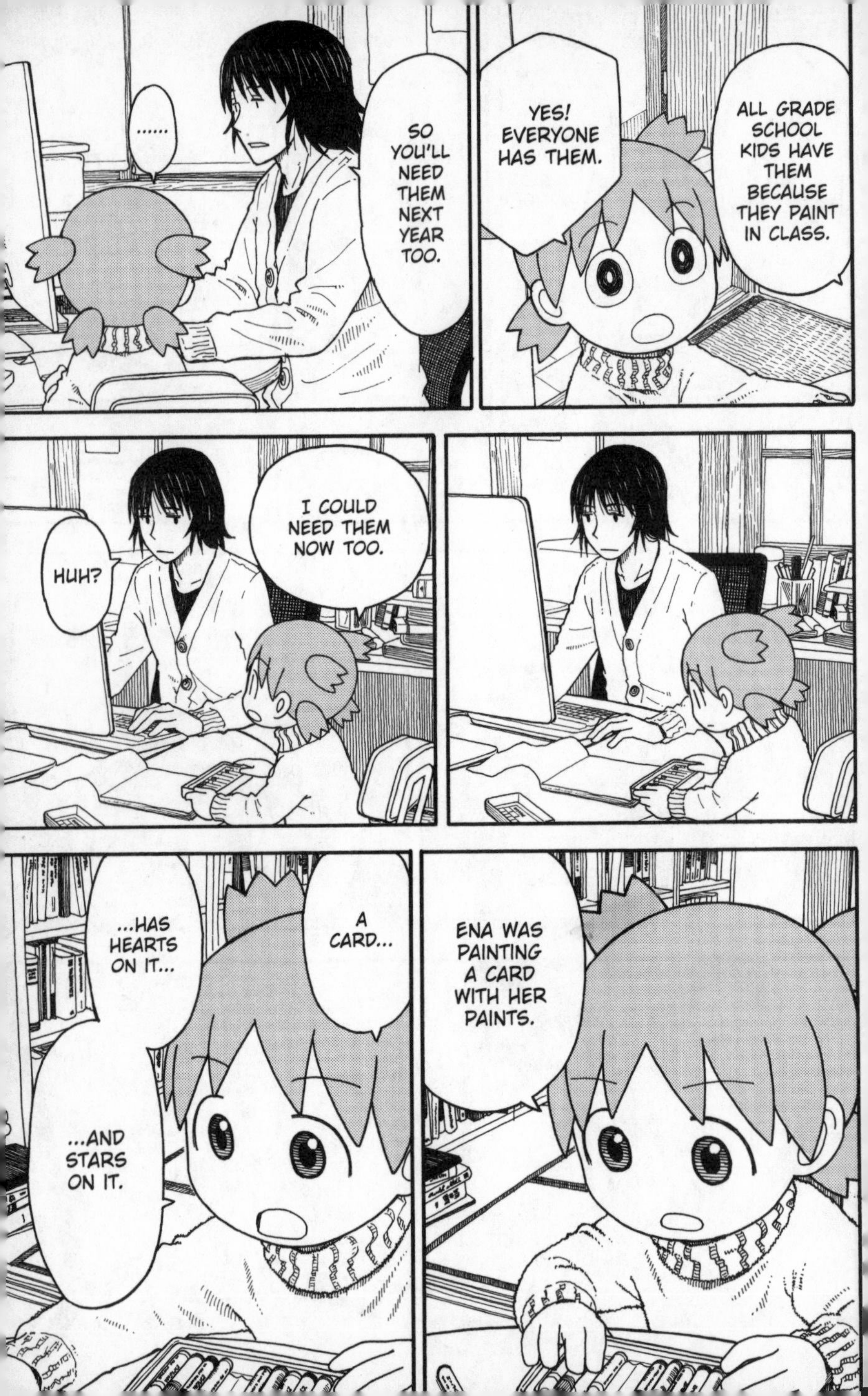
ALL GRADE SCHOOL KIDS HAVE THEM BECAUSE THEY PAINT IN CLASS.
YES! EVERYONE HAS THEM.
SO YOU'LL NEED THEM NEXT YEAR TOO.
......
I COULD NEED THEM NOW TOO.
HUH?
ENA WAS PAINTING A CARD WITH HER PAINTS.
A CARD...
...HAS HEARTS ON IT...
...AND STARS ON IT.

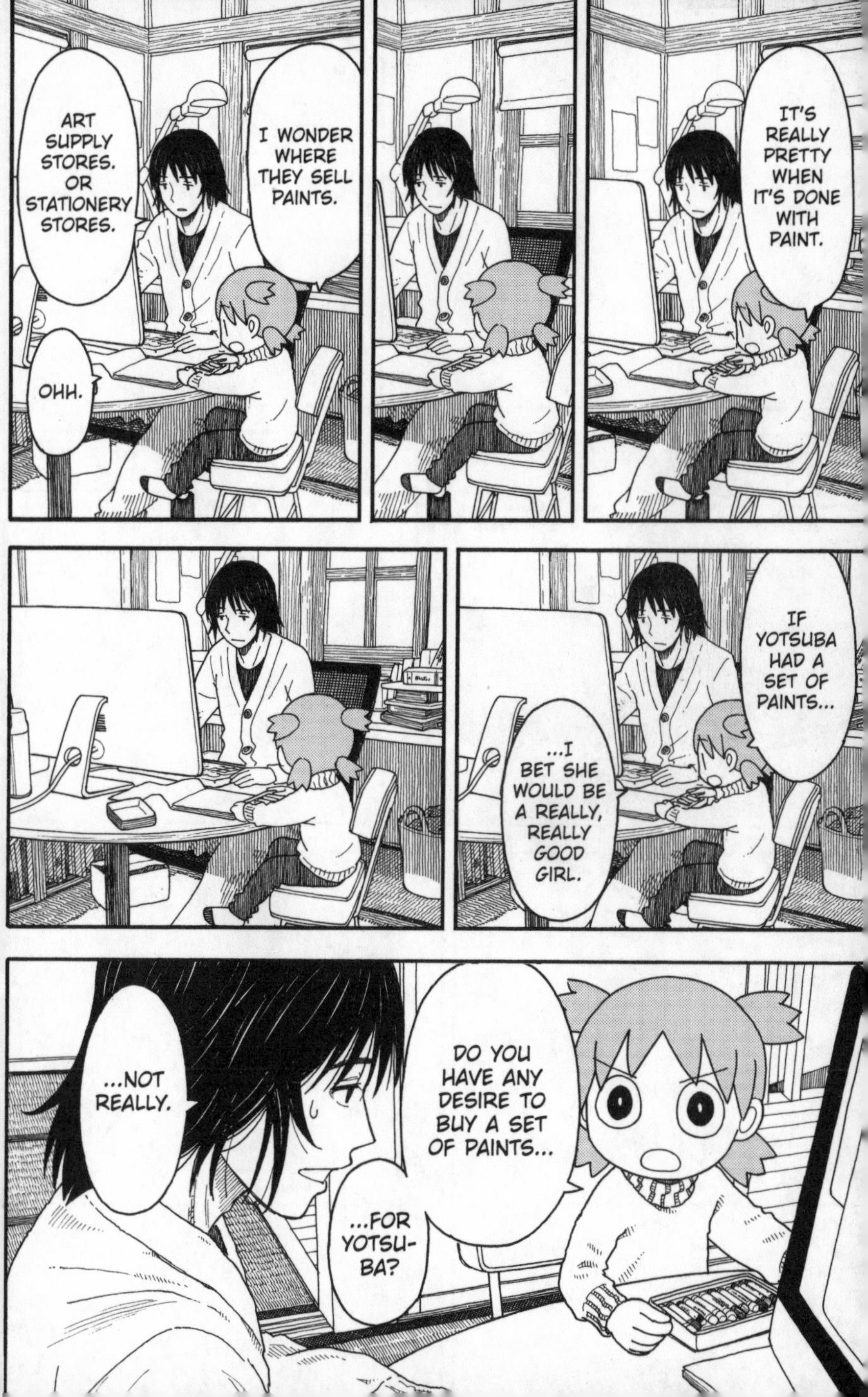
IT'S REALLY PRETTY WHEN IT'S DONE WITH PAINT.
I WONDER WHERE THEY SELL PAINTS.
ART SUPPLY STORES. OR STATIONERY STORES.
OHH.
IF YOTSUBA HAD A SET OF PAINTS...
...I BET SHE WOULD BE A REALLY, REALLY GOOD GIRL.
DO YOU HAVE ANY DESIRE TO BUY A SET OF PAINTS...
...FOR YOTSU-BA?
...NOT REALLY.

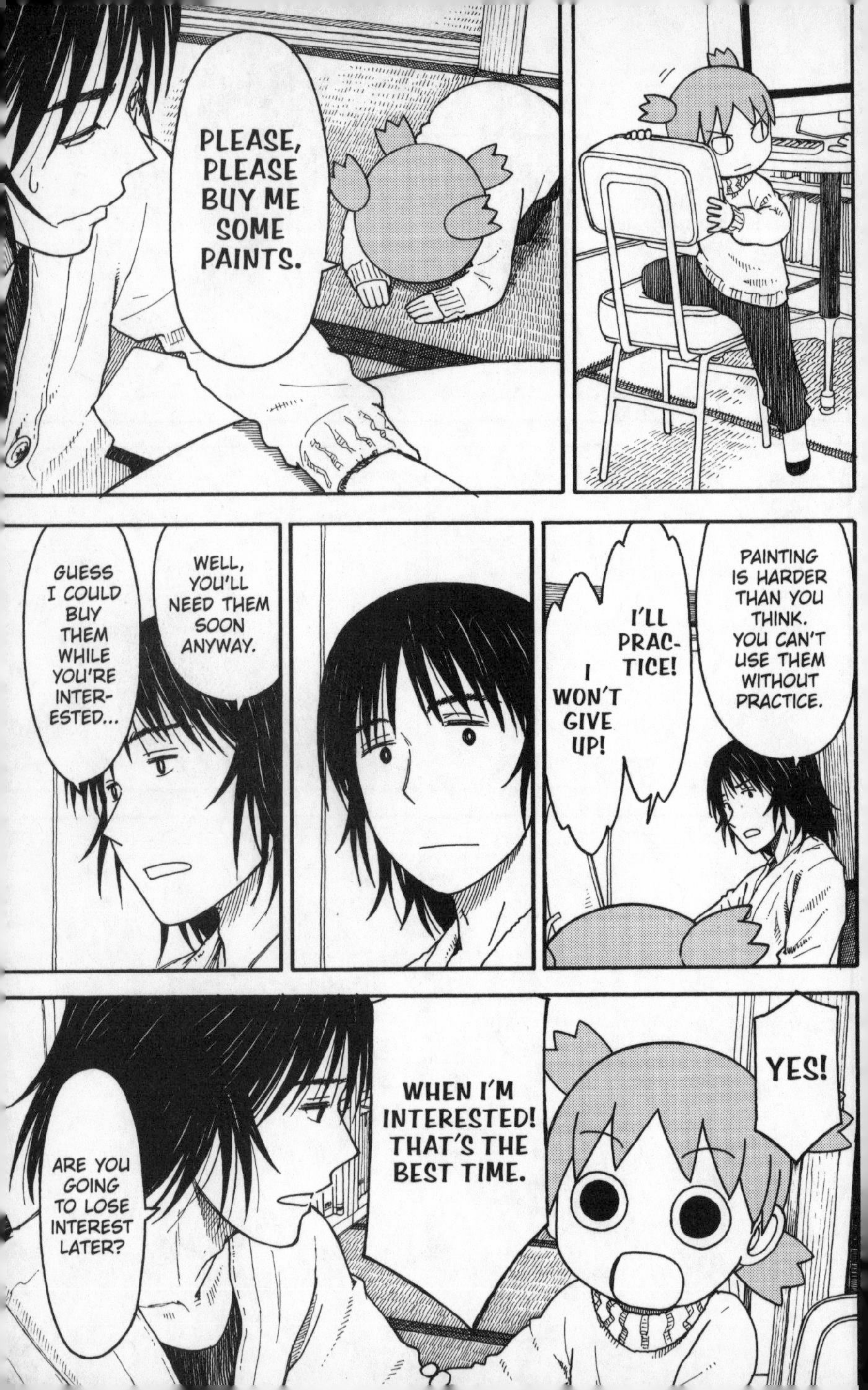
PLEASE, PLEASE BUY ME SOME PAINTS.
PAINTING IS HARDER THAN YOU THINK. YOU CAN'T USE THEM WITHOUT PRACTICE.
I'LL PRAC-TICE!
I WON'T GIVE UP!
WELL, YOU'LL NEED THEM SOON ANYWAY.
GUESS I COULD BUY THEM WHILE YOU'RE INTER-ESTED...
YES!
WHEN I'M INTERESTED! THAT'S THE BEST TIME.
ARE YOU GOING TO LOSE INTEREST LATER?

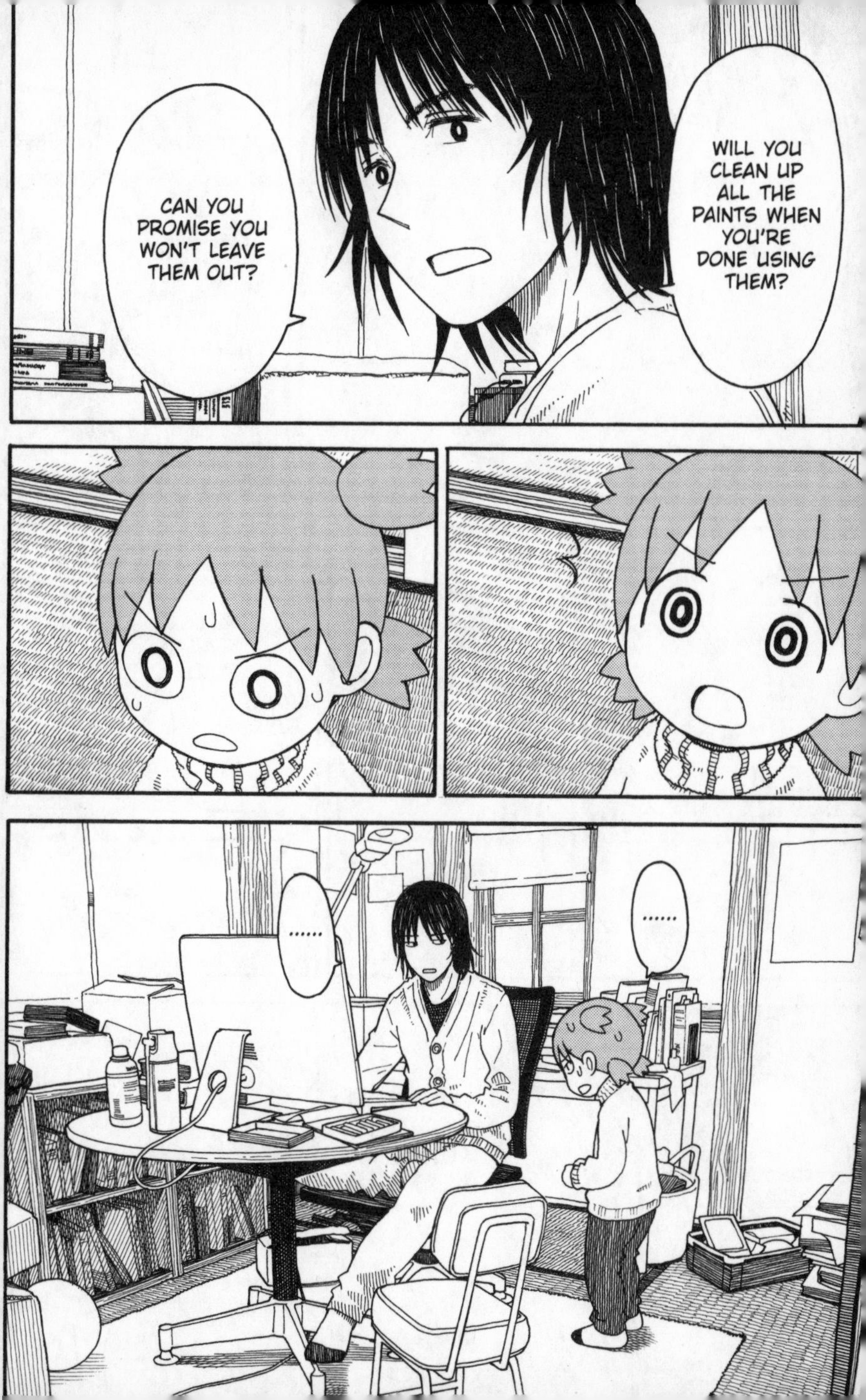
WILL YOU CLEAN UP ALL THE PAINTS WHEN YOU'RE DONE USING THEM?
CAN YOU PROMISE YOU WON'T LEAVE THEM OUT?
......
......

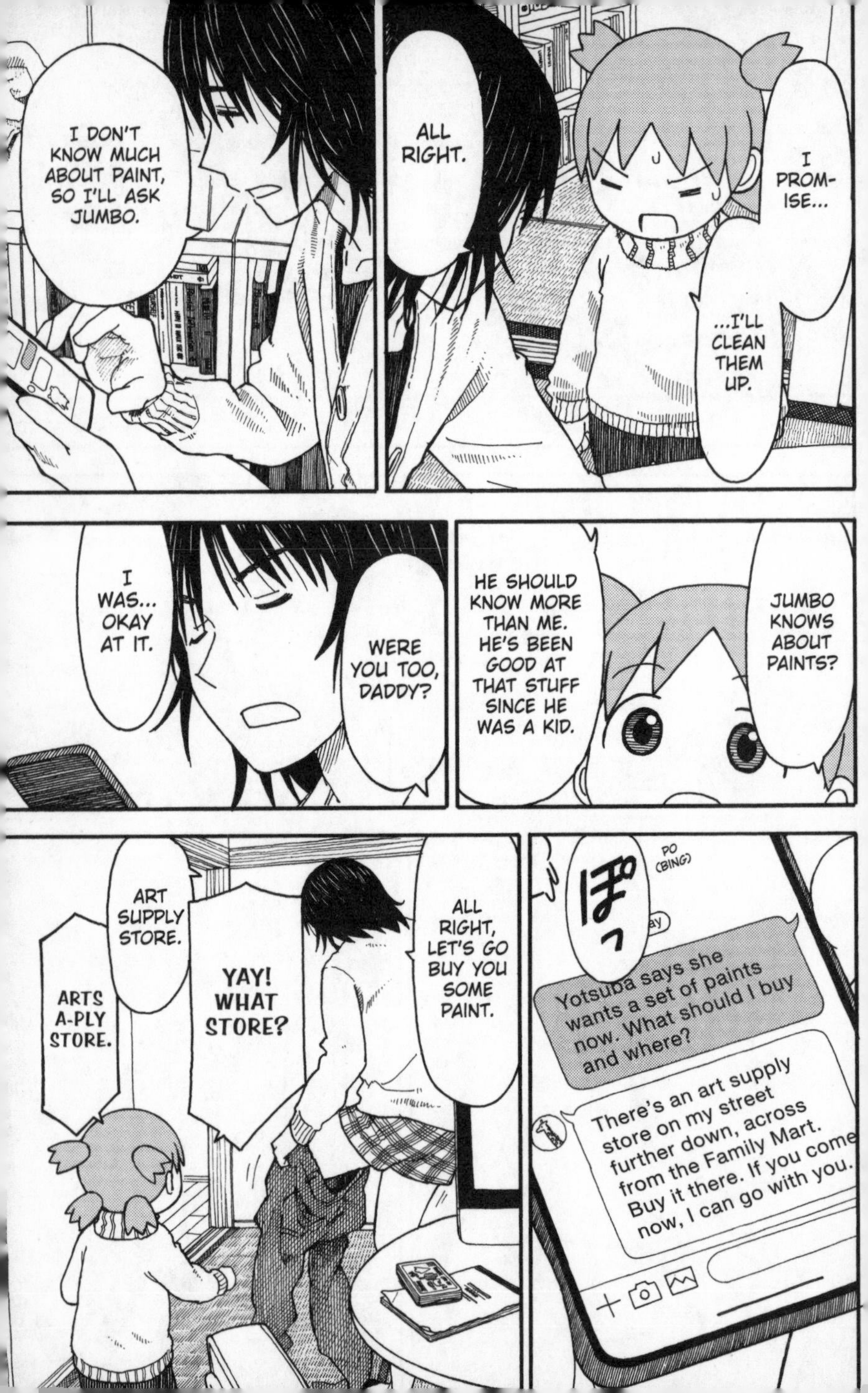
I PROMISE...
...I'LL CLEAN THEM UP.
ALL RIGHT.
I DON'T KNOW MUCH ABOUT PAINT, SO I'LL ASK JUMBO.
JUMBO KNOWS ABOUT PAINTS?
HE SHOULD KNOW MORE THAN ME. HE'S BEEN GOOD AT THAT STUFF SINCE HE WAS A KID.
WERE YOU TOO, DADDY?
I WAS... OKAY AT IT.
ぽっ
PO (BING)
Yotsuba says she wants a set of paints now. What should I buy and where?
There's an art supply store on my street further down, across from the Family Mart. Buy it there. If you come now, I can go with you.
ALL RIGHT, LET'S GO BUY YOU SOME PAINT.
YAY! WHAT STORE?
ART SUPPLY STORE.
ARTS A-PLY STORE.

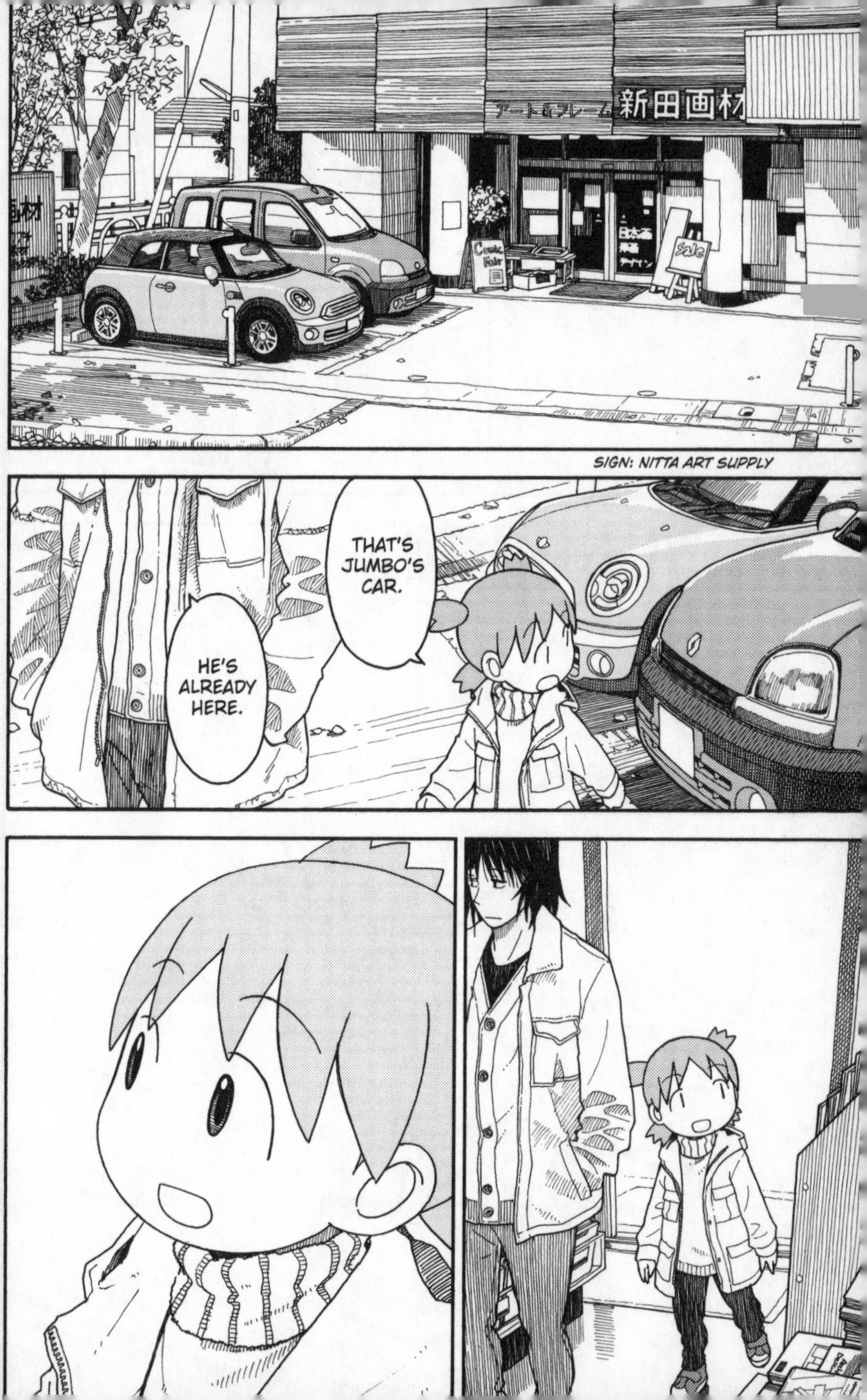
アート＆フレーム 新田画材
Sale
SIGN: NITTA ART SUPPLY
THAT'S JUMBO'S CAR.
HE'S ALREADY HERE.

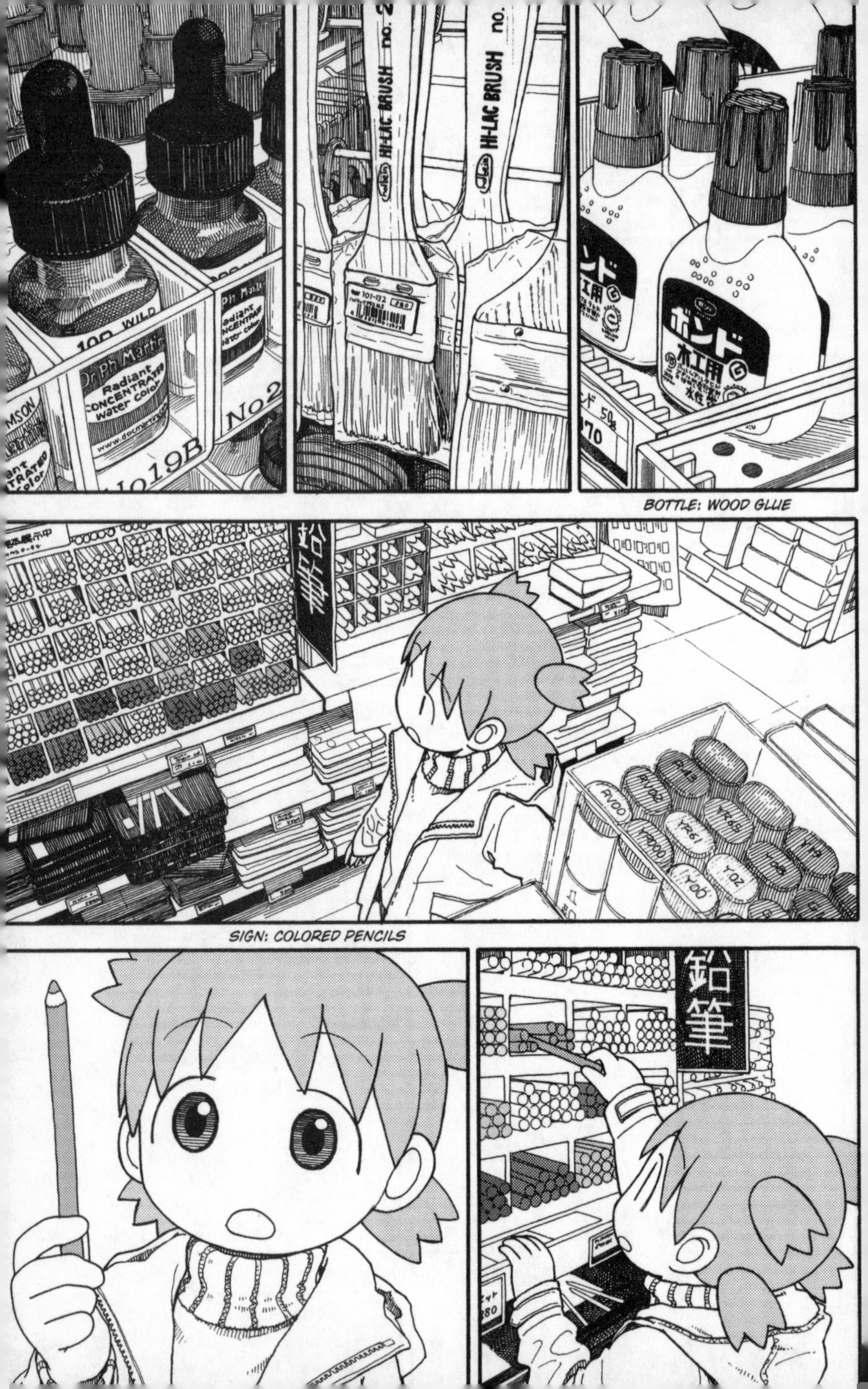
ボンド
木工用
BOTTLE: WOOD GLUE
HI-LAC BRUSH
HI-LAC BRUSH
10D WILD
Dr.Ph.Martin's
Radiant CONCENTRATED Water Color
No19B
No2
鉛筆
SIGN: COLORED PENCILS
鉛筆

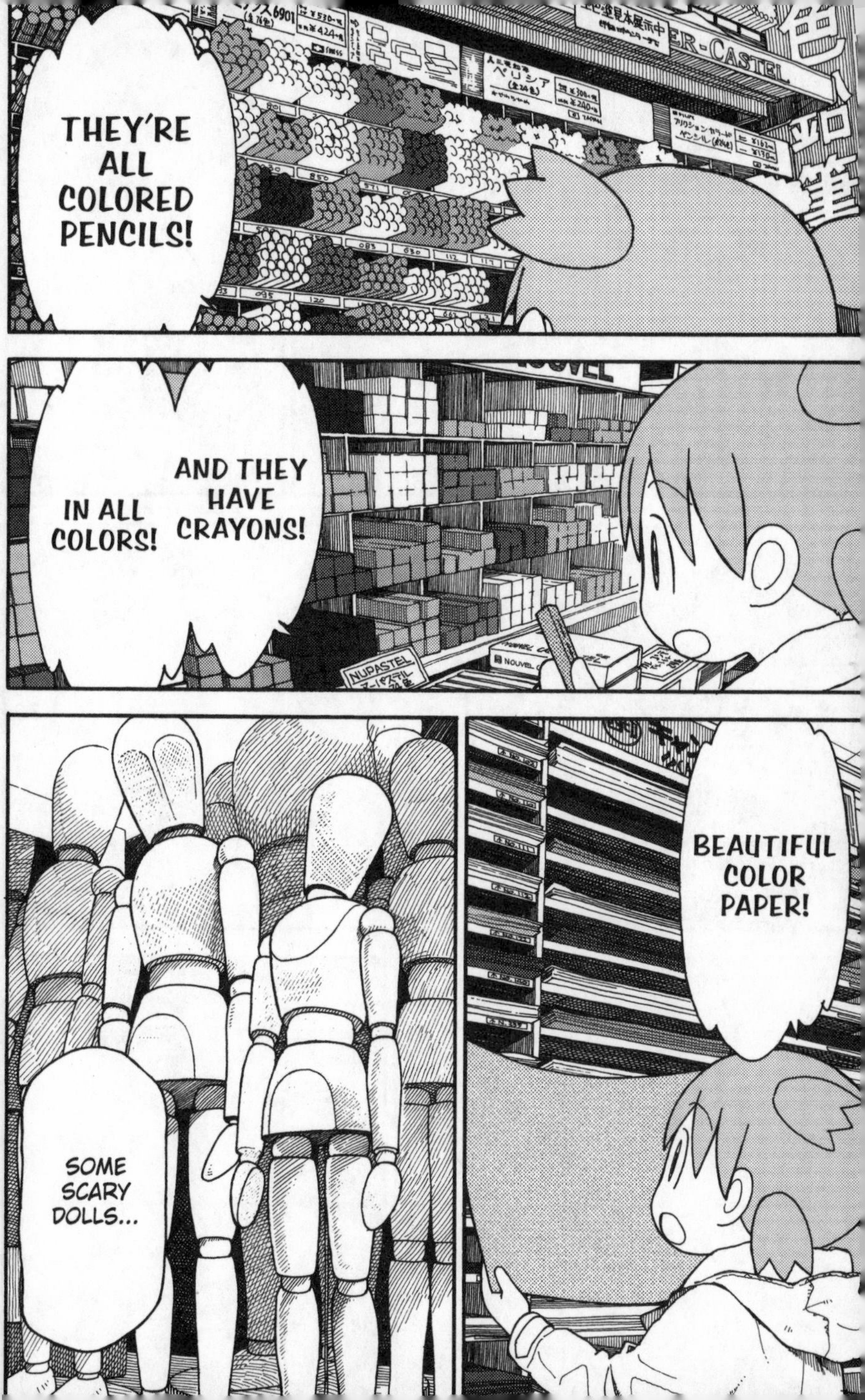
THEY'RE ALL COLORED PENCILS!
AND THEY HAVE CRAYONS!
IN ALL COLORS!
NUPASTEL
BEAUTIFUL COLOR PAPER!
SOME SCARY DOLLS...

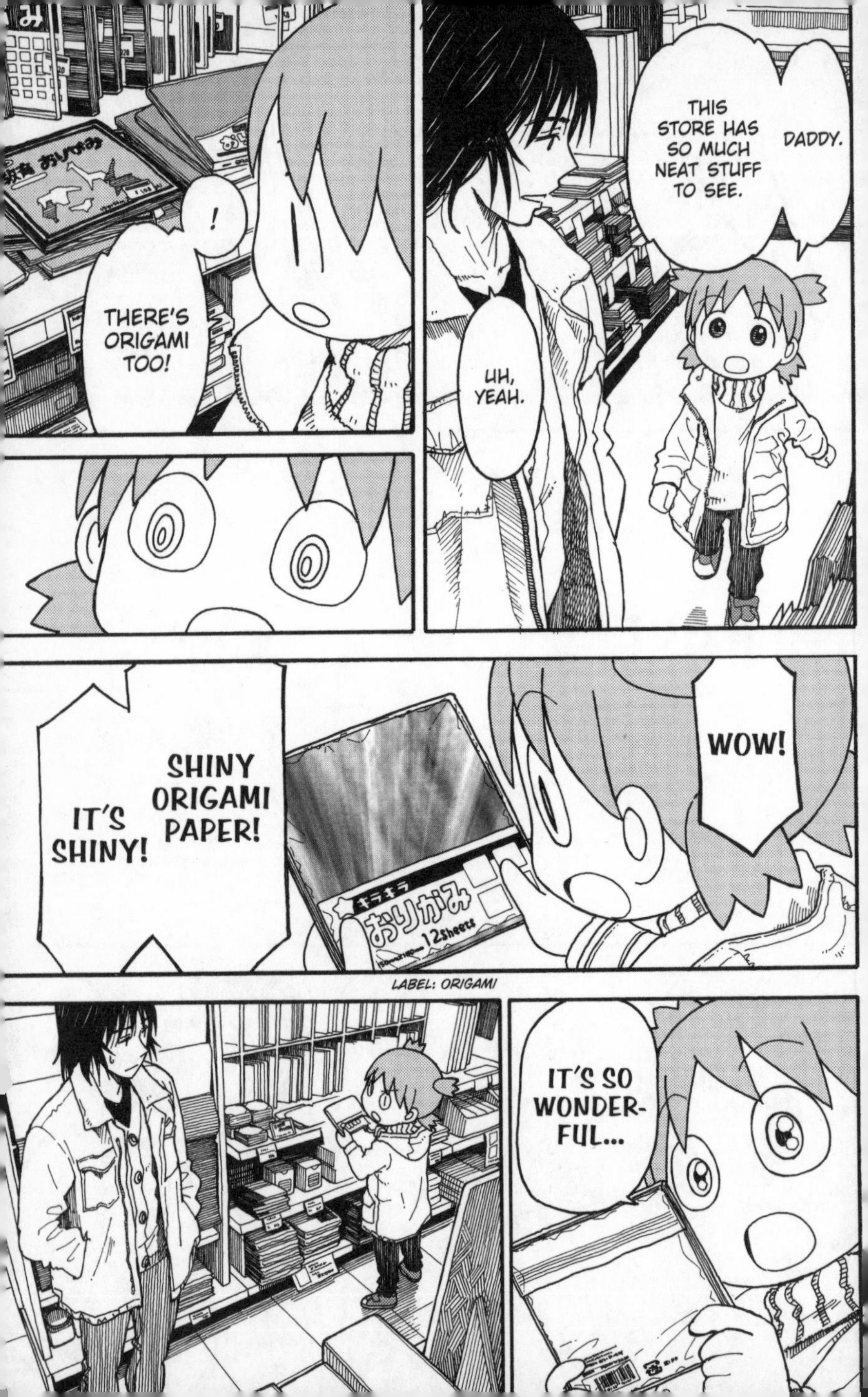
DADDY.
THIS STORE HAS SO MUCH NEAT STUFF TO SEE.
UH, YEAH.
!
THERE'S ORIGAMI TOO!
WOW!
SHINY ORIGAMI PAPER!
IT'S SHINY!
キラキラ
おりがみ
12Sheets
LABEL: ORIGAMI
IT'S SO WONDERFUL...

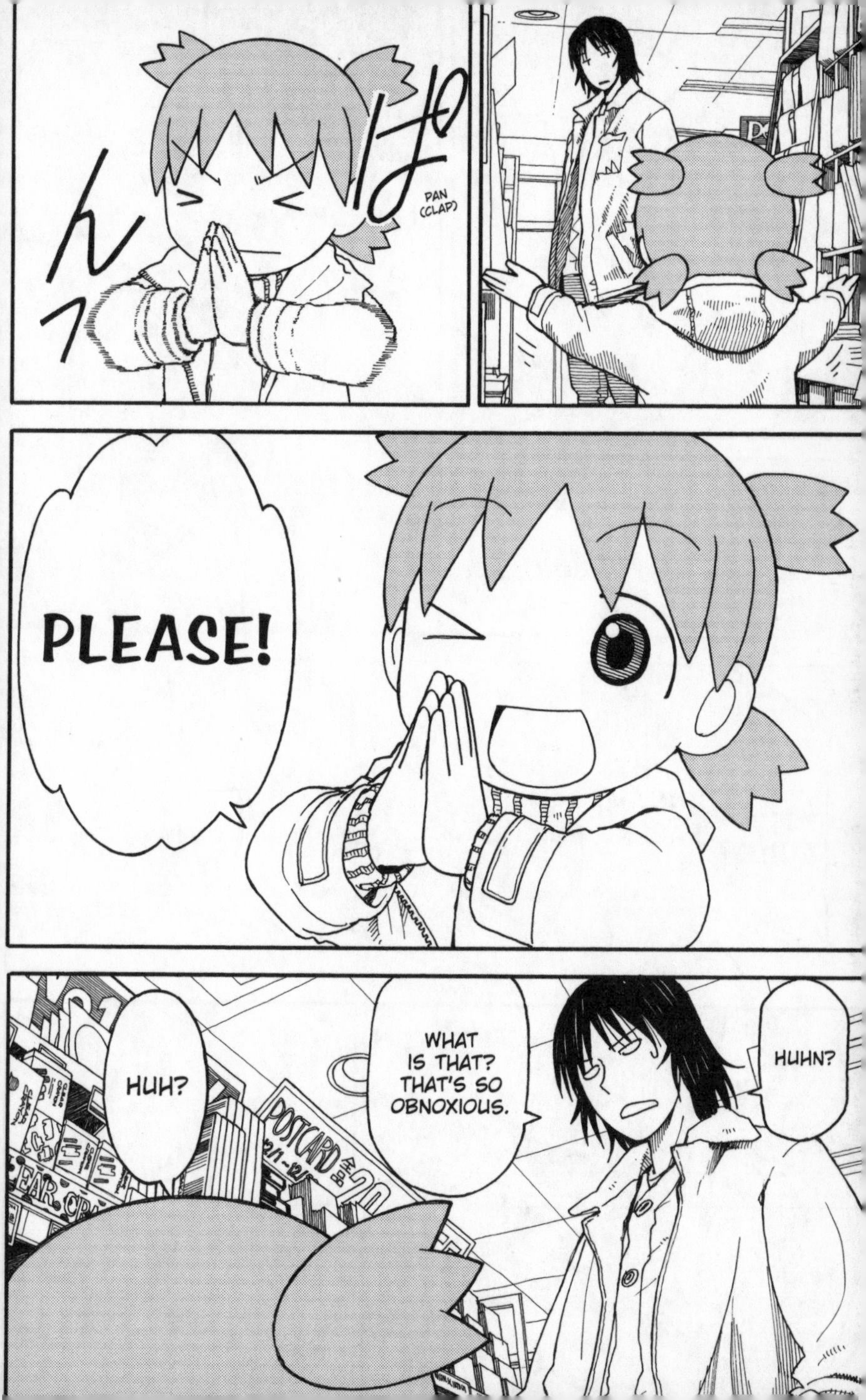
PAN (CLAP)
PLEASE!
HUHN?
WHAT IS THAT? THAT'S SO OBNOXIOUS.
HUH?
POSTCARD

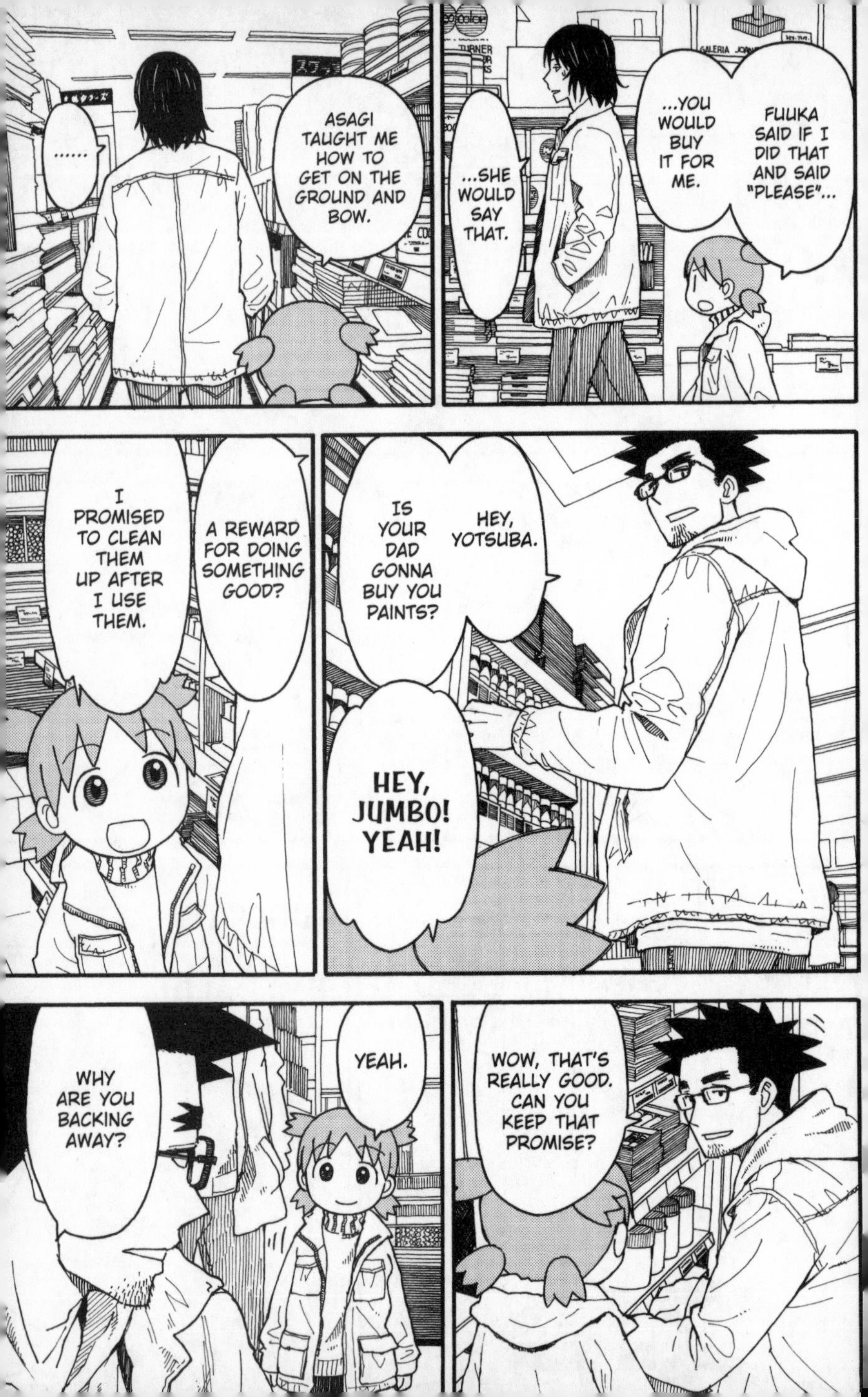
FUUKA SAID IF I DID THAT AND SAID "PLEASE"...
...YOU WOULD BUY IT FOR ME.
...SHE WOULD SAY THAT.
ASAGI TAUGHT ME HOW TO GET ON THE GROUND AND BOW.
......
HEY, YOTSUBA.
IS YOUR DAD GONNA BUY YOU PAINTS?
HEY, JUMBO! YEAH!
A REWARD FOR DOING SOMETHING GOOD?
I PROMISED TO CLEAN THEM UP AFTER I USE THEM.
WOW, THAT'S REALLY GOOD. CAN YOU KEEP THAT PROMISE?
YEAH.
WHY ARE YOU BACKING AWAY?

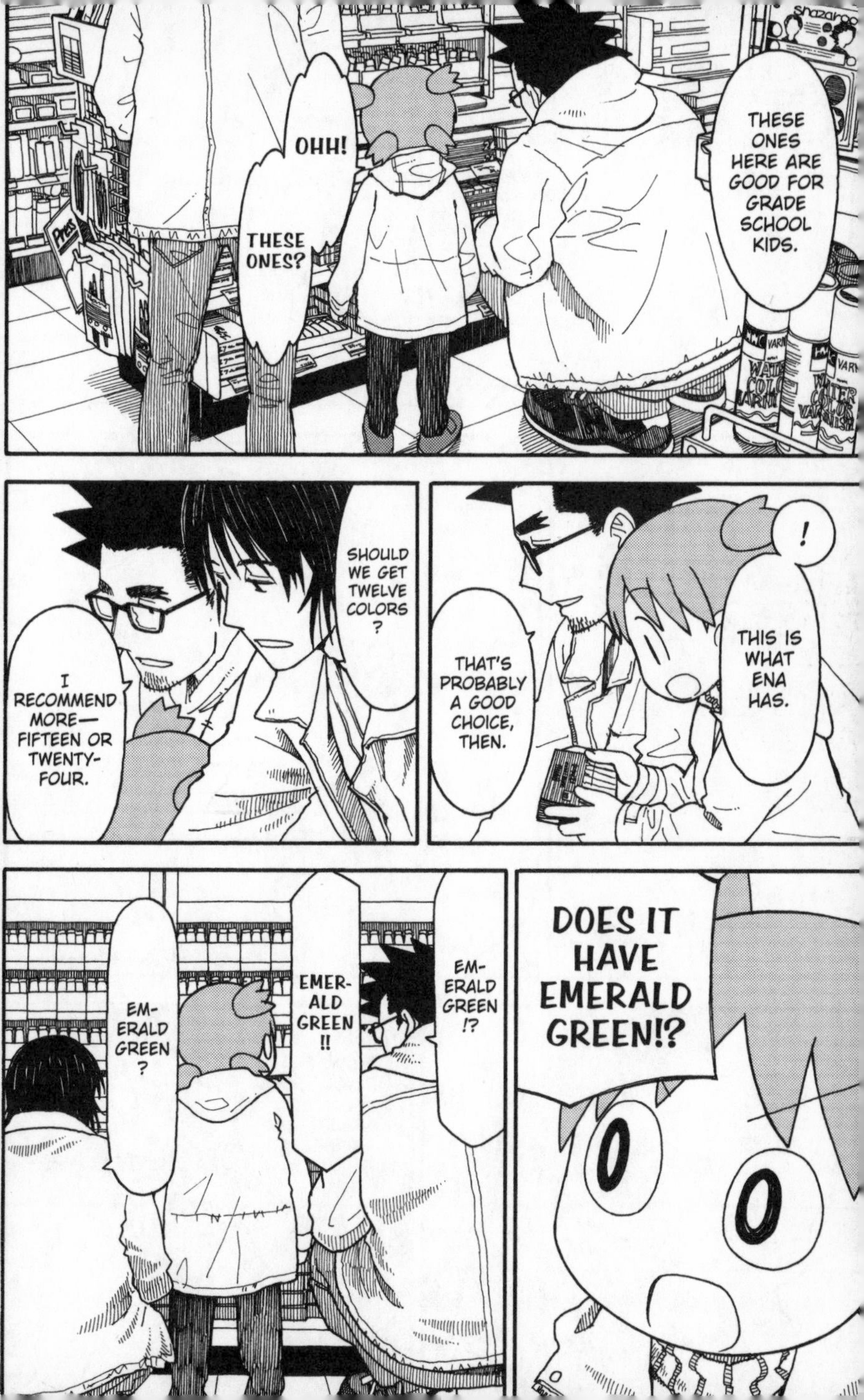
THESE ONES HERE ARE GOOD FOR GRADE SCHOOL KIDS.
OHH!
THESE ONES?
!
THIS IS WHAT ENA HAS.
THAT'S PROBABLY A GOOD CHOICE, THEN.
SHOULD WE GET TWELVE COLORS?
I RECOMMEND MORE—FIFTEEN OR TWENTY-FOUR.
DOES IT HAVE EMERALD GREEN!?
EMERALD GREEN!?
EMERALD GREEN!!
EMERALD GREEN?

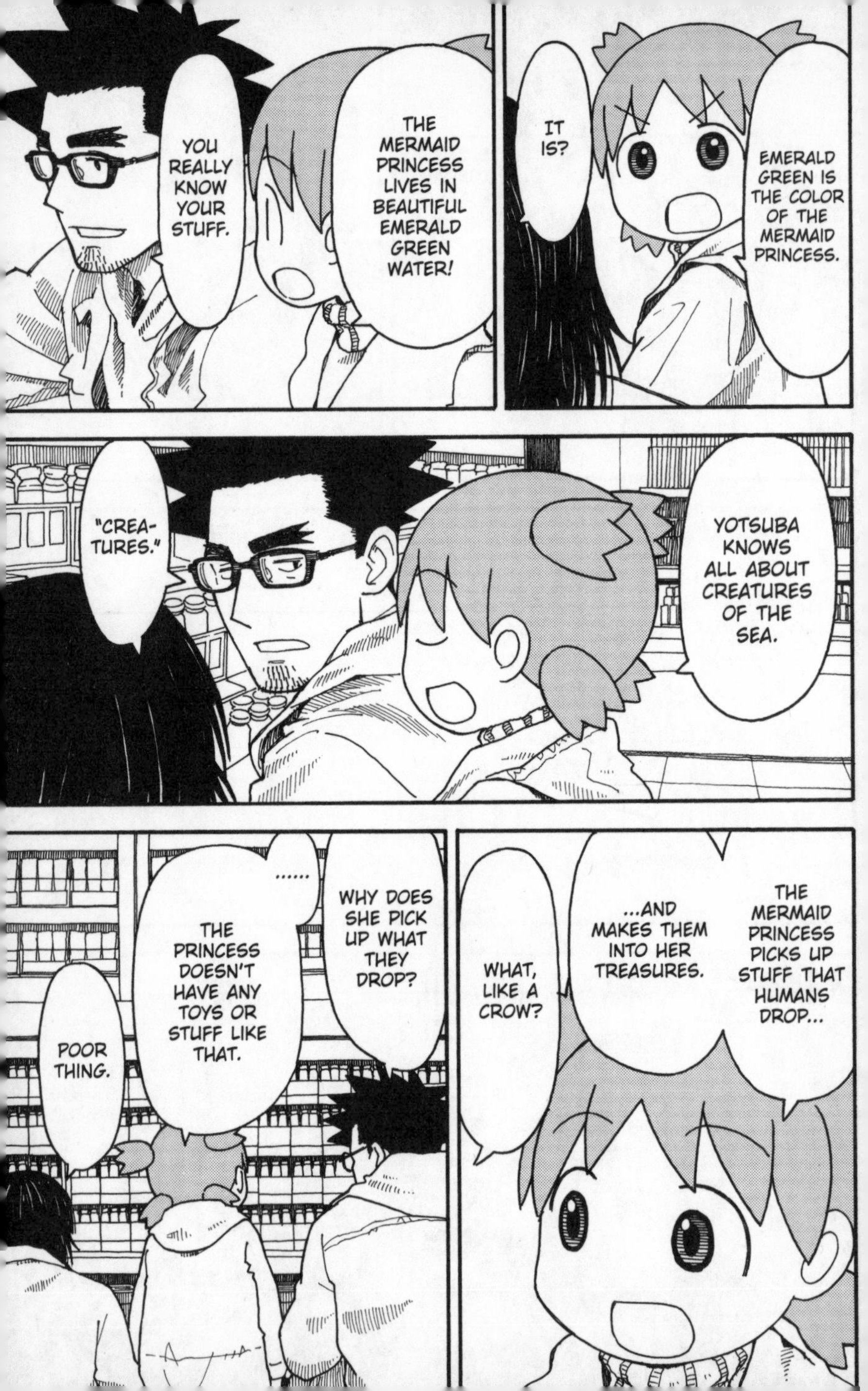
EMERALD GREEN IS THE COLOR OF THE MERMAID PRINCESS.
IT IS?
THE MERMAID PRINCESS LIVES IN BEAUTIFUL EMERALD GREEN WATER!
YOU REALLY KNOW YOUR STUFF.
YOTSUBA KNOWS ALL ABOUT CREATURES OF THE SEA.
"CREA-TURES."
THE MERMAID PRINCESS PICKS UP STUFF THAT HUMANS DROP...
...AND MAKES THEM INTO HER TREASURES.
WHAT, LIKE A CROW?
WHY DOES SHE PICK UP WHAT THEY DROP?
......
THE PRINCESS DOESN'T HAVE ANY TOYS OR STUFF LIKE THAT.
POOR THING.

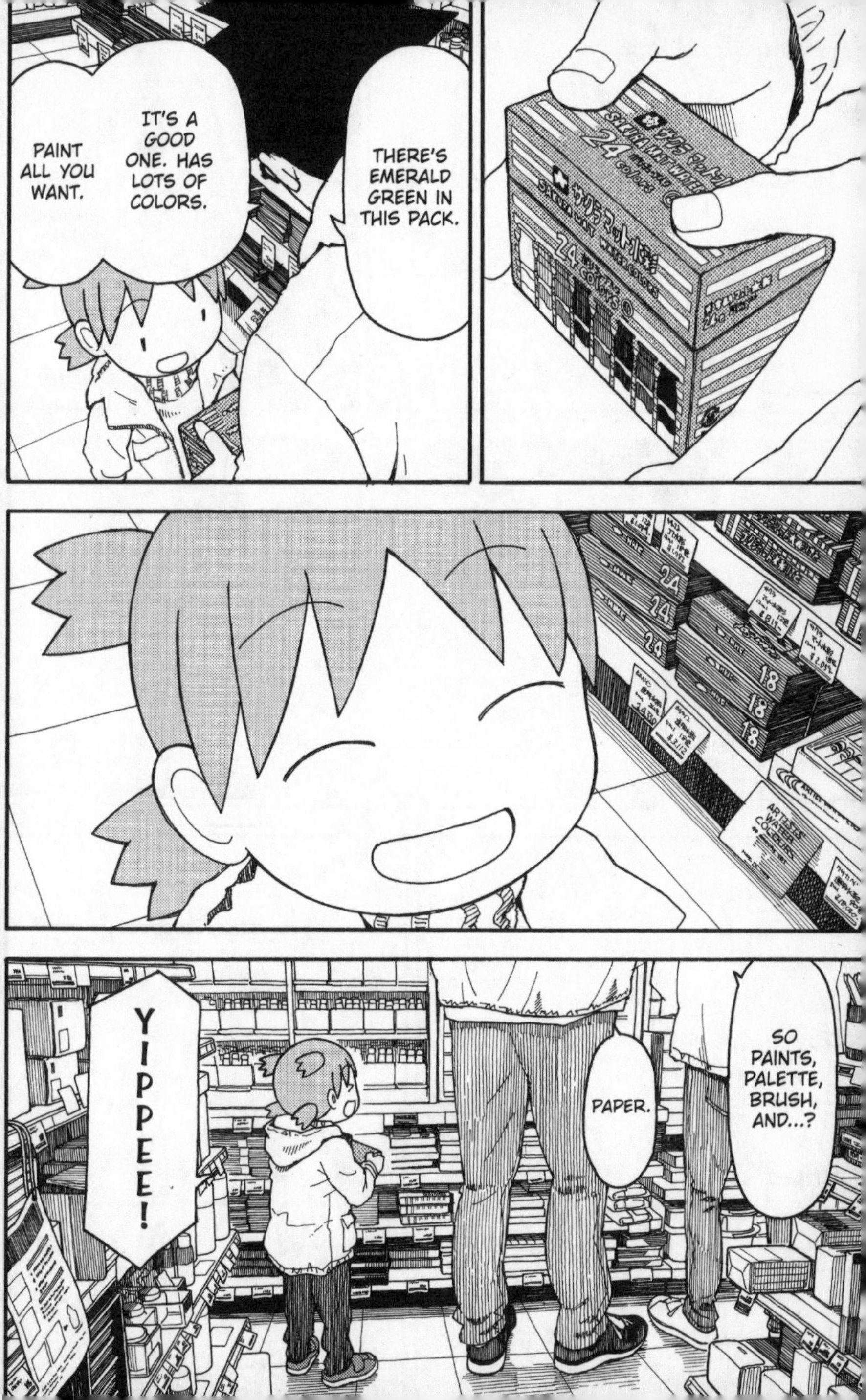
THERE'S EMERALD GREEN IN THIS PACK.
IT'S A GOOD ONE. HAS LOTS OF COLORS.
PAINT ALL YOU WANT.
SO PAINTS, PALETTE, BRUSH, AND...?
PAPER.
YIPPEEE!

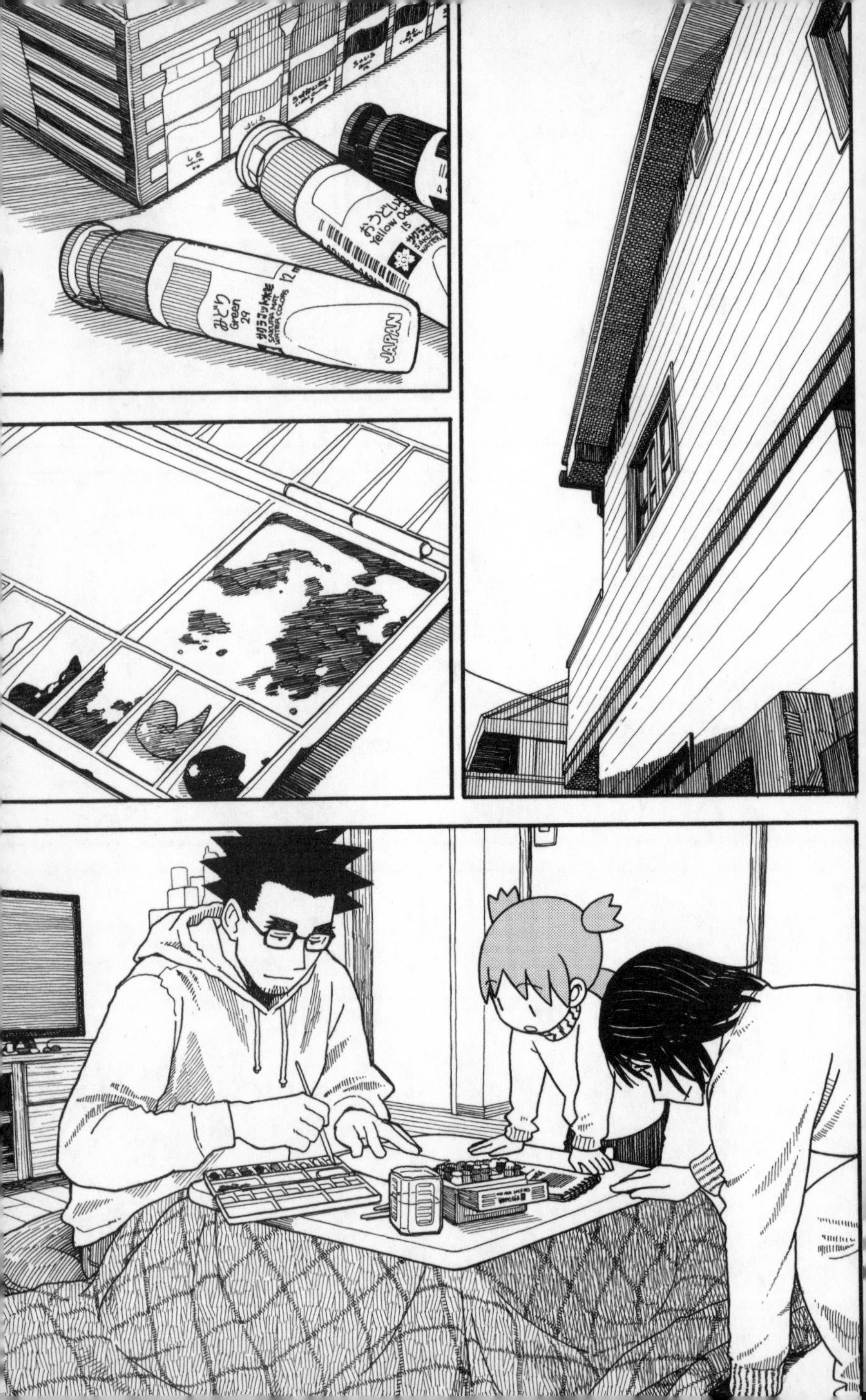

みどり
Green 29
SAKURA MAT WATER COLORS
JAPAN
15

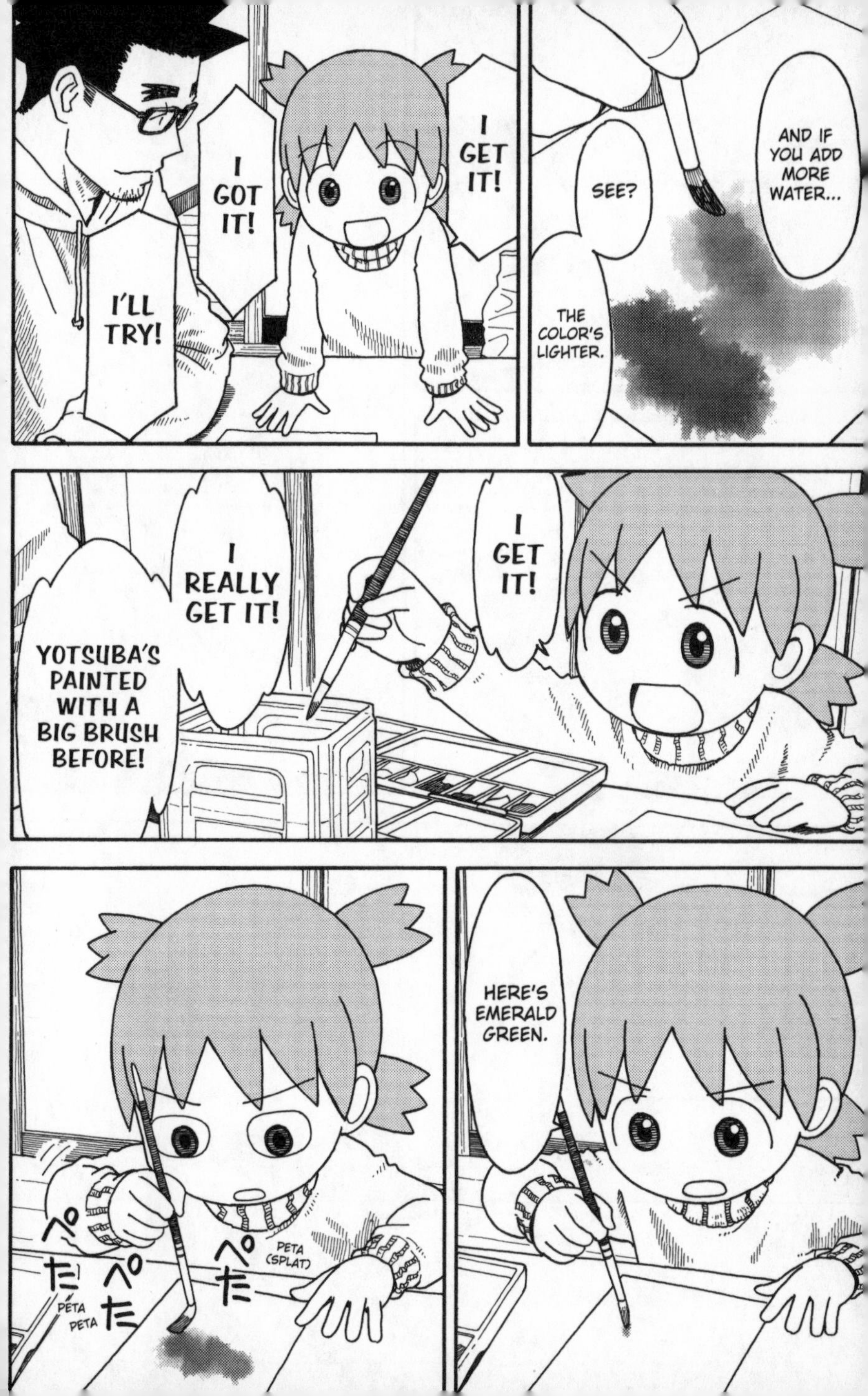
AND IF YOU ADD MORE WATER...
SEE?
THE COLOR'S LIGHTER.
I GET IT!
I GOT IT!
I'LL TRY!
I GET IT!
I REALLY GET IT!
YOTSUBA'S PAINTED WITH A BIG BRUSH BEFORE!
HERE'S EMERALD GREEN.
ぺた
PETA (SPLAT)
ぺた
ぺた
PETA PETA

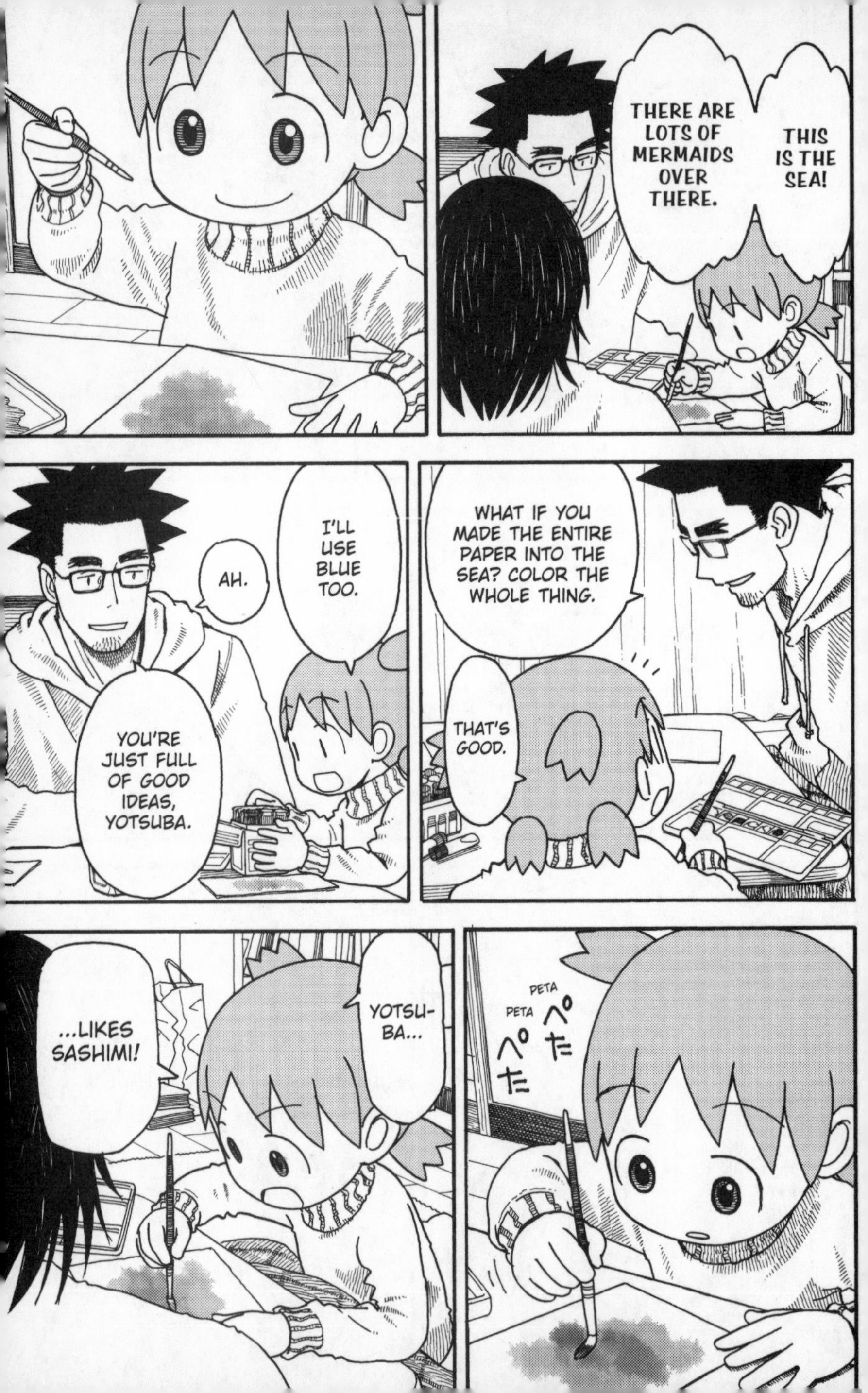
THIS IS THE SEA!
THERE ARE LOTS OF MERMAIDS OVER THERE.
WHAT IF YOU MADE THE ENTIRE PAPER INTO THE SEA? COLOR THE WHOLE THING.
THAT'S GOOD.
I'LL USE BLUE TOO.
AH.
YOU'RE JUST FULL OF GOOD IDEAS, YOTSUBA.
PETA
ぺた
PETA
ぺた
YOTSU-BA...
...LIKES SASHIMI!

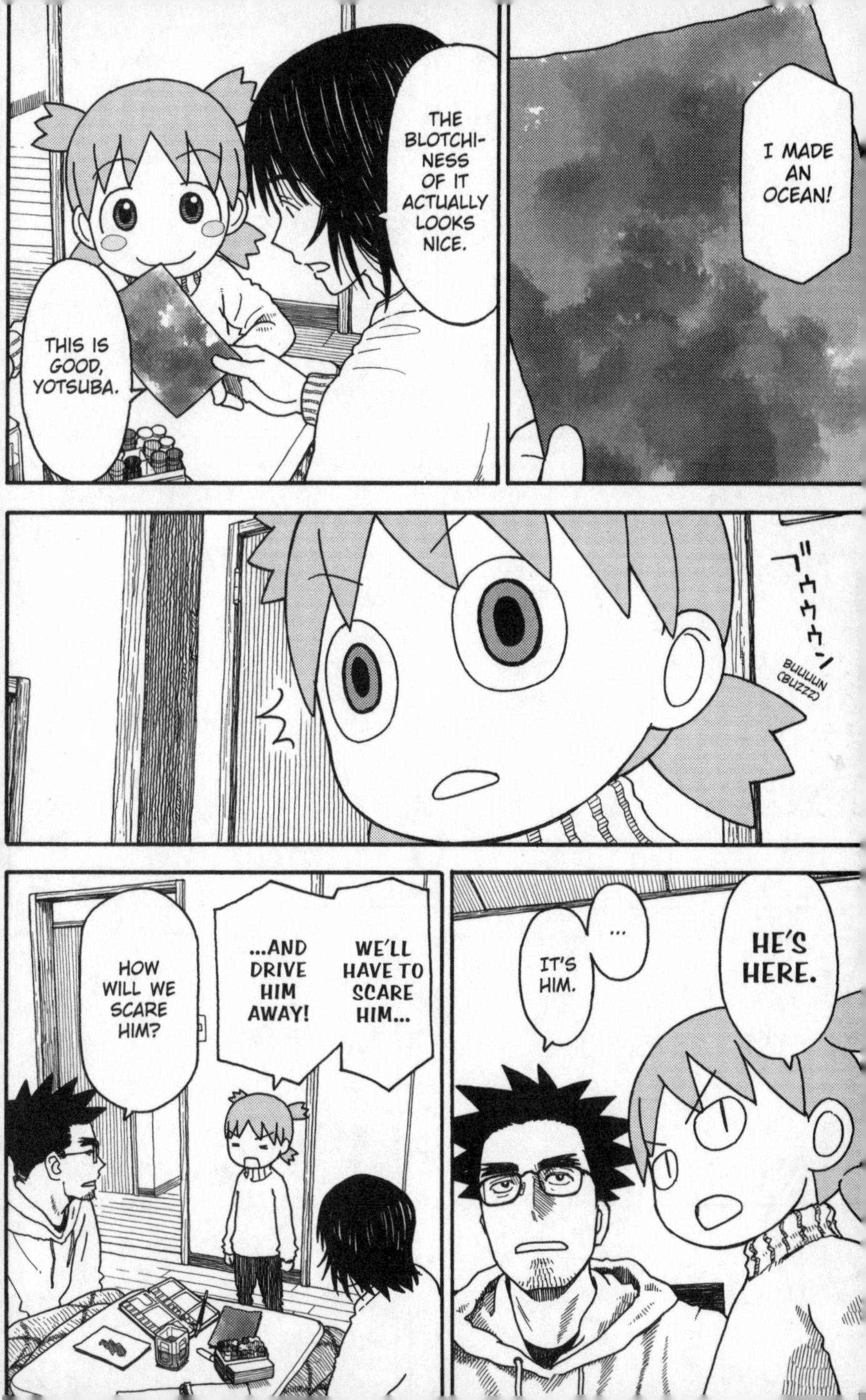
I MADE AN OCEAN!
THE BLOTCHINESS OF IT ACTUALLY LOOKS NICE.
THIS IS GOOD, YOTSUBA.
ブウウウン
BUUUUN (BUZZZ)
HE'S HERE.
...
IT'S HIM.
WE'LL HAVE TO SCARE HIM...
...AND DRIVE HIM AWAY!
HOW WILL WE SCARE HIM?

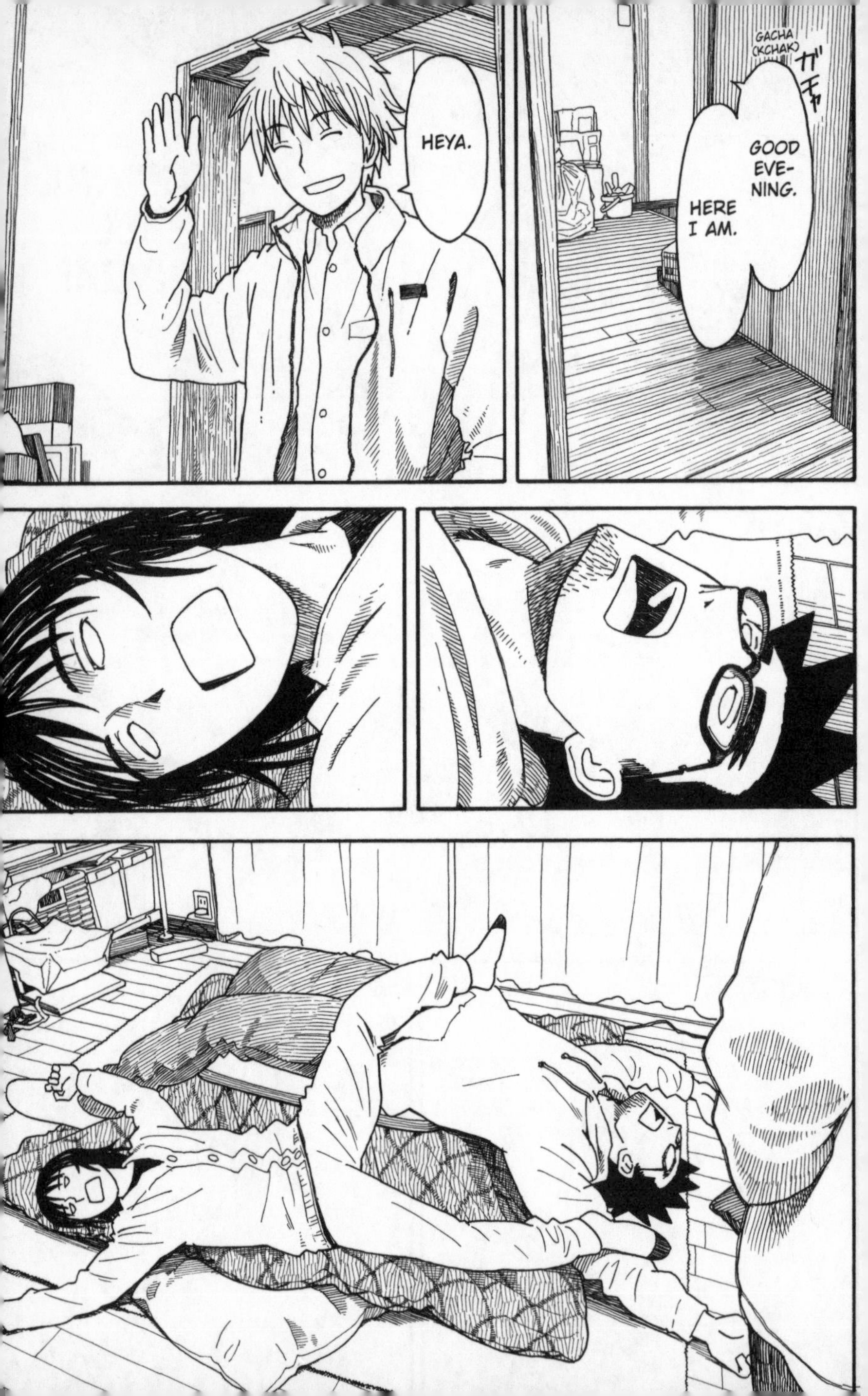
GACHA (KCHAK)
ガチャ
GOOD EVE-NING. HERE I AM.
HEYA.

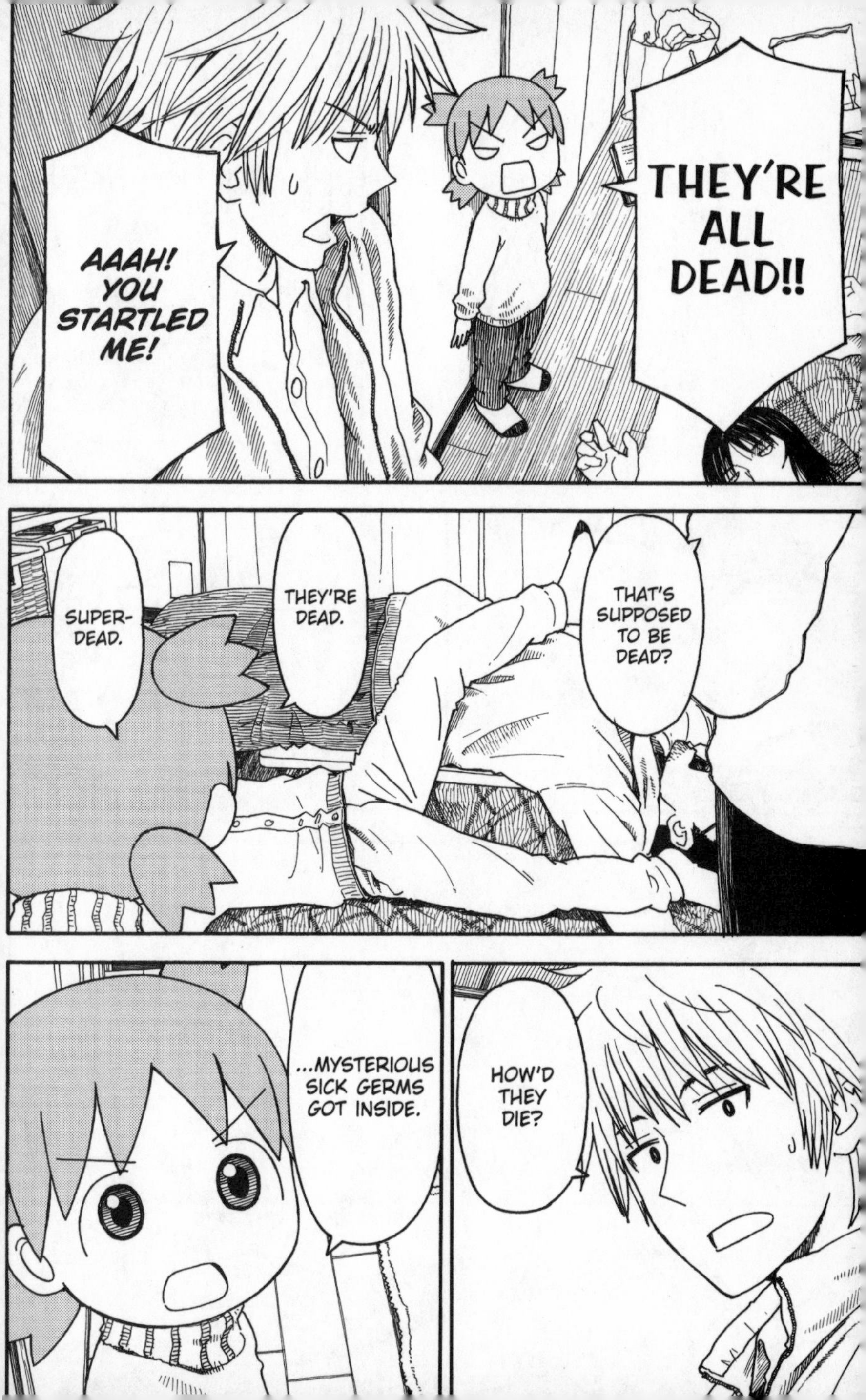
THEY'RE ALL DEAD!!
AAAH! YOU STARTLED ME!
THAT'S SUPPOSED TO BE DEAD?
THEY'RE DEAD.
SUPER-DEAD.
HOW'D THEY DIE?
...MYSTERIOUS SICK GERMS GOT INSIDE.

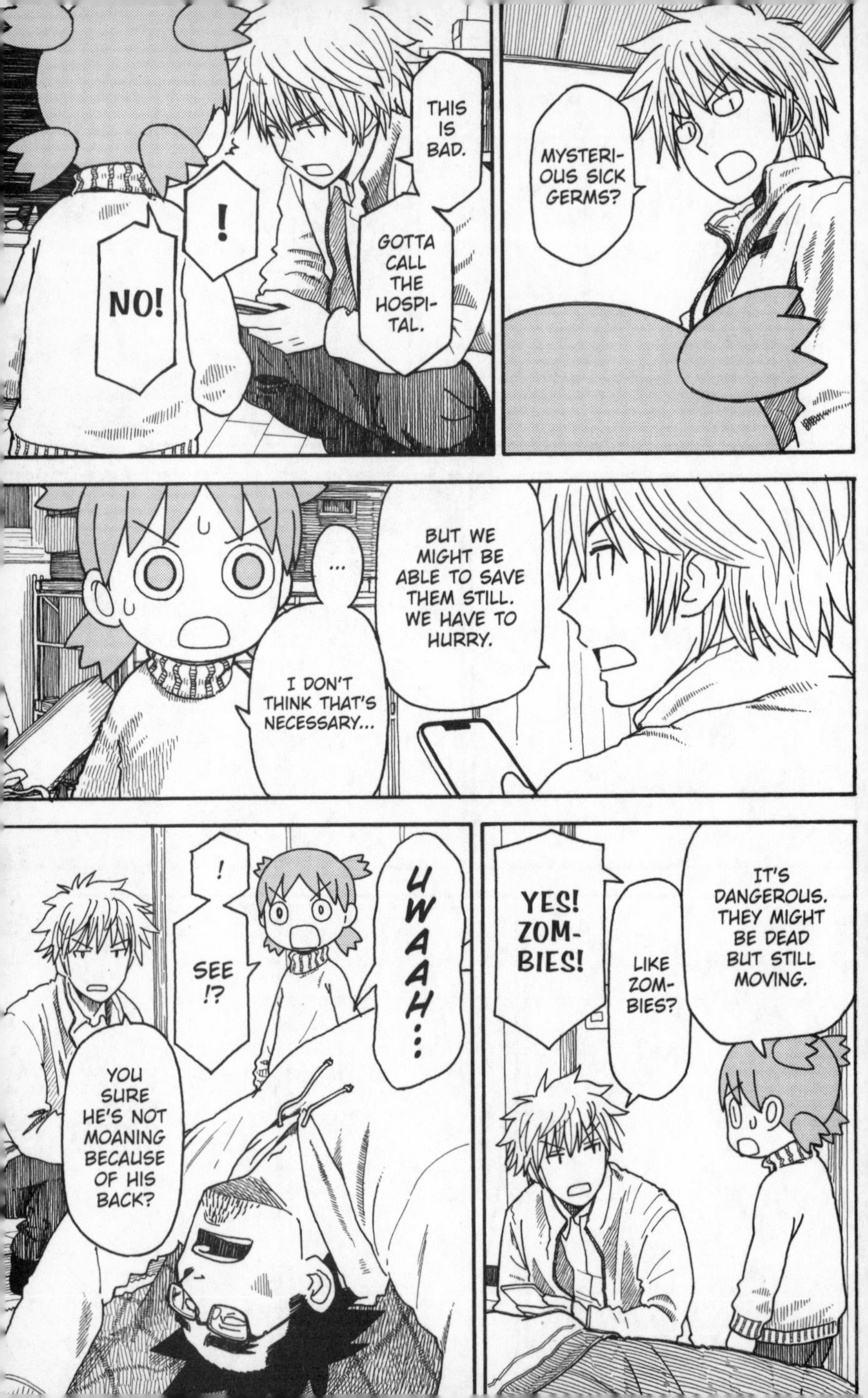
MYSTERIOUS SICK GERMS?
THIS IS BAD.
GOTTA CALL THE HOSPITAL.
!
NO!
BUT WE MIGHT BE ABLE TO SAVE THEM STILL. WE HAVE TO HURRY.
...
I DON'T THINK THAT'S NECESSARY...
IT'S DANGEROUS. THEY MIGHT BE DEAD BUT STILL MOVING.
LIKE ZOMBIES?
YES! ZOMBIES!
UWAAAH...
!
SEE!?
YOU SURE HE'S NOT MOANING BECAUSE OF HIS BACK?

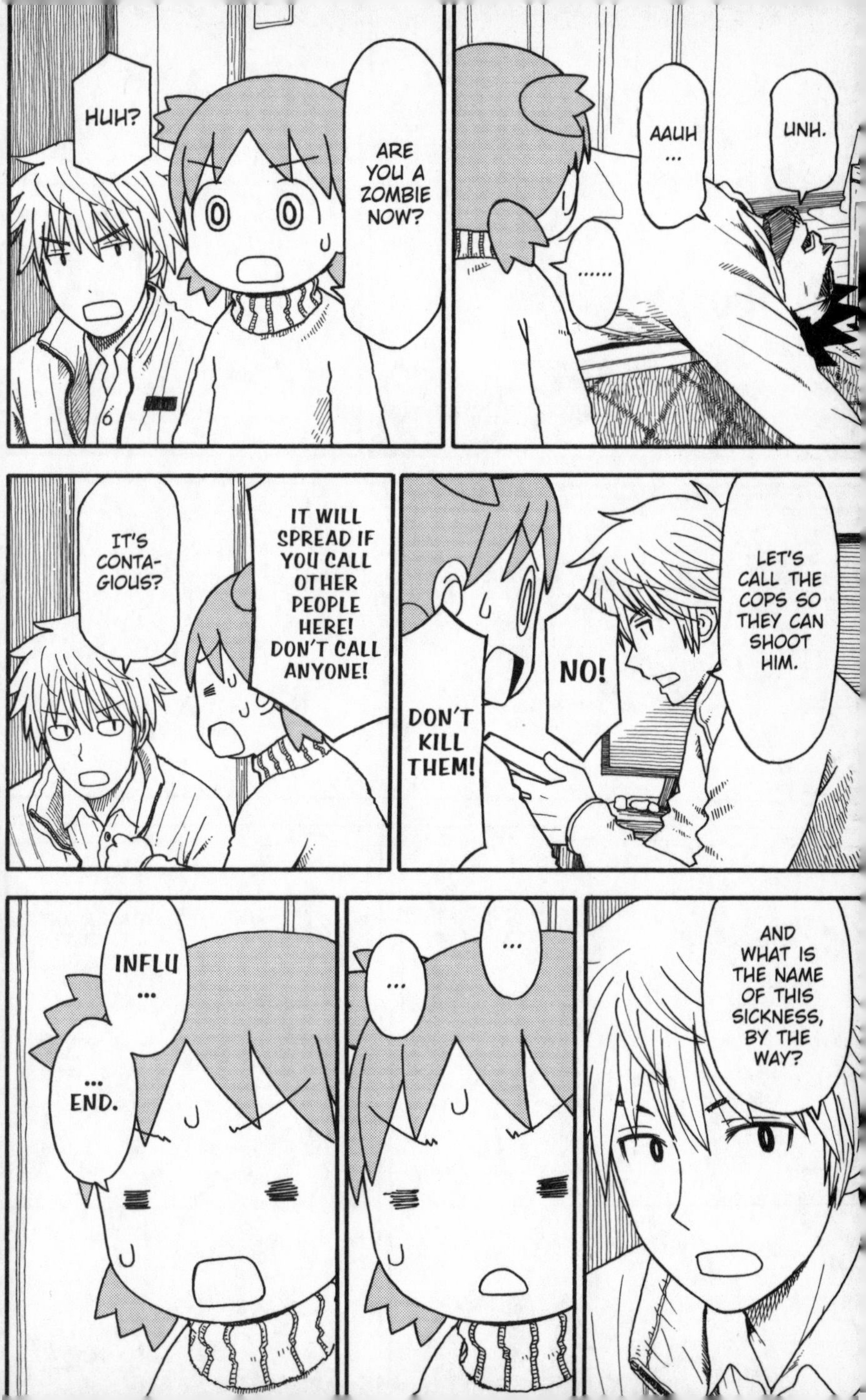
UNH.
AAUH ...
......
ARE YOU A ZOMBIE NOW?
HUH?
LET'S CALL THE COPS SO THEY CAN SHOOT HIM.
NO!
DON'T KILL THEM!
IT WILL SPREAD IF YOU CALL OTHER PEOPLE HERE! DON'T CALL ANYONE!
IT'S CONTA-GIOUS?
AND WHAT IS THE NAME OF THIS SICKNESS, BY THE WAY?
...
...
INFLU ...
... END.

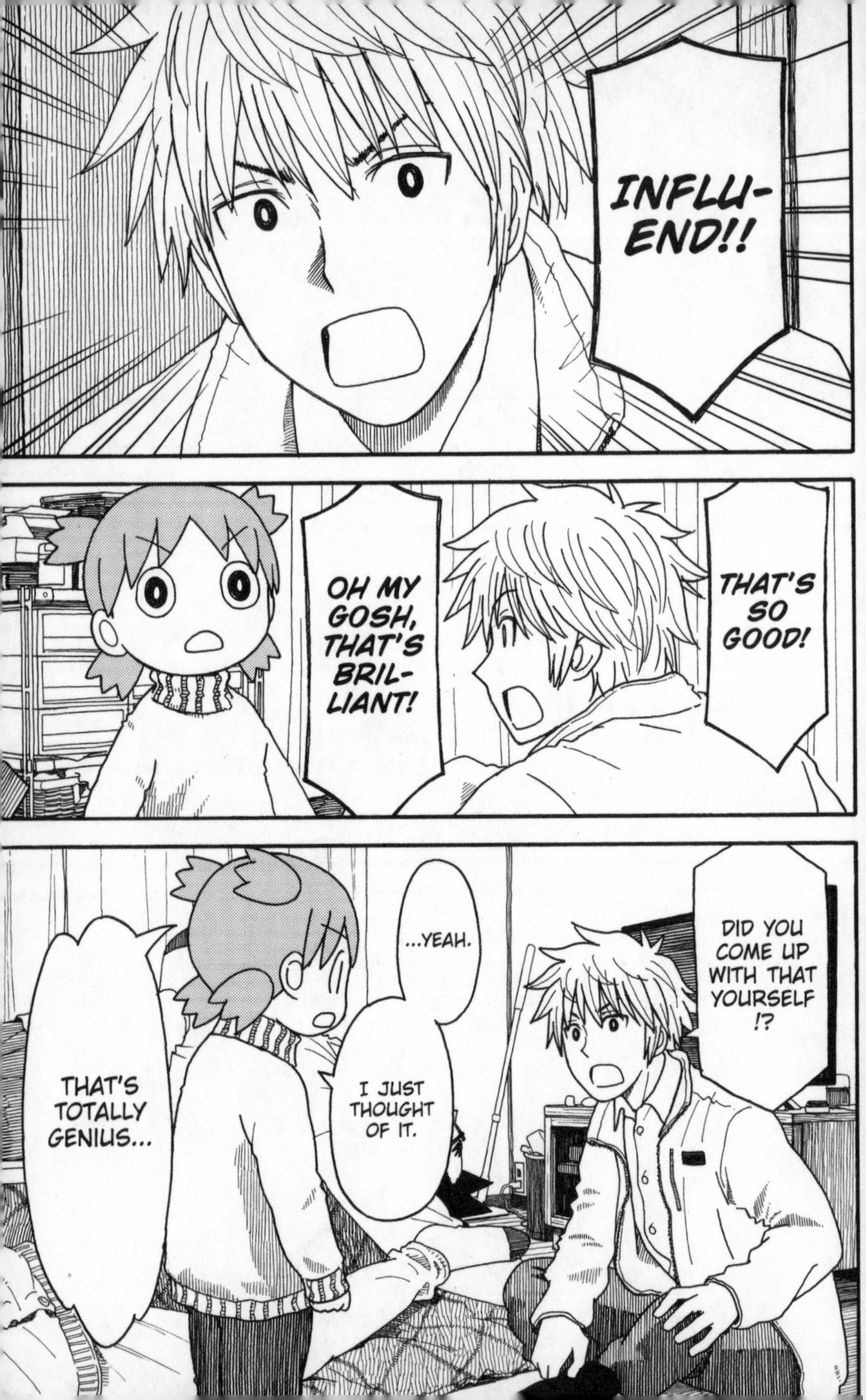
INFLU-END!!
THAT'S SO GOOD!
OH MY GOSH, THAT'S BRIL-LIANT!
DID YOU COME UP WITH THAT YOURSELF !?
...YEAH.
I JUST THOUGHT OF IT.
THAT'S TOTALLY GENIUS...

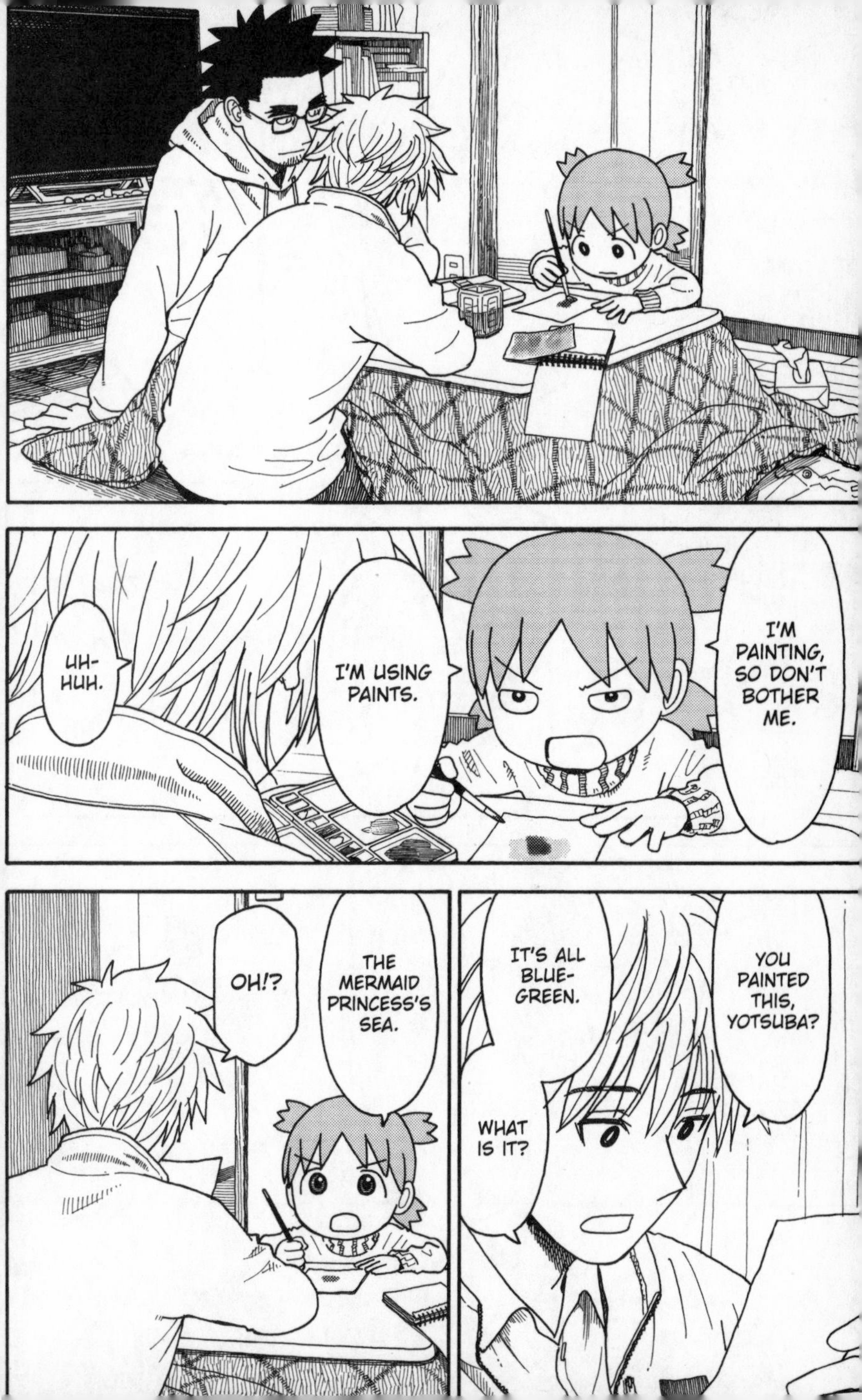
I'M PAINTING, SO DON'T BOTHER ME.
I'M USING PAINTS.
UH-HUH.
YOU PAINTED THIS, YOTSUBA?
IT'S ALL BLUE-GREEN.
WHAT IS IT?
THE MERMAID PRINCESS'S SEA.
OH!?

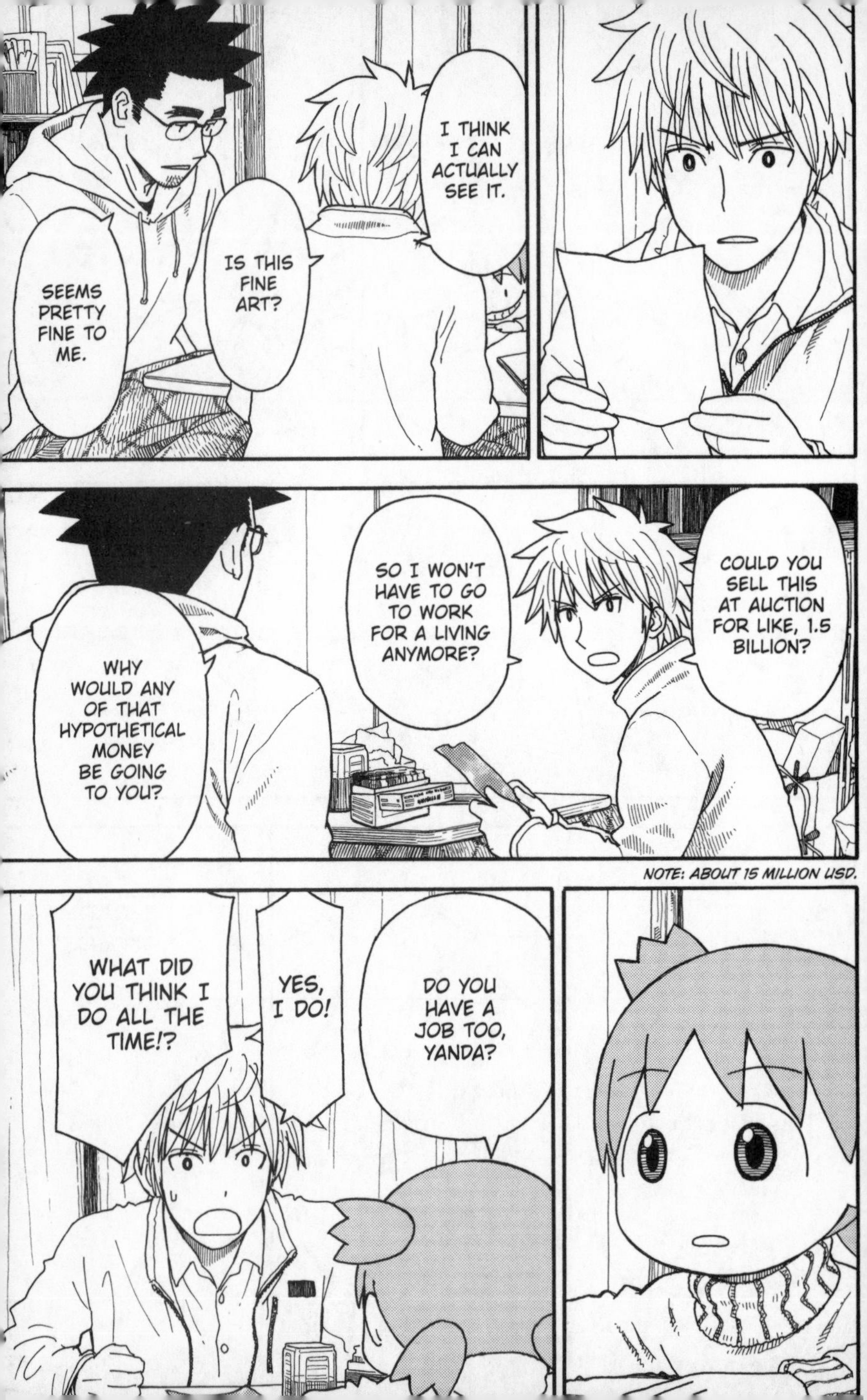
I THINK I CAN ACTUALLY SEE IT.
IS THIS FINE ART?
SEEMS PRETTY FINE TO ME.
COULD YOU SELL THIS AT AUCTION FOR LIKE, 1.5 BILLION?
SO I WON'T HAVE TO GO TO WORK FOR A LIVING ANYMORE?
WHY WOULD ANY OF THAT HYPOTHETICAL MONEY BE GOING TO YOU?
DO YOU HAVE A JOB TOO, YANDA?
YES, I DO!
WHAT DID YOU THINK I DO ALL THE TIME!?

NOTE: ABOUT 15 MILLION USD.

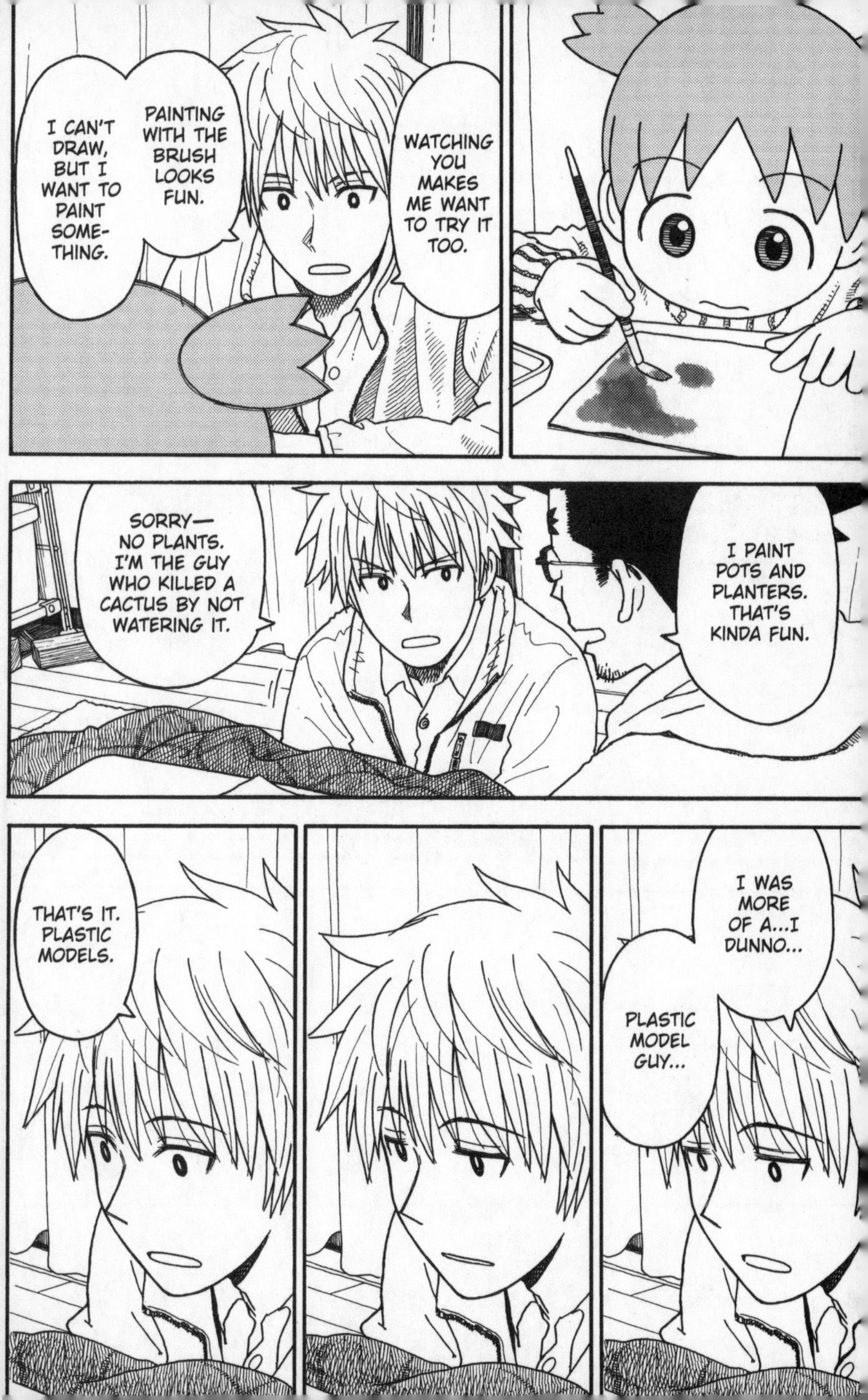
WATCHING YOU MAKES ME WANT TO TRY IT TOO.
PAINTING WITH THE BRUSH LOOKS FUN.
I CAN'T DRAW, BUT I WANT TO PAINT SOME-THING.
I PAINT POTS AND PLANTERS. THAT'S KINDA FUN.
SORRY— NO PLANTS. I'M THE GUY WHO KILLED A CACTUS BY NOT WATERING IT.
I WAS MORE OF A...I DUNNO...
PLASTIC MODEL GUY...
THAT'S IT. PLASTIC MODELS.

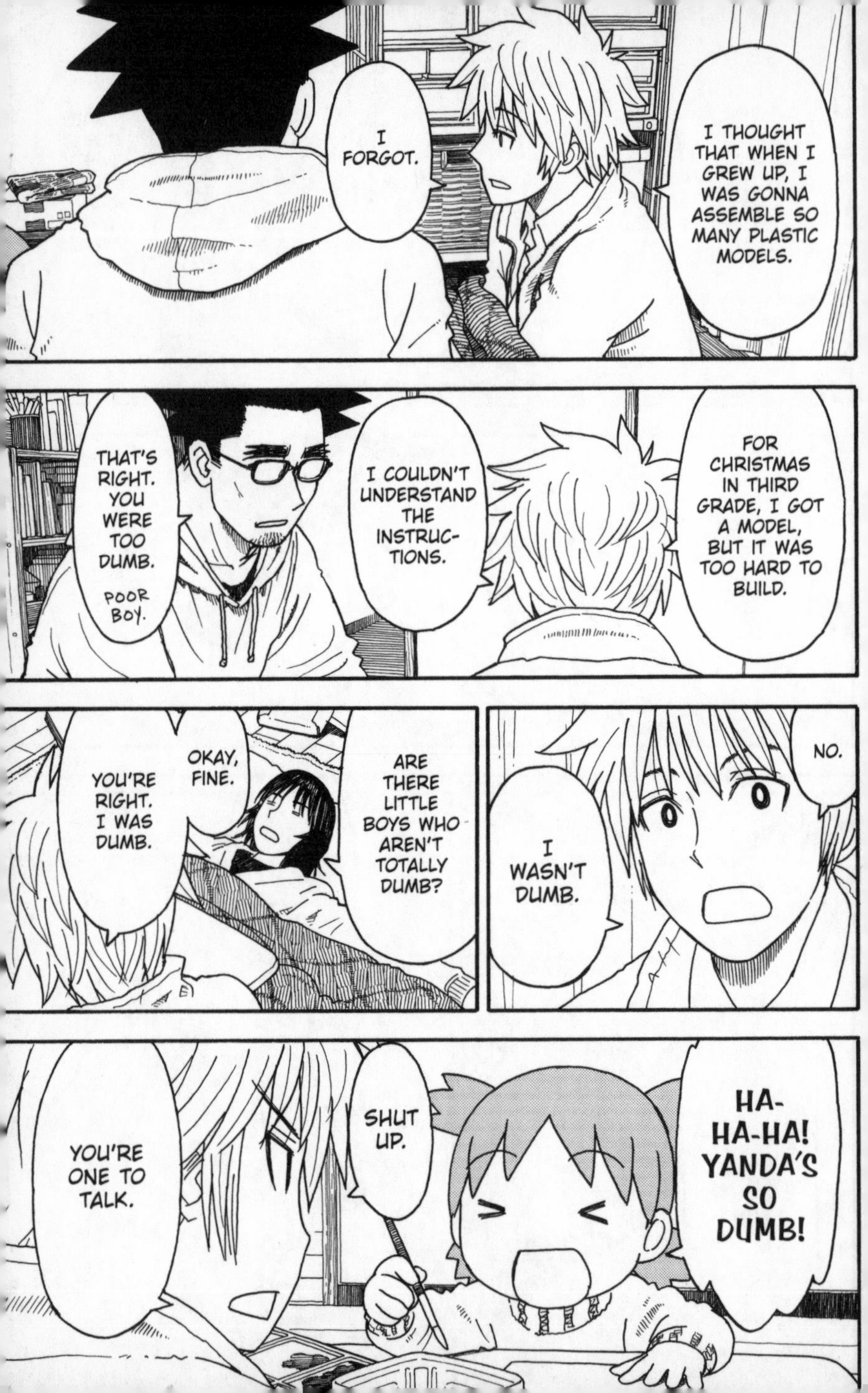
I THOUGHT THAT WHEN I GREW UP, I WAS GONNA ASSEMBLE SO MANY PLASTIC MODELS.
I FORGOT.
FOR CHRISTMAS IN THIRD GRADE, I GOT A MODEL, BUT IT WAS TOO HARD TO BUILD.
I COULDN'T UNDERSTAND THE INSTRUCTIONS.
THAT'S RIGHT. YOU WERE TOO DUMB.
POOR BOY.
NO.
I WASN'T DUMB.
ARE THERE LITTLE BOYS WHO AREN'T TOTALLY DUMB?
OKAY, FINE.
YOU'RE RIGHT. I WAS DUMB.
HA-HA-HA! YANDA'S SO DUMB!
SHUT UP.
YOU'RE ONE TO TALK.

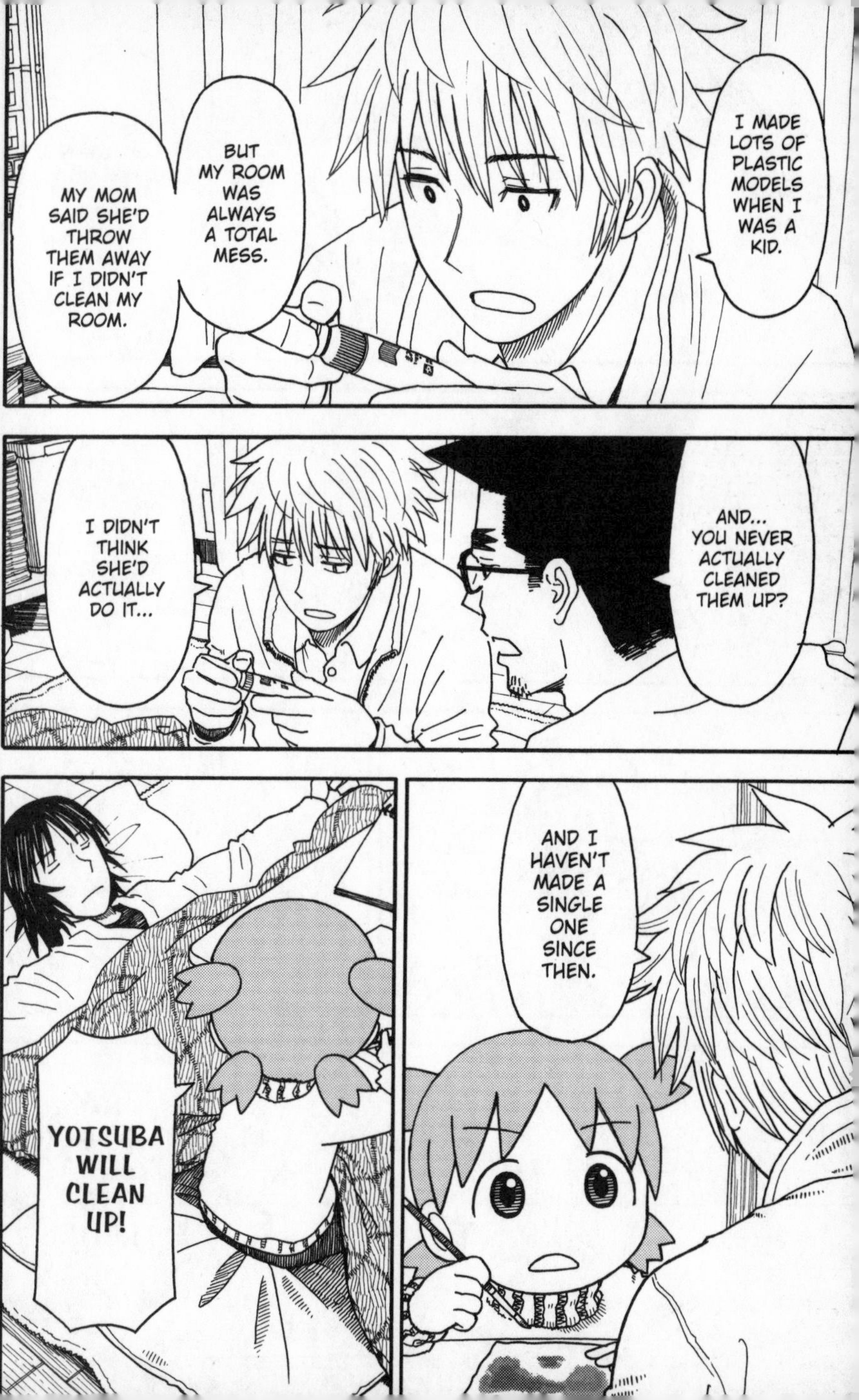
I MADE LOTS OF PLASTIC MODELS WHEN I WAS A KID.
BUT MY ROOM WAS ALWAYS A TOTAL MESS.
MY MOM SAID SHE'D THROW THEM AWAY IF I DIDN'T CLEAN MY ROOM.
AND... YOU NEVER ACTUALLY CLEANED THEM UP?
I DIDN'T THINK SHE'D ACTUALLY DO IT...
AND I HAVEN'T MADE A SINGLE ONE SINCE THEN.
YOTSUBA WILL CLEAN UP!

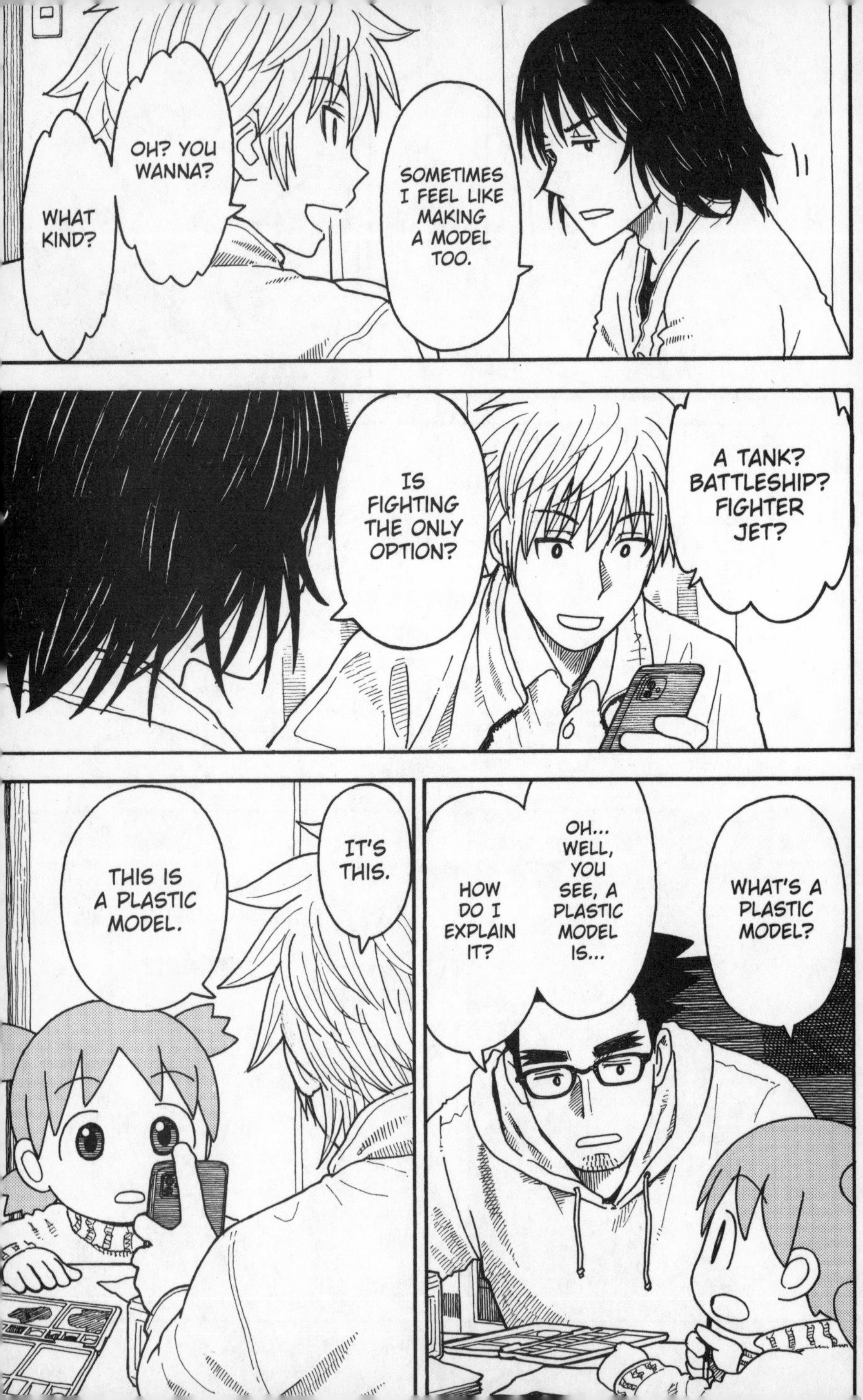
SOMETIMES I FEEL LIKE MAKING A MODEL TOO.
OH? YOU WANNA?
WHAT KIND?
A TANK? BATTLESHIP? FIGHTER JET?
IS FIGHTING THE ONLY OPTION?
WHAT'S A PLASTIC MODEL?
OH... WELL, YOU SEE, A PLASTIC MODEL IS...
HOW DO I EXPLAIN IT?
IT'S THIS.
THIS IS A PLASTIC MODEL.

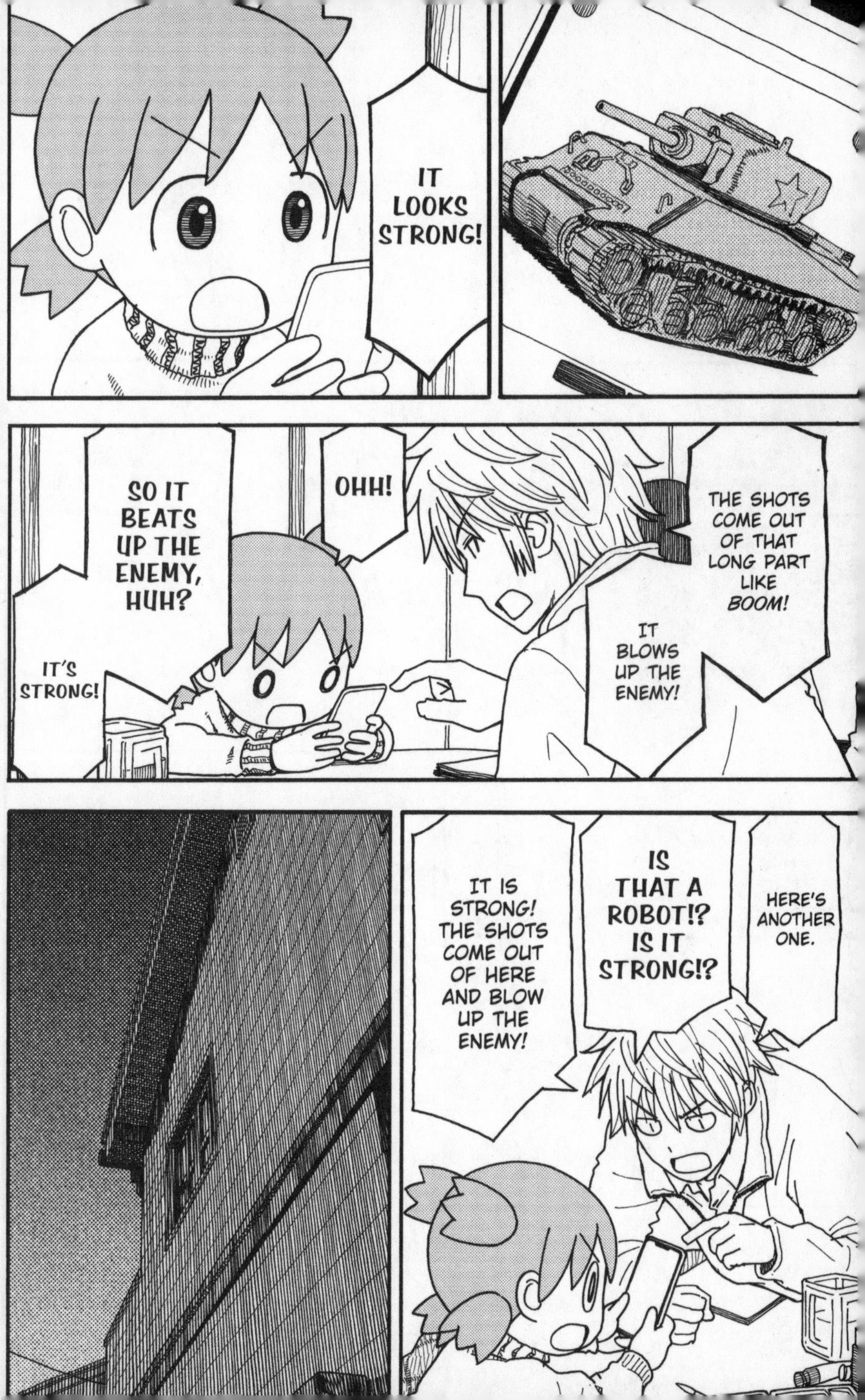
IT LOOKS STRONG!
THE SHOTS COME OUT OF THAT LONG PART LIKE *BOOM!*
IT BLOWS UP THE ENEMY!
OHH!
SO IT BEATS UP THE ENEMY, HUH?
IT'S STRONG!
HERE'S ANOTHER ONE.
IS THAT A ROBOT!? IS IT STRONG!?
IT IS STRONG! THE SHOTS COME OUT OF HERE AND BLOW UP THE ENEMY!

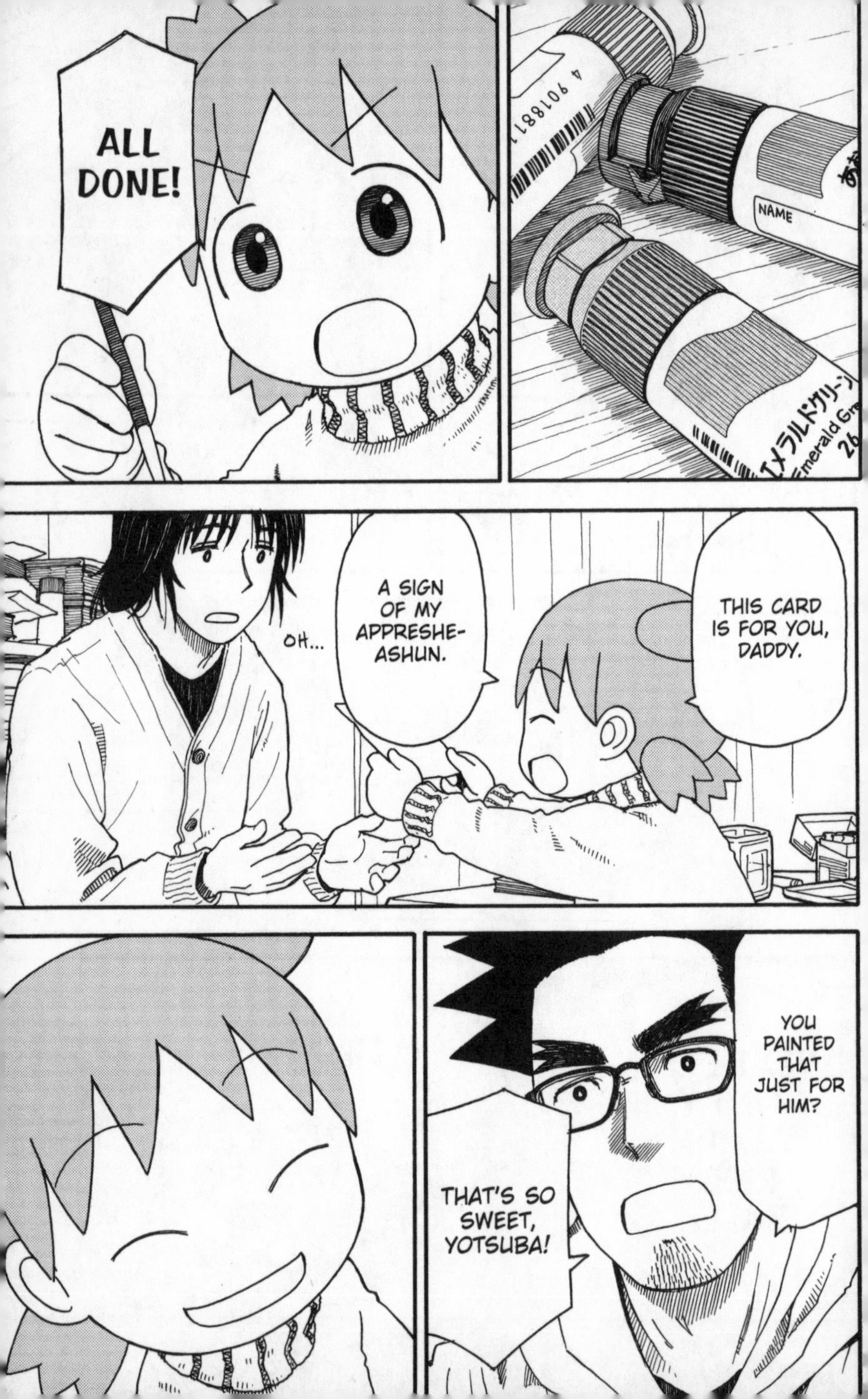
NAME
エメラルドグリーン
ALL DONE!
THIS CARD IS FOR YOU, DADDY.
A SIGN OF MY APPRESHE-ASHUN.
OH...
YOU PAINTED THAT JUST FOR HIM?
THAT'S SO SWEET, YOTSUBA!

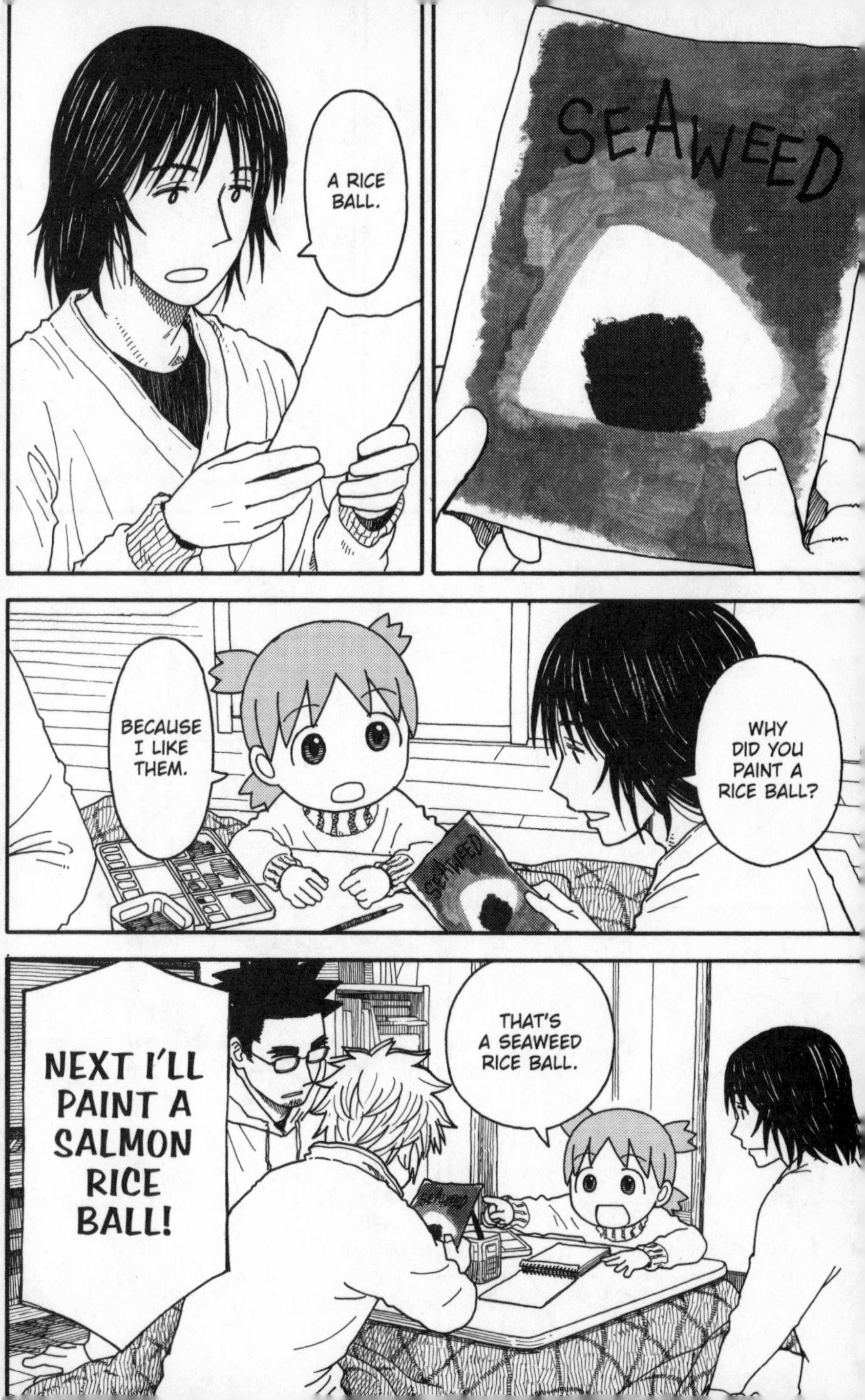
SEAWEED
A RICE BALL.
WHY DID YOU PAINT A RICE BALL?
BECAUSE I LIKE THEM.
THAT'S A SEAWEED RICE BALL.
NEXT I'LL PAINT A SALMON RICE BALL!

YOTSUBA&!

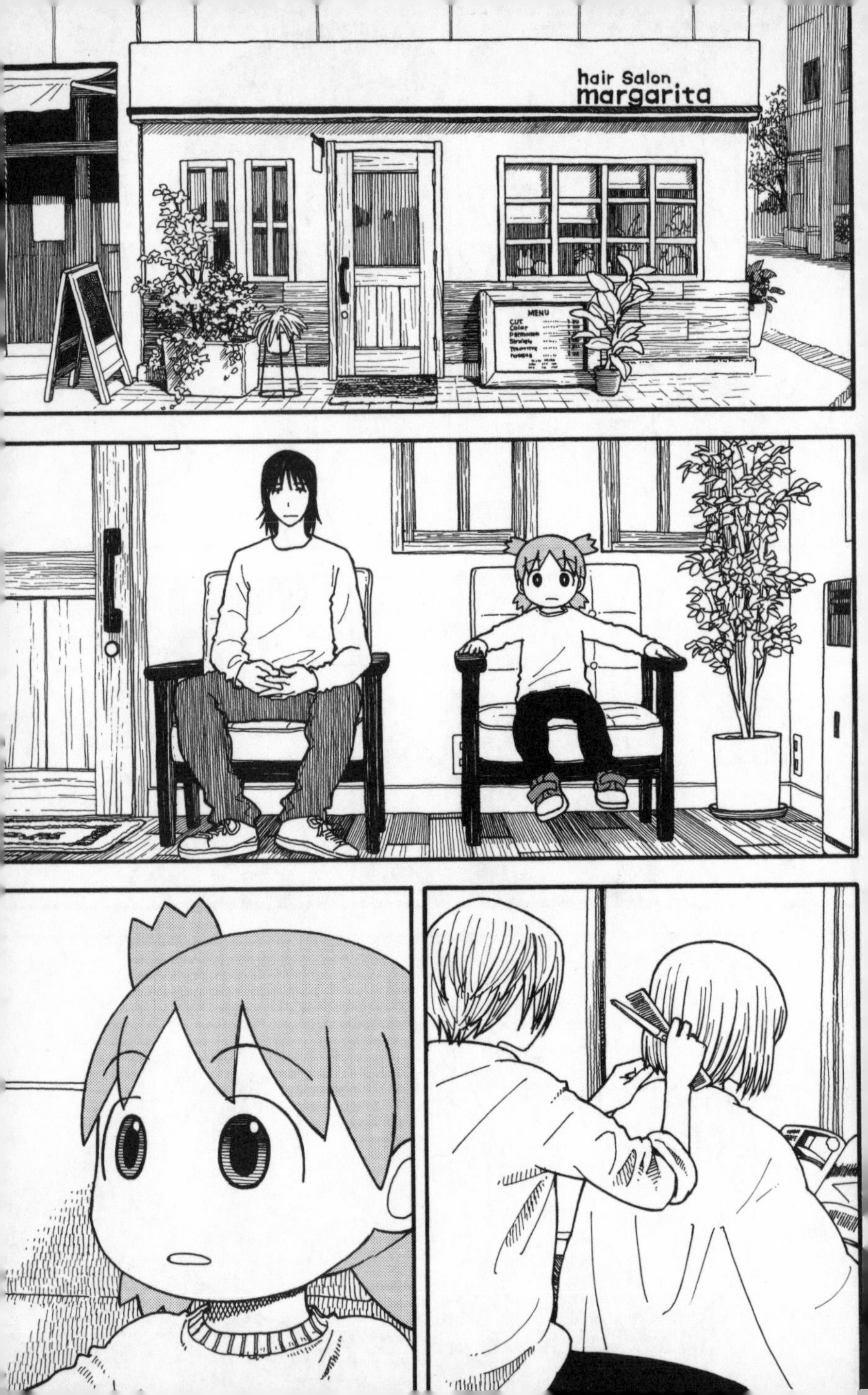
hair Salon
margarita
MENU
CUT
Color

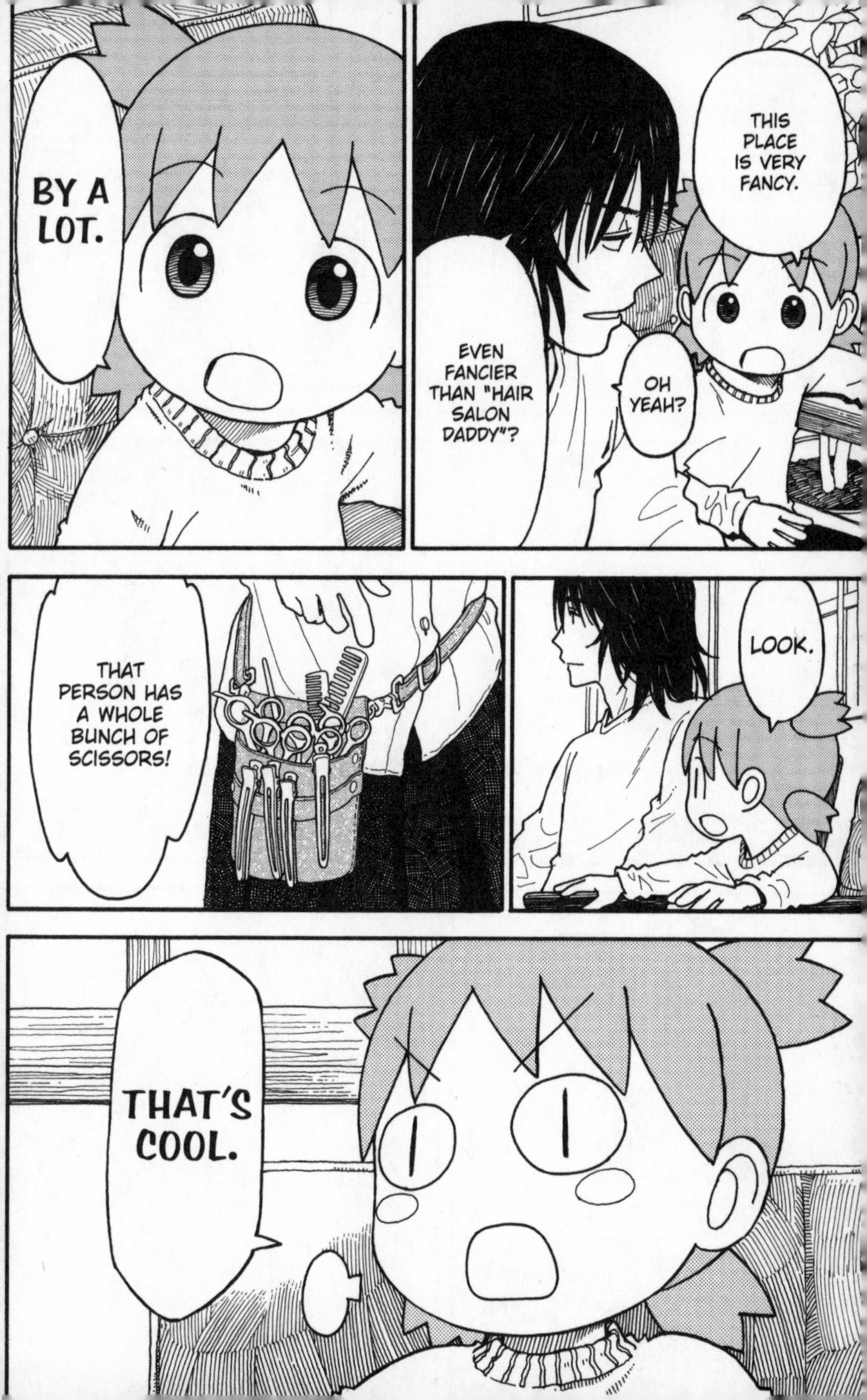
THIS PLACE IS VERY FANCY.
OH YEAH?
EVEN FANCIER THAN "HAIR SALON DADDY"?
BY A LOT.
LOOK.
THAT PERSON HAS A WHOLE BUNCH OF SCISSORS!
THAT'S COOL.

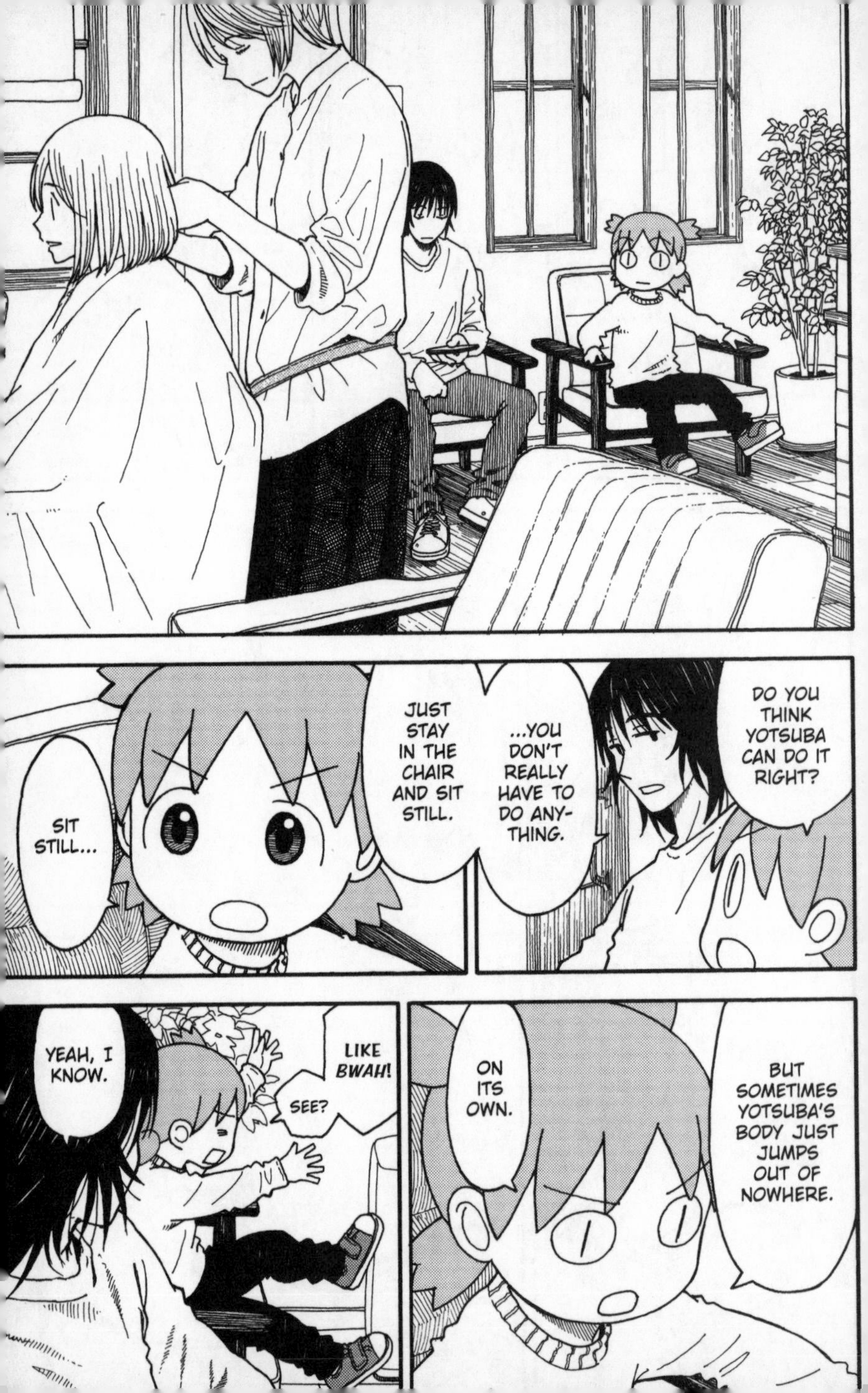
DO YOU THINK YOTSUBA CAN DO IT RIGHT?
...YOU DON'T REALLY HAVE TO DO ANYTHING.
JUST STAY IN THE CHAIR AND SIT STILL.
SIT STILL...
BUT SOMETIMES YOTSUBA'S BODY JUST JUMPS OUT OF NOWHERE.
ON ITS OWN.
LIKE *BWAH*!
SEE?
YEAH, I KNOW.

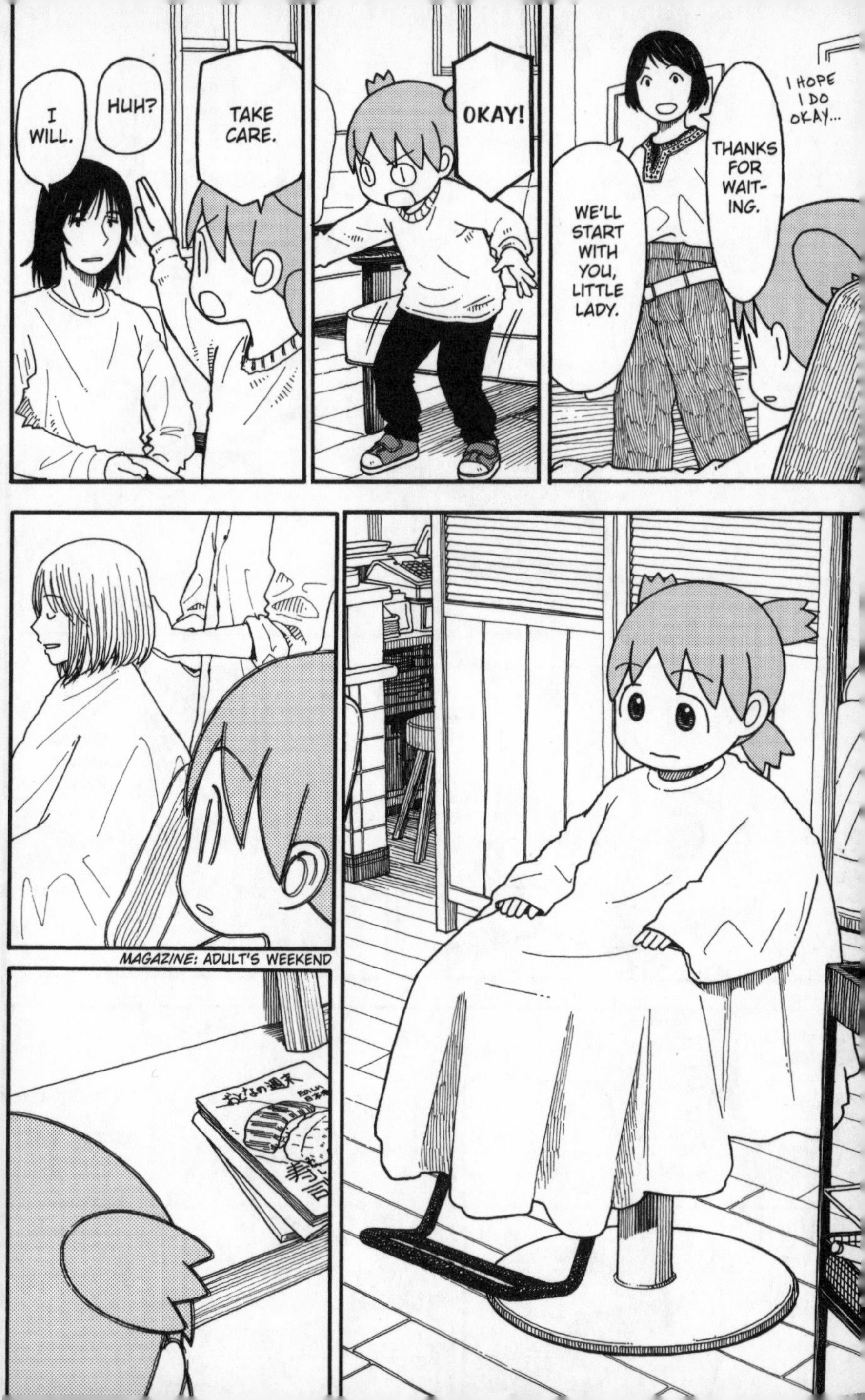
I HOPE I DO OKAY...
THANKS FOR WAIT-ING.
WE'LL START WITH YOU, LITTLE LADY.
OKAY!
TAKE CARE.
HUH?
I WILL.
MAGAZINE: ADULT'S WEEKEND
おとなの週末

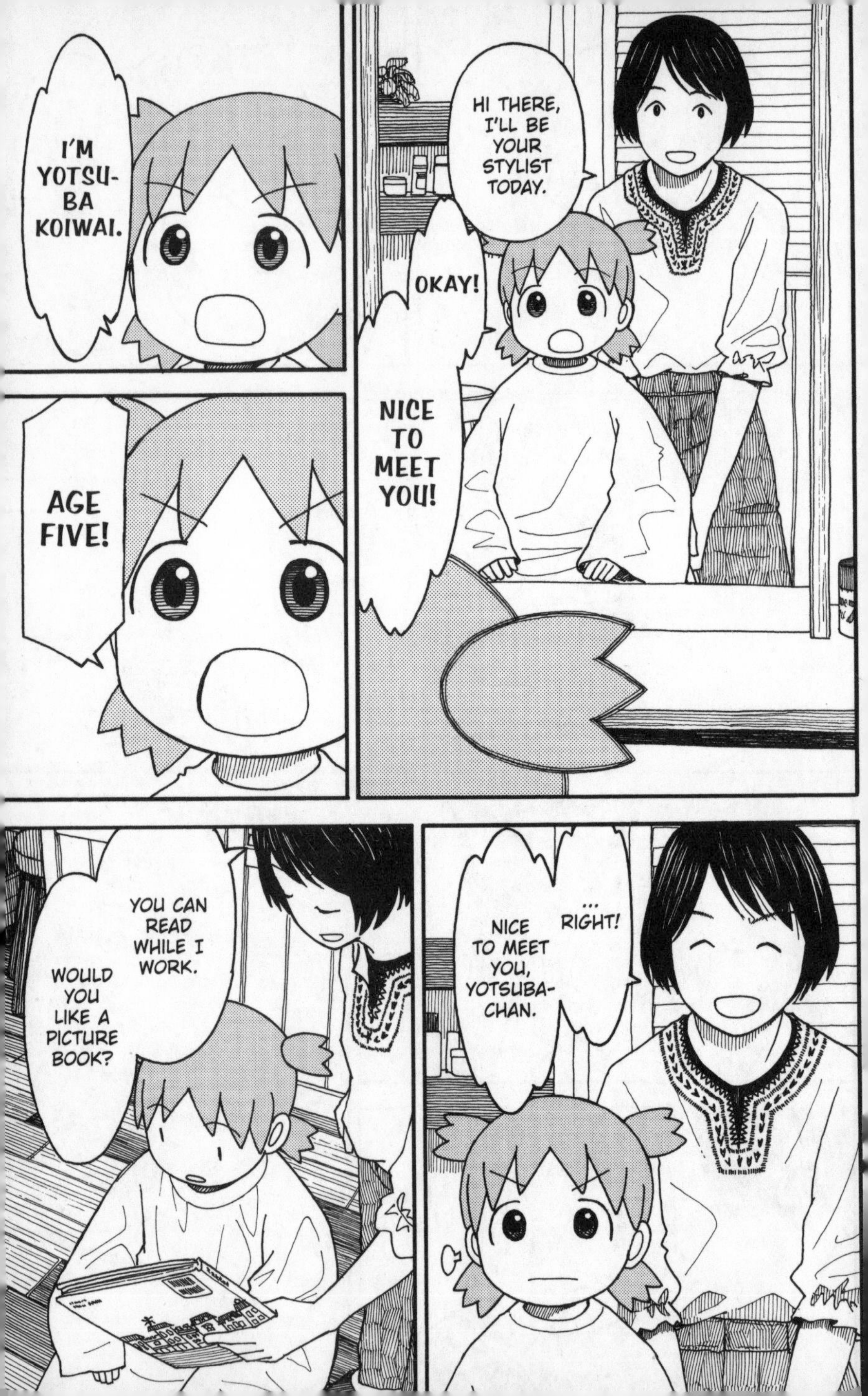
HI THERE, I'LL BE YOUR STYLIST TODAY.
OKAY!
NICE TO MEET YOU!
I'M YOTSU-BA KOIWAI.
AGE FIVE!
...RIGHT!
NICE TO MEET YOU, YOTSUBA-CHAN.
YOU CAN READ WHILE I WORK.
WOULD YOU LIKE A PICTURE BOOK?

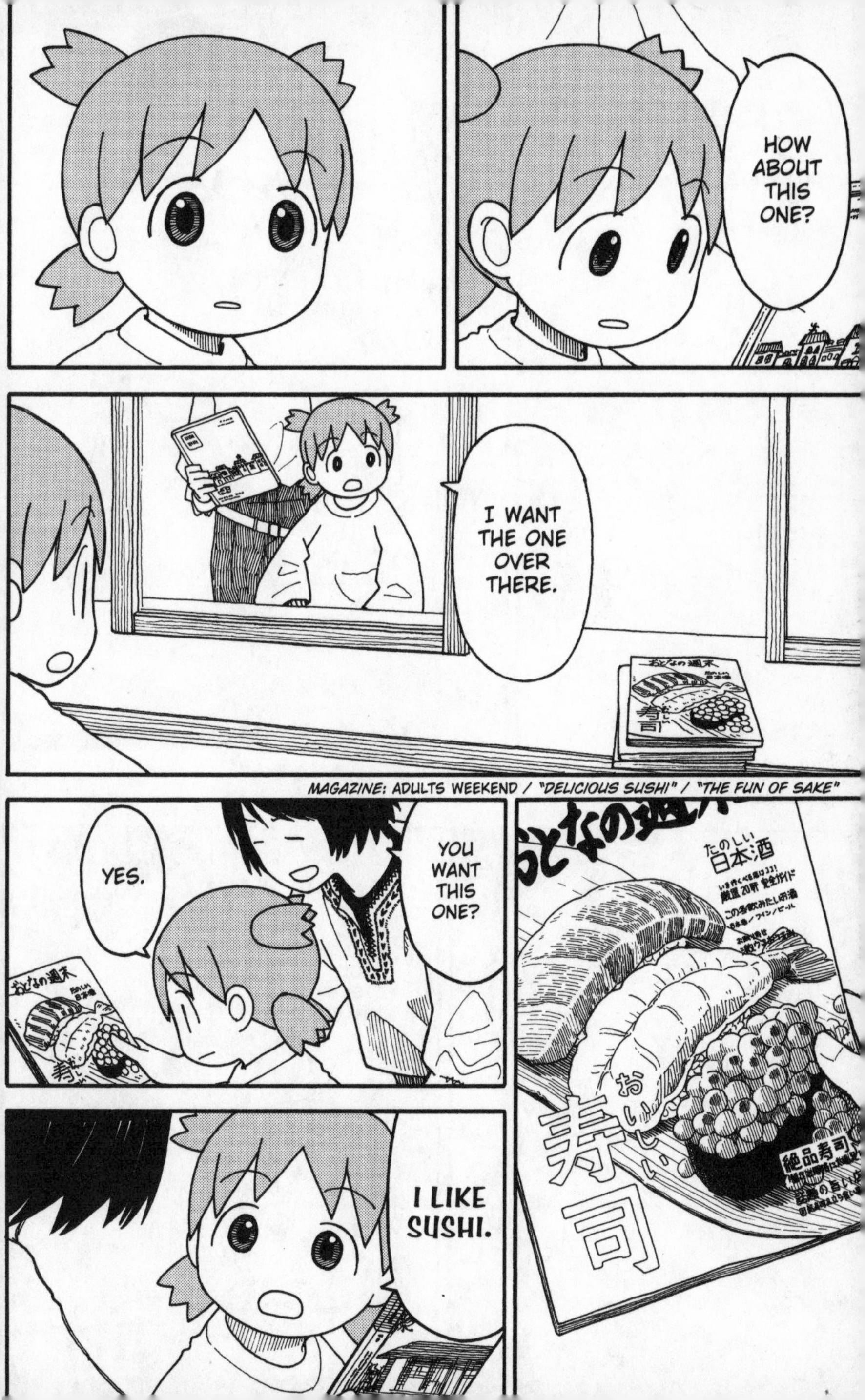
HOW ABOUT THIS ONE?
I WANT THE ONE OVER THERE.
MAGAZINE: ADULTS WEEKEND / "DELICIOUS SUSHI" / "THE FUN OF SAKE"
たのしい日本酒
寿司
絶品寿司
YOU WANT THIS ONE?
YES.
I LIKE SUSHI.

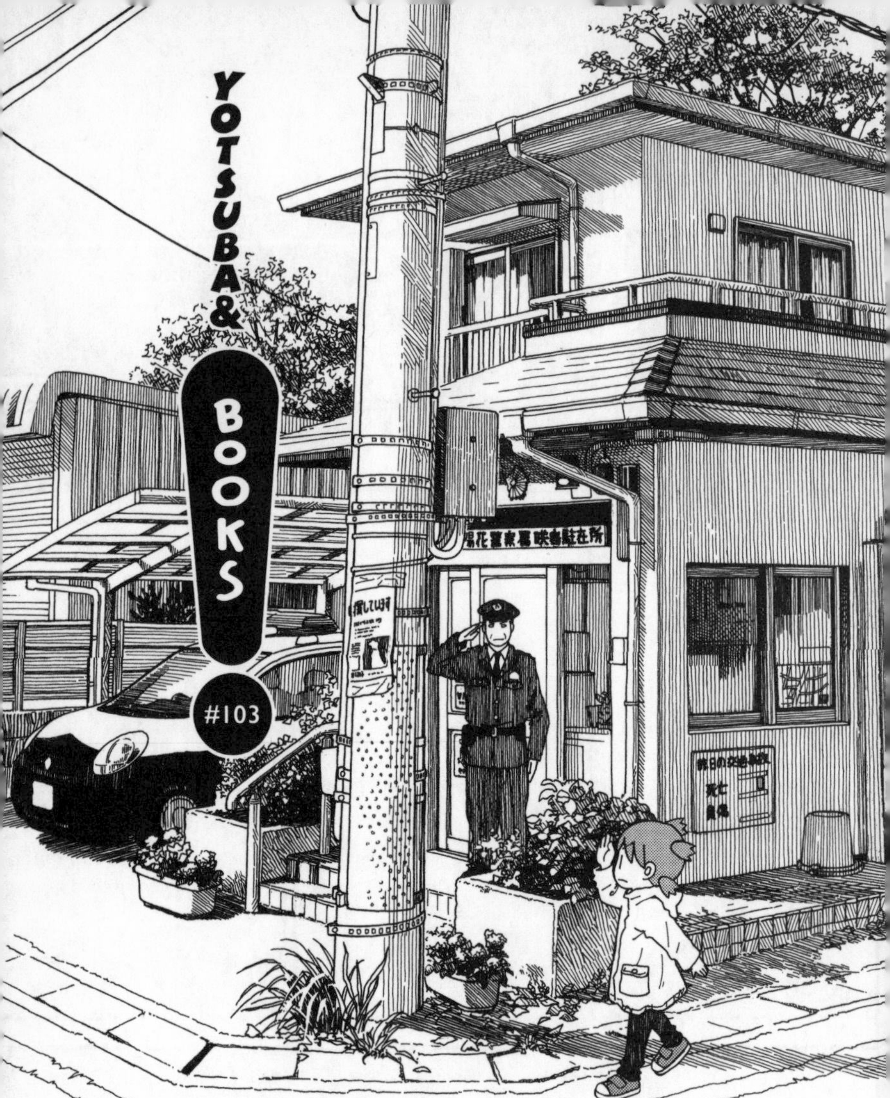
YOTSUBA&!
BOOKS
#103

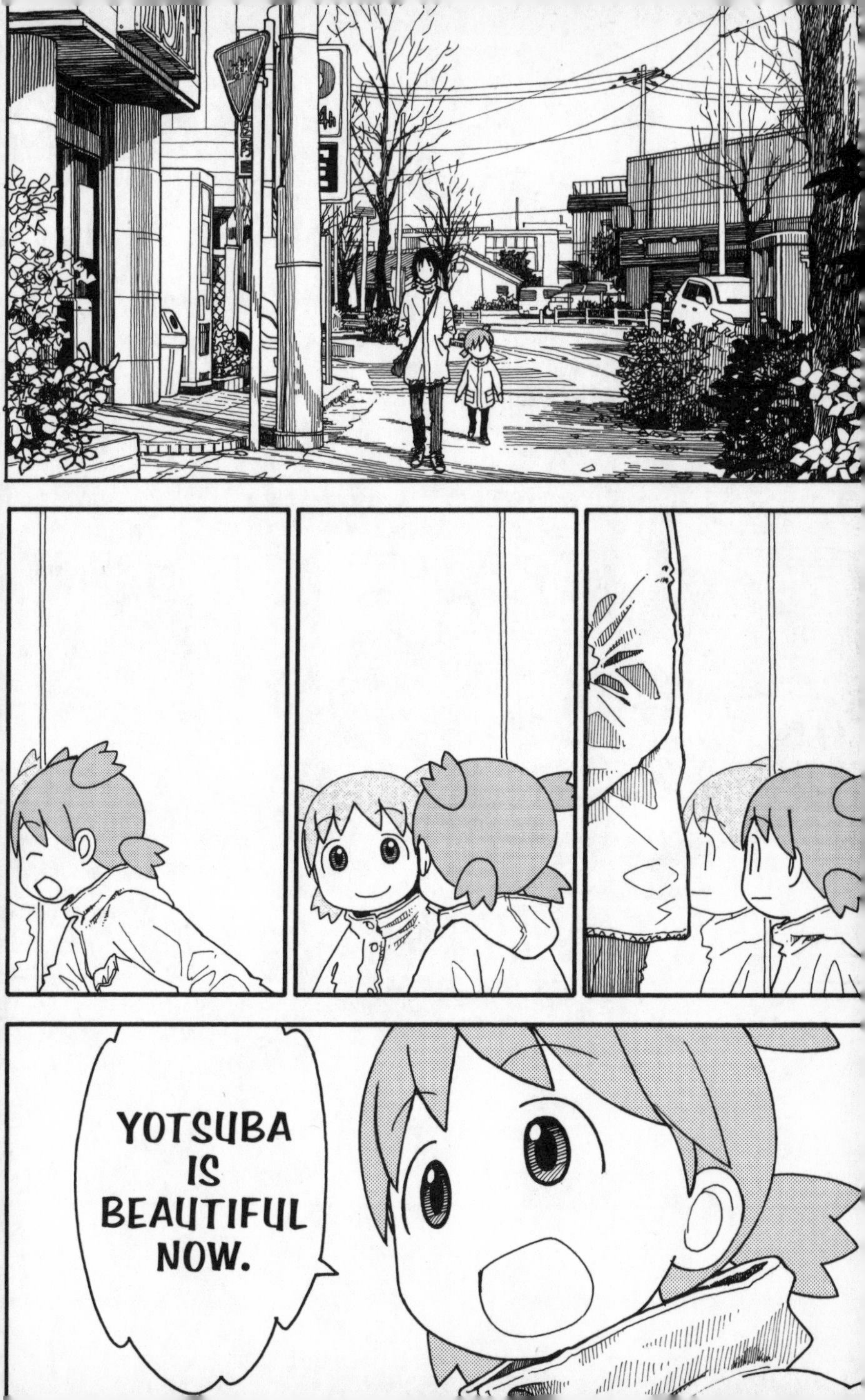
YOTSUBA IS BEAUTIFUL NOW.

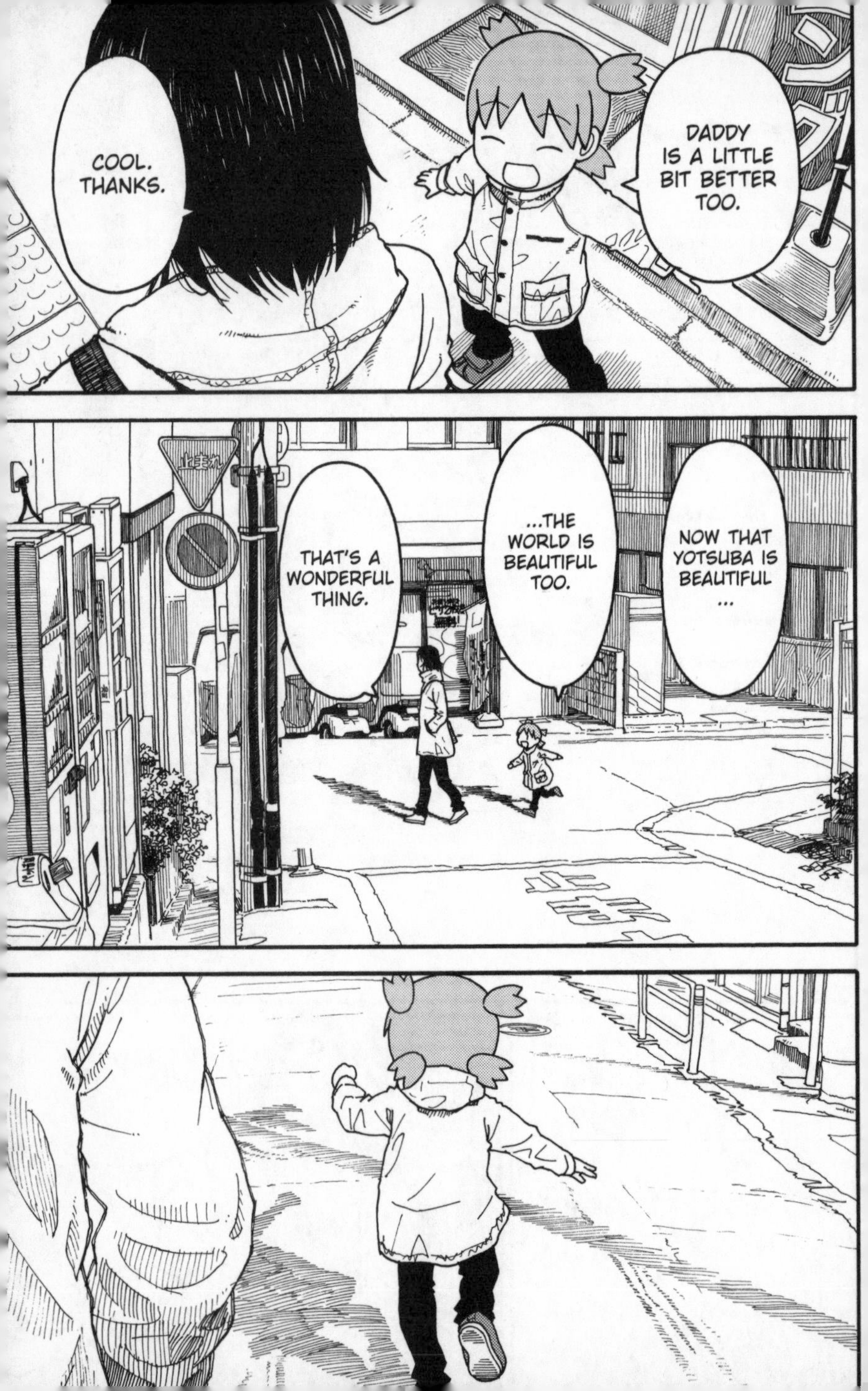
DADDY IS A LITTLE BIT BETTER TOO.
COOL. THANKS.
NOW THAT YOTSUBA IS BEAUTIFUL ...
...THE WORLD IS BEAUTIFUL TOO.
THAT'S A WONDERFUL THING.

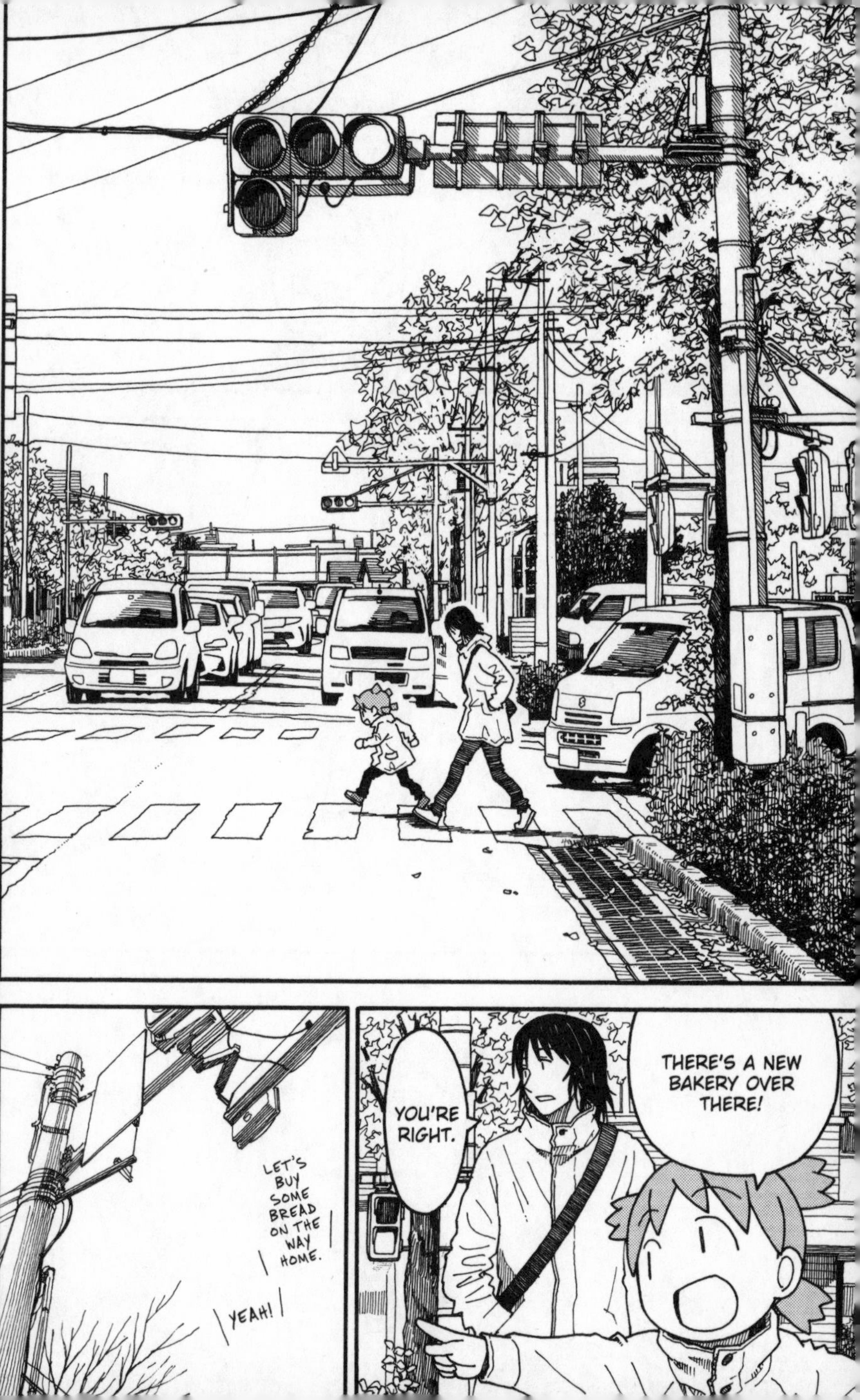
THERE'S A NEW BAKERY OVER THERE!
YOU'RE RIGHT.
LET'S BUY SOME BREAD ON THE WAY HOME.
YEAH!

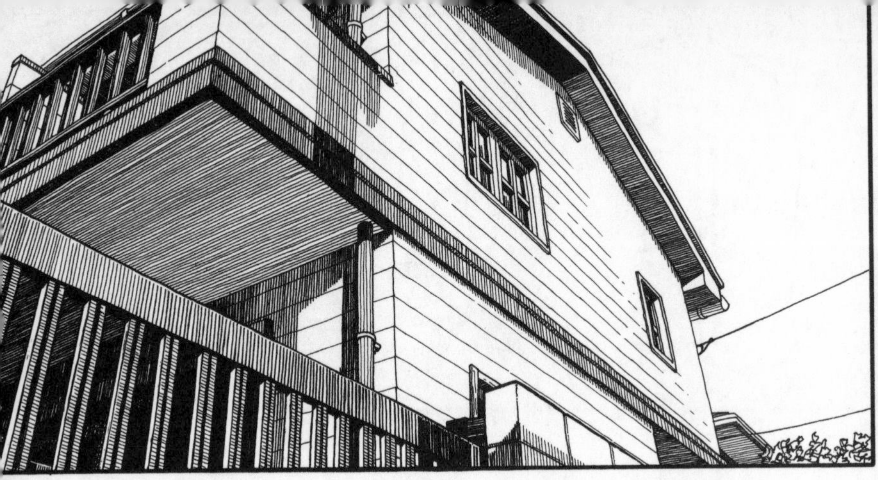

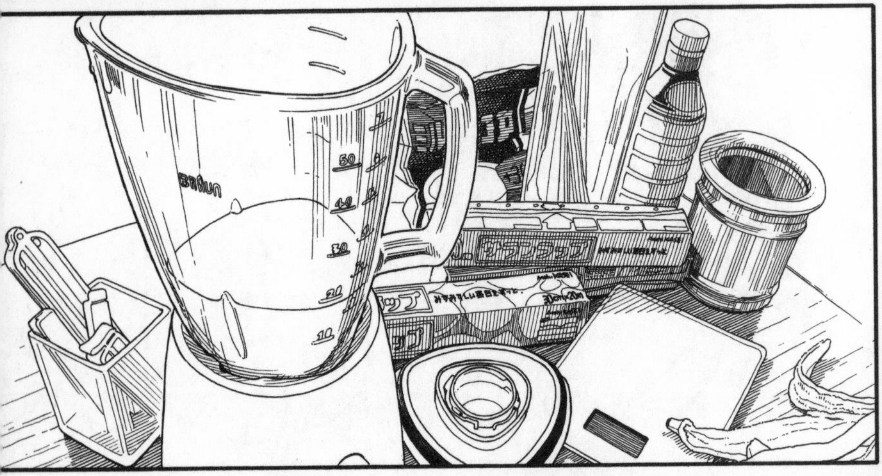
サランラップ

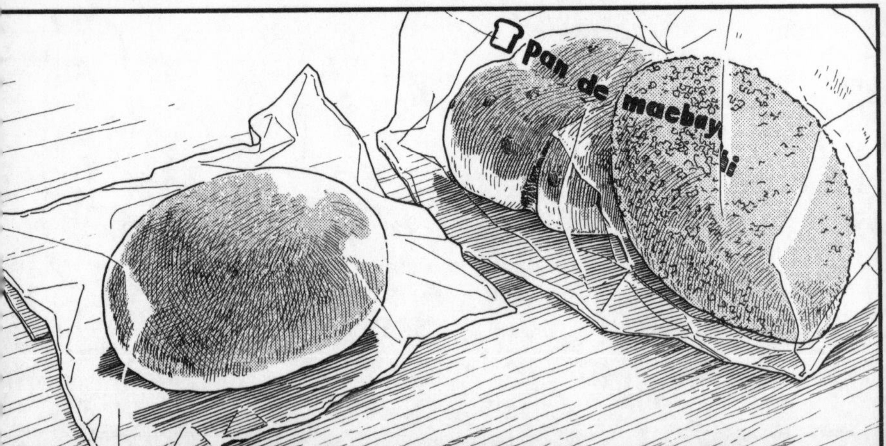
pan de

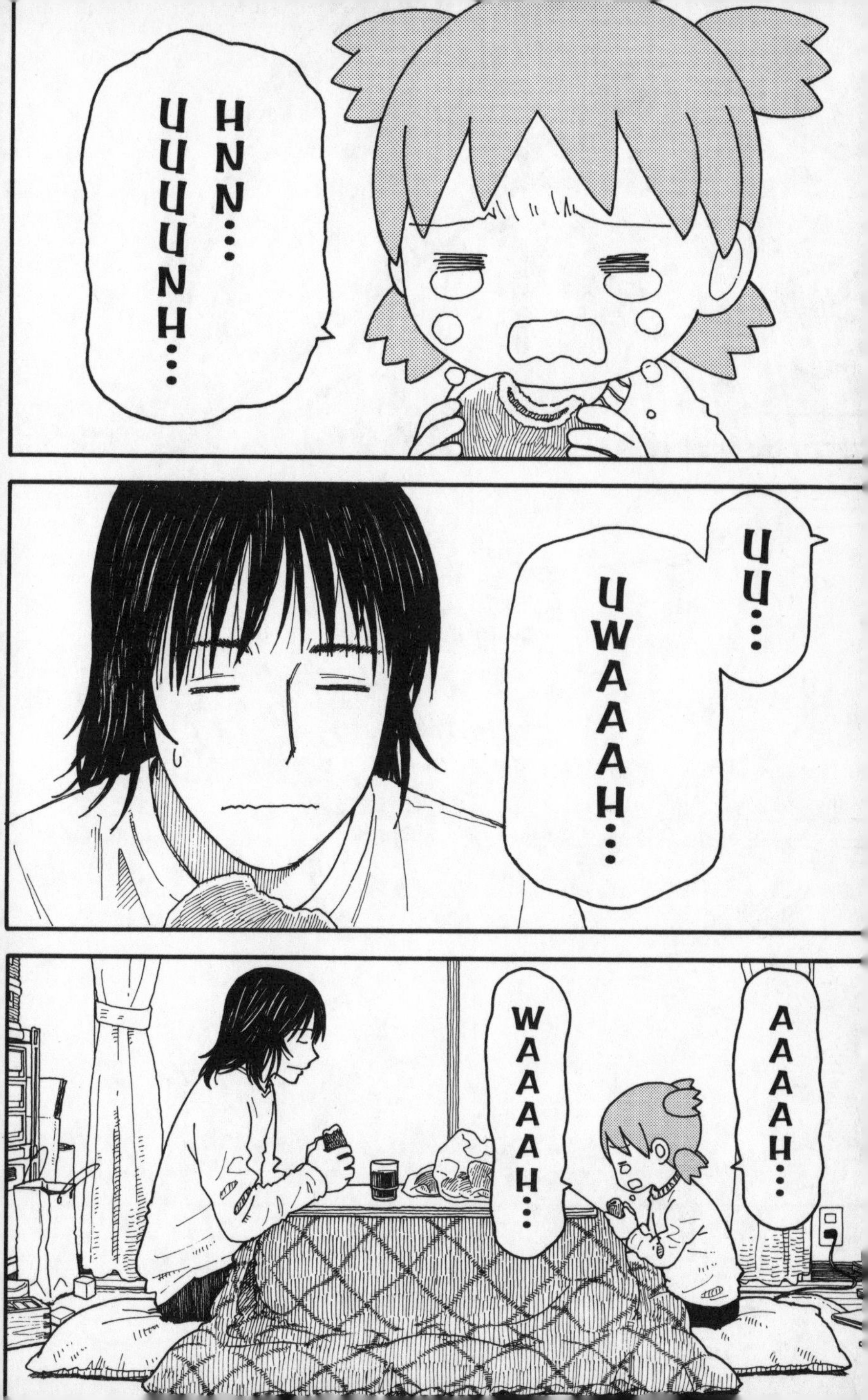
HNN...
UUUUUNH...
UU...
UWAAAAH...
AAAAH...
WAAAAAH...

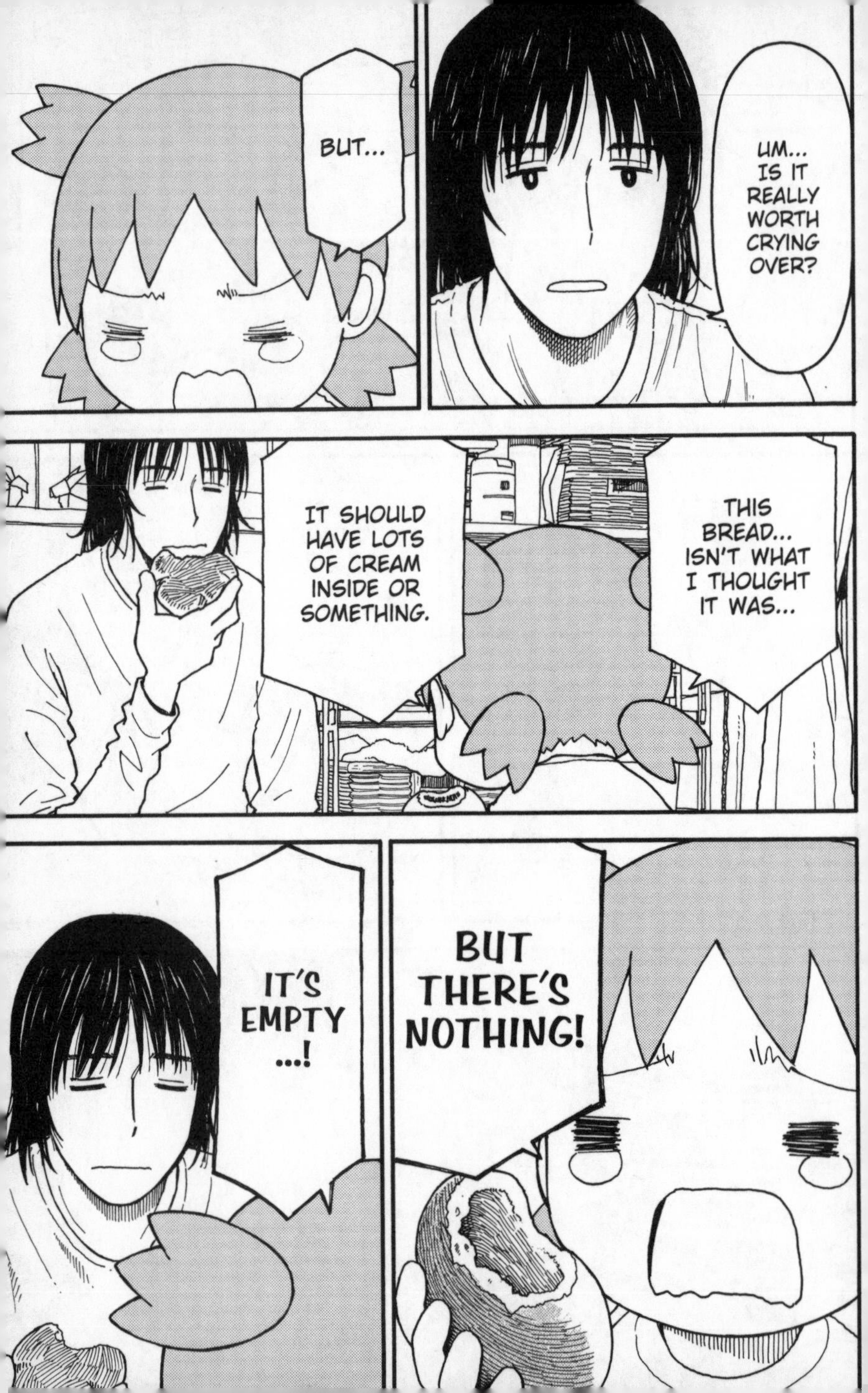
UM... IS IT REALLY WORTH CRYING OVER?
BUT...
THIS BREAD... ISN'T WHAT I THOUGHT IT WAS...
IT SHOULD HAVE LOTS OF CREAM INSIDE OR SOMETHING.
BUT THERE'S NOTHING!
IT'S EMPTY ...!

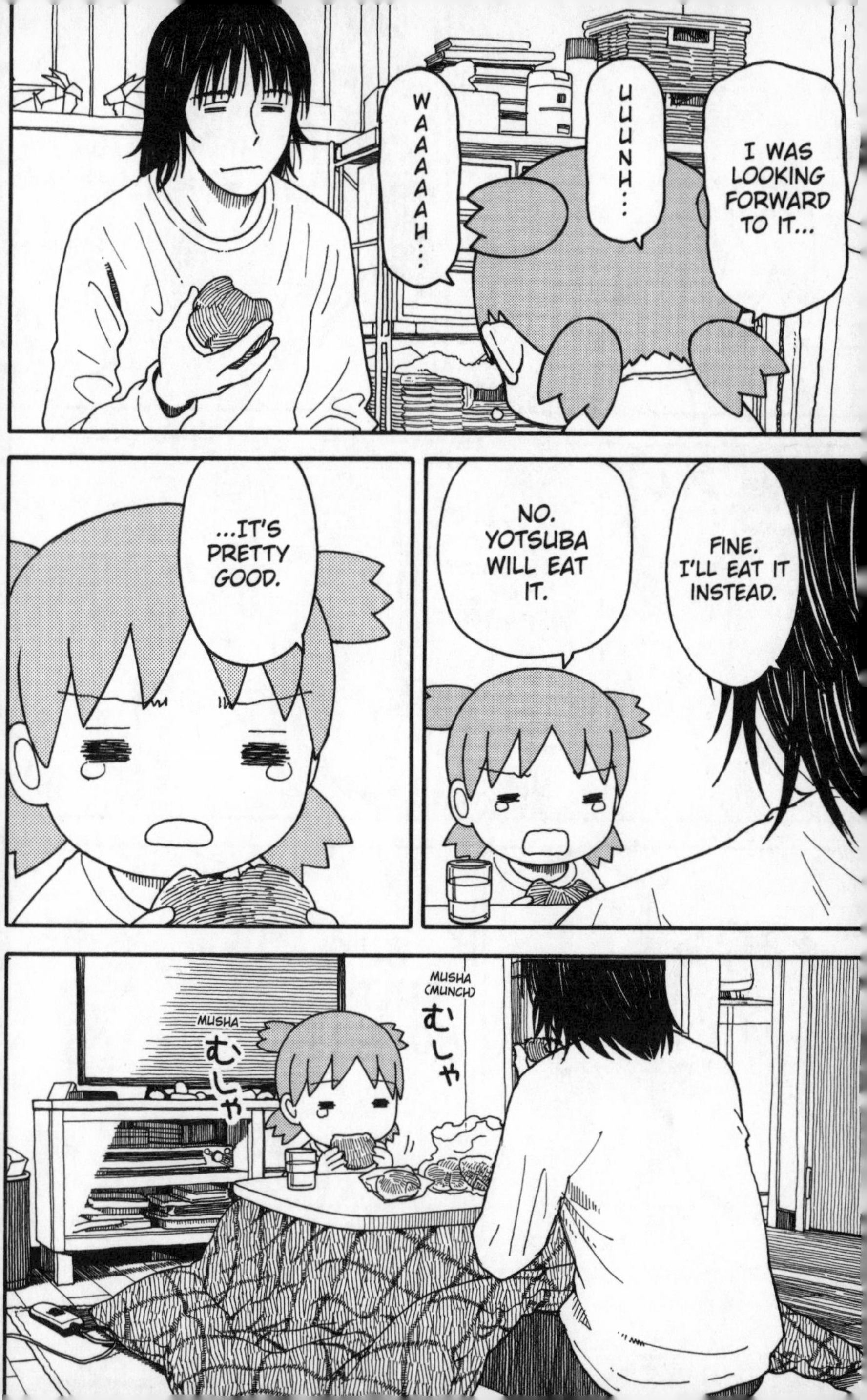
I WAS LOOKING FORWARD TO IT...
UUUNH...
WAAAAAAH...
FINE. I'LL EAT IT INSTEAD.
NO. YOTSUBA WILL EAT IT.
...IT'S PRETTY GOOD.
MUSHA (MUNCH)
むしゃ
MUSHA
むしゃ

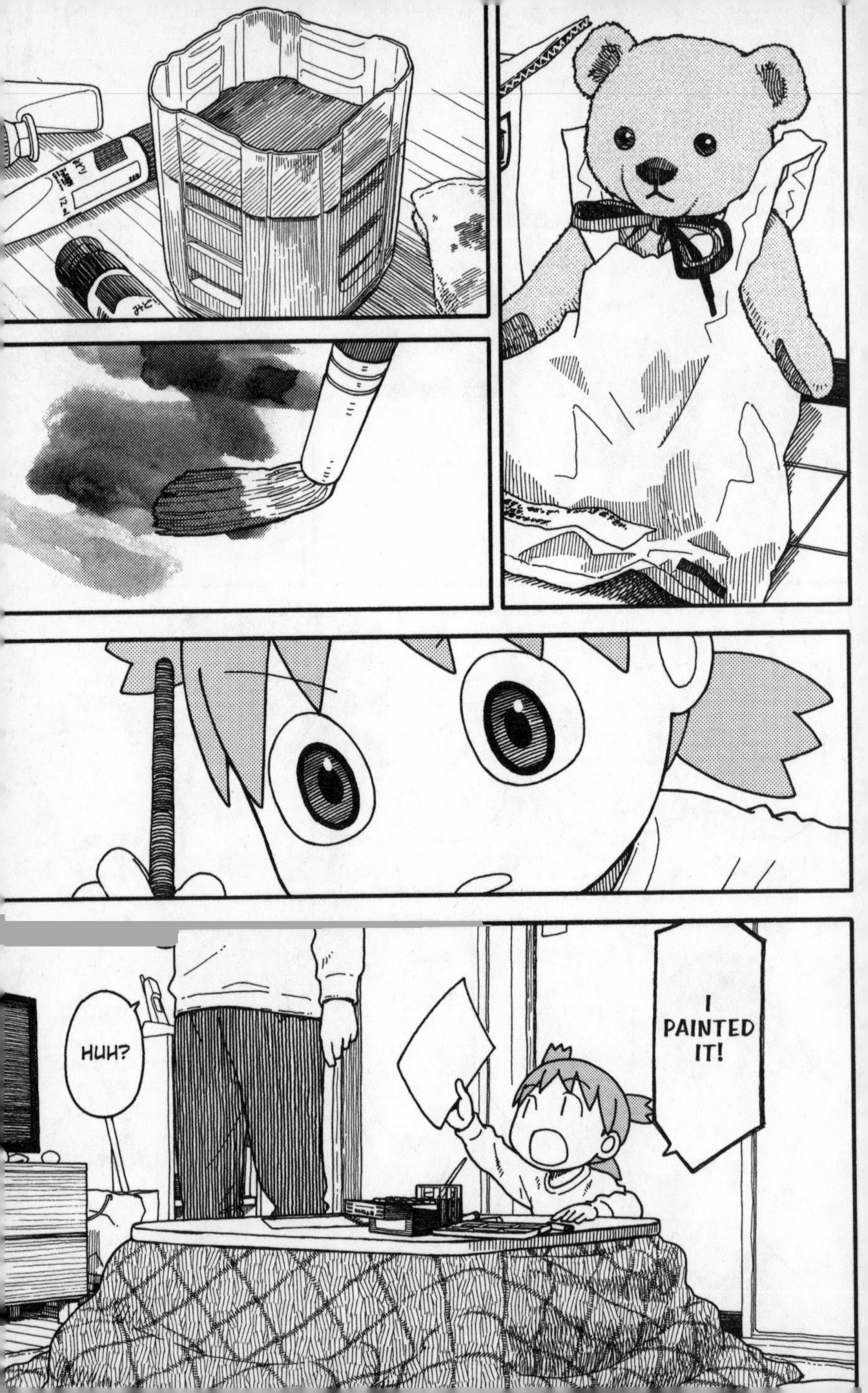
I PAINTED IT!
HUH?

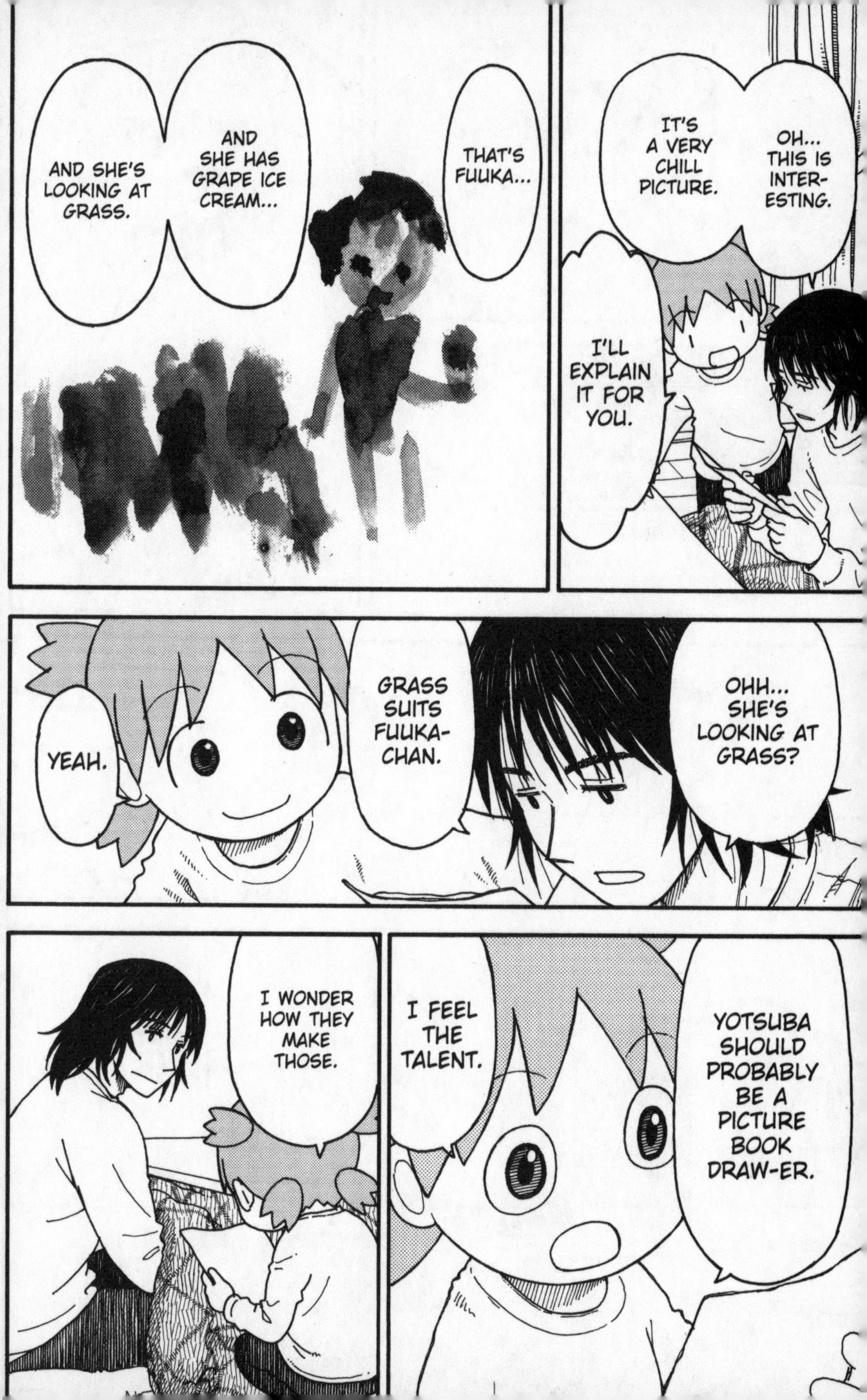
OH... THIS IS INTER-ESTING.
IT'S A VERY CHILL PICTURE.
I'LL EXPLAIN IT FOR YOU.
THAT'S FUUKA...
AND SHE HAS GRAPE ICE CREAM...
AND SHE'S LOOKING AT GRASS.
OHH... SHE'S LOOKING AT GRASS?
GRASS SUITS FUUKA-CHAN.
YEAH.
YOTSUBA SHOULD PROBABLY BE A PICTURE BOOK DRAW-ER.
I FEEL THE TALENT.
I WONDER HOW THEY MAKE THOSE.

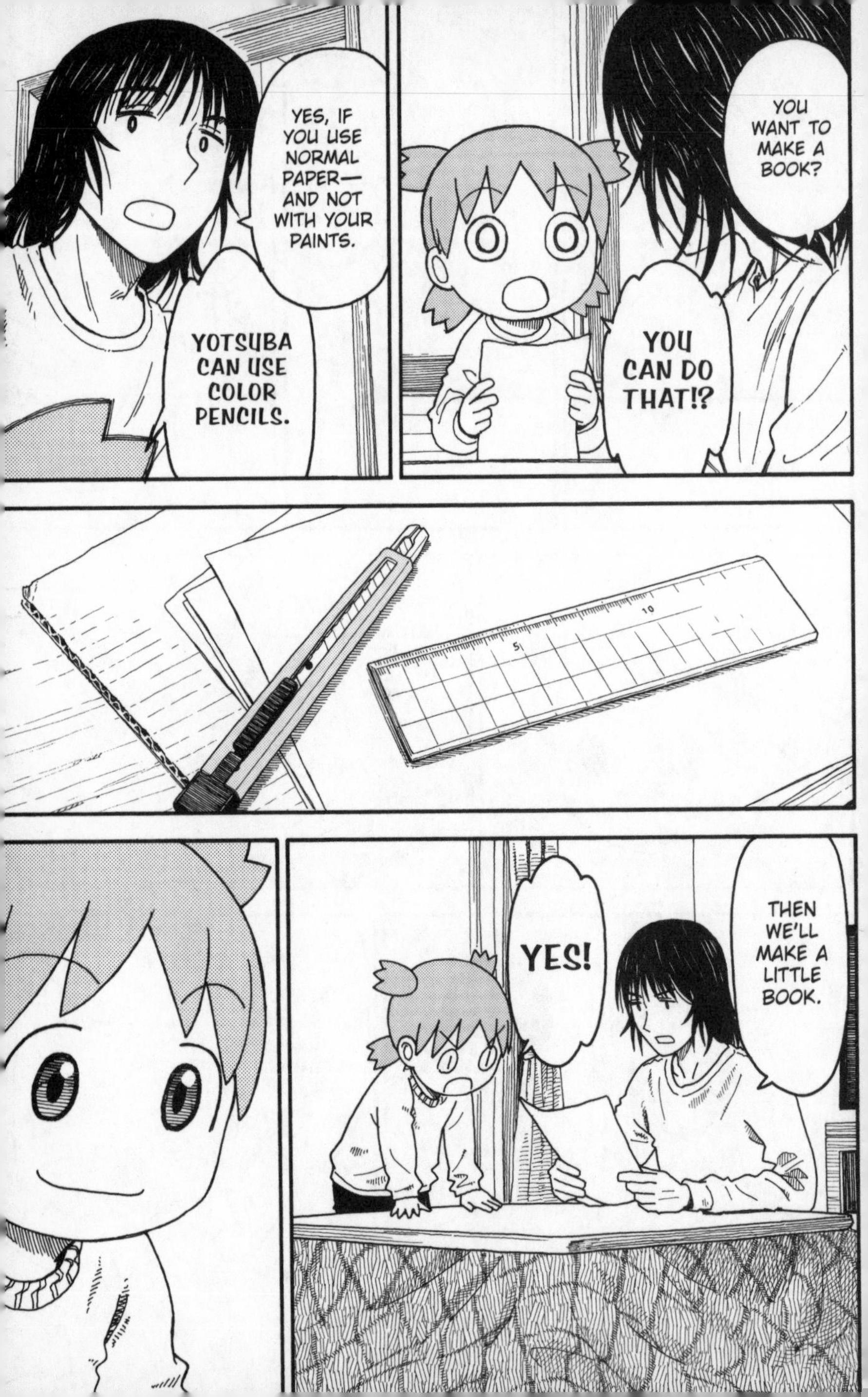

YOU WANT TO MAKE A BOOK?
YOU CAN DO THAT!?
YES, IF YOU USE NORMAL PAPER—AND NOT WITH YOUR PAINTS.
YOTSUBA CAN USE COLOR PENCILS.
THEN WE'LL MAKE A LITTLE BOOK.
YES!

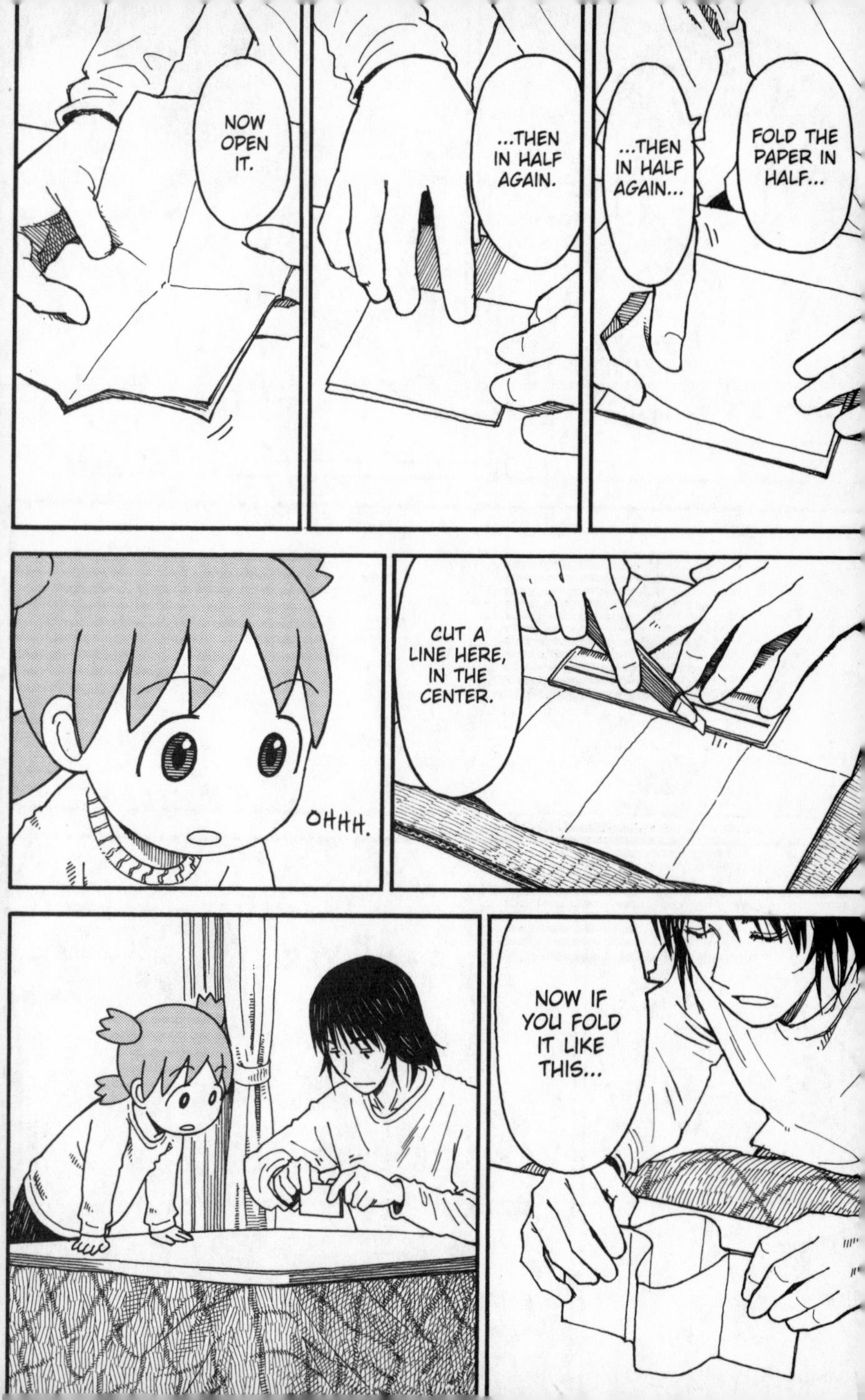
FOLD THE PAPER IN HALF...
...THEN IN HALF AGAIN...
...THEN IN HALF AGAIN.
NOW OPEN IT.
CUT A LINE HERE, IN THE CENTER.
OHHH.
NOW IF YOU FOLD IT LIKE THIS...

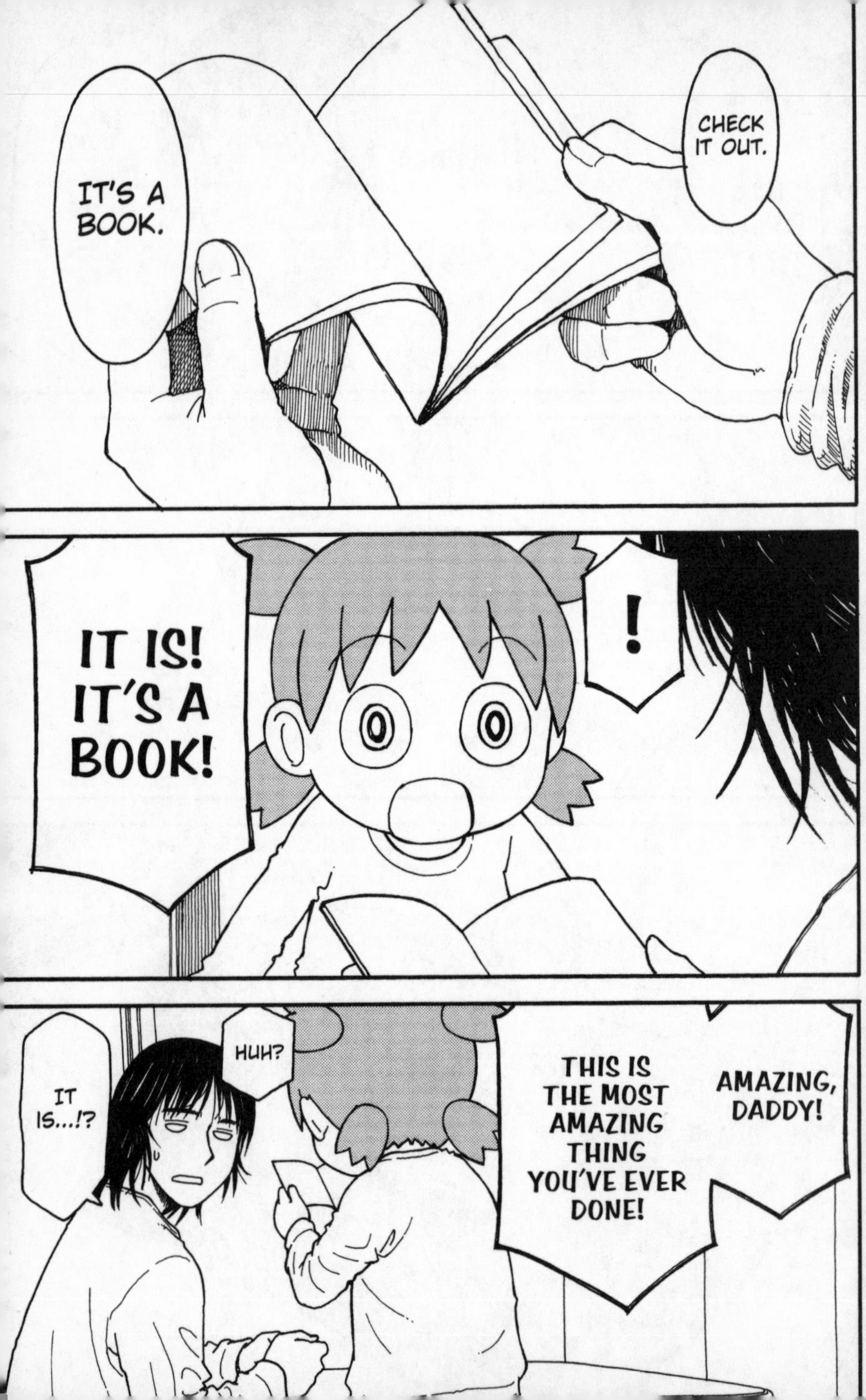
CHECK IT OUT.
IT'S A BOOK.
!
IT IS! IT'S A BOOK!
AMAZING, DADDY!
THIS IS THE MOST AMAZING THING YOU'VE EVER DONE!
HUH?
IT IS...!?

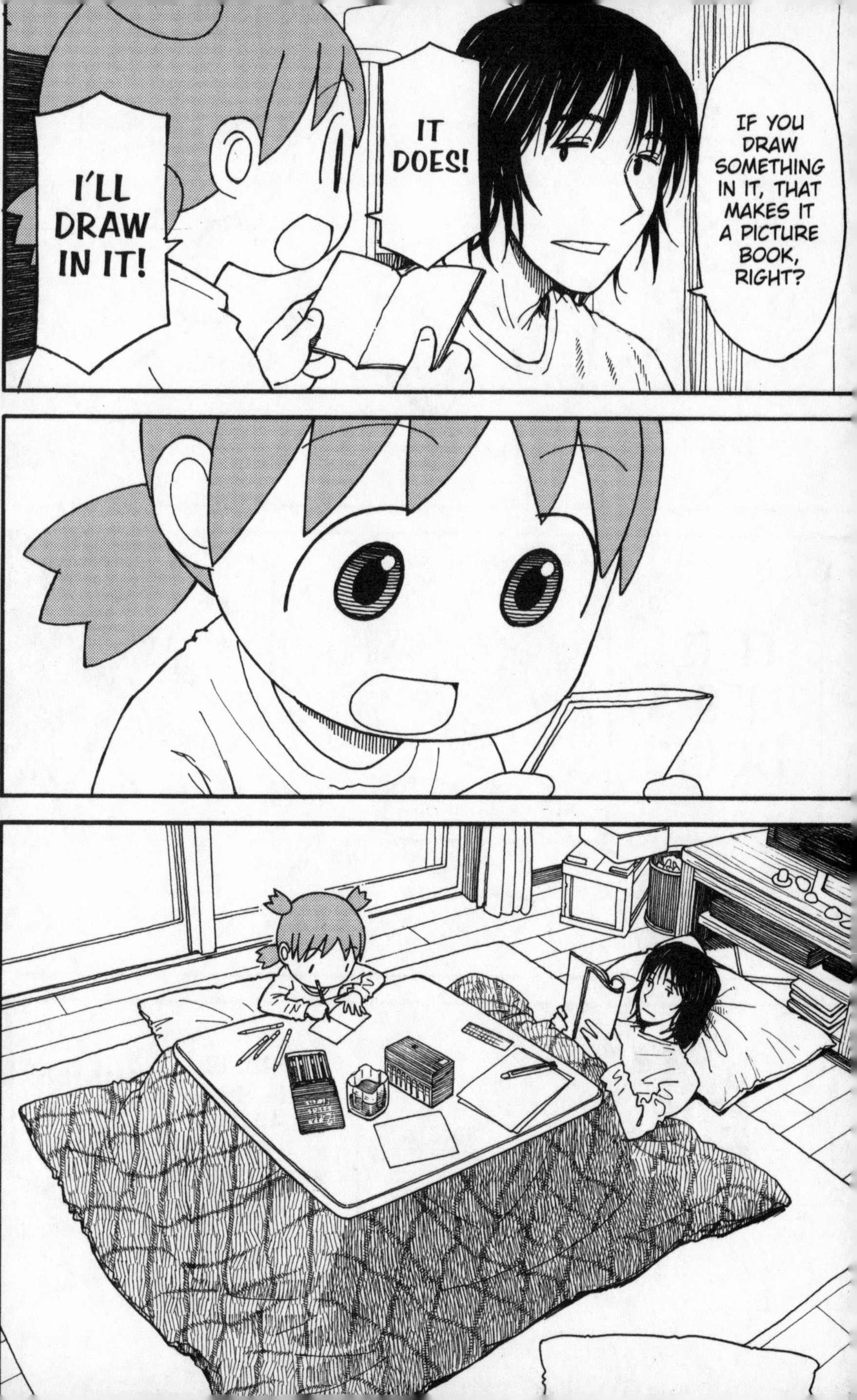
IF YOU DRAW SOMETHING IN IT, THAT MAKES IT A PICTURE BOOK, RIGHT?
IT DOES!
I'LL DRAW IN IT!

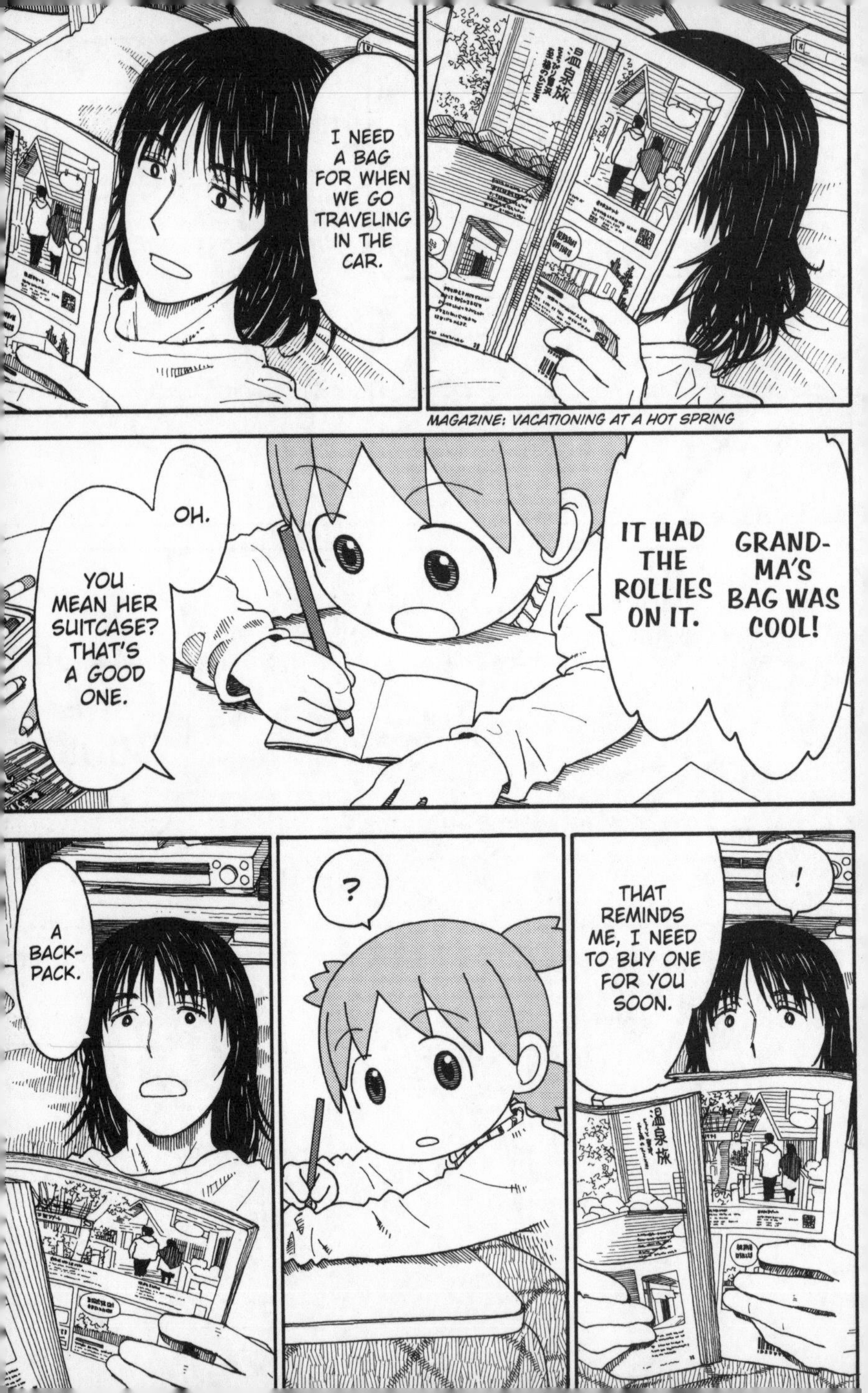
MAGAZINE: VACATIONING AT A HOT SPRING
I NEED A BAG FOR WHEN WE GO TRAVELING IN THE CAR.
GRAND-MA'S BAG WAS COOL!
IT HAD THE ROLLIES ON IT.
OH.
YOU MEAN HER SUITCASE? THAT'S A GOOD ONE.
!
THAT REMINDS ME, I NEED TO BUY ONE FOR YOU SOON.
?
A BACK-PACK.

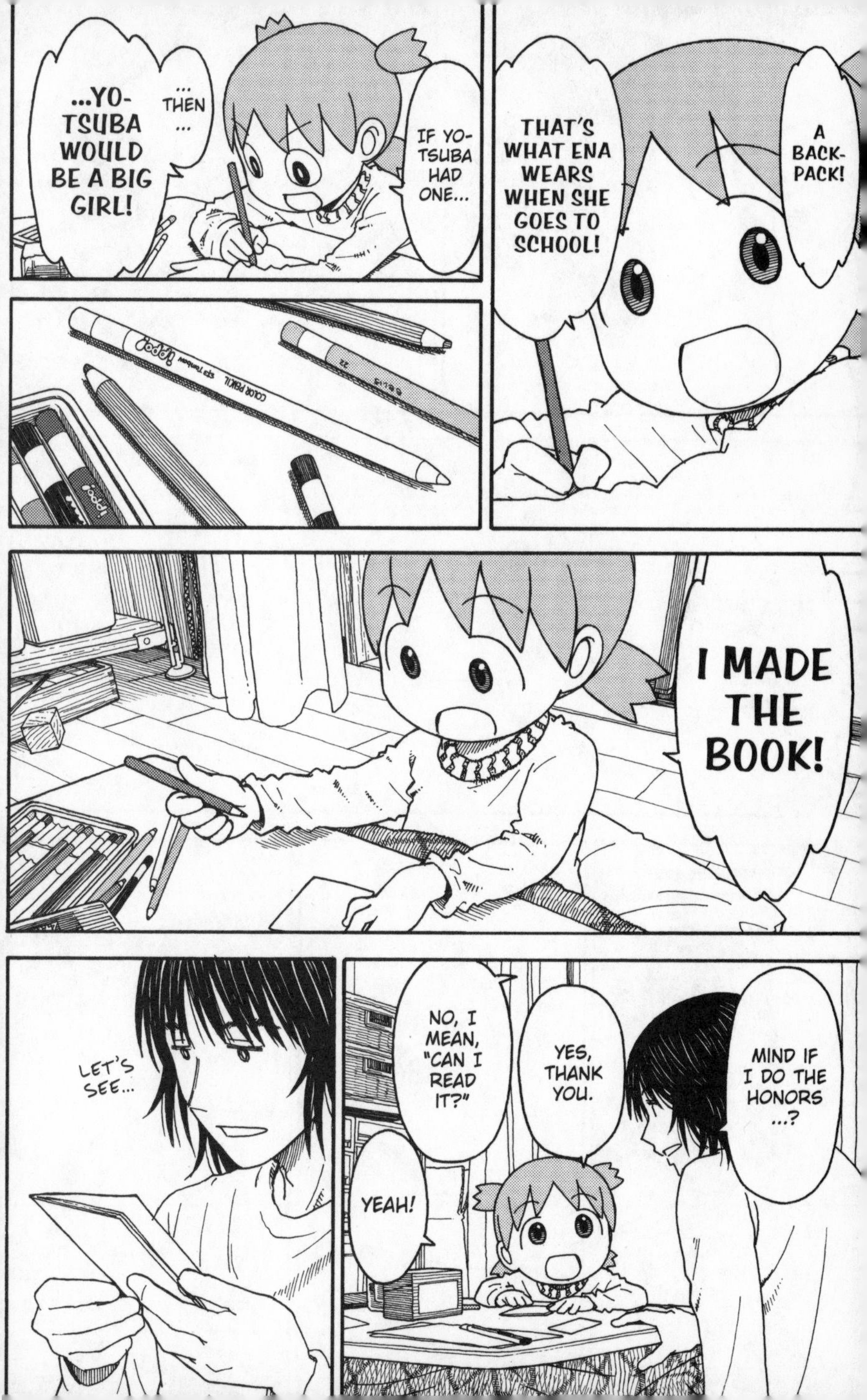
A BACK-PACK!
THAT'S WHAT ENA WEARS WHEN SHE GOES TO SCHOOL!
IF YO-TSUBA HAD ONE...
... THEN ...
...YO-TSUBA WOULD BE A BIG GIRL!
I MADE THE BOOK!
MIND IF I DO THE HONORS ...?
YES, THANK YOU.
NO, I MEAN, "CAN I READ IT?"
YEAH!
LET'S SEE...

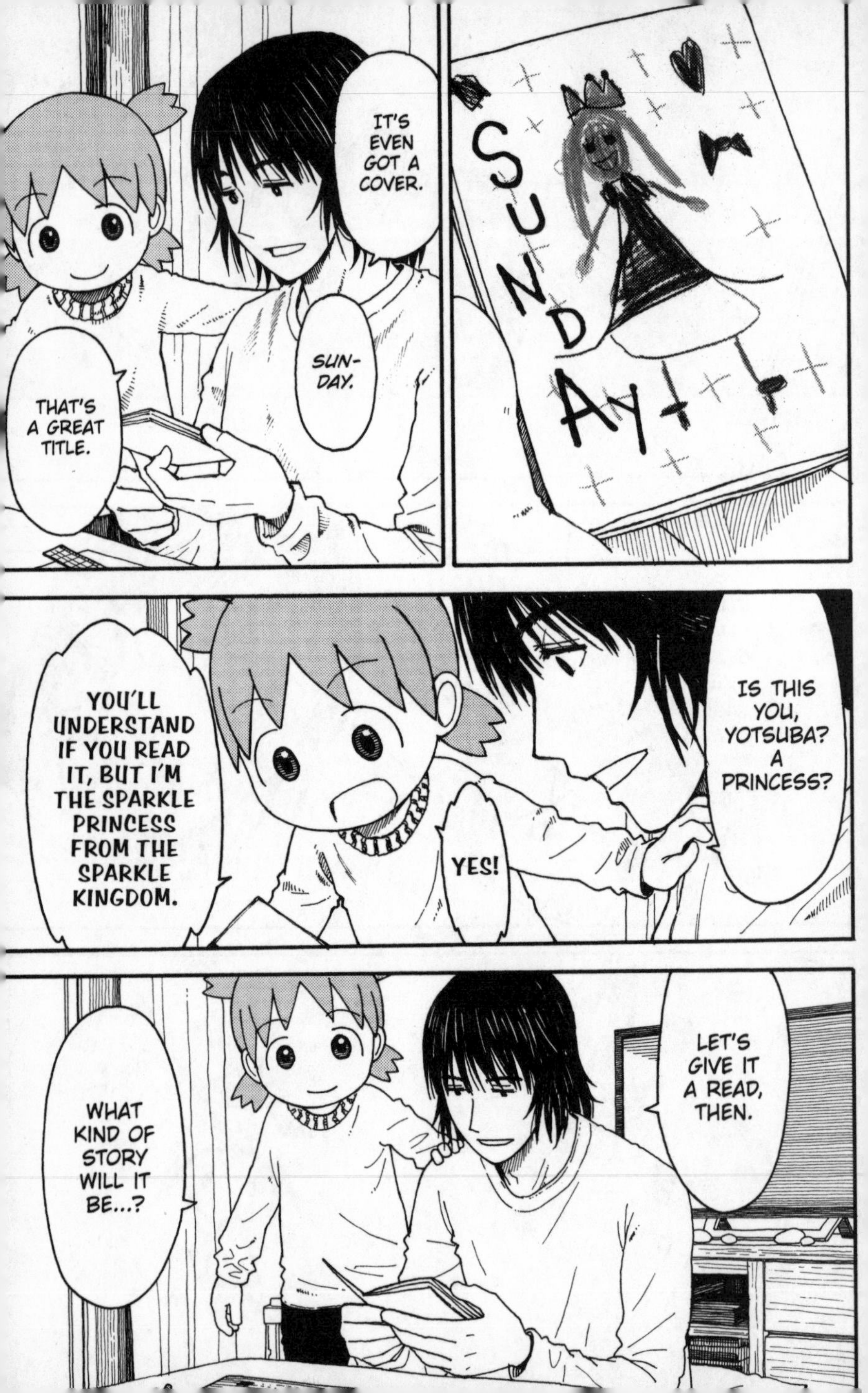
SUNDAY
IT'S EVEN GOT A COVER.
SUN-DAY.
THAT'S A GREAT TITLE.
IS THIS YOU, YOTSUBA? A PRINCESS?
YES!
YOU'LL UNDERSTAND IF YOU READ IT, BUT I'M THE SPARKLE PRINCESS FROM THE SPARKLE KINGDOM.
LET'S GIVE IT A READ, THEN.
WHAT KIND OF STORY WILL IT BE...?

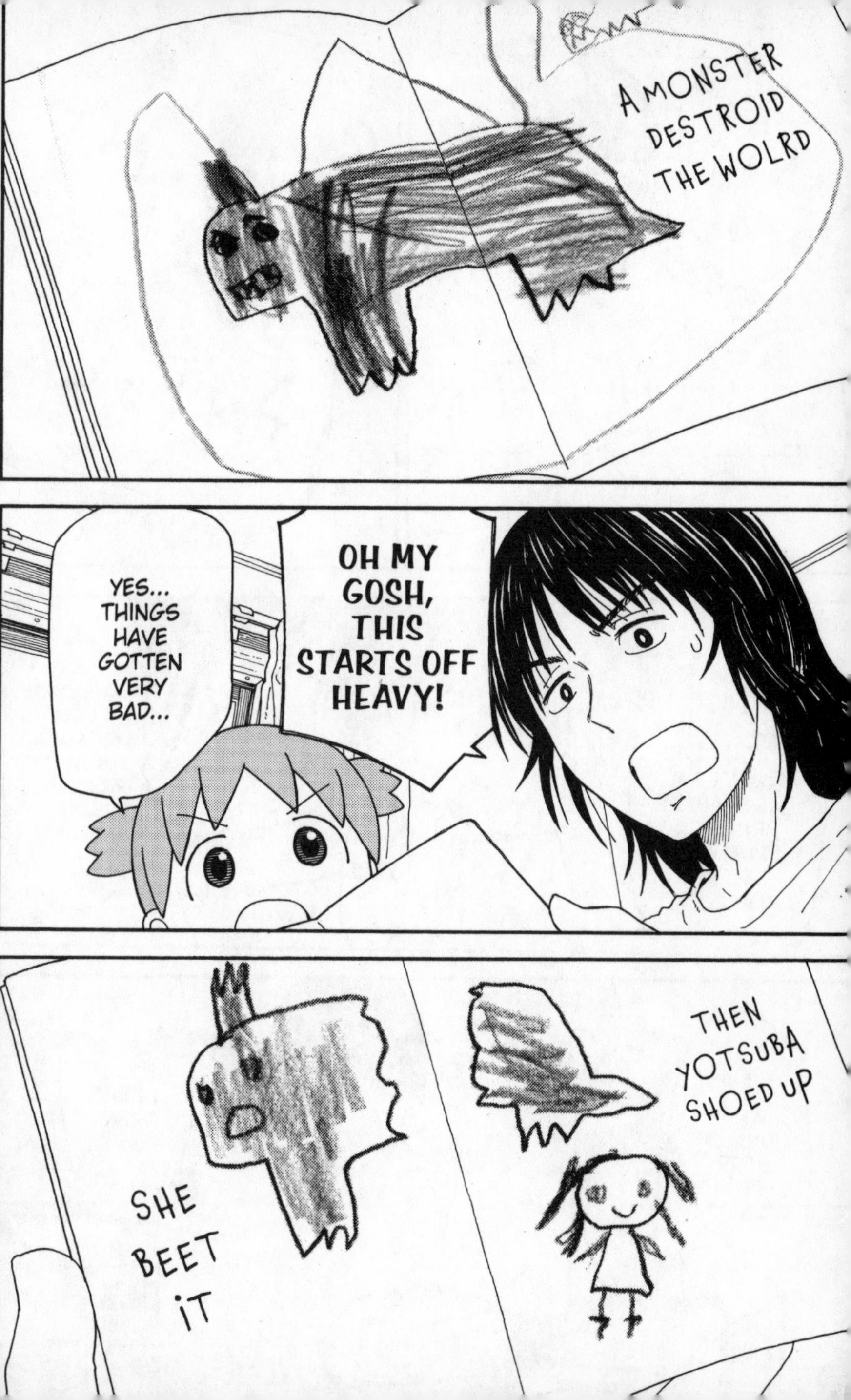
A MONSTER DESTROID THE WOLRD
OH MY GOSH, THIS STARTS OFF HEAVY!
YES... THINGS HAVE GOTTEN VERY BAD...
THEN YOTSUBA SHOED UP
SHE BEET IT

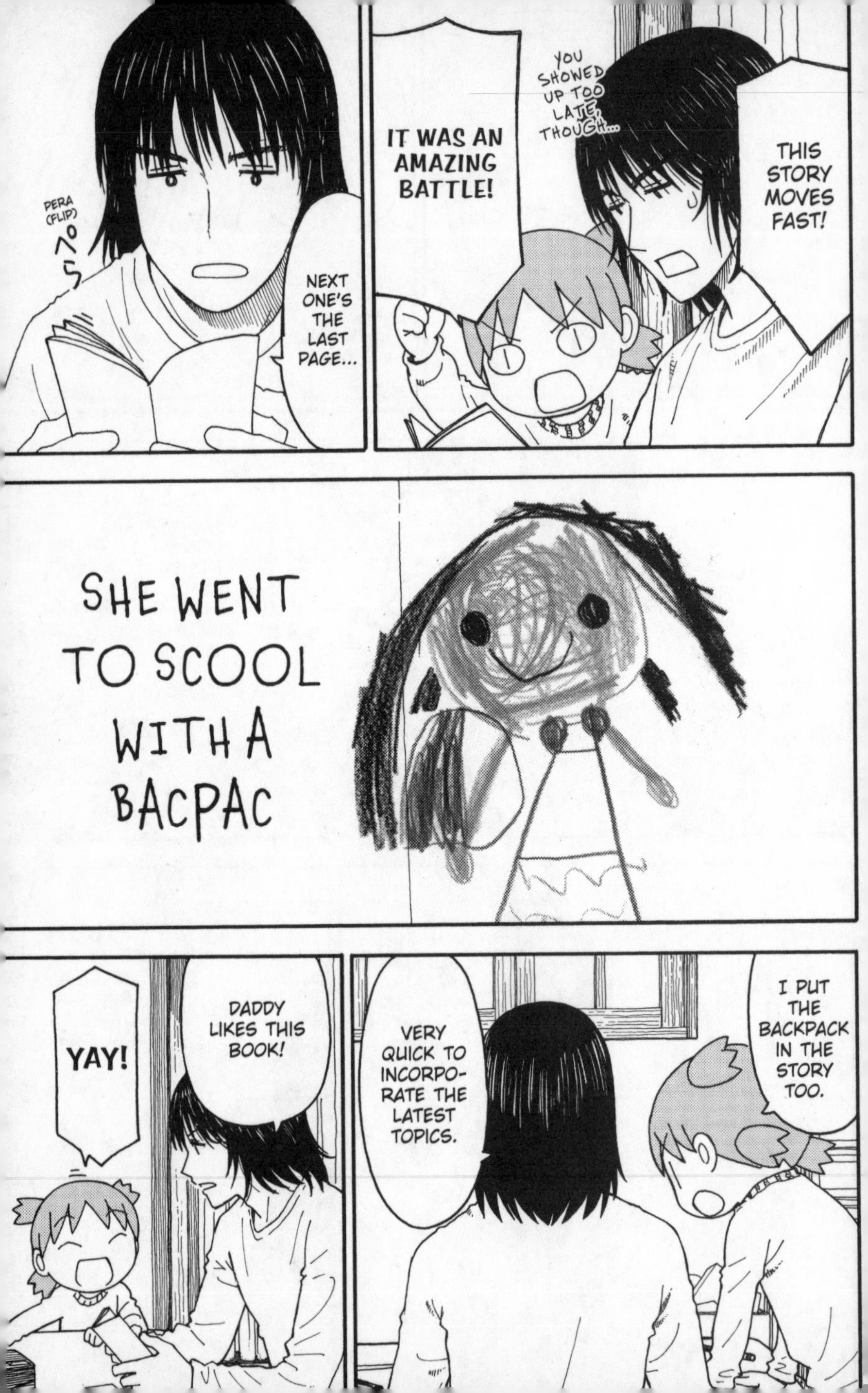
THIS STORY MOVES FAST!
YOU SHOWED UP TOO LATE, THOUGH...
IT WAS AN AMAZING BATTLE!
NEXT ONE'S THE LAST PAGE...
PERA (FLIP)
SHE WENT TO SCOOL WITH A BACPAC
I PUT THE BACKPACK IN THE STORY TOO.
VERY QUICK TO INCORPORATE THE LATEST TOPICS.
DADDY LIKES THIS BOOK!
YAY!

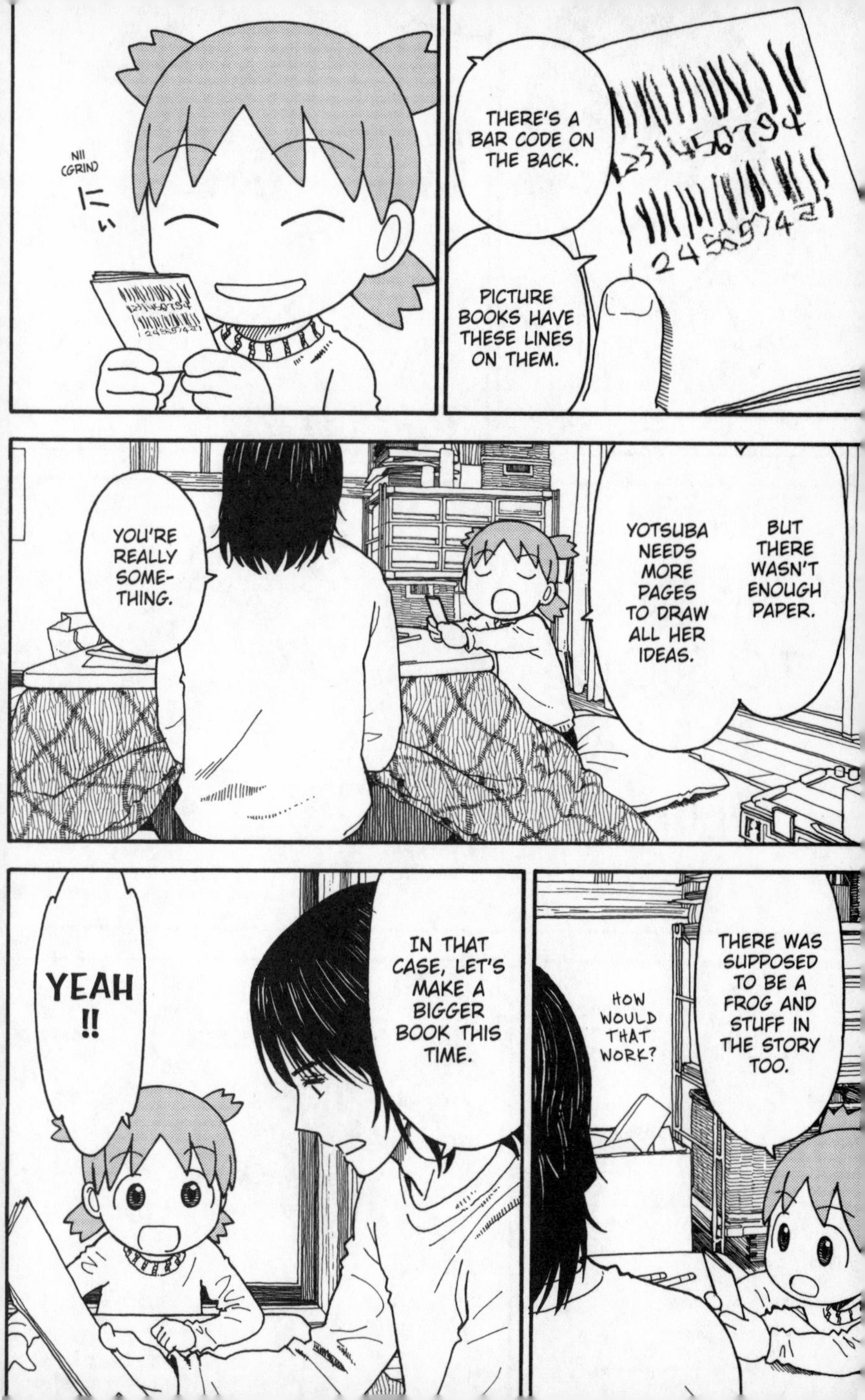
THERE'S A BAR CODE ON THE BACK.
PICTURE BOOKS HAVE THESE LINES ON THEM.
NII (GRIND)
にい
BUT THERE WASN'T ENOUGH PAPER.
YOTSUBA NEEDS MORE PAGES TO DRAW ALL HER IDEAS.
YOU'RE REALLY SOME-THING.
THERE WAS SUPPOSED TO BE A FROG AND STUFF IN THE STORY TOO.
HOW WOULD THAT WORK?
IN THAT CASE, LET'S MAKE A BIGGER BOOK THIS TIME.
YEAH !!

YOTSUBA&!

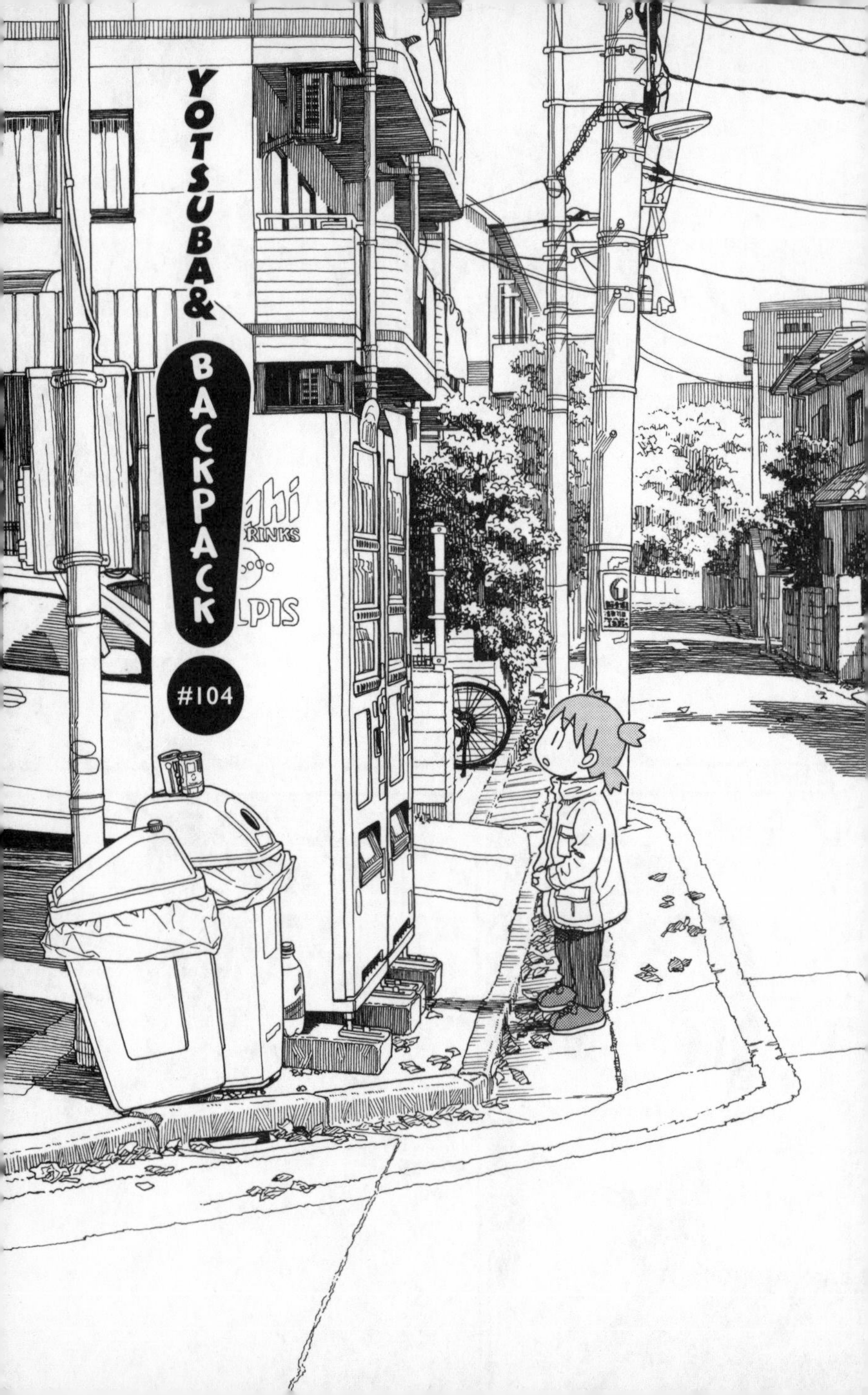
YOTSUBA&
BACKPACK
#104
ahi
RINKS
LPIS

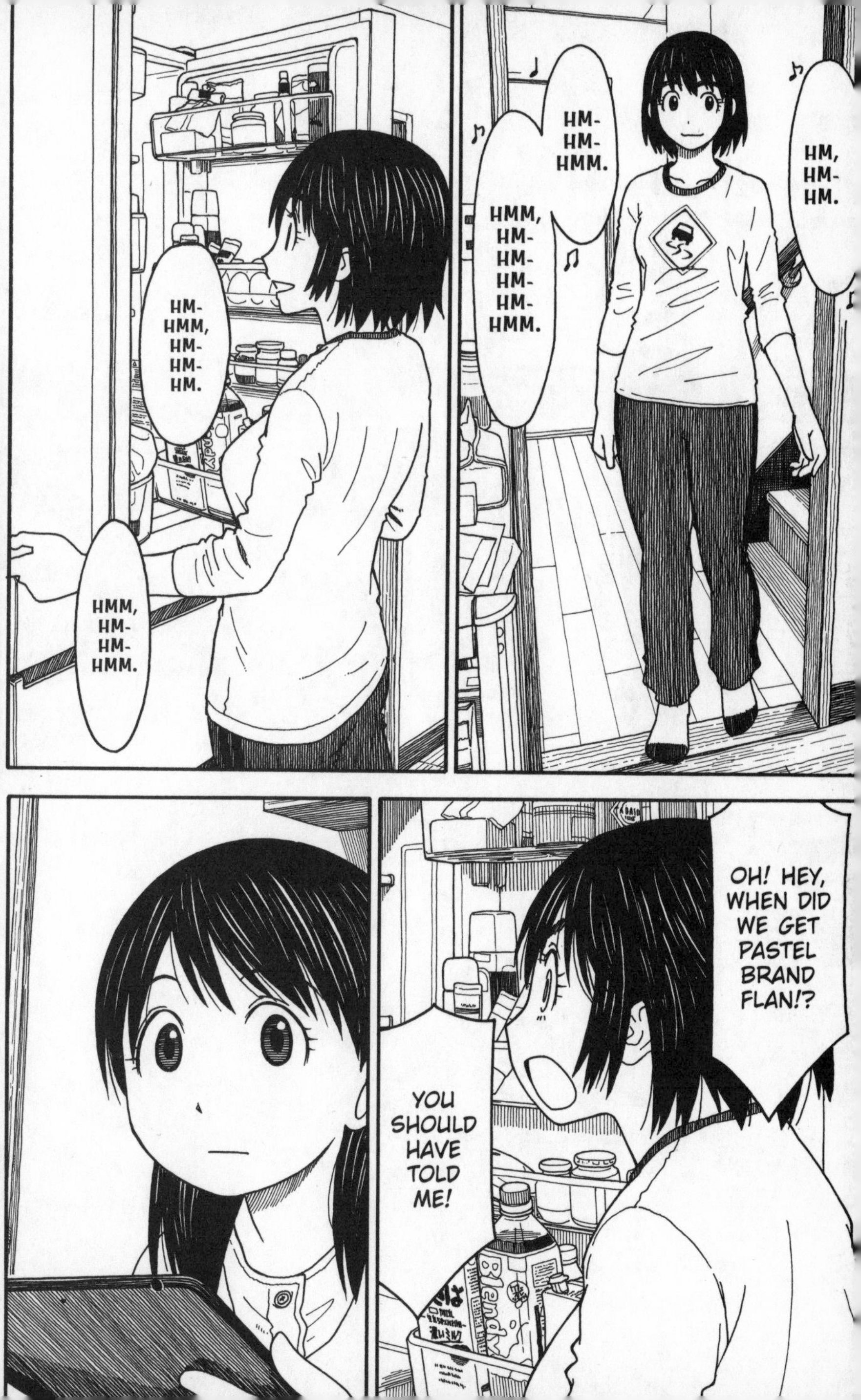
HM, HM-HM.
HM-HM-HMM.
HMM, HM-HM-HM-HM-HMM.
HM-HMM, HM-HM-HM.
HMM, HM-HM-HMM.
OH! HEY, WHEN DID WE GET PASTEL BRAND FLAN!?
YOU SHOULD HAVE TOLD ME!

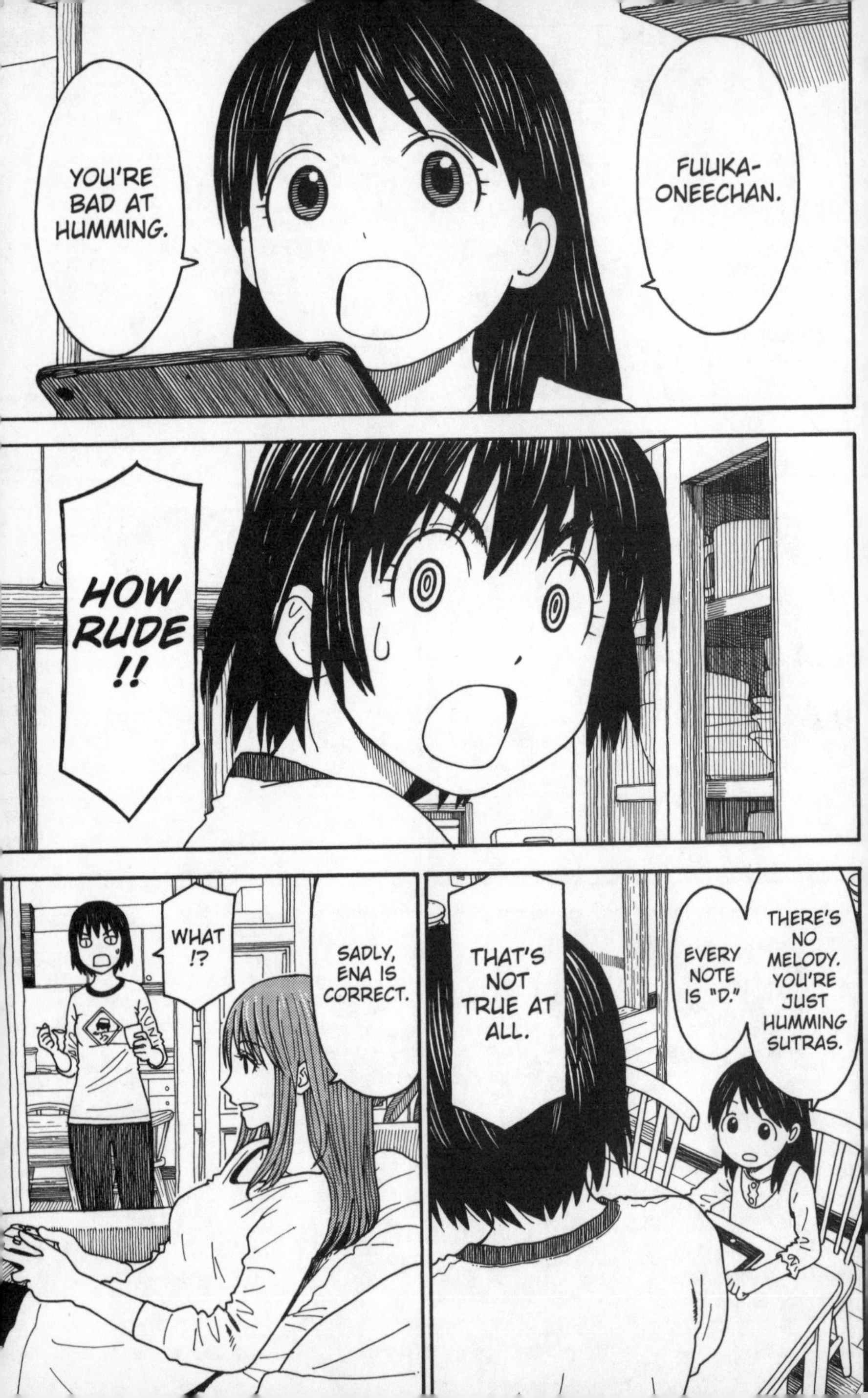
FUUKA-ONEECHAN.
YOU'RE BAD AT HUMMING.
HOW RUDE!!
THERE'S NO MELODY. YOU'RE JUST HUMMING SUTRAS.
EVERY NOTE IS "D."
THAT'S NOT TRUE AT ALL.
SADLY, ENA IS CORRECT.
WHAT!?

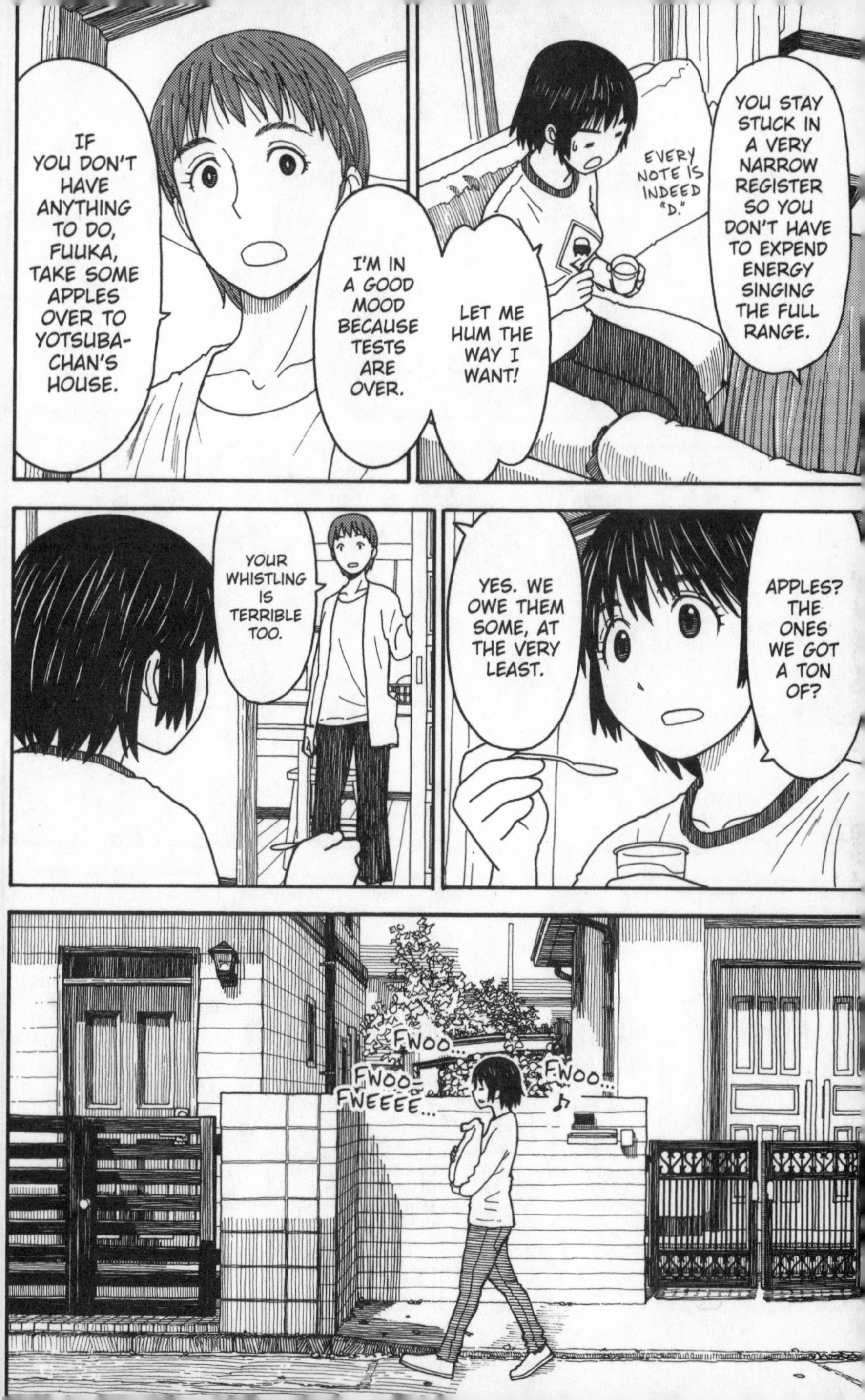
YOU STAY STUCK IN A VERY NARROW REGISTER SO YOU DON'T HAVE TO EXPEND ENERGY SINGING THE FULL RANGE.
EVERY NOTE IS INDEED "D."
LET ME HUM THE WAY I WANT!
I'M IN A GOOD MOOD BECAUSE TESTS ARE OVER.
IF YOU DON'T HAVE ANYTHING TO DO, FUUKA, TAKE SOME APPLES OVER TO YOTSUBA-CHAN'S HOUSE.
APPLES? THE ONES WE GOT A TON OF?
YES. WE OWE THEM SOME, AT THE VERY LEAST.
YOUR WHISTLING IS TERRIBLE TOO.
FWOO... ♪
FWOO...
FWOO-FWEEEEE...

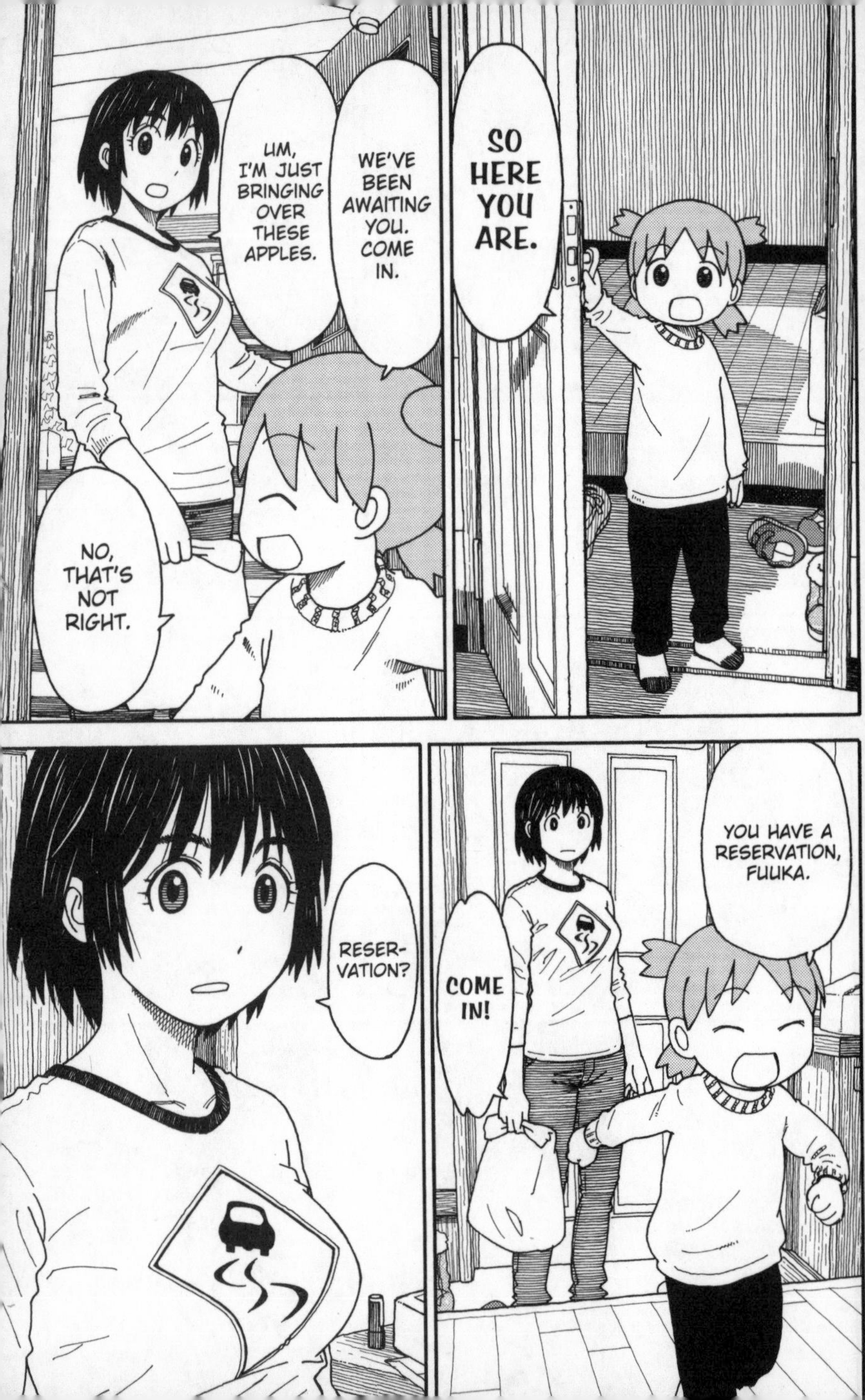
SO HERE YOU ARE.
WE'VE BEEN AWAITING YOU. COME IN.
UM, I'M JUST BRINGING OVER THESE APPLES.
NO, THAT'S NOT RIGHT.
YOU HAVE A RESERVATION, FUUKA.
COME IN!
RESER-VATION?

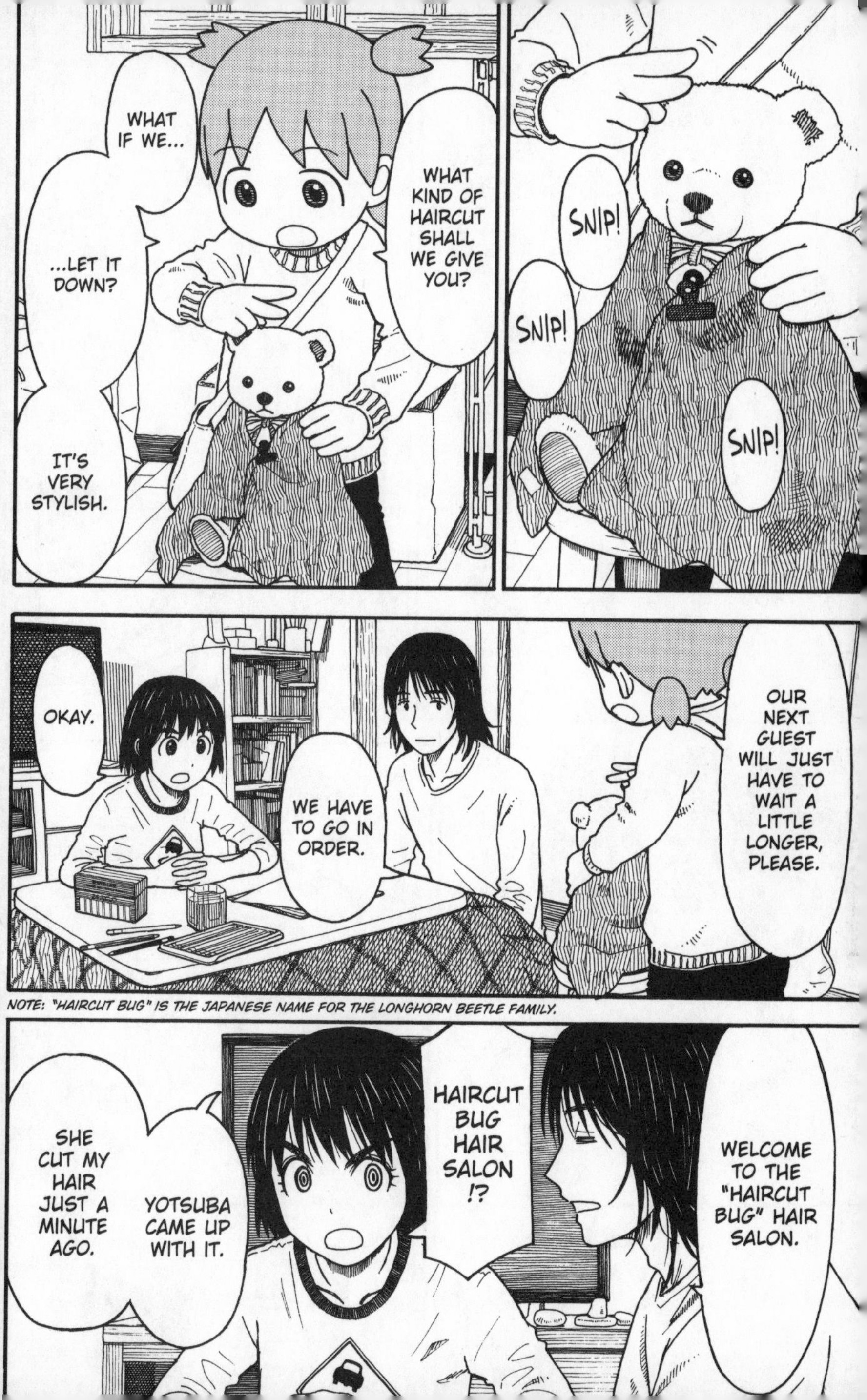
SNIP!
SNIP!
SNIP!
WHAT KIND OF HAIRCUT SHALL WE GIVE YOU?
WHAT IF WE...
...LET IT DOWN?
IT'S VERY STYLISH.
OUR NEXT GUEST WILL JUST HAVE TO WAIT A LITTLE LONGER, PLEASE.
WE HAVE TO GO IN ORDER.
OKAY.
WELCOME TO THE "HAIRCUT BUG" HAIR SALON.
HAIRCUT BUG HAIR SALON!?
YOTSUBA CAME UP WITH IT.
SHE CUT MY HAIR JUST A MINUTE AGO.
NOTE: "HAIRCUT BUG" IS THE JAPANESE NAME FOR THE LONGHORN BEETLE FAMILY.

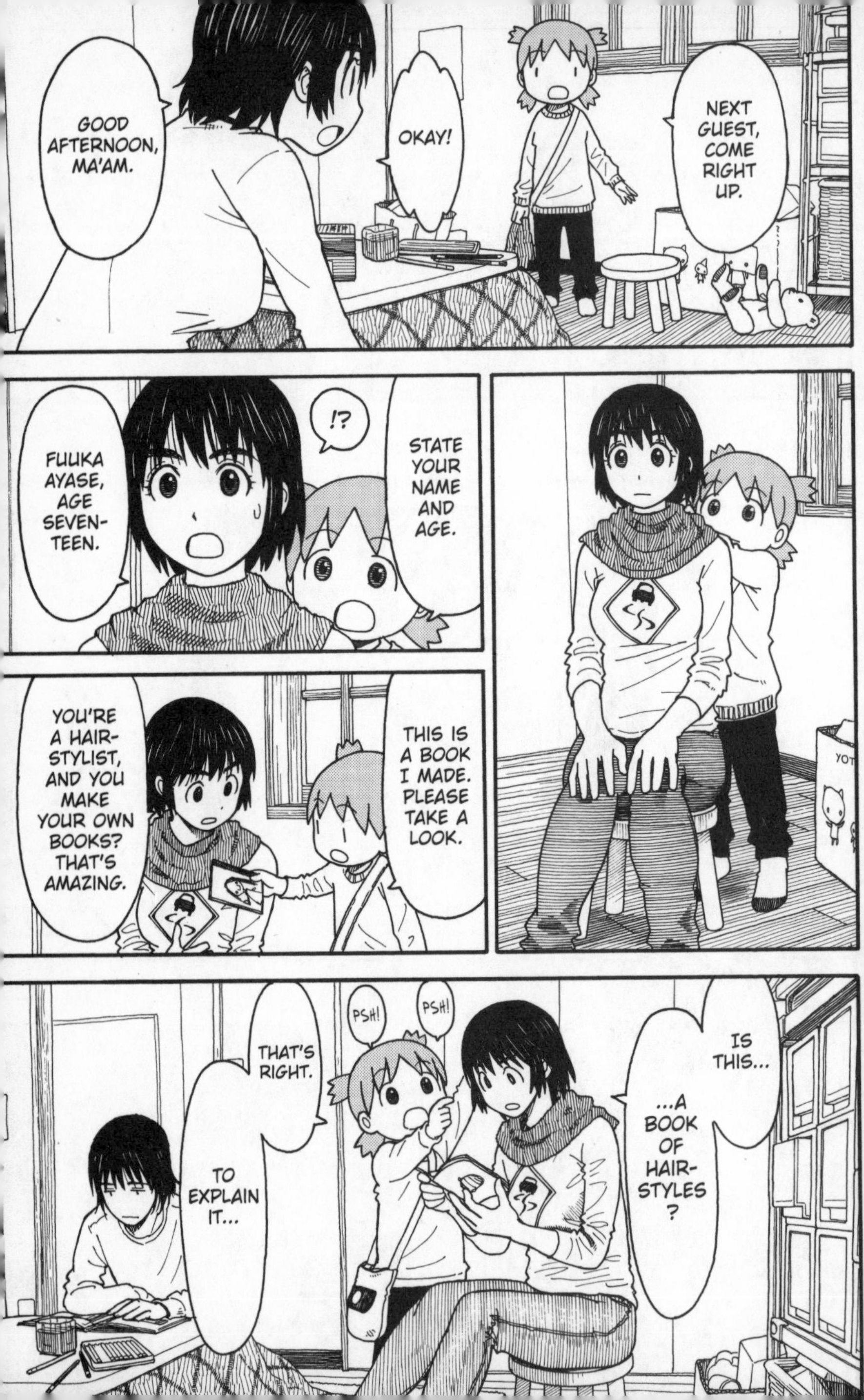
NEXT GUEST, COME RIGHT UP.
OKAY!
GOOD AFTERNOON, MA'AM.
STATE YOUR NAME AND AGE.
!?
FUUKA AYASE, AGE SEVEN-TEEN.
THIS IS A BOOK I MADE. PLEASE TAKE A LOOK.
YOU'RE A HAIR-STYLIST, AND YOU MAKE YOUR OWN BOOKS? THAT'S AMAZING.
IS THIS...
...A BOOK OF HAIR-STYLES?
PSH!
PSH!
THAT'S RIGHT.
TO EXPLAIN IT...

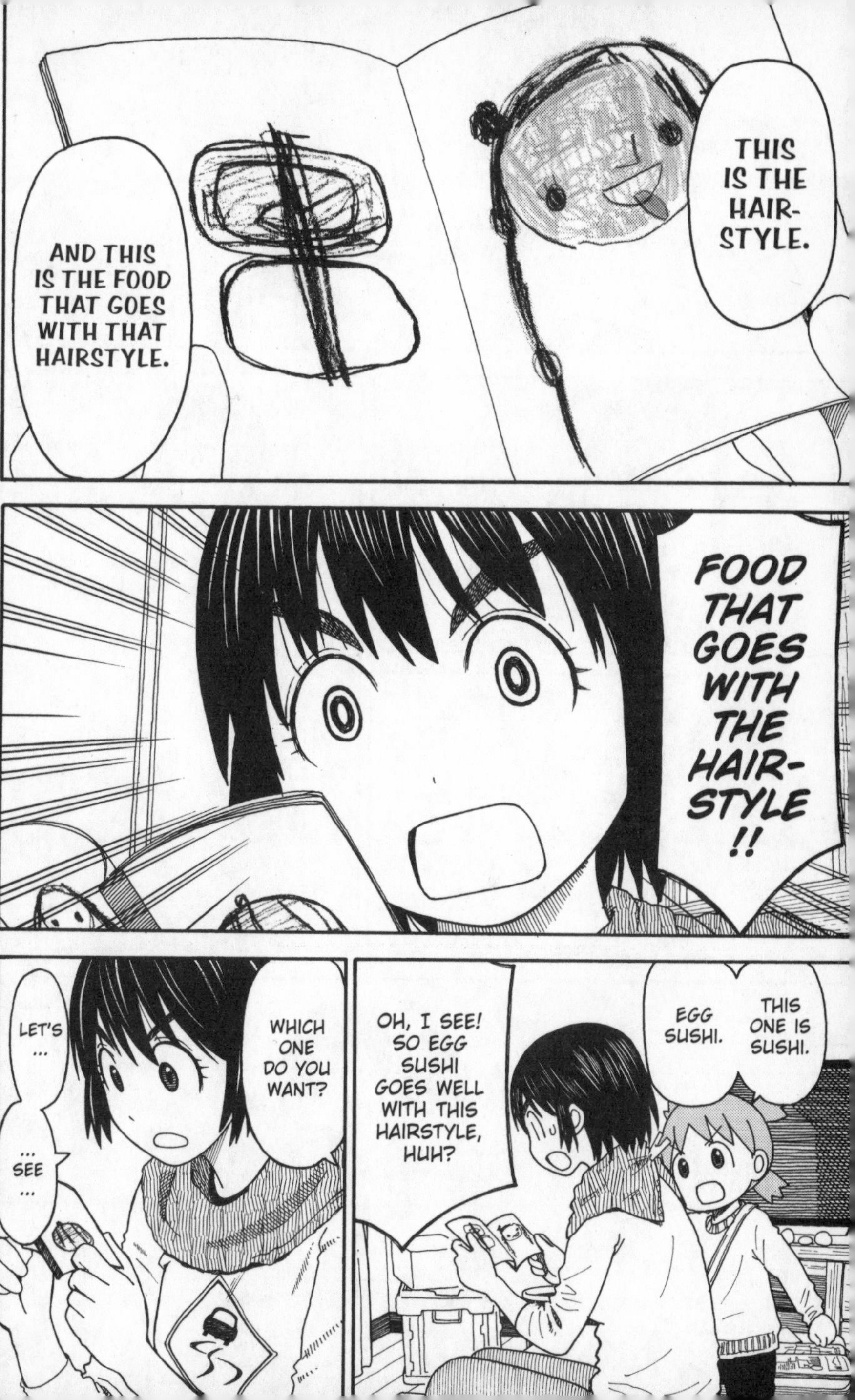
THIS IS THE HAIR-STYLE.
AND THIS IS THE FOOD THAT GOES WITH THAT HAIRSTYLE.
FOOD THAT GOES WITH THE HAIR-STYLE !!
THIS ONE IS SUSHI.
EGG SUSHI.
OH, I SEE! SO EGG SUSHI GOES WELL WITH THIS HAIRSTYLE, HUH?
WHICH ONE DO YOU WANT?
LET'S ...
... SEE ...

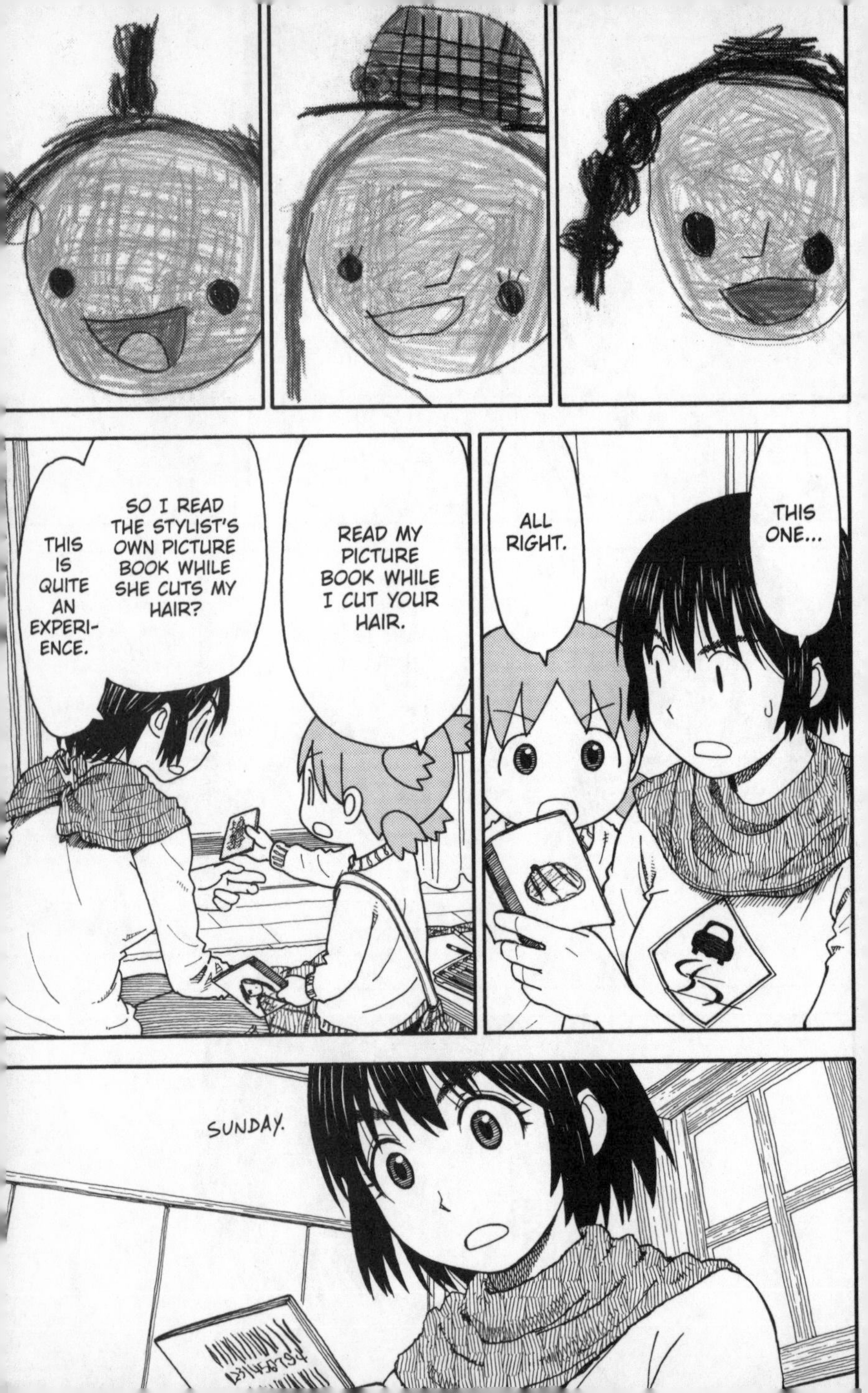
THIS ONE...
ALL RIGHT.
READ MY PICTURE BOOK WHILE I CUT YOUR HAIR.
SO I READ THE STYLIST'S OWN PICTURE BOOK WHILE SHE CUTS MY HAIR?
THIS IS QUITE AN EXPERIENCE.
SUNDAY.

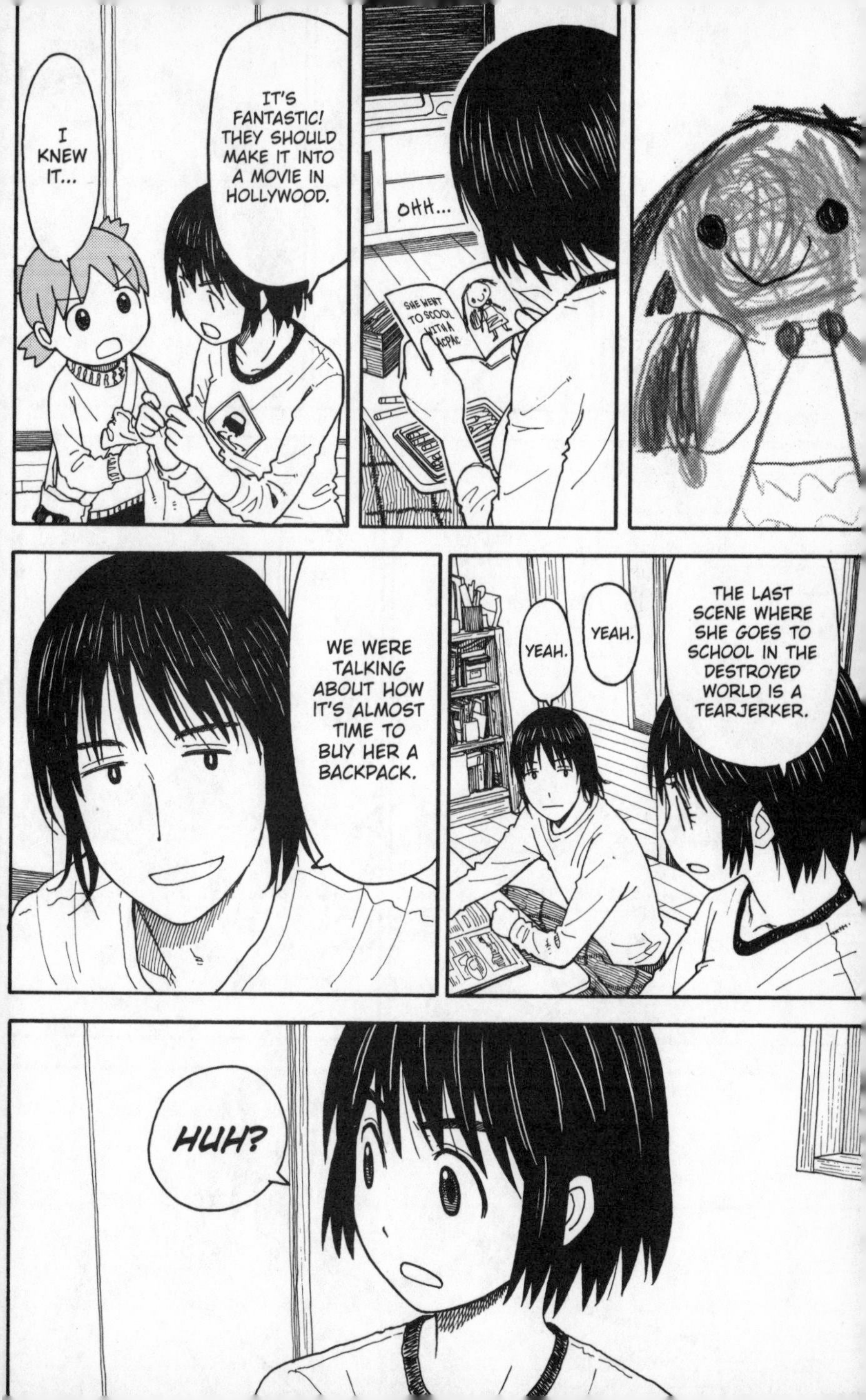

OHH...
SHE WENT TO SCOOL WITH A ACPAC
IT'S FANTASTIC! THEY SHOULD MAKE IT INTO A MOVIE IN HOLLYWOOD.
I KNEW IT...
THE LAST SCENE WHERE SHE GOES TO SCHOOL IN THE DESTROYED WORLD IS A TEARJERKER.
YEAH.
YEAH.
WE WERE TALKING ABOUT HOW IT'S ALMOST TIME TO BUY HER A BACKPACK.
HUH?

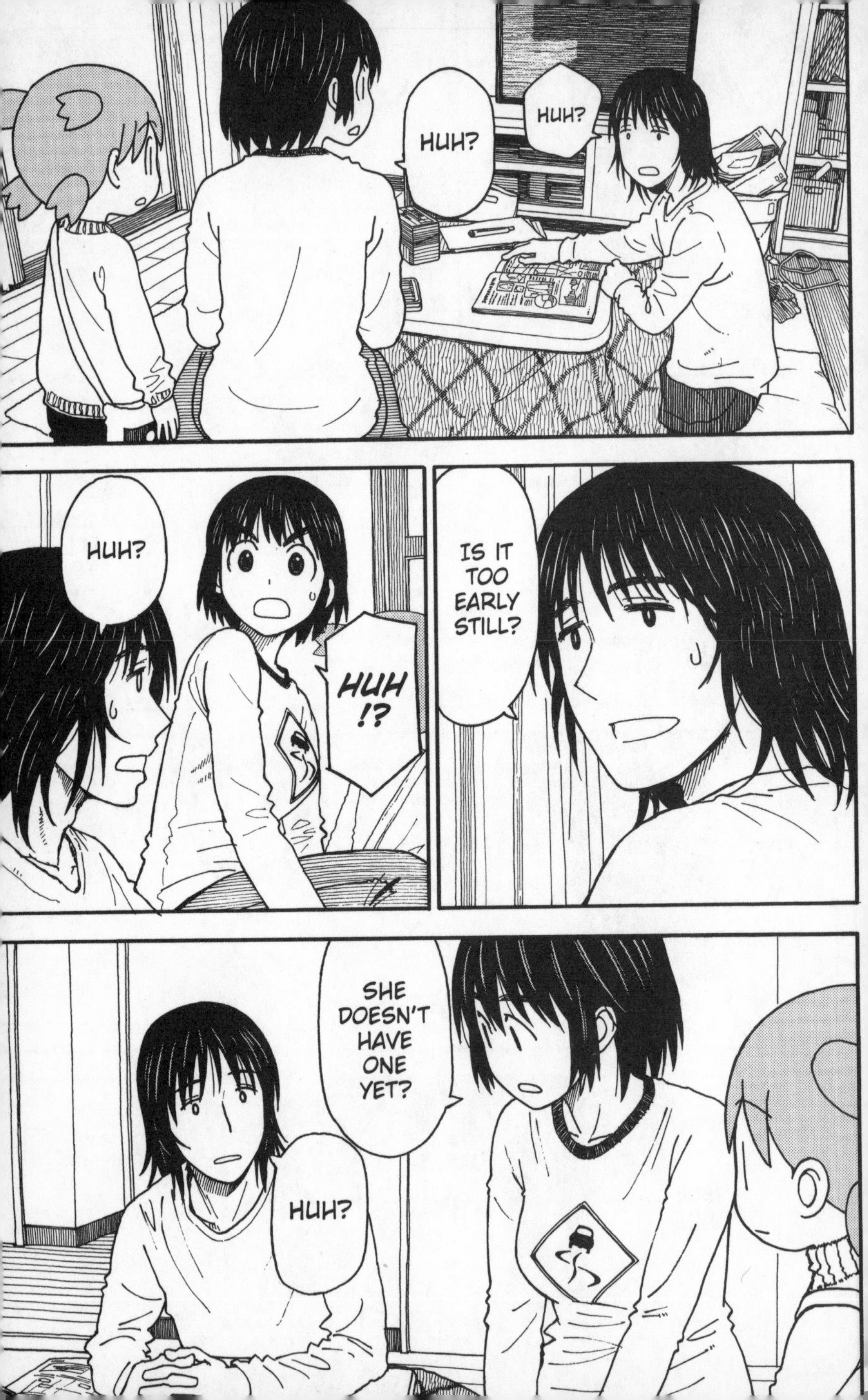
HUH?
HUH?
IS IT TOO EARLY STILL?
HUH?
HUH!?
SHE DOESN'T HAVE ONE YET?
HUH?

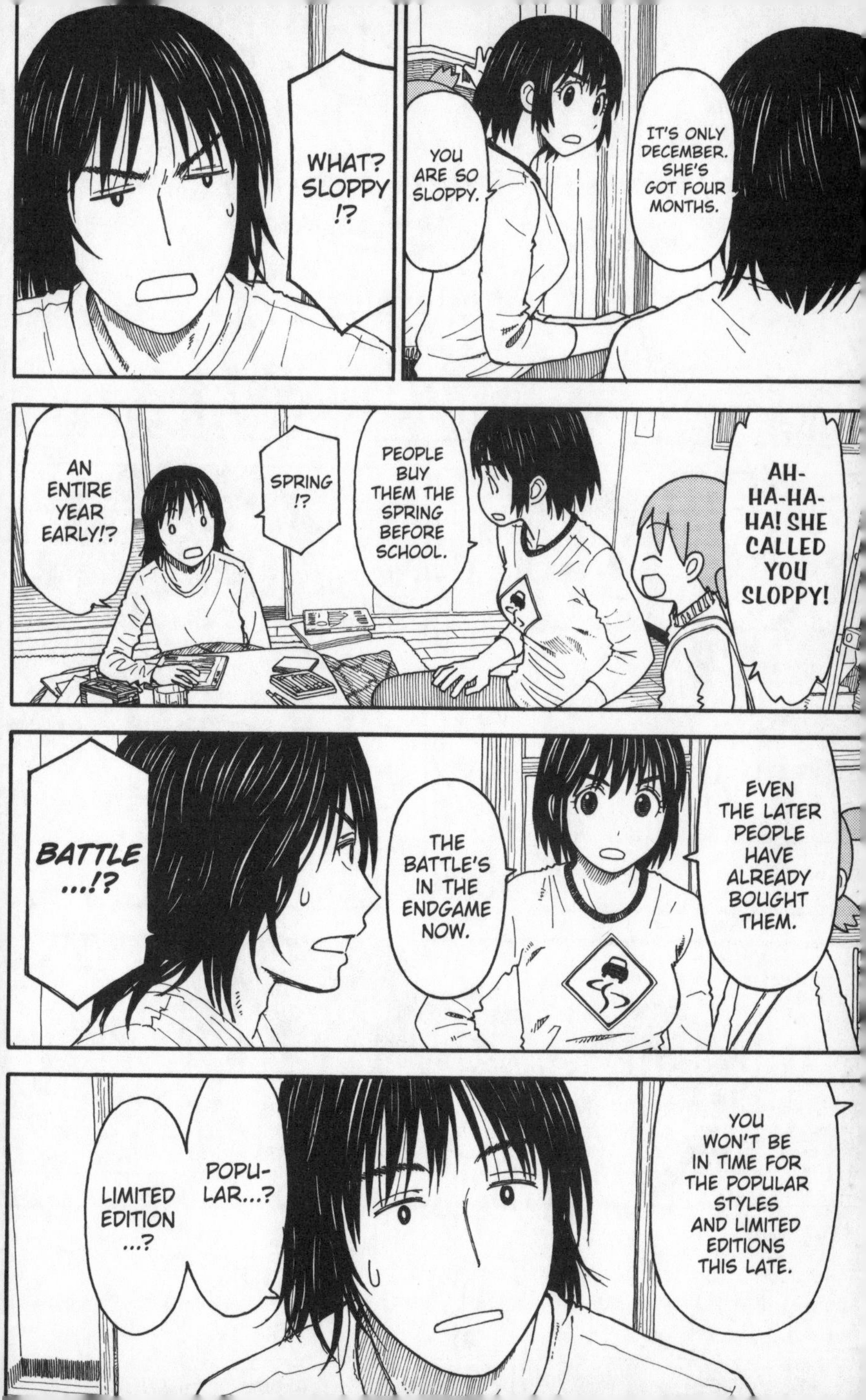
IT'S ONLY DECEMBER. SHE'S GOT FOUR MONTHS.
YOU ARE SO SLOPPY.
WHAT? SLOPPY!?
AH-HA-HA-HA! SHE CALLED YOU SLOPPY!
PEOPLE BUY THEM THE SPRING BEFORE SCHOOL.
SPRING!?
AN ENTIRE YEAR EARLY!?
EVEN THE LATER PEOPLE HAVE ALREADY BOUGHT THEM.
THE BATTLE'S IN THE ENDGAME NOW.
BATTLE...!?
YOU WON'T BE IN TIME FOR THE POPULAR STYLES AND LIMITED EDITIONS THIS LATE.
POPU-LAR...?
LIMITED EDITION...?

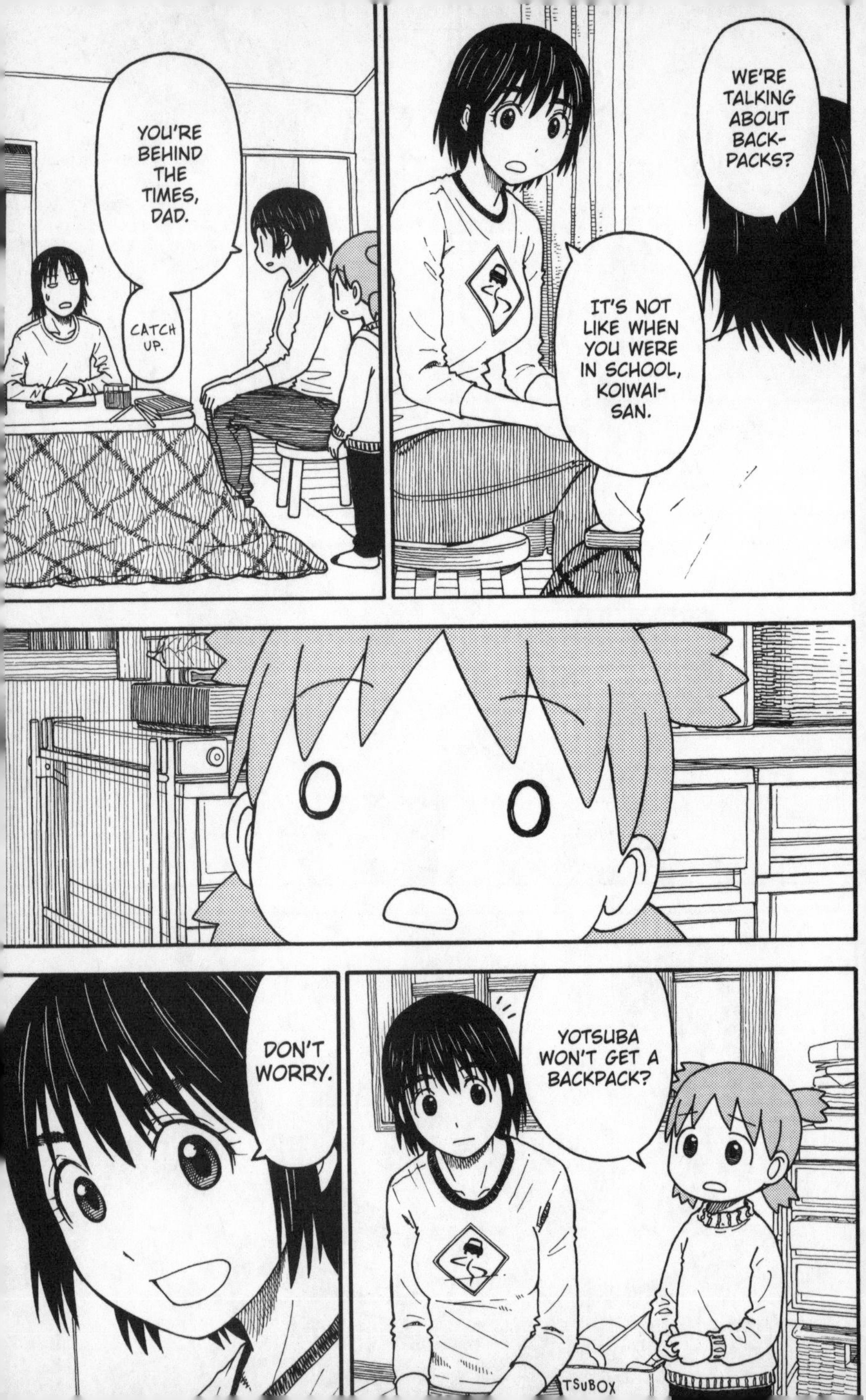
WE'RE TALKING ABOUT BACK-PACKS?
IT'S NOT LIKE WHEN YOU WERE IN SCHOOL, KOIWAI-SAN.
YOU'RE BEHIND THE TIMES, DAD.
CATCH UP.
YOTSUBA WON'T GET A BACKPACK?
TSUBOX
DON'T WORRY.

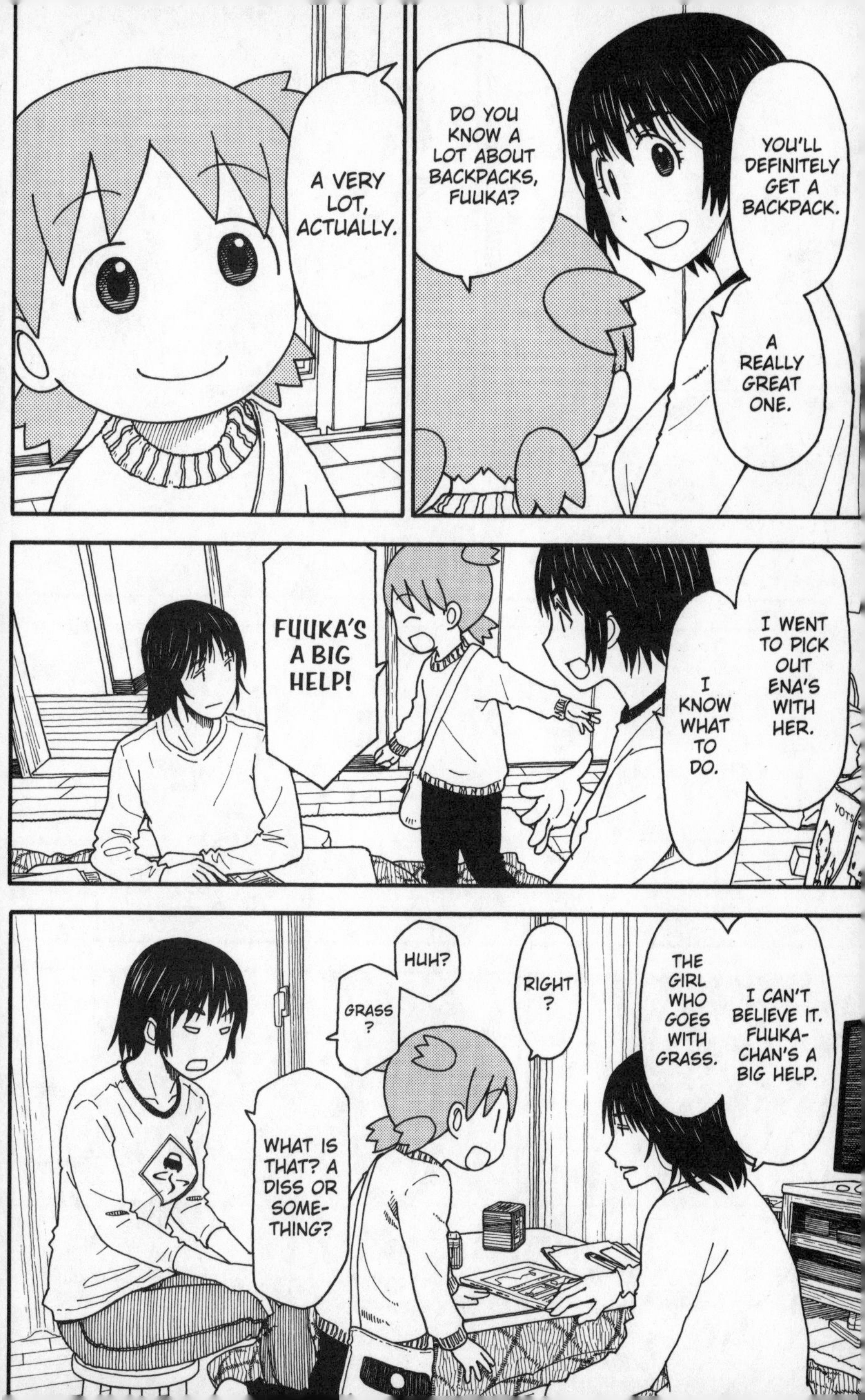
YOU'LL DEFINITELY GET A BACKPACK.
A REALLY GREAT ONE.
DO YOU KNOW A LOT ABOUT BACKPACKS, FUUKA?
A VERY LOT, ACTUALLY.
I WENT TO PICK OUT ENA'S WITH HER.
I KNOW WHAT TO DO.
FUUKA'S A BIG HELP!
I CAN'T BELIEVE IT. FUUKA-CHAN'S A BIG HELP.
THE GIRL WHO GOES WITH GRASS.
RIGHT?
HUH?
GRASS?
WHAT IS THAT? A DISS OR SOME-THING?

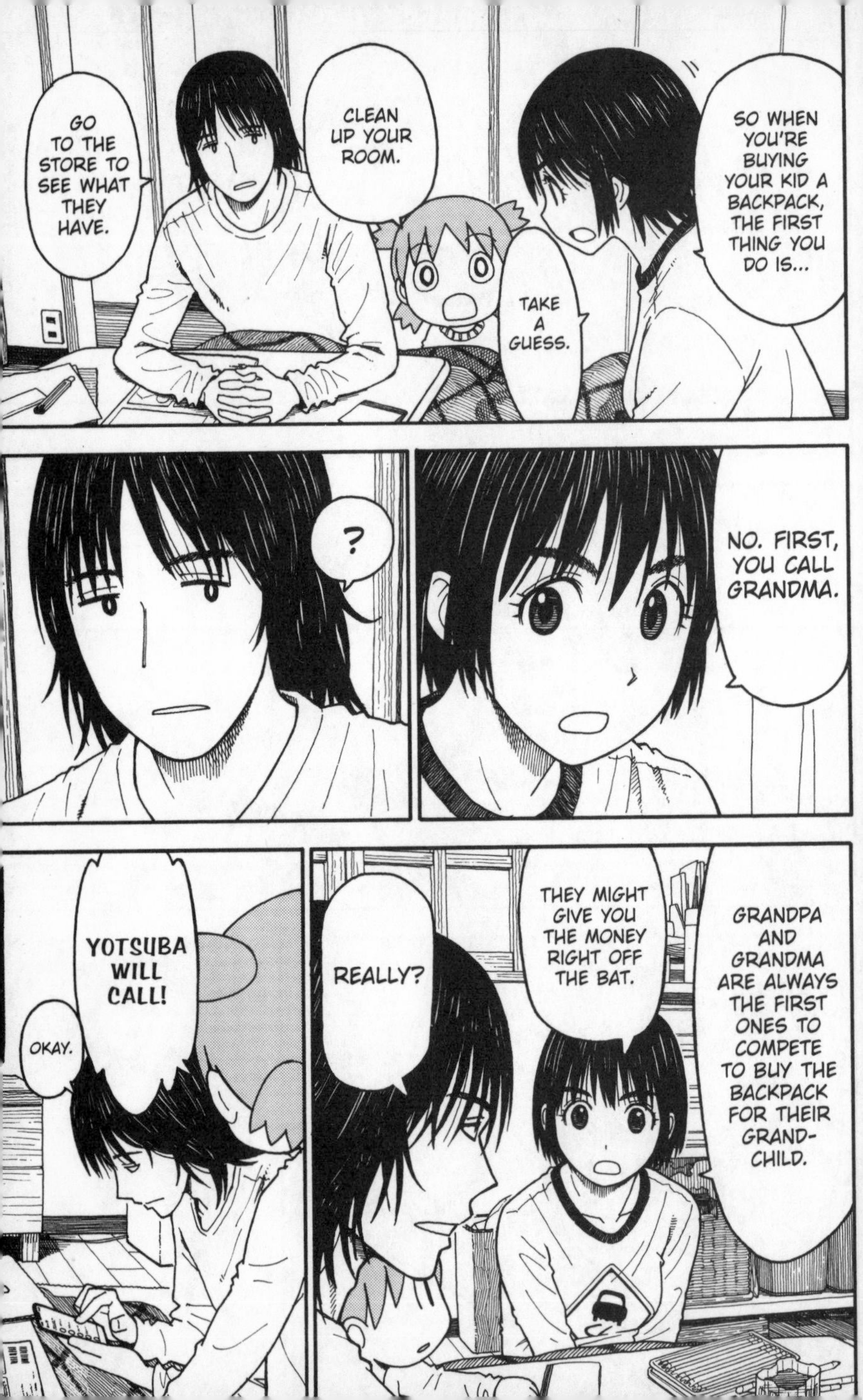
SO WHEN YOU'RE BUYING YOUR KID A BACKPACK, THE FIRST THING YOU DO IS...
TAKE A GUESS.
CLEAN UP YOUR ROOM.
GO TO THE STORE TO SEE WHAT THEY HAVE.
NO. FIRST, YOU CALL GRANDMA.
?
GRANDPA AND GRANDMA ARE ALWAYS THE FIRST ONES TO COMPETE TO BUY THE BACKPACK FOR THEIR GRAND-CHILD.
THEY MIGHT GIVE YOU THE MONEY RIGHT OFF THE BAT.
REALLY?
YOTSUBA WILL CALL!
OKAY.

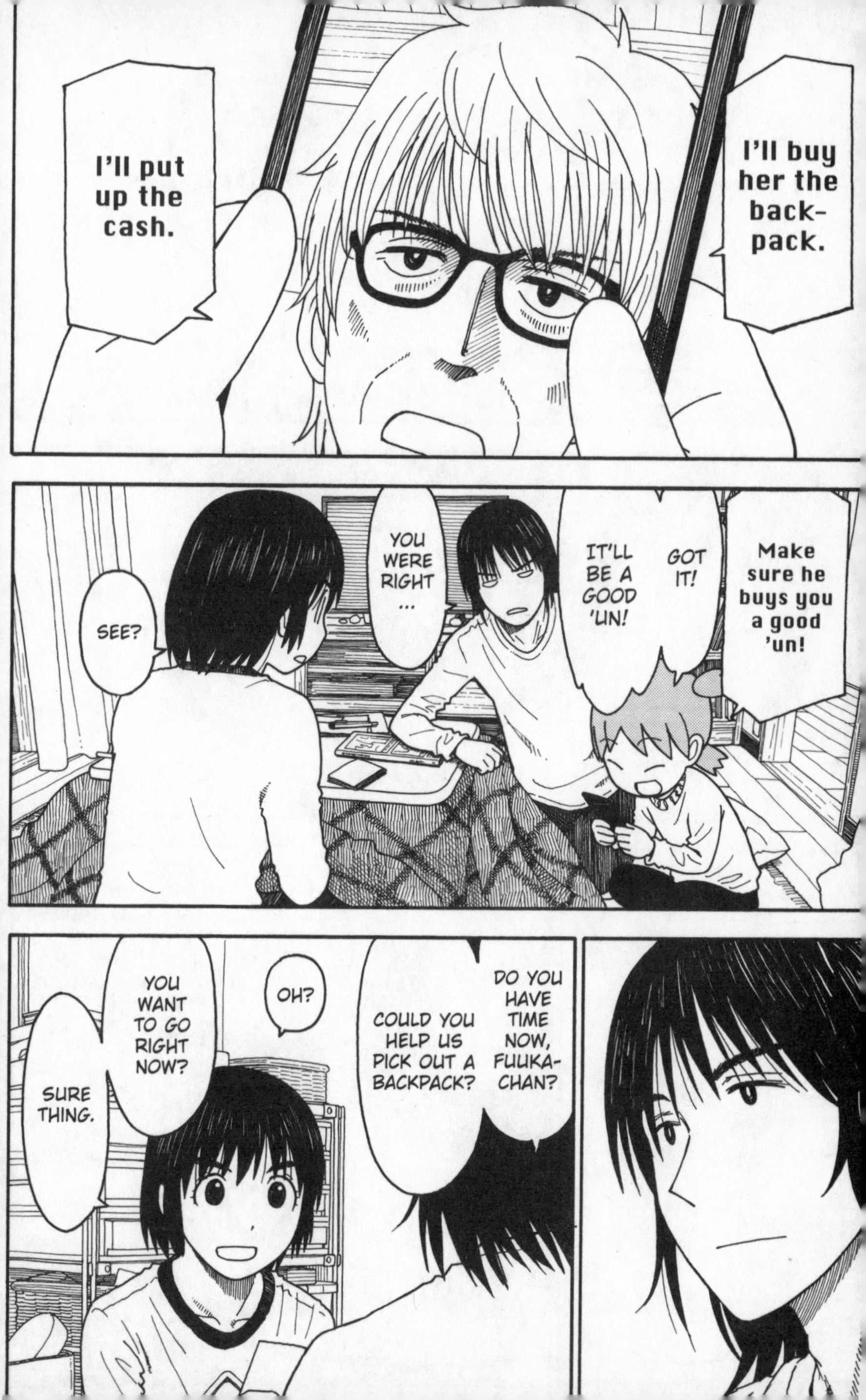
I'll buy her the back-pack.
I'll put up the cash.
Make sure he buys you a good 'un!
GOT IT!
IT'LL BE A GOOD 'UN!
YOU WERE RIGHT ...
SEE?
DO YOU HAVE TIME NOW, FUUKA-CHAN?
COULD YOU HELP US PICK OUT A BACKPACK?
OH?
YOU WANT TO GO RIGHT NOW?
SURE THING.

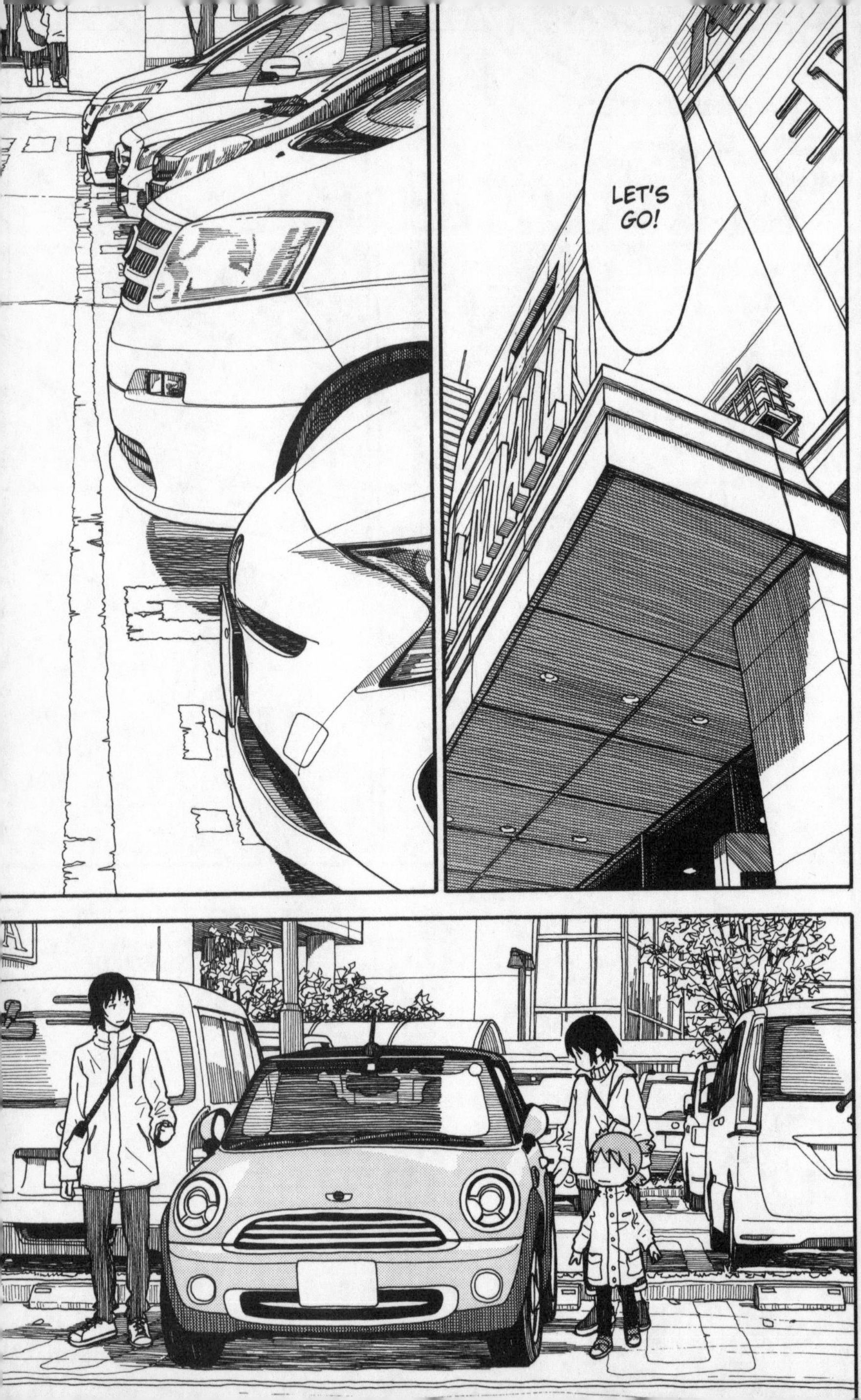
LET'S GO!

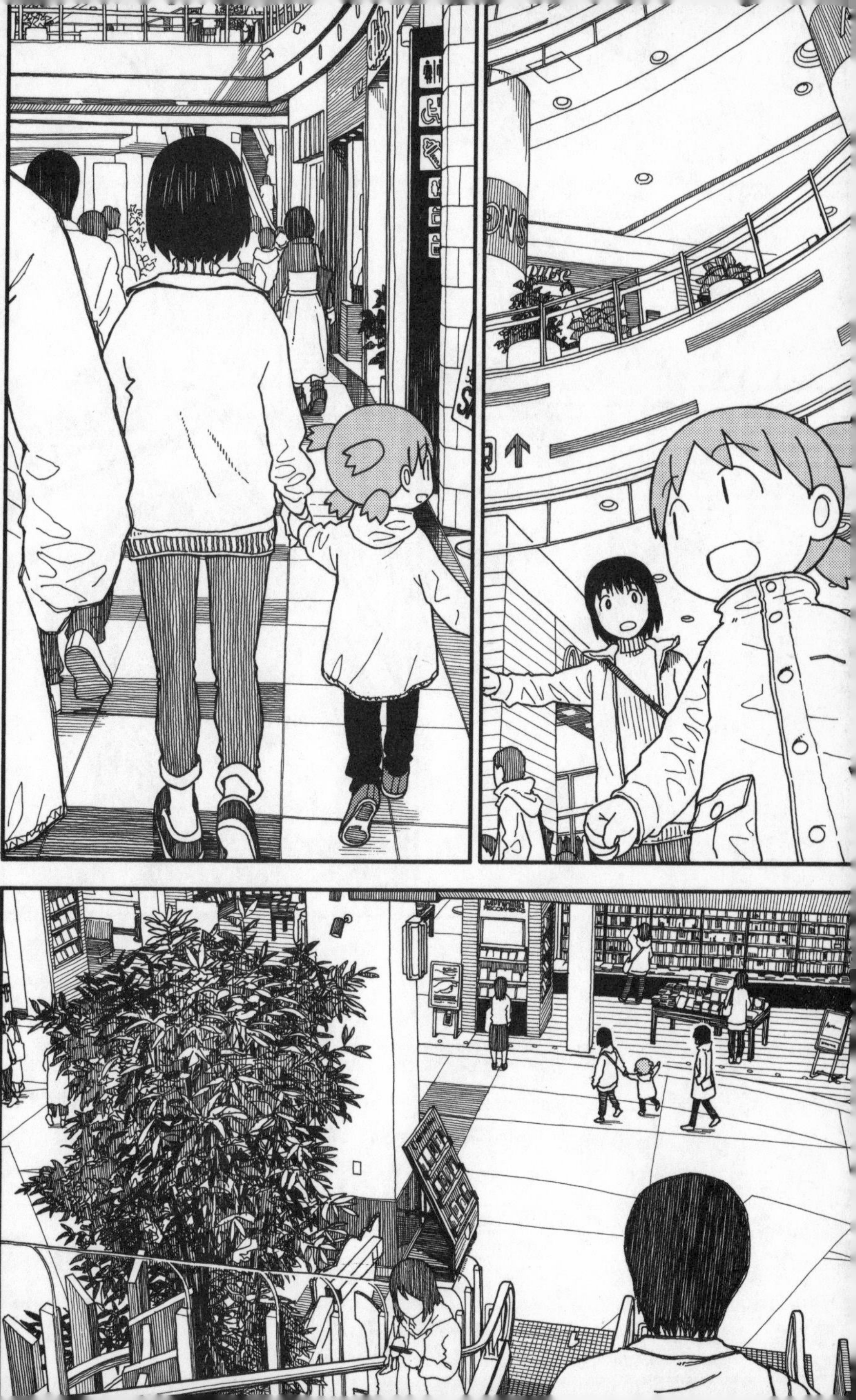

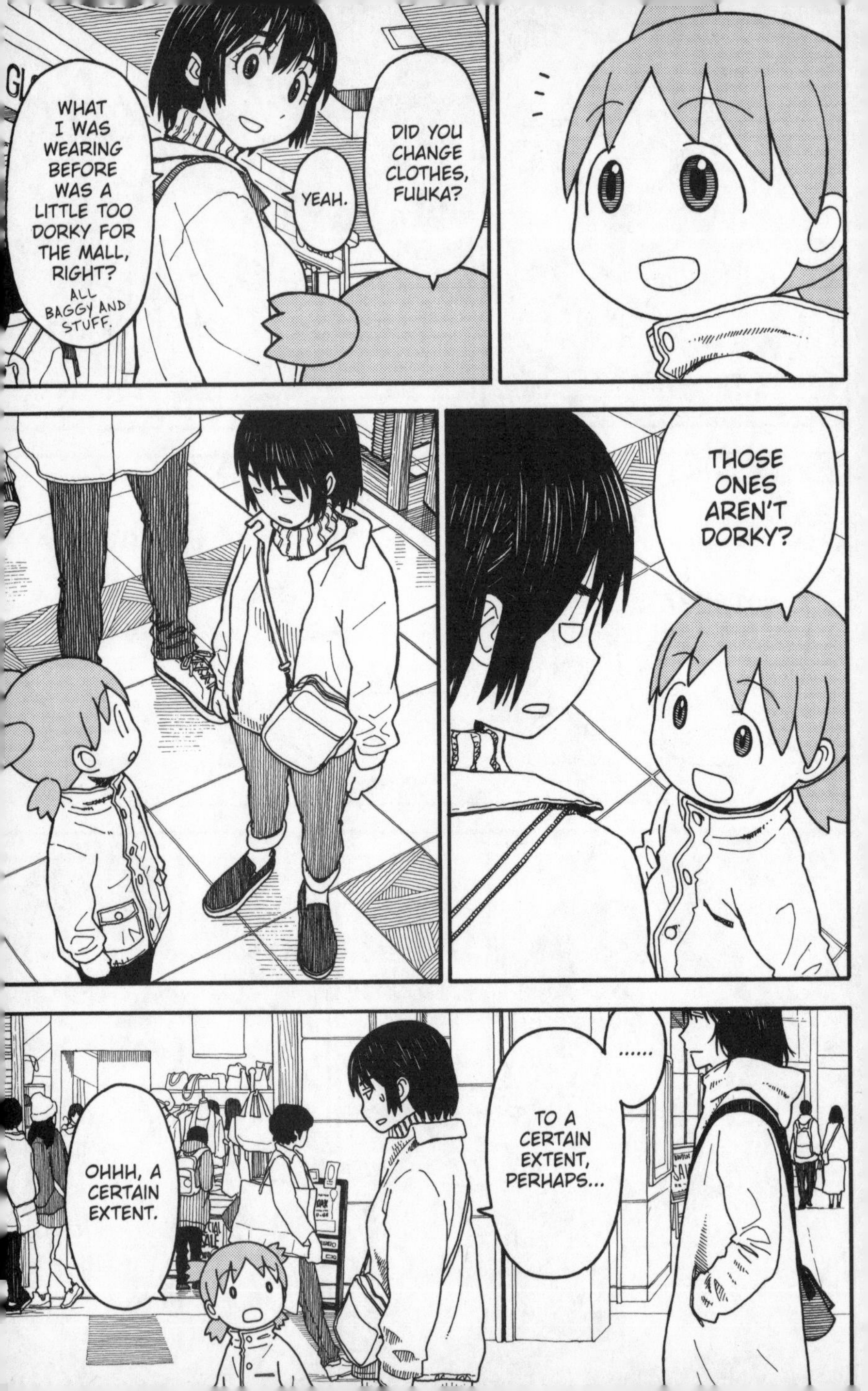
DID YOU CHANGE CLOTHES, FUUKA?
YEAH.
WHAT I WAS WEARING BEFORE WAS A LITTLE TOO DORKY FOR THE MALL, RIGHT?
ALL BAGGY AND STUFF.
THOSE ONES AREN'T DORKY?
......
TO A CERTAIN EXTENT, PERHAPS...
OHHH, A CERTAIN EXTENT.

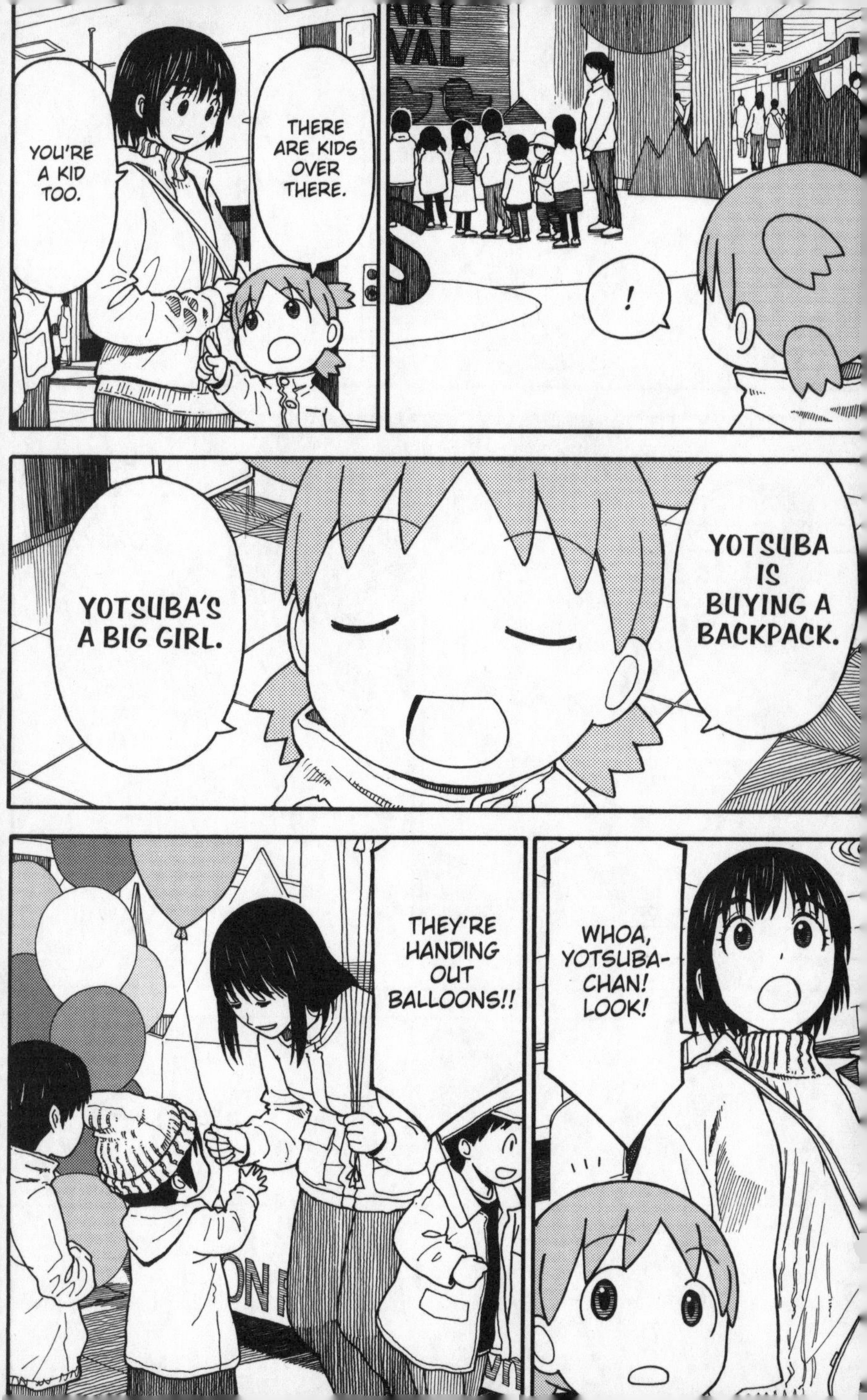
!
THERE ARE KIDS OVER THERE.
YOU'RE A KID TOO.
YOTSUBA IS BUYING A BACKPACK.
YOTSUBA'S A BIG GIRL.
WHOA, YOTSUBA-CHAN! LOOK!
THEY'RE HANDING OUT BALLOONS!!

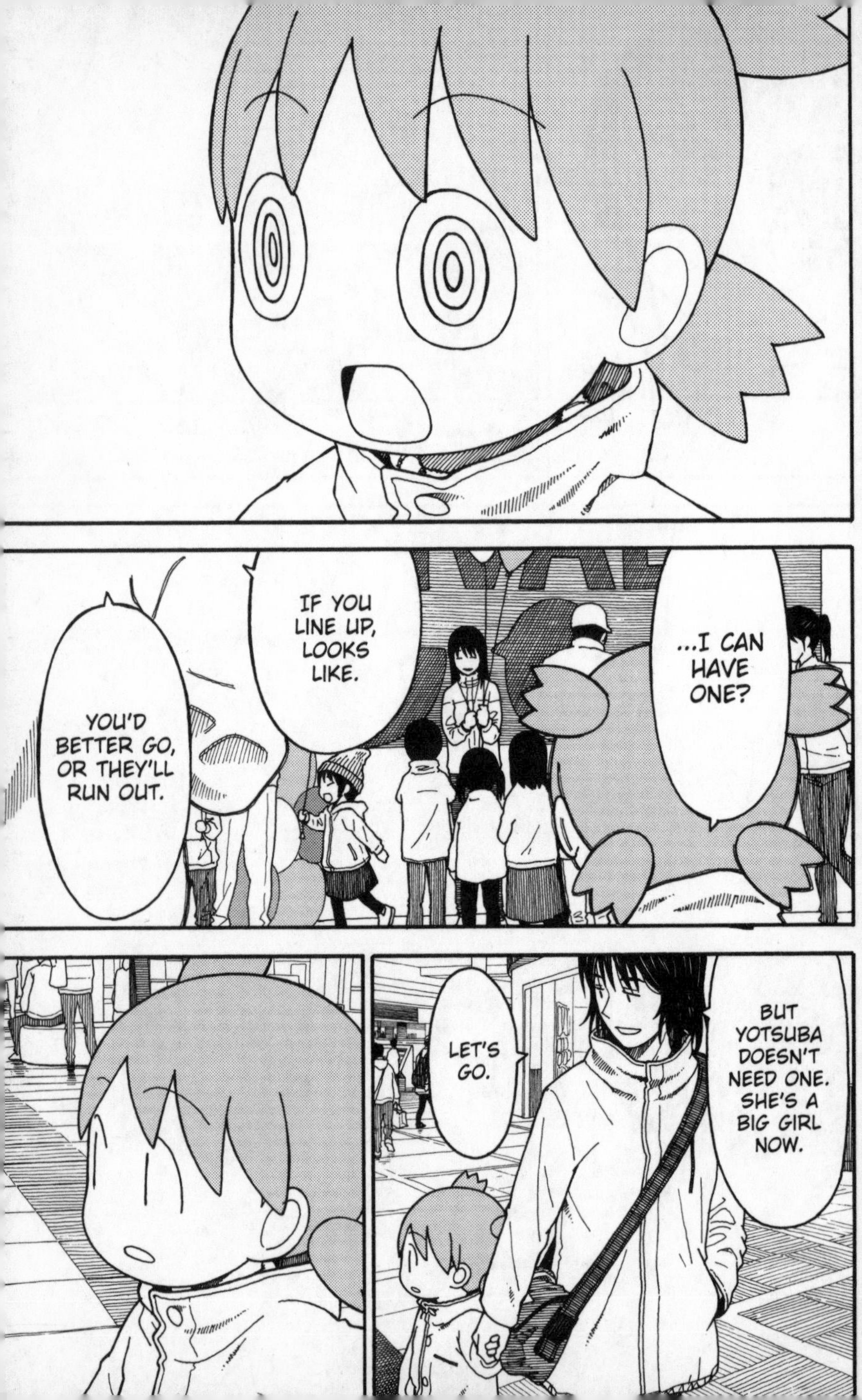
...I CAN HAVE ONE?
IF YOU LINE UP, LOOKS LIKE.
YOU'D BETTER GO, OR THEY'LL RUN OUT.
BUT YOTSUBA DOESN'T NEED ONE. SHE'S A BIG GIRL NOW.
LET'S GO.

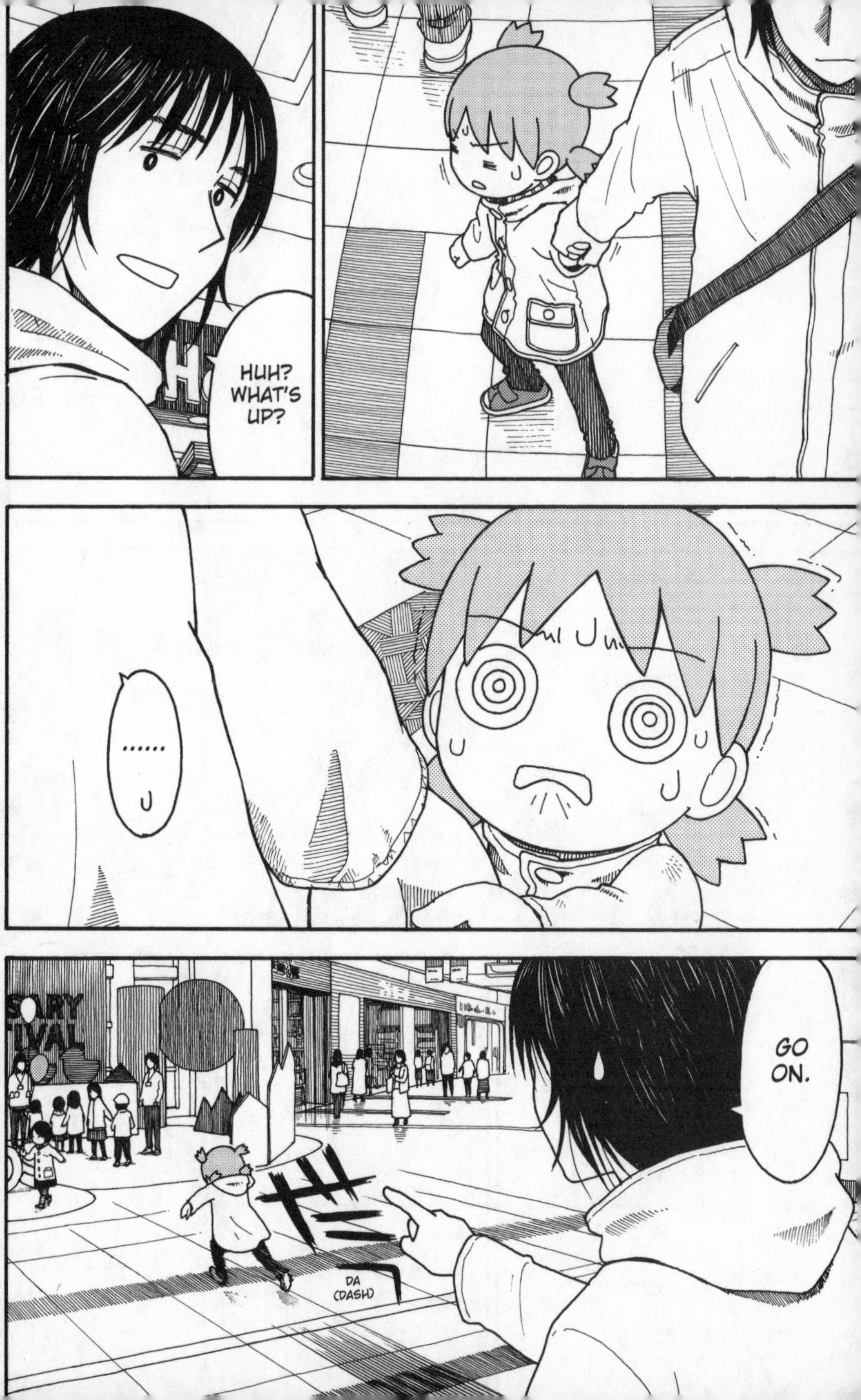
HUH? WHAT'S UP?
......
GO ON.
DA (DASH)

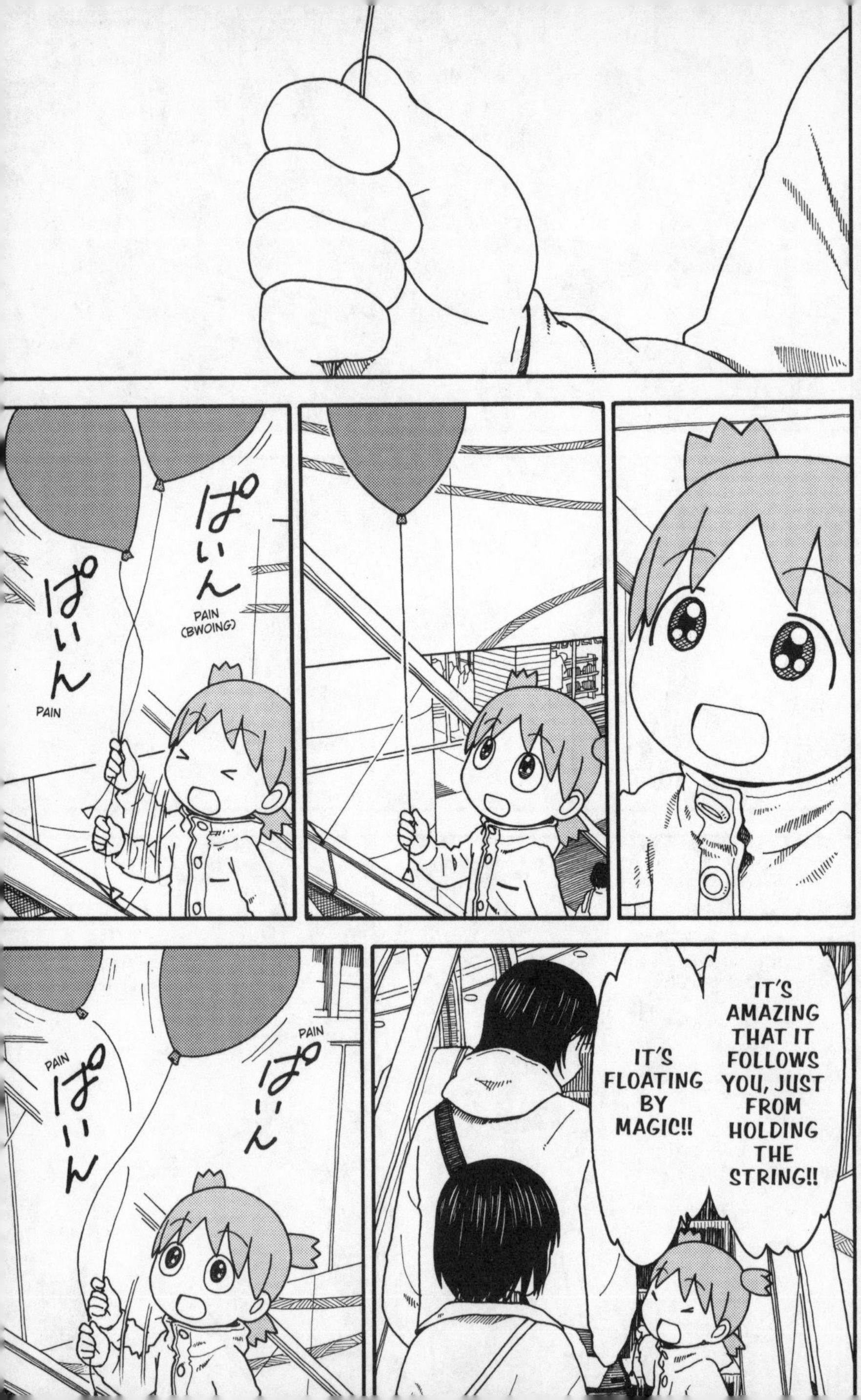
ぱいん
PAIN (BWOING)
ぱいん
PAIN
IT'S AMAZING THAT IT FOLLOWS YOU, JUST FROM HOLDING THE STRING!!
IT'S FLOATING BY MAGIC!!
ぱいん
PAIN
ぱいん
PAIN

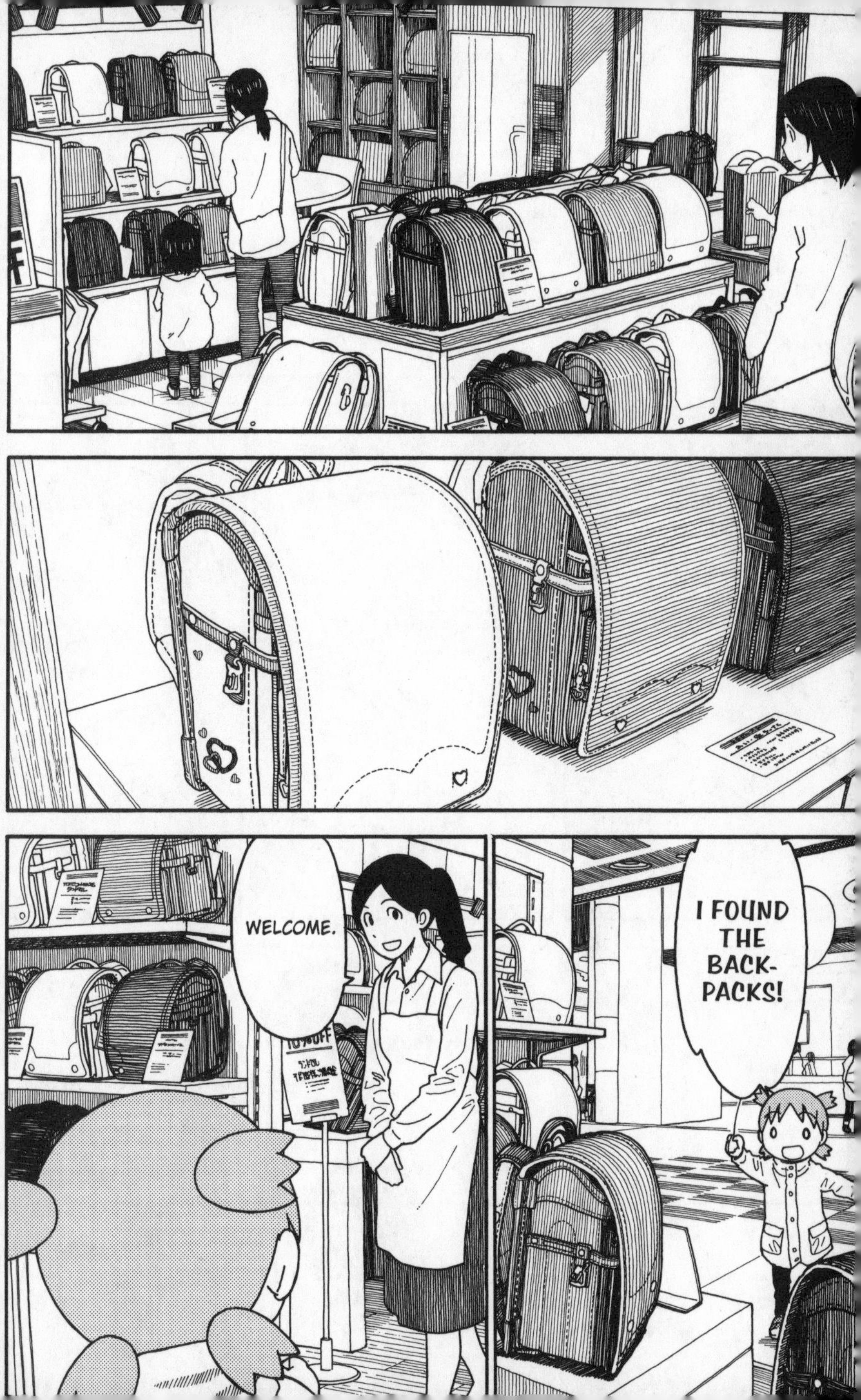
I FOUND THE BACK- PACKS!
WELCOME.

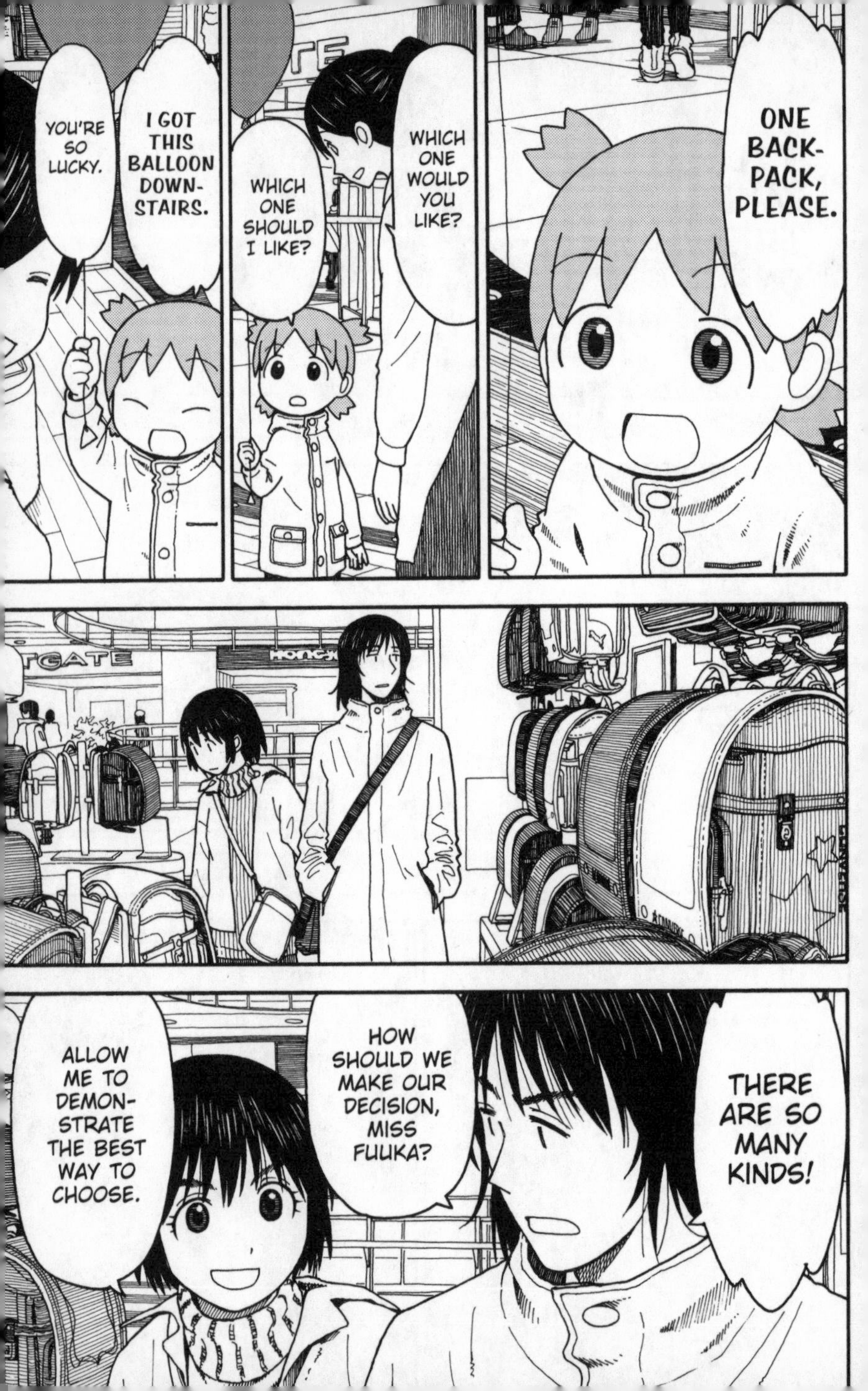
ONE BACK-PACK, PLEASE.
WHICH ONE WOULD YOU LIKE?
WHICH ONE SHOULD I LIKE?
I GOT THIS BALLOON DOWN-STAIRS.
YOU'RE SO LUCKY.
THERE ARE SO MANY KINDS!
HOW SHOULD WE MAKE OUR DECISION, MISS FUUKA?
ALLOW ME TO DEMON-STRATE THE BEST WAY TO CHOOSE.

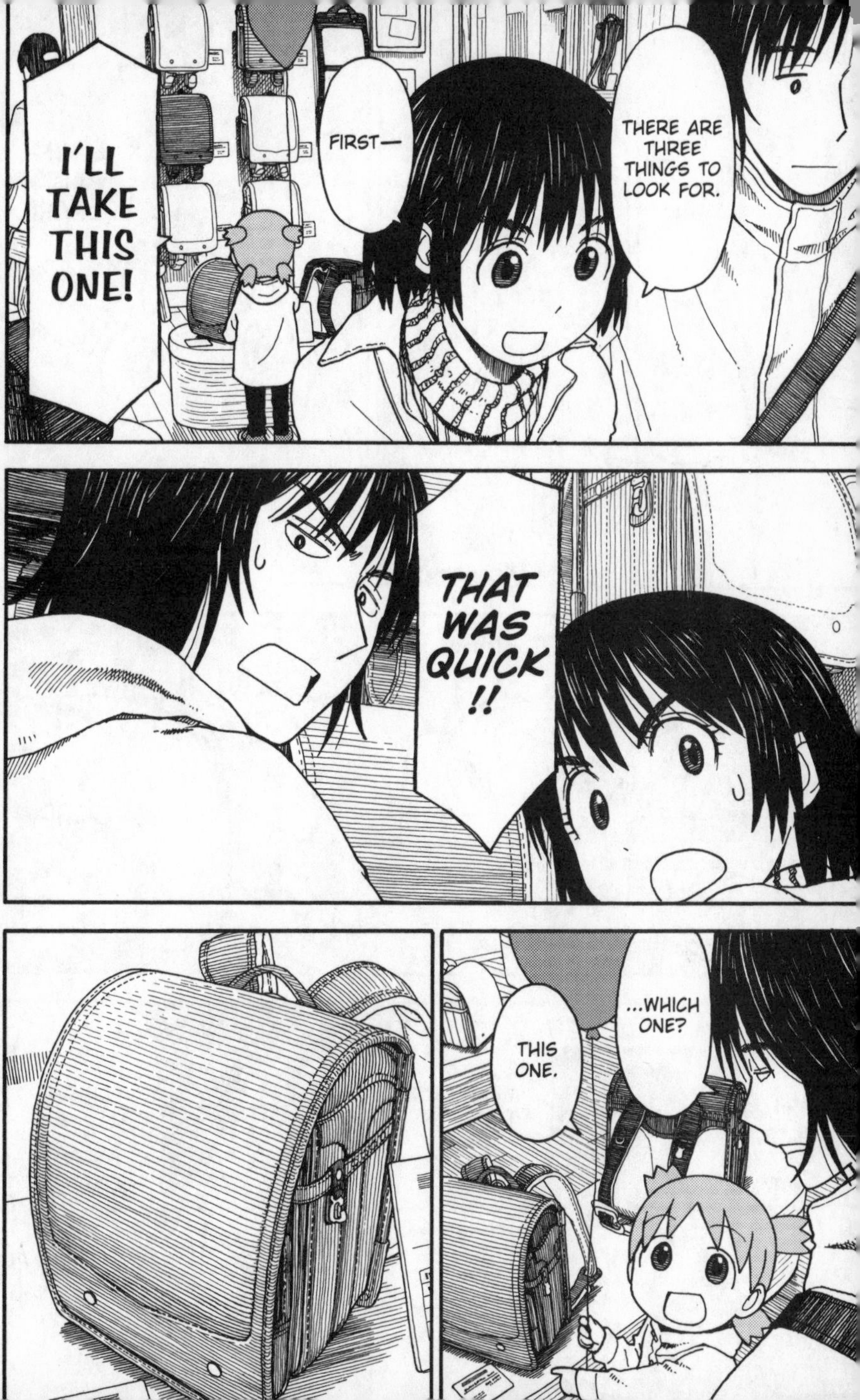
THERE ARE THREE THINGS TO LOOK FOR.
FIRST—
I'LL TAKE THIS ONE!
THAT WAS QUICK!!
...WHICH ONE?
THIS ONE.

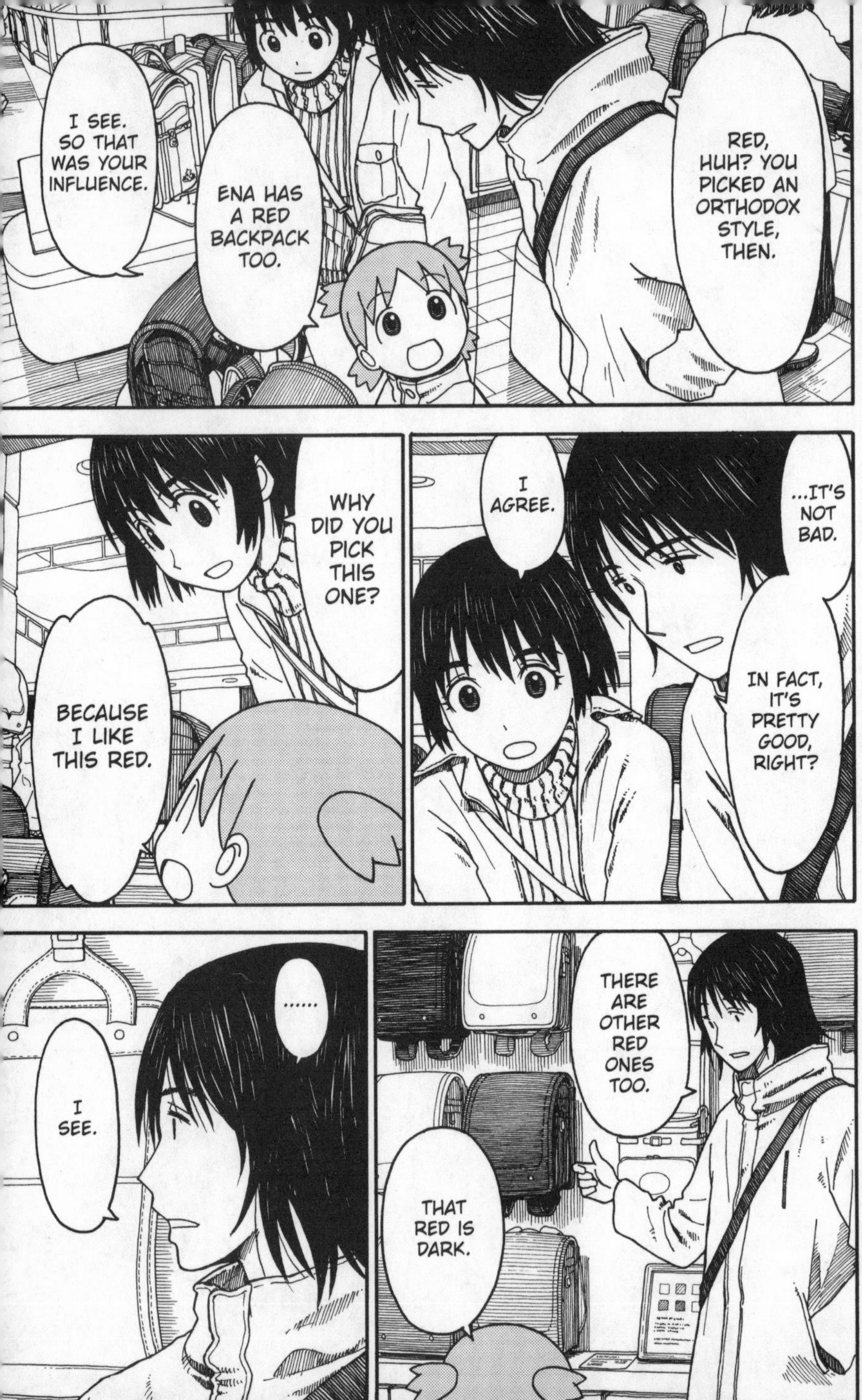
RED, HUH? YOU PICKED AN ORTHODOX STYLE, THEN.
ENA HAS A RED BACKPACK TOO.
I SEE. SO THAT WAS YOUR INFLUENCE.
...IT'S NOT BAD.
I AGREE.
IN FACT, IT'S PRETTY GOOD, RIGHT?
WHY DID YOU PICK THIS ONE?
BECAUSE I LIKE THIS RED.
THERE ARE OTHER RED ONES TOO.
THAT RED IS DARK.
......
I SEE.

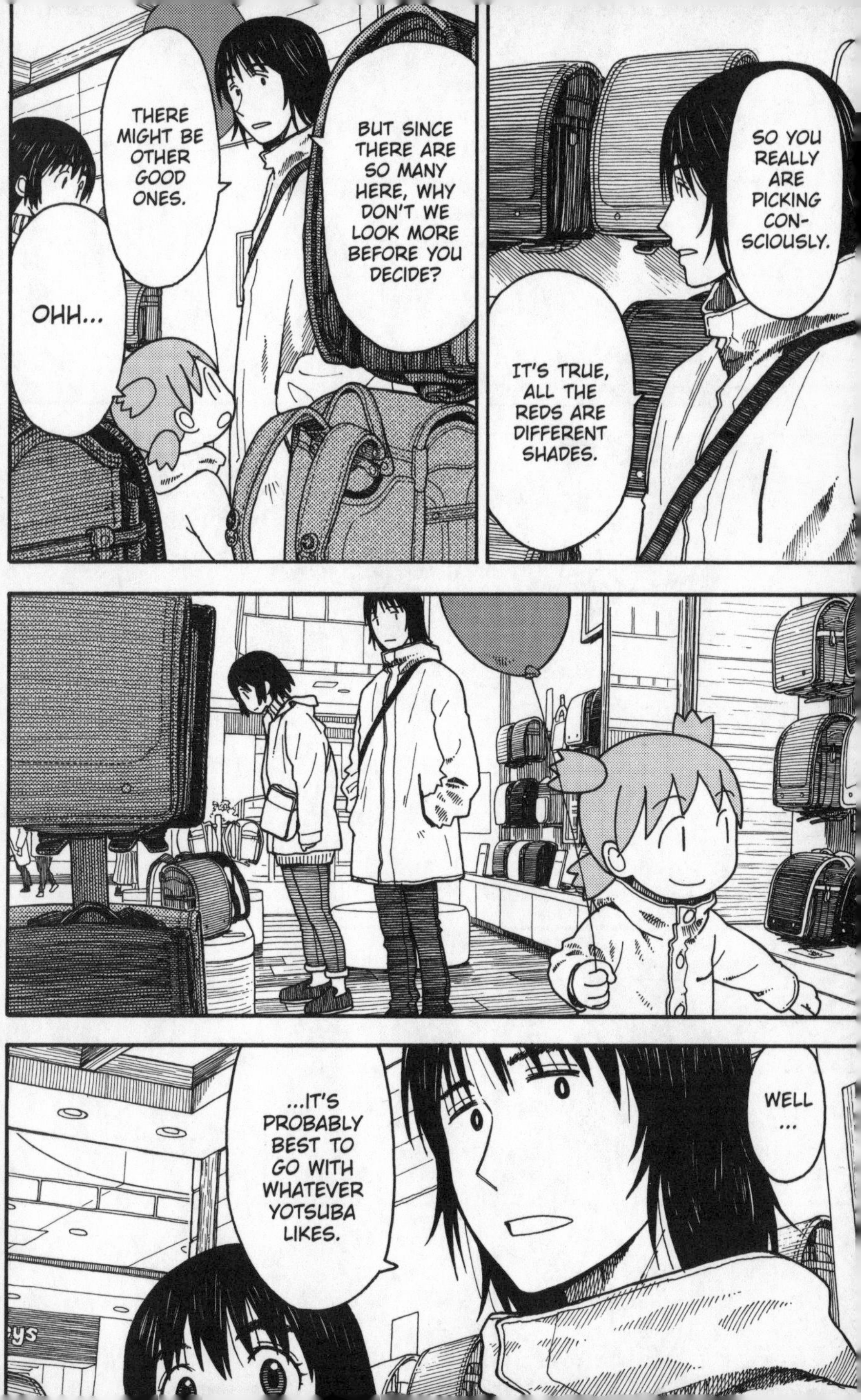
SO YOU REALLY ARE PICKING CON-SCIOUSLY.
IT'S TRUE, ALL THE REDS ARE DIFFERENT SHADES.
BUT SINCE THERE ARE SO MANY HERE, WHY DON'T WE LOOK MORE BEFORE YOU DECIDE?
THERE MIGHT BE OTHER GOOD ONES.
OHH...
WELL ...
...IT'S PROBABLY BEST TO GO WITH WHATEVER YOTSUBA LIKES.

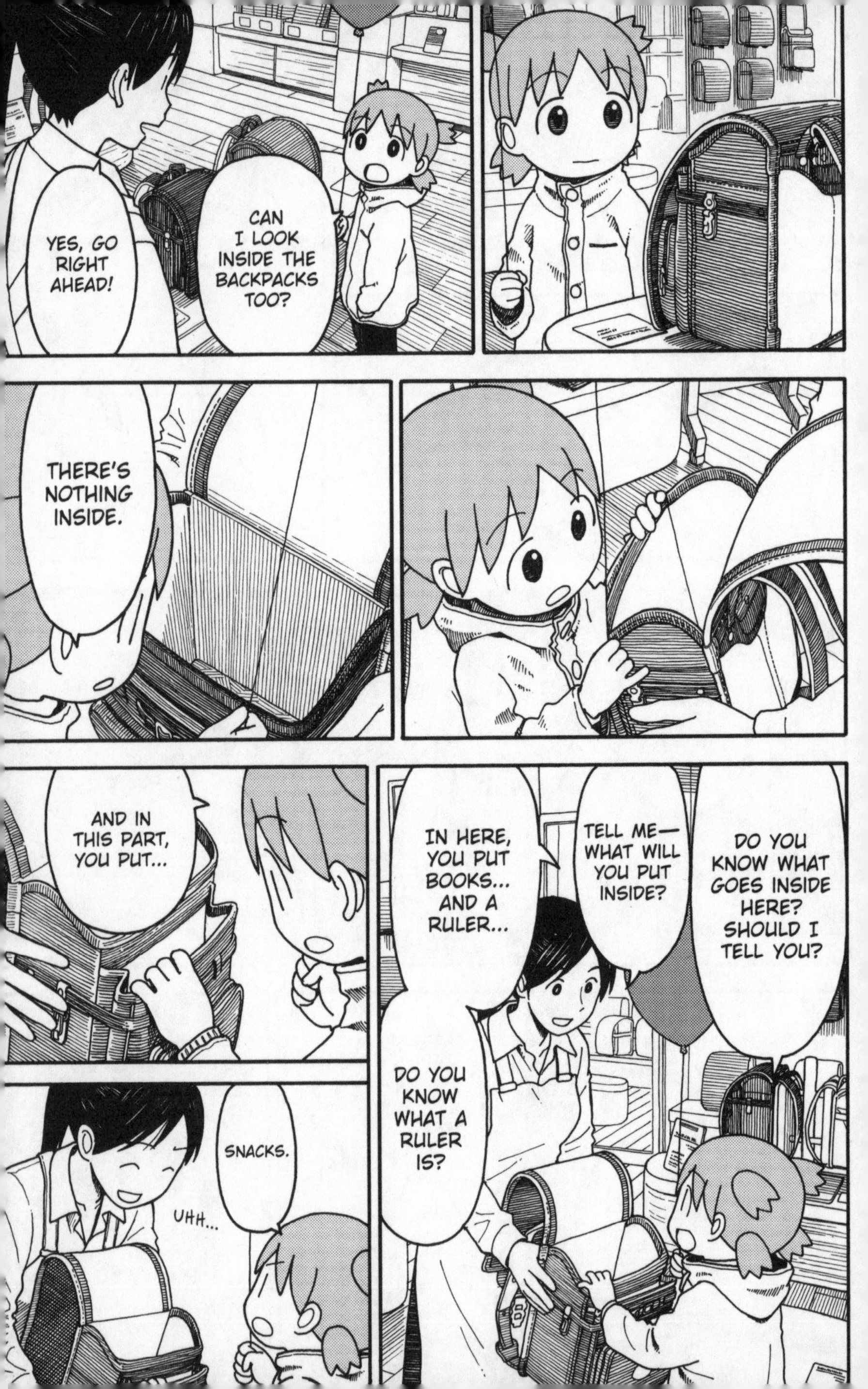
CAN I LOOK INSIDE THE BACKPACKS TOO?
YES, GO RIGHT AHEAD!
THERE'S NOTHING INSIDE.
DO YOU KNOW WHAT GOES INSIDE HERE? SHOULD I TELL YOU?
TELL ME— WHAT WILL YOU PUT INSIDE?
IN HERE, YOU PUT BOOKS... AND A RULER...
DO YOU KNOW WHAT A RULER IS?
AND IN THIS PART, YOU PUT...
SNACKS.
UHH...

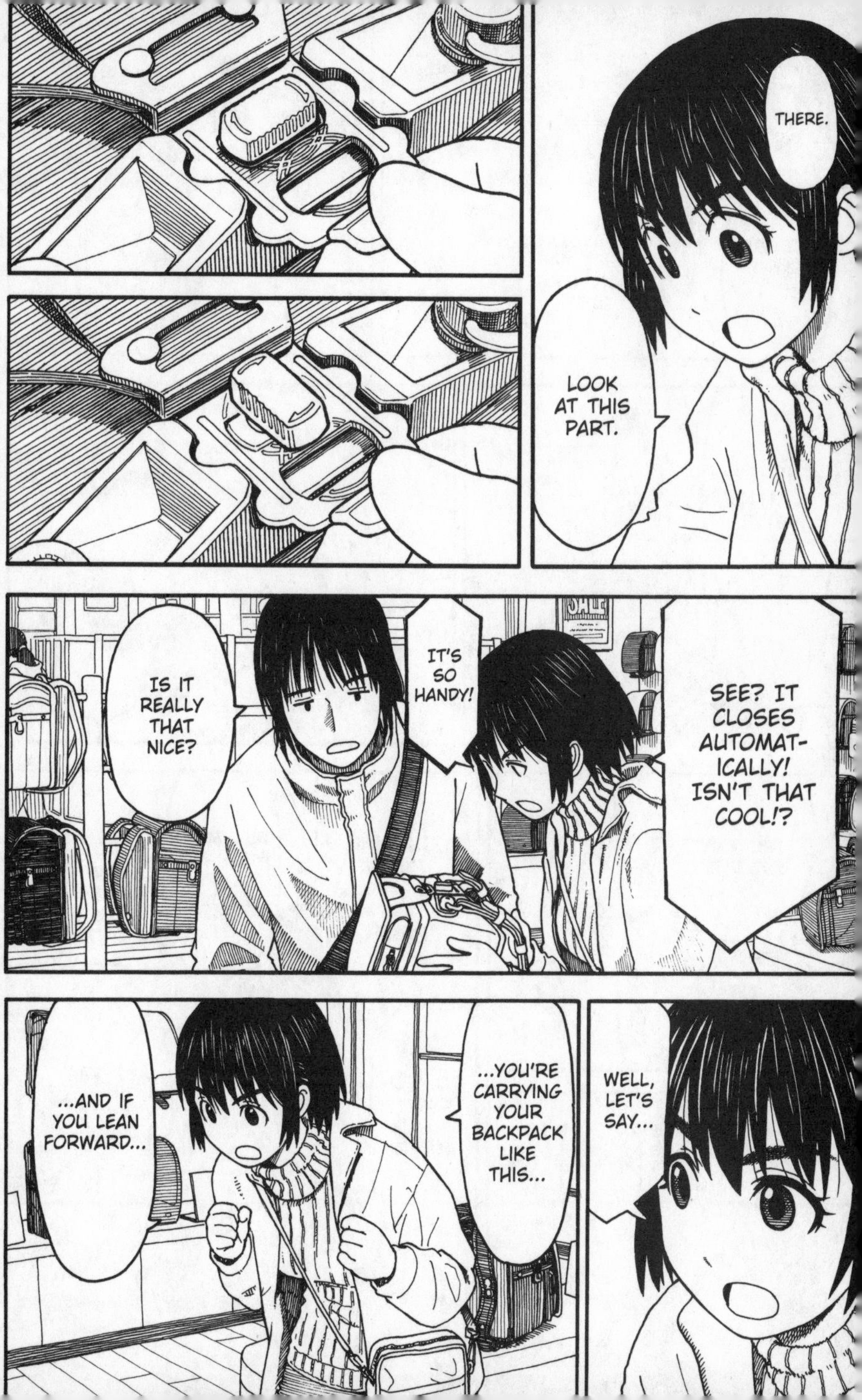
THERE.
LOOK AT THIS PART.
SEE? IT CLOSES AUTOMAT-ICALLY! ISN'T THAT COOL!?
IT'S SO HANDY!
IS IT REALLY THAT NICE?
WELL, LET'S SAY...
...YOU'RE CARRYING YOUR BACKPACK LIKE THIS...
...AND IF YOU LEAN FORWARD...

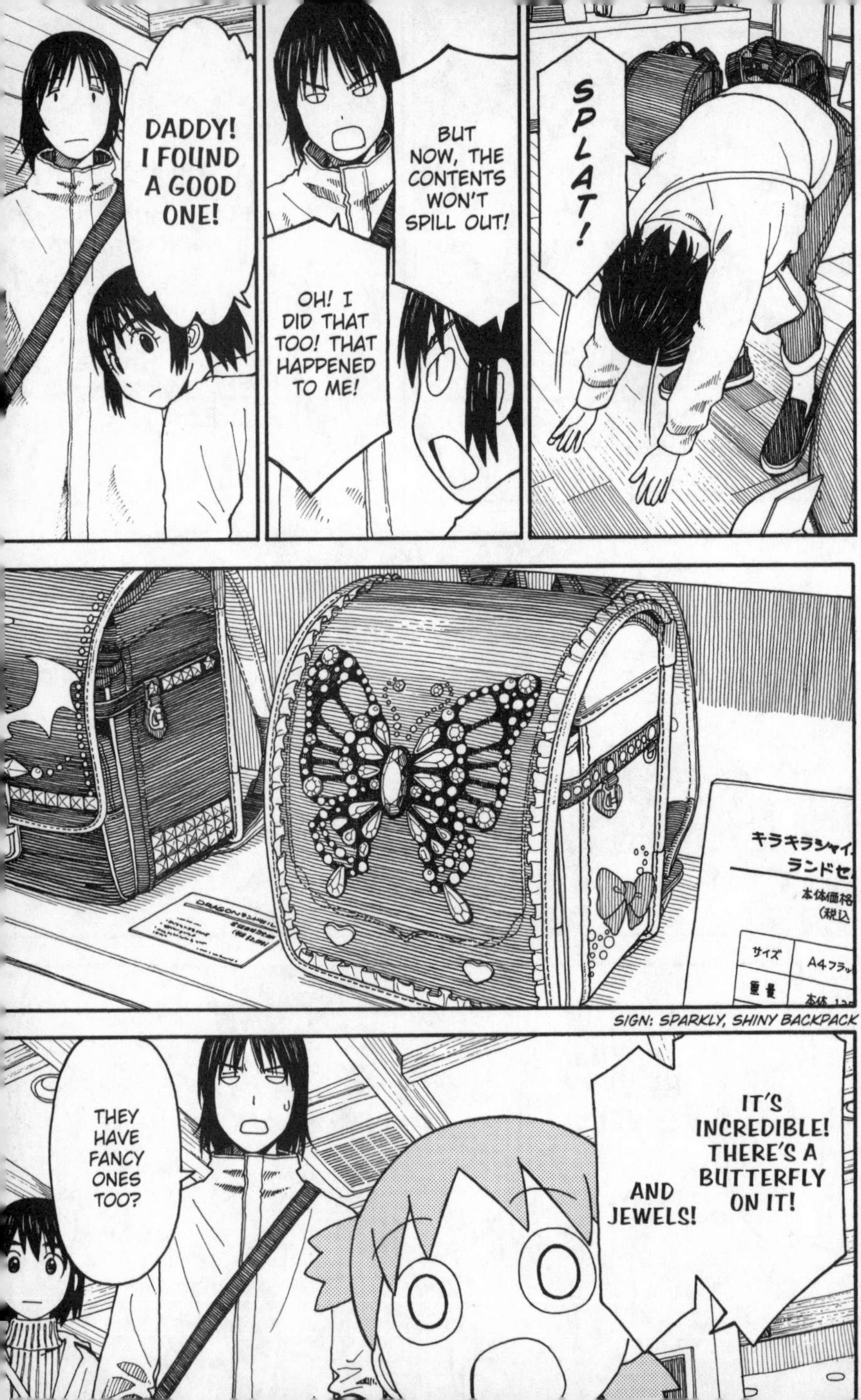
SPLAT!
BUT NOW, THE CONTENTS WON'T SPILL OUT!
OH! I DID THAT TOO! THAT HAPPENED TO ME!
DADDY! I FOUND A GOOD ONE!
キラキラシャイ
ランドセ
本体価格
(税込
サイズ
A4フラッ
重量
本体
DRAGON
SIGN: SPARKLY, SHINY BACKPACK
IT'S INCREDIBLE! THERE'S A BUTTERFLY ON IT!
AND JEWELS!
THEY HAVE FANCY ONES TOO?

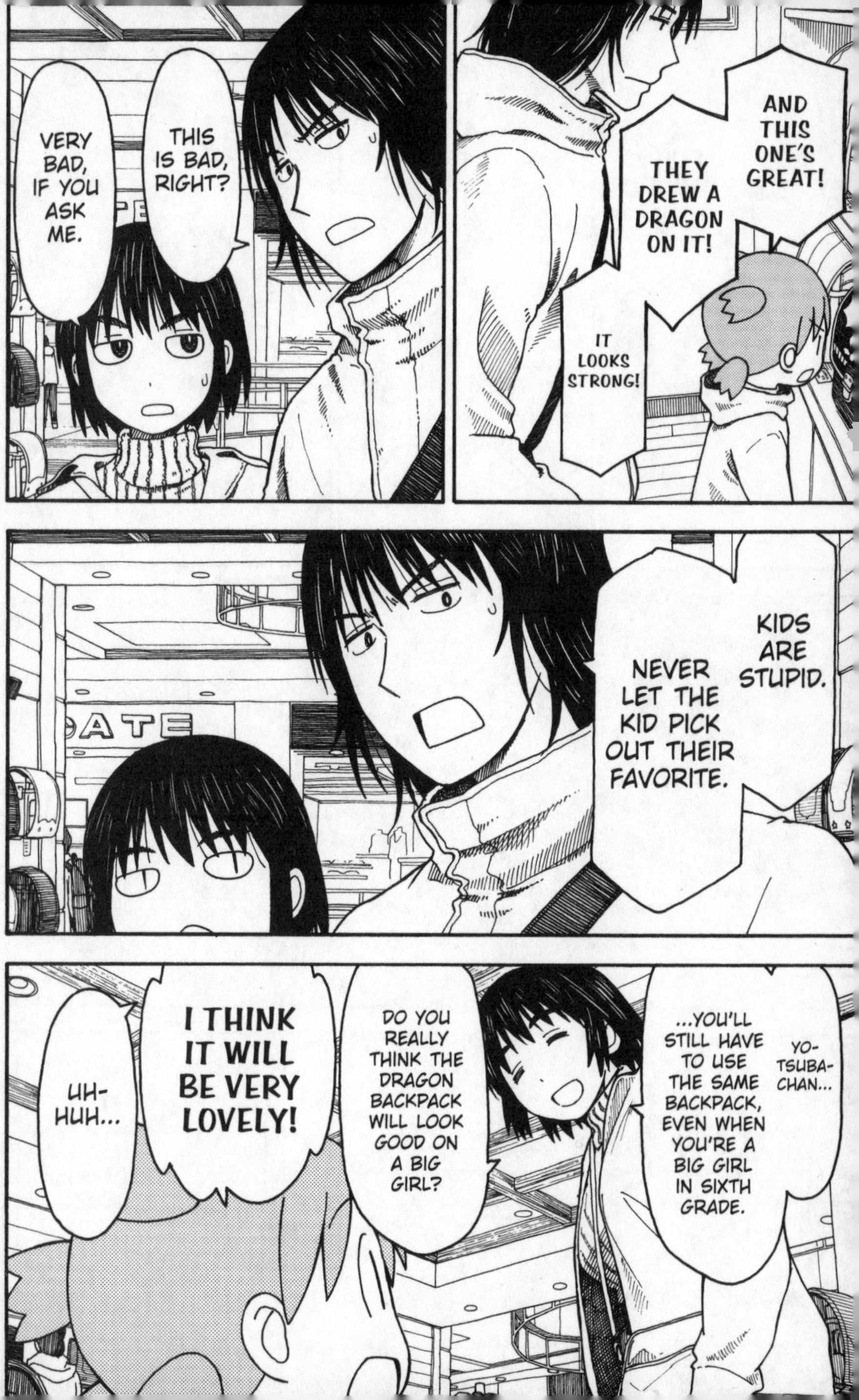
AND THIS ONE'S GREAT!
THEY DREW A DRAGON ON IT!
IT LOOKS STRONG!
THIS IS BAD, RIGHT?
VERY BAD, IF YOU ASK ME.
KIDS ARE STUPID.
NEVER LET THE KID PICK OUT THEIR FAVORITE.
YO-TSUBA-CHAN...
...YOU'LL STILL HAVE TO USE THE SAME BACKPACK, EVEN WHEN YOU'RE A BIG GIRL IN SIXTH GRADE.
DO YOU REALLY THINK THE DRAGON BACKPACK WILL LOOK GOOD ON A BIG GIRL?
I THINK IT WILL BE VERY LOVELY!
UH-HUH...

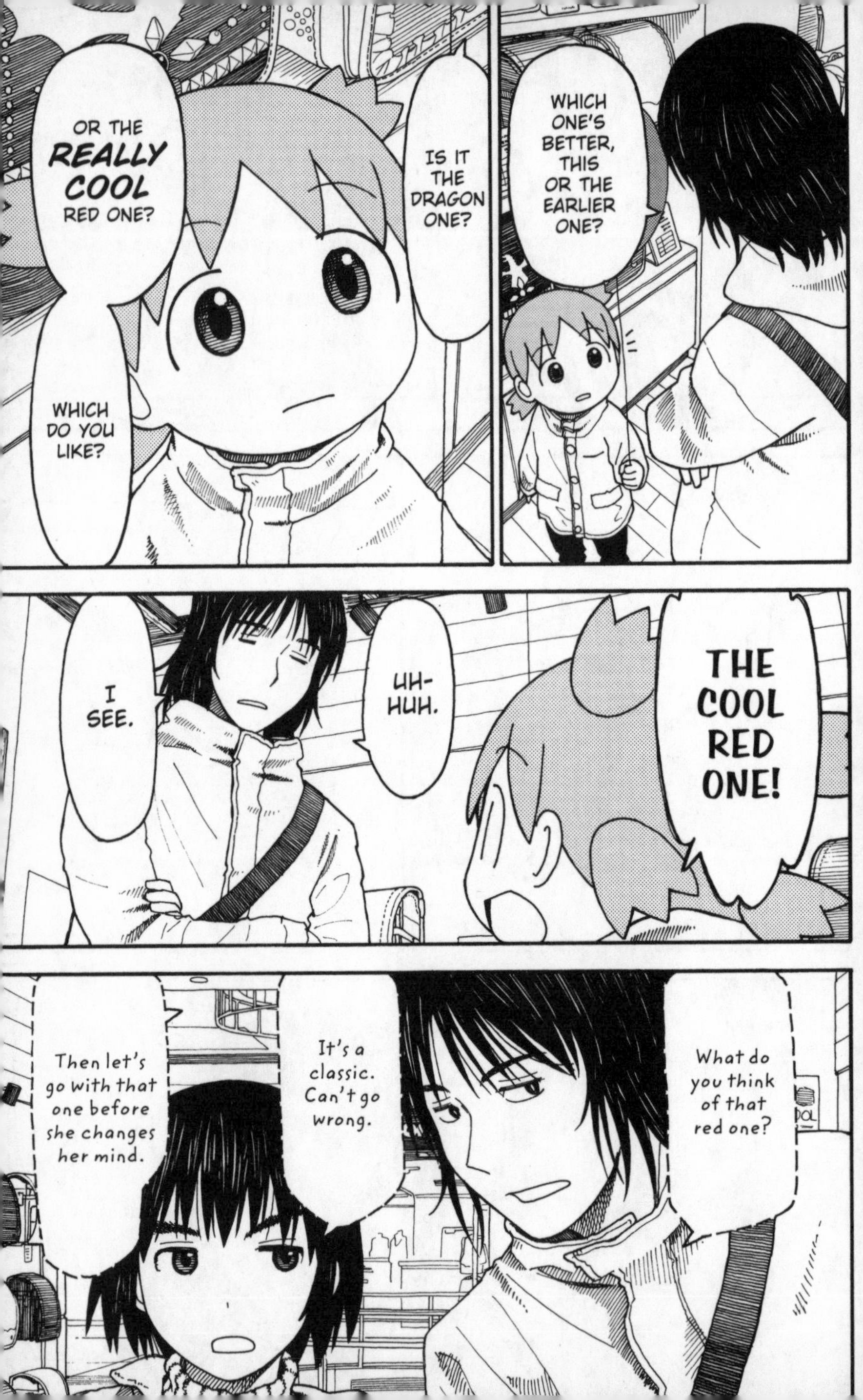
WHICH ONE'S BETTER, THIS OR THE EARLIER ONE?
IS IT THE DRAGON ONE?
OR THE REALLY COOL RED ONE?
WHICH DO YOU LIKE?
THE COOL RED ONE!
UH-HUH.
I SEE.
What do you think of that red one?
It's a classic. Can't go wrong.
Then let's go with that one before she changes her mind.

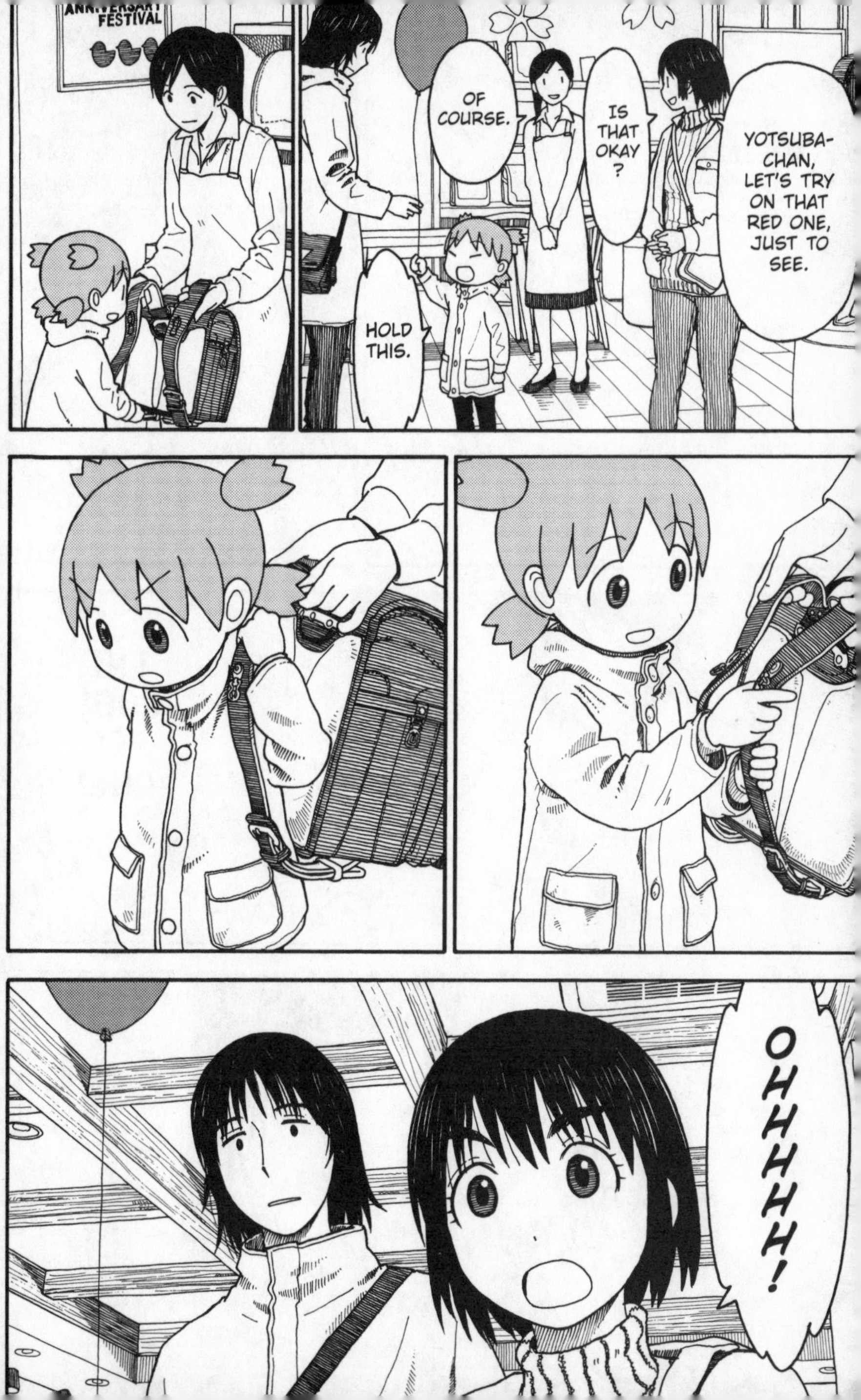
YOTSUBA-CHAN, LET'S TRY ON THAT RED ONE, JUST TO SEE.
IS THAT OKAY?
OF COURSE.
HOLD THIS.
ANNIVERSARY FESTIVAL
OHHHHH!

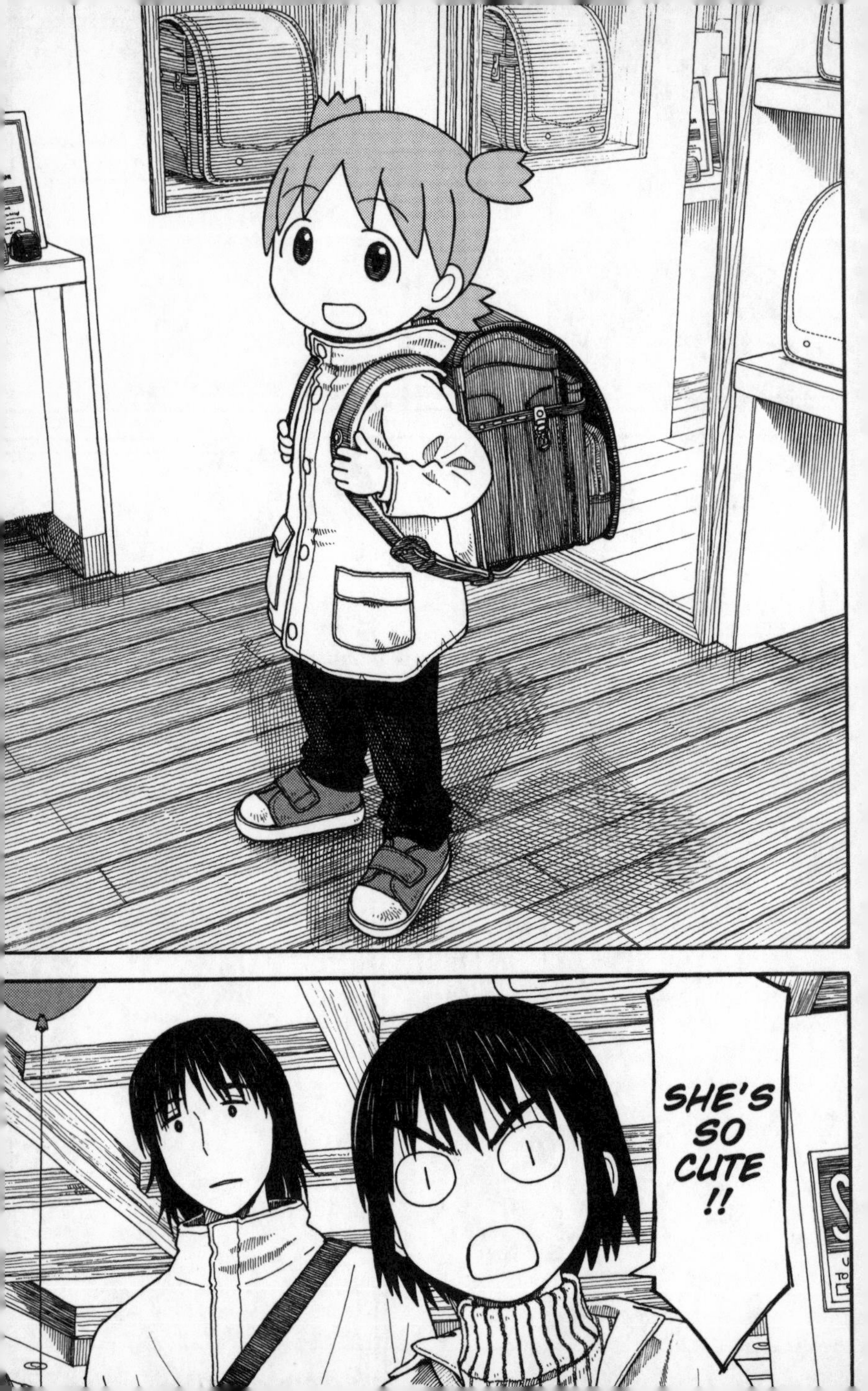
SHE'S SO CUTE !!

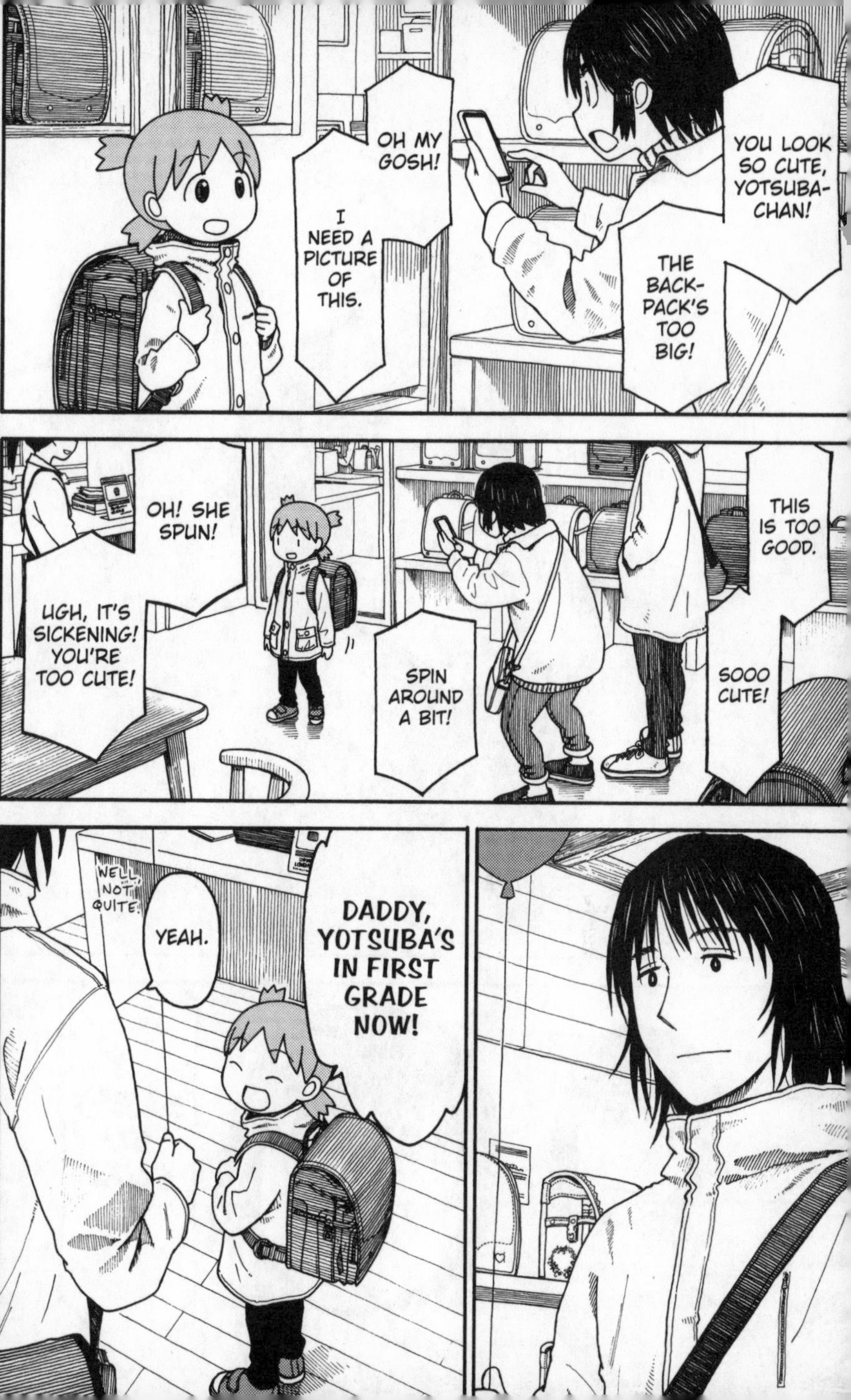
YOU LOOK SO CUTE, YOTSUBA-CHAN!
THE BACK-PACK'S TOO BIG!
OH MY GOSH!
I NEED A PICTURE OF THIS.
THIS IS TOO GOOD.
SOOO CUTE!
SPIN AROUND A BIT!
OH! SHE SPUN!
UGH, IT'S SICKENING! YOU'RE TOO CUTE!
DADDY, YOTSUBA'S IN FIRST GRADE NOW!
YEAH.
WELL, NOT QUITE.

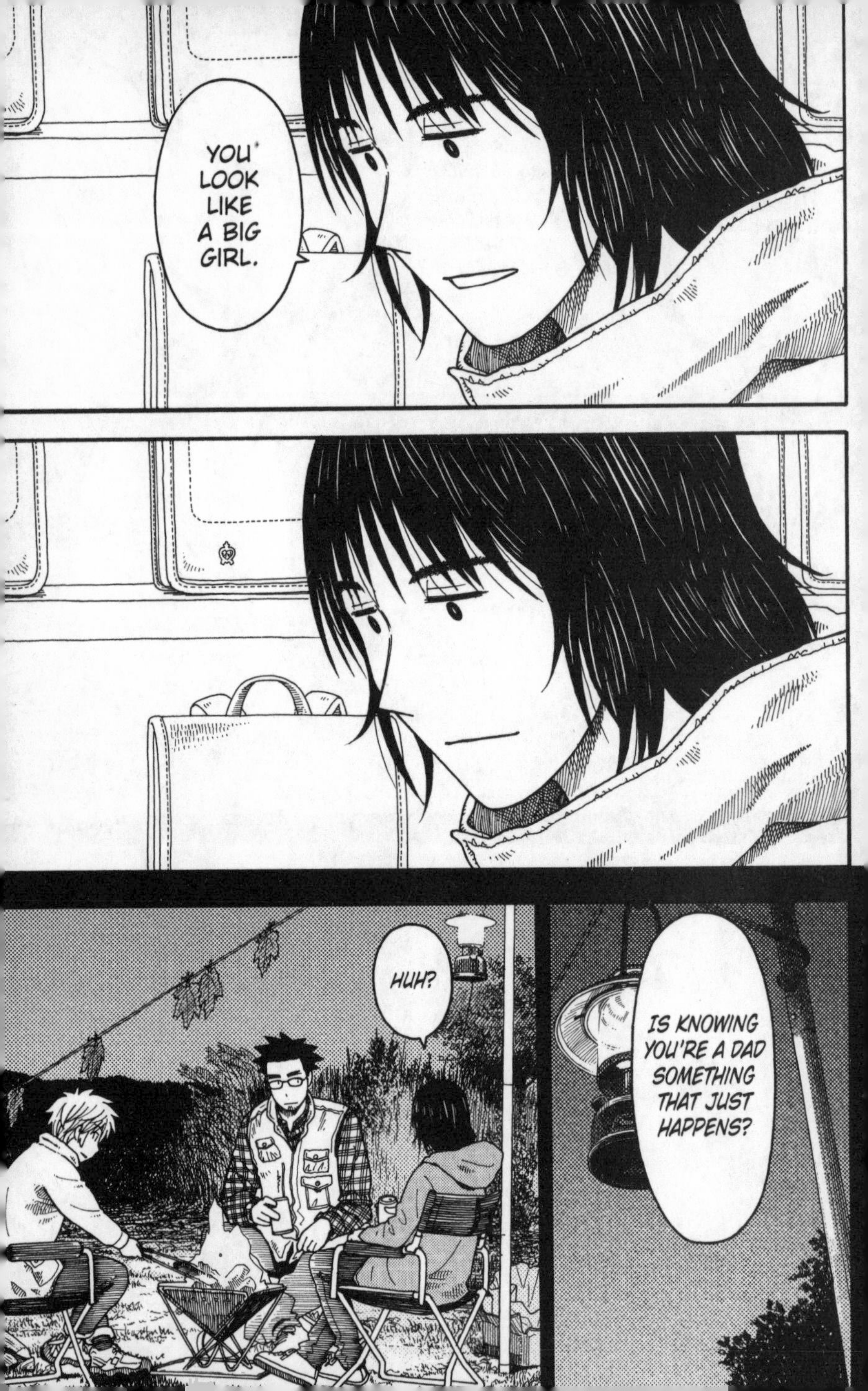
YOU LOOK LIKE A BIG GIRL.
IS KNOWING YOU'RE A DAD SOMETHING THAT JUST HAPPENS?
HUH?

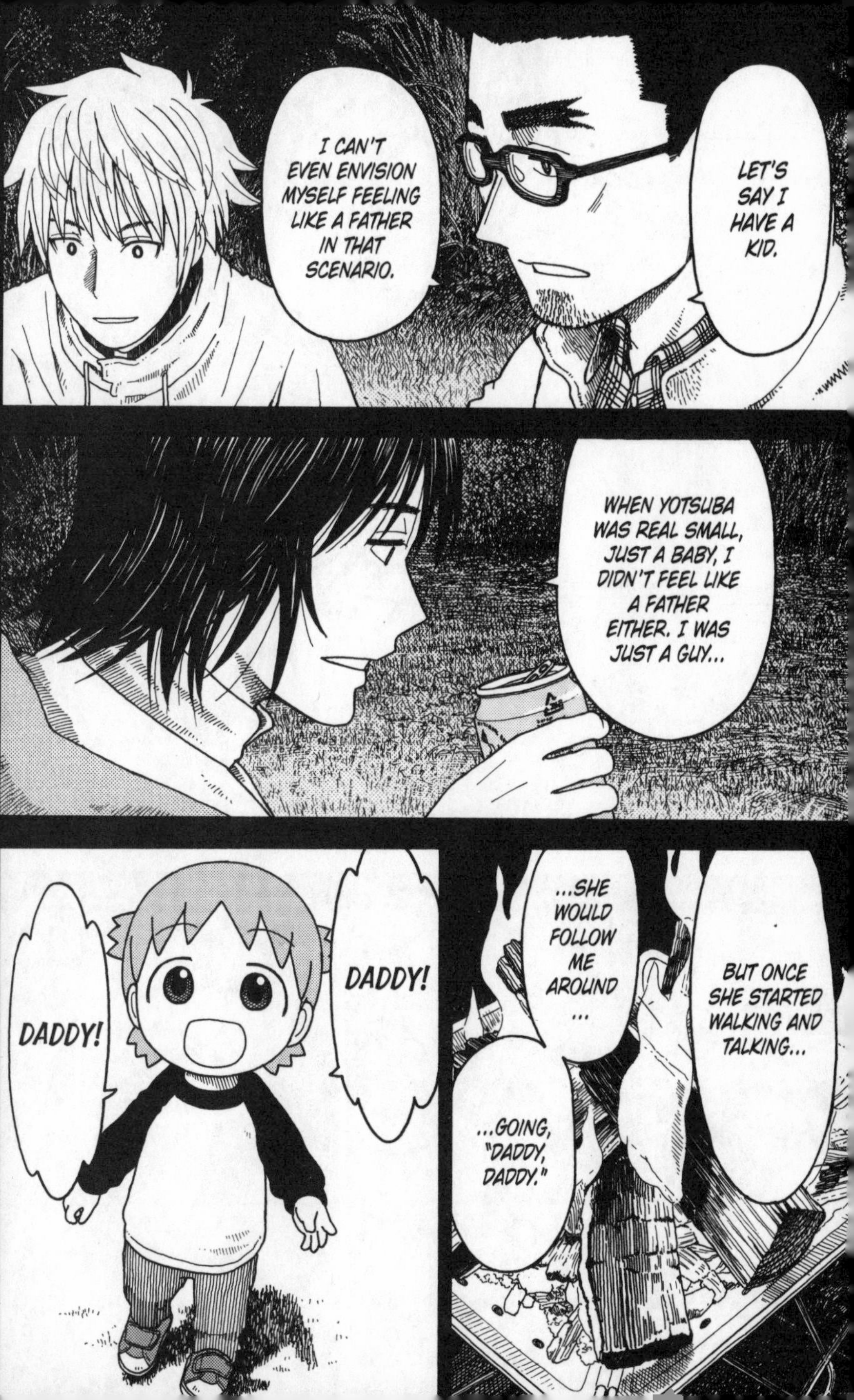
LET'S SAY I HAVE A KID.
I CAN'T EVEN ENVISION MYSELF FEELING LIKE A FATHER IN THAT SCENARIO.
WHEN YOTSUBA WAS REAL SMALL, JUST A BABY, I DIDN'T FEEL LIKE A FATHER EITHER. I WAS JUST A GUY...
BUT ONCE SHE STARTED WALKING AND TALKING...
...SHE WOULD FOLLOW ME AROUND ...
...GOING, "DADDY, DADDY."
DADDY!
DADDY!

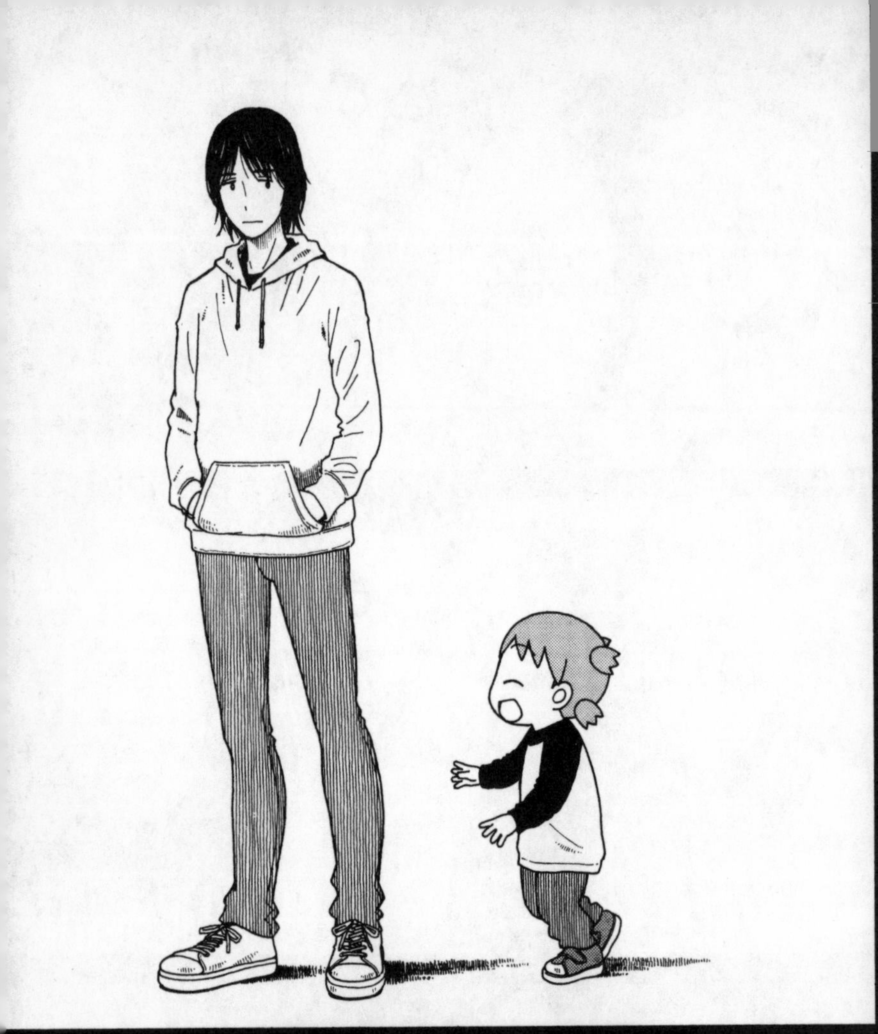
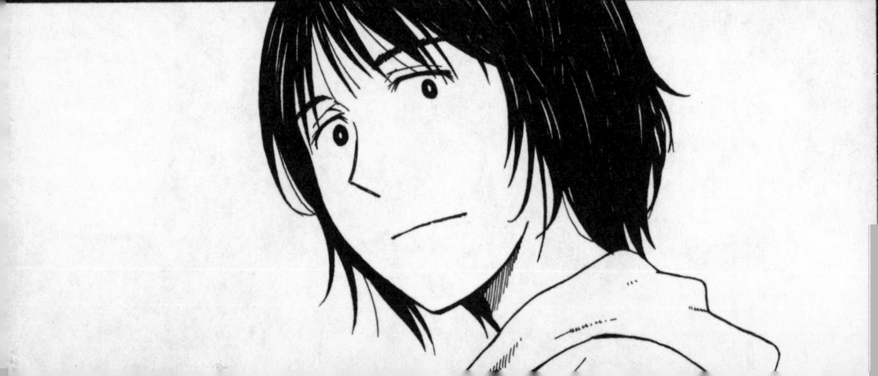

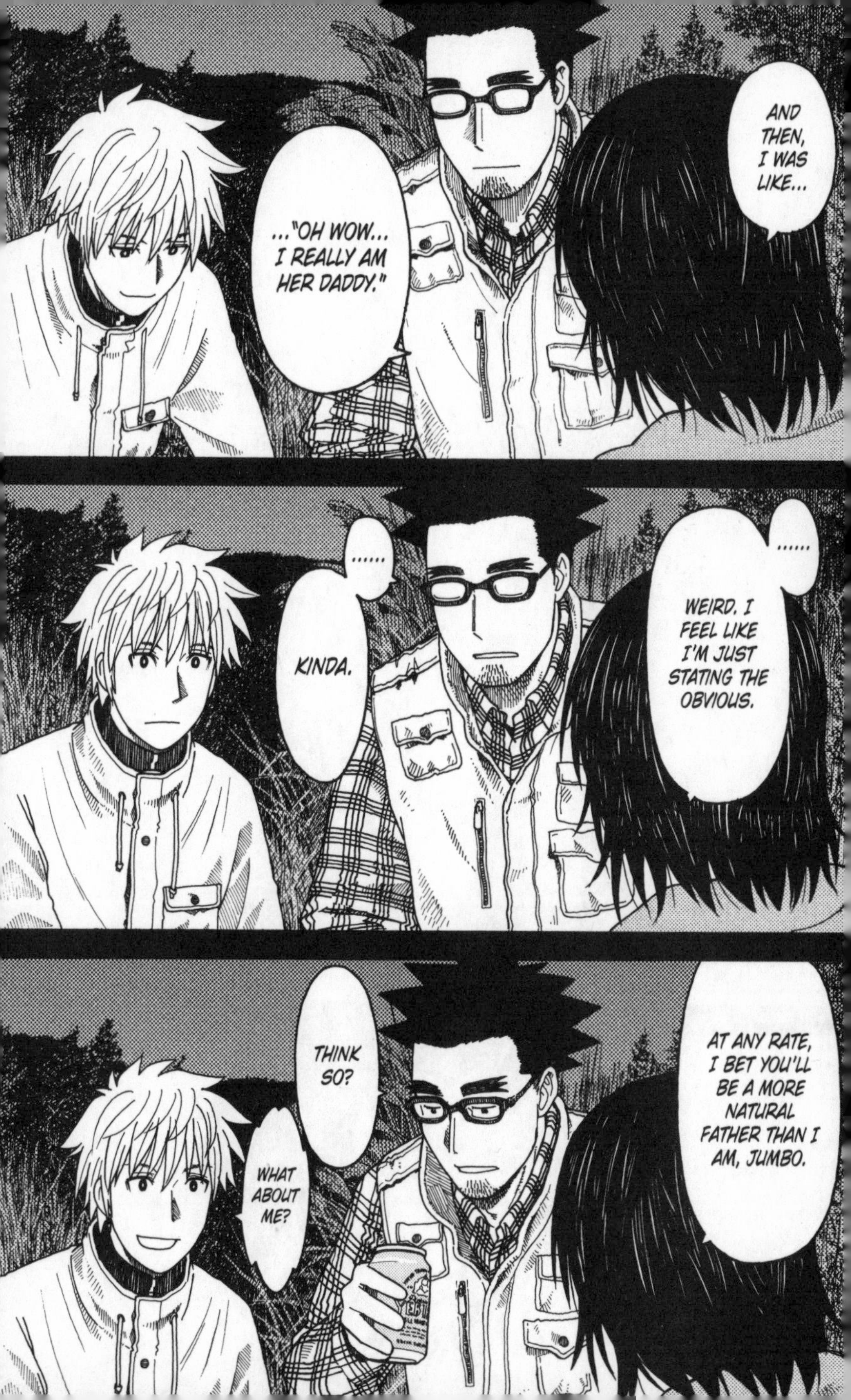
AND THEN, I WAS LIKE...
..."OH WOW... I REALLY AM HER DADDY."
......
WEIRD. I FEEL LIKE I'M JUST STATING THE OBVIOUS.
......
KINDA.
AT ANY RATE, I BET YOU'LL BE A MORE NATURAL FATHER THAN I AM, JUMBO.
THINK SO?
WHAT ABOUT ME?

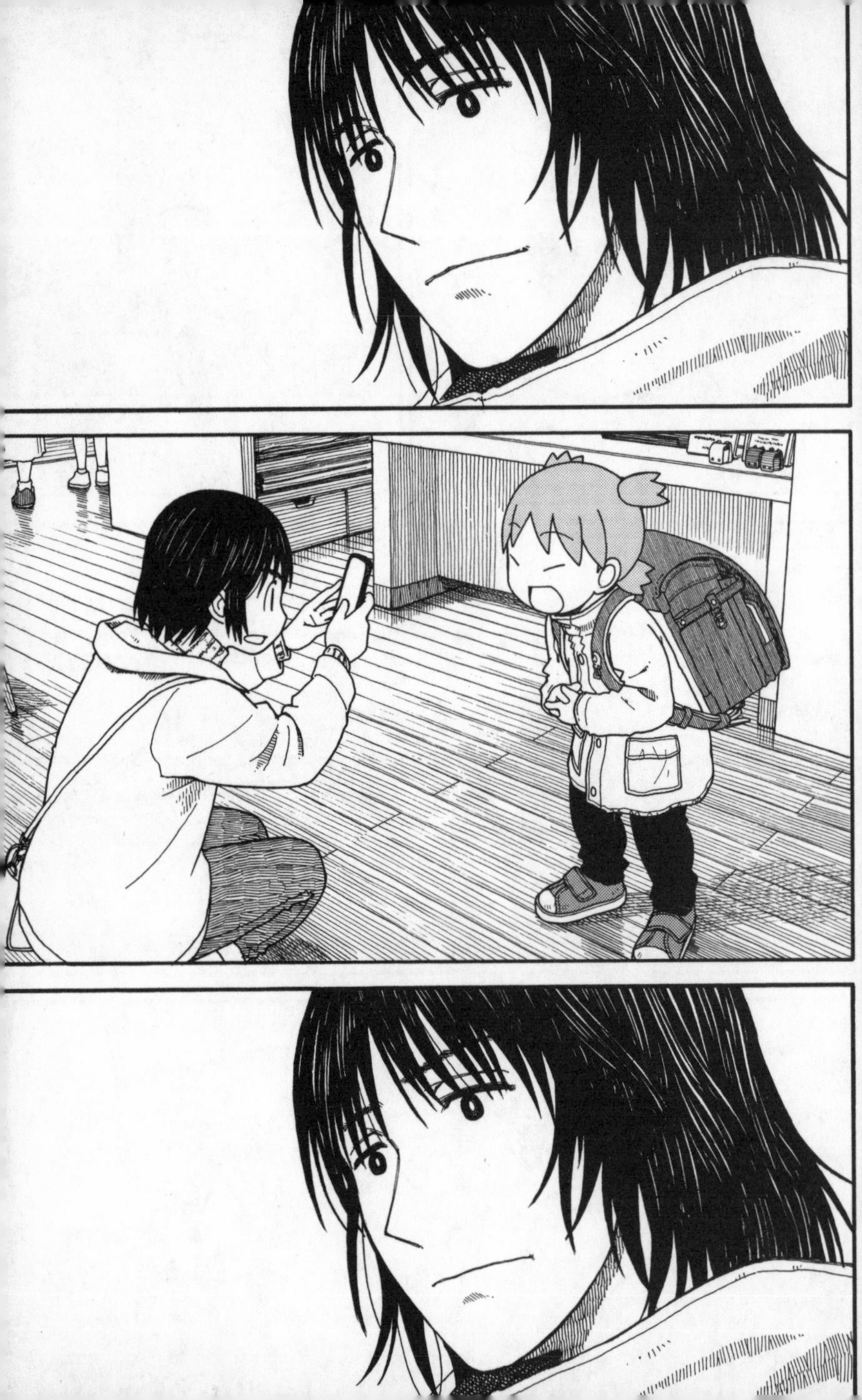

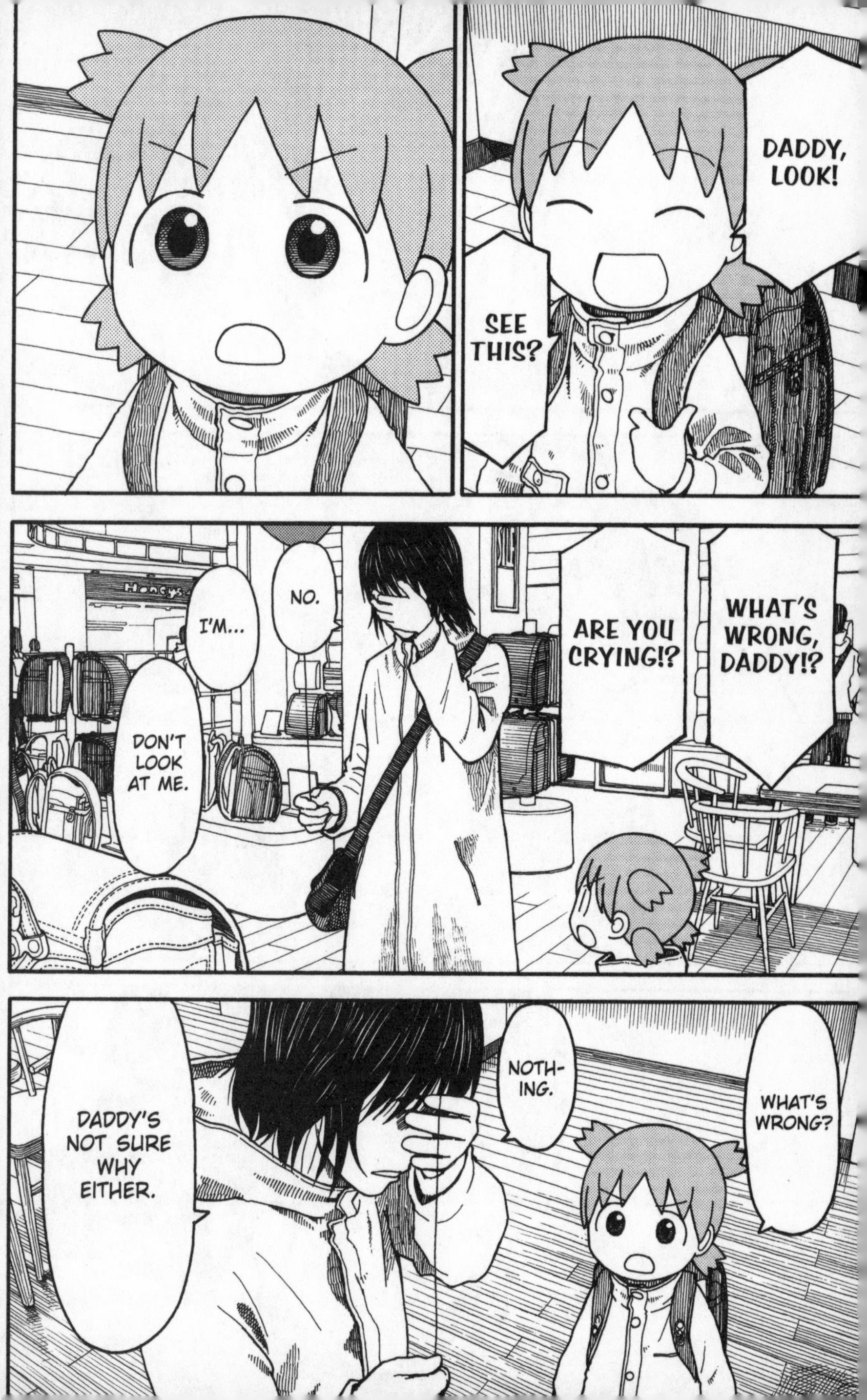
DADDY, LOOK!
SEE THIS?
WHAT'S WRONG, DADDY!?
ARE YOU CRYING!?
NO.
I'M...
DON'T LOOK AT ME.
WHAT'S WRONG?
NOTH-ING.
DADDY'S NOT SURE WHY EITHER.

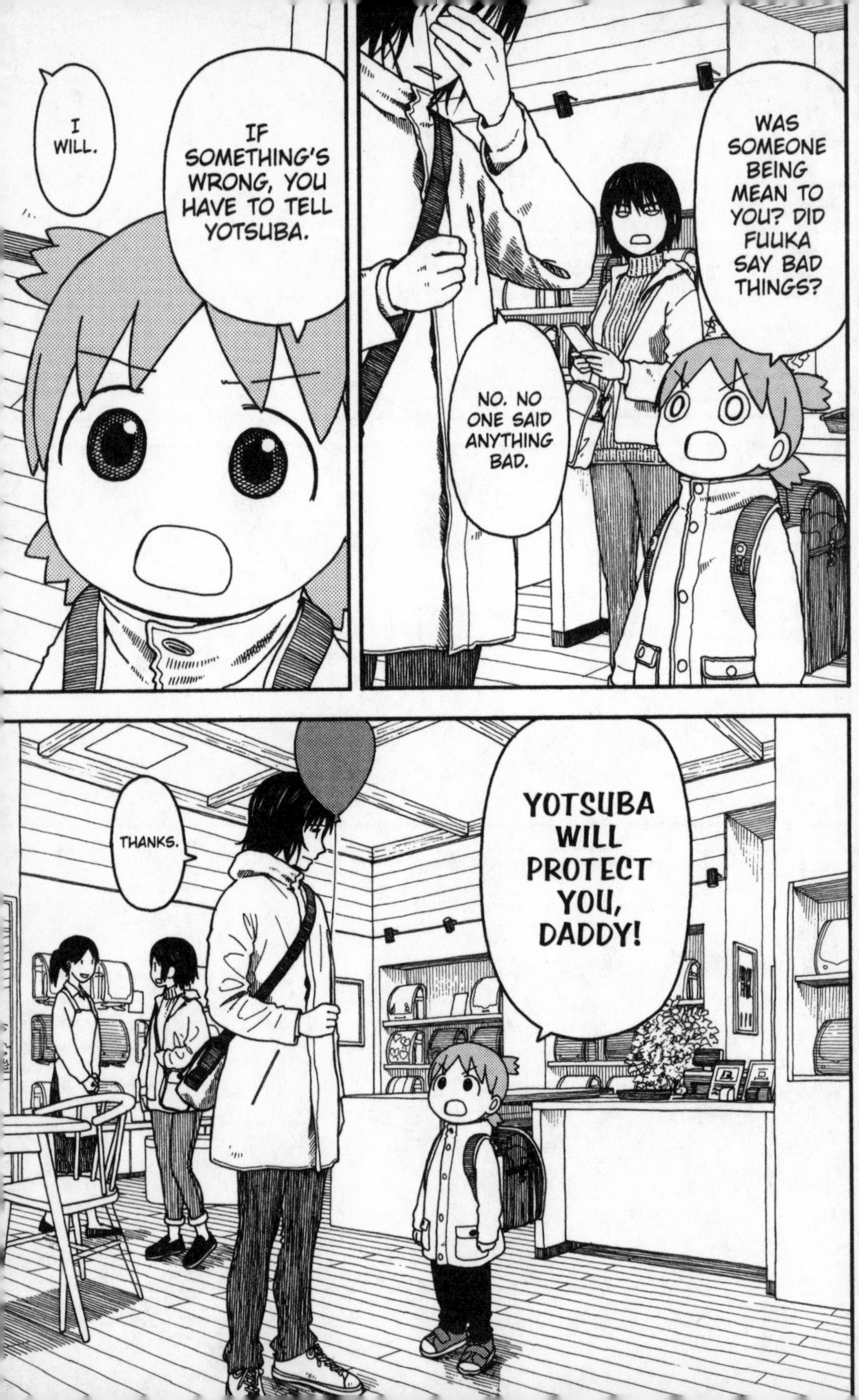
WAS SOMEONE BEING MEAN TO YOU? DID FUUKA SAY BAD THINGS?
NO. NO ONE SAID ANYTHING BAD.
IF SOMETHING'S WRONG, YOU HAVE TO TELL YOTSUBA.
I WILL.
YOTSUBA WILL PROTECT YOU, DADDY!
THANKS.

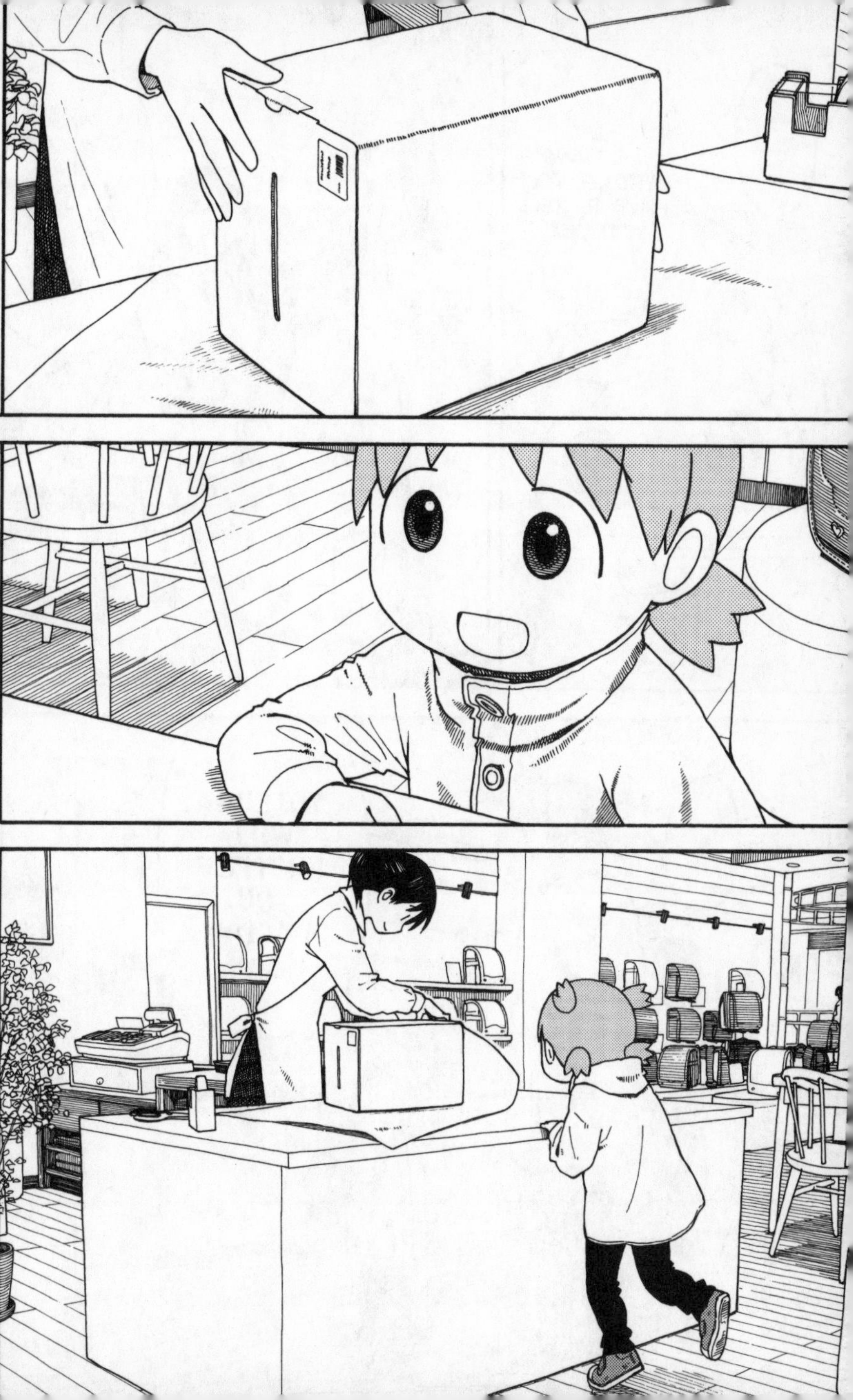

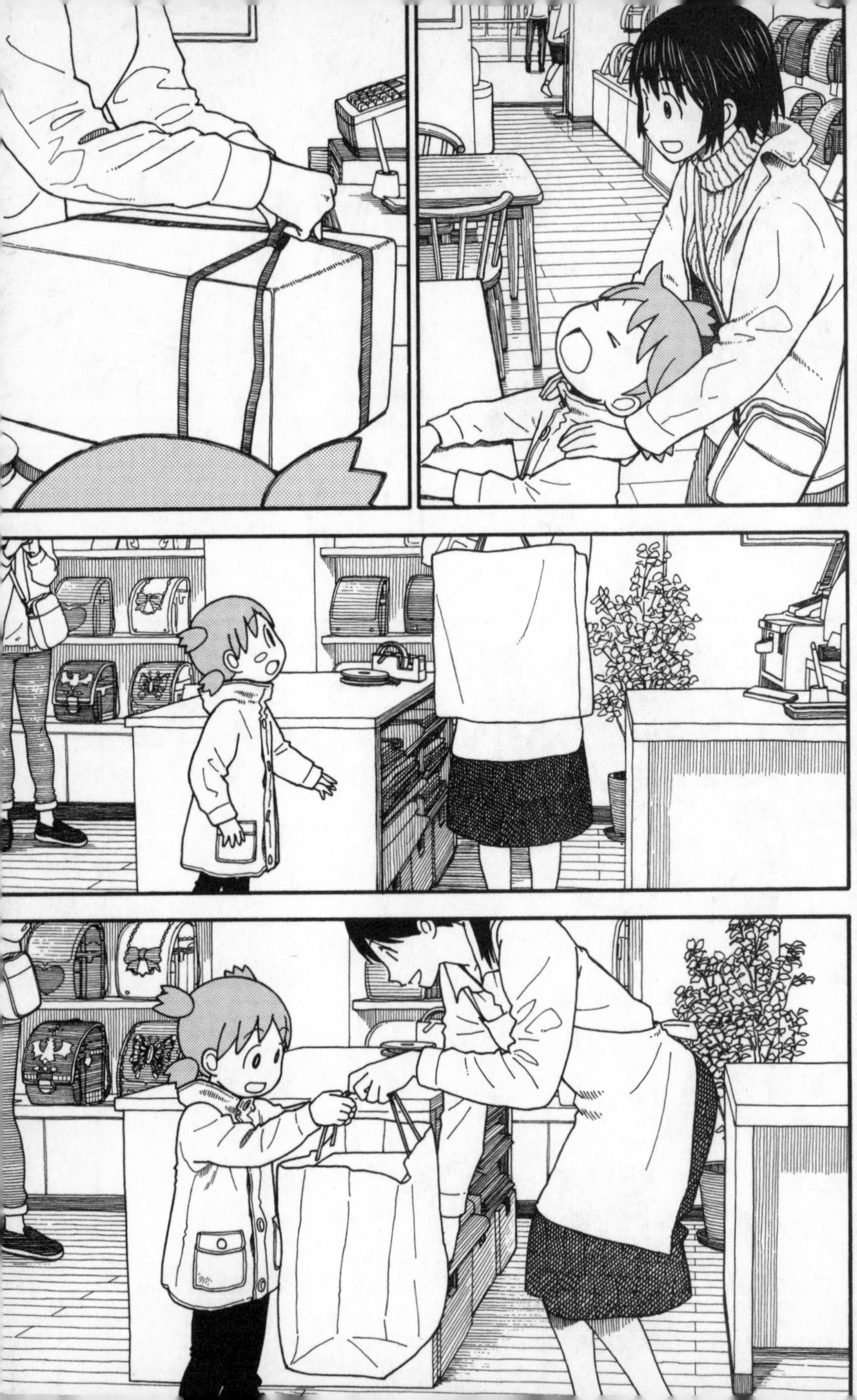

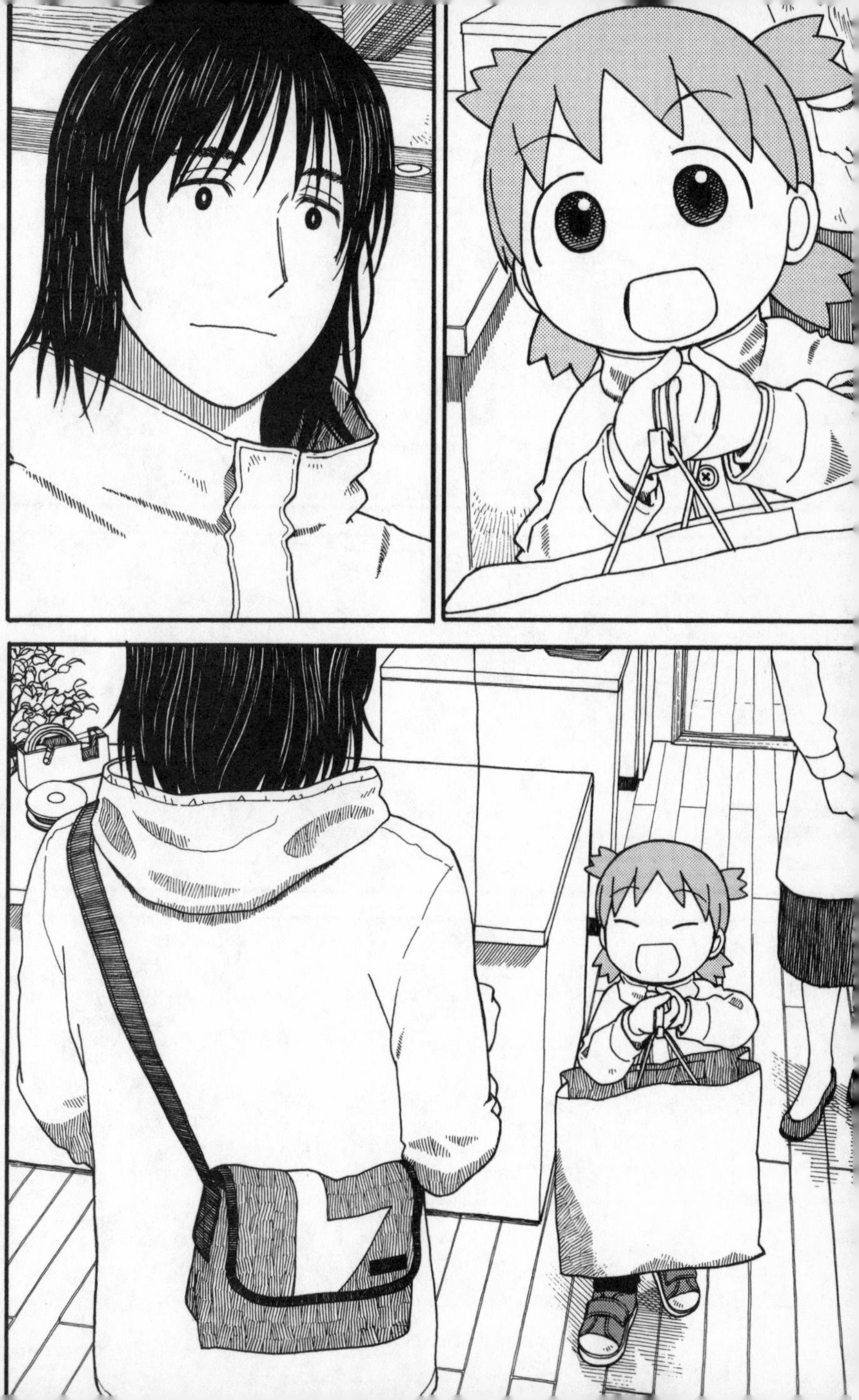

YOTSUBA&!

YOTSUBA&! 15
KIYOHIKO AZUMA

Translation: Stephen Paul
Lettering: Abigail Blackman

YOTSUBA&! Vol. 15 © KIYOHIKO AZUMA/YOTUBA SUTAZIO 2021
First published in Japan in 2021 by KADOKAWA CORPORATION., Tokyo.
English translation rights arranged with KADOKAWA CORPORATION, Tokyo through Tuttle-Mori Agency, Inc., Tokyo.

English translation © 2021 by Yen Press, LLC

Yen Press • 150 West 30th Street, 19th Floor • New York, NY 10001

Visit us at yenpress.com • facebook.com/yenpress • twitter.com/yenpress • yenpress.tumblr.com • instagram.com/yenpress

First Yen Press Print Edition: September 2021

Yen Press is an imprint of Yen Press, LLC.
The Yen Press name and logo are trademarks of Yen Press, LLC.

Library of Congress Control Number: 2016932334

ISBNs: 978-1-9753-3609-7 (paperback)
       978-1-9753-3610-3 (ebook)

10 9 8 7 6 5 4 3 2

WOR

Printed in the United States of America

TO BE CONTINUED!

YOTSUBA&!

ENJOY EVERYTHING.